# International monetary economics, 1870–1960

# International monetary economics, 1870–1960

## Between the classical and the new classical

M. JUNE FLANDERS

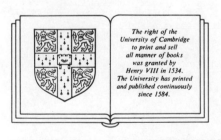

The right of the
University of Cambridge
to print and sell
all manner of books
was granted by
Henry VIII in 1534.
The University has printed
and published continuously
since 1584.

*CAMBRIDGE UNIVERSITY PRESS*

*Cambridge*
*New York   Port Chester   Melbourne   Sydney*

Published by the Press Syndicate of the University of Cambridge
The Pitt Building, Trumpington Street, Cambridge CB2 1RP
40 West 20th Street, New York, NY 10011, USA
10 Stamford Road, Oakleigh, Melbourne 3166, Australia

First published 1989

Printed in Great Britain at the University Press, Cambridge

*British Library cataloguing in publication data*

Flanders, M. June
International monetary economics, 1870–1960: between
the classical and the new classical.
1. International monetary systems. Theories, history
I. Title
332.4'5

Library of Congress cataloguing in publication data

Flanders, M. June, 1927–
International monetary economics. 1870–1960: between the
classical and the new classical / M. June Flanders
      p.   cm.
Bibliography
Includes index.
ISBN 0-521-36170-2
1. International finance   2. Monetary policy.   I. Title.
HG3881.F537   1989
332'.042–dc20   89-9811

ISBN 0 521 36170 2

*I dedicate this book to the memory of two people who taught me much: Abraham White and Lloyd Metzler*

# Contents

# Preface

This book has been simmering on a back burner in my mind for some time. I brought it to a boil and clarified it when I was able to go away on leave; here, after the second sabbatical, is the result.

I feel like the man in Aesop's Fable with the son and the donkey. Everybody he met on the road had a conflicting view of the proper allocation of labor between the three. In his good-natured attempts to listen to all advice, he lost his donkey and all his earthly goods. I have heard much excellent advice. Following it all was by definition impossible, since many admonitions were mutually incompatible. I listened seriously to all who ventured an opinion; to those whose advice I did not, or could not, in spite of all, follow – apologies.

My greatest intellectual debt is to Lloyd Metzler. My deepest regret is that I was forced to leave the city and the University of Chicago before partaking more of the stimulation that emanated from his gentle wisdom, low-key but brilliant. On a broader scale, I have benefited from contacts over many countries and continents – and many decades. Specific help, comments, and advice in the writing of this book has likewise come from a number of sources.

The heroes, who must not remain unsung, are the two friends who heroically struggled through all of an early and very rough draft. They are Arthur Bloomfield and John Whitaker. Discussions, in writing and in person, improved the final result more than they know, albeit surely less than they hoped. My arguments with the latter, in Thomas Jefferson's cloisters at the University of Virginia, served wonderfully to help concentrate my attention and direct my effort to straightening out a number of problems.

Useful comments, facts, references, encouragement, and discussions helped the research; arguments convinced me of my error or helped me to understand myself. These came from: Hans Brems, Richard Caves, A. W. Coats, Jonathan Eaton, Stanley Engerman, Marvin Goodfriend, R. M. Hartwell, Elhanan Helpman, Peter Kenen, Adam Klug, David Laidler, Axel Leijonhufvud, Donald Moggridge, Assaf Razin. Parts of the work were presented at seminars, where helpful criticism was offered, at: The California Institute of Technology, Duke, University of California at Los Angeles,

xi

University of North Carolina, Princeton, University of Rochester, the Institute for International Economic Studies, Stockholm, and the University of Western Ontario. Graduate students at the University of Virginia and at Tel Aviv University helped greatly, often unknowingly.

My thanks to Craufurd Goodwin for his support and encouragement in the project, and to the editors of the *History of political economy* for permission to use material first published there.

The first sabbatical leave during which I began to think seriously about some of the issues herein discussed was spent partly at the Institute for International Economic Studies in Stockholm. The combination of a friendly, active group of colleagues, and an infrastructure consisting of a fantastically efficient and helpful staff made being there an intellectual as well as a personal pleasure. The stay at the University of Virginia, where a splendid research library and a roomful of computers and printers combined with curious students and lively colleagues, was likewise simultaneously restful and invigorating.

My appreciation also to the Foerder Institute of Tel Aviv University for technical assistance, to Daniel Brod for checking the references, and to the gracious and helpful librarians in the Social Science Faculty at Tel Aviv University who for some reason never learned that a librarian's job is to protect books from potential readers.

To my son Daveed, loving thanks for his invaluable editorial and proof-reading help; to him and his brother Zvi, deep gratitude for their constant moral support and encouragement.

For help with the typing, thanks are due to WordPerfect and my IBM PC aka The Golem.

# 1

## Preliminaries

# CHAPTER 1

# Introduction

### The adjustment mechanism

This study deals with some topics in the development of the theory of international adjustment. Other names for it are: international monetary economics, the macroeconomics of an open economy, the theory of the balance of payments (or the theory of exchange rates). It sometimes includes some well-known specific sets of questions, such as the "transfer problem", and the "theory of devaluation".

There are those who argue that there is no such thing as a separate theory of the balance of payments, or of exchange rates. This is true in the same sense that there is not a separate theory of labor market adjustments, of investment, or of taxation. All of these are (correctly) viewed as part of a general equilibrium system. Most economists, nevertheless, find it convenient for various purposes to single out pieces of that general model and scrutinize them more closely. As long as there are different "countries" (which can be defined as units with their own money and monetary institutions) and as long as transactions with residents of the same country are viewed differently from those involving residents of other countries – so long does it make sense to look at this section of a general-equilibrium system with a closeup lens. This in no way denies its "general equilibriumness". In any event, I am dealing here with the history of ideas. I did not invent the field – I am merely studying it.

Expressed most generally, we are dealing with analysis of responses to disturbances. By this I mean, quite simply, the following. Given the basic balance of payments (the current account plus autonomous capital flows) – given trade between countries in goods, services, and financial assets – anything which affects any of those flows will upset the equality between payments to foreigners and receipts from foreigners. Then one asks:

1  Is there any automatic mechanism which will tend to redress the imbalance and restore equality? And if there is, how does it work?
2  If not, are there government policies which can or should be applied to take the place of an automatic mechanism, or to aid a faltering one?

3  How do either automatic or policy-induced adjustments in balances
   between countries impinge on the domestic economies of the countries
   concerned or on third countries?

4  Do the answers to the above questions depend on whether or not
   exchange rates are determined in a free market or pegged by government
   decree and intervention? If pegged, what is an appropriate level of
   exchange rates? When should they be changed? How will market-
   determined exchange rates behave (and how will their changes affect the
   internal economy)?

This list is not exhaustive, but it represents a fair statement of the kind of
issue I am concerned with. It is to the development of such theories during
the last quarter of the previous century and the first half of the present one
that I turn my attention.

The theory(ies) of international adjustment can be classified into groups.
(I shall occasionally use the word "schools", but more for the purpose of
verbal variety than to suggest that these are necessarily schools, doctrines, or
even, in all cases, research programs, to use Latsis's 1976 terminology.) I
shall argue, however, that in each case, the members of the group have
something in common with respect to the way they attack the questions
sketched above. My main reason for undertaking this classification is
necessity: I was forced into it by the material. When I set about writing a
sequential, chronological story I got chaos. Ideas, trends, approaches, and
analytical frameworks seemed to be scattered in total disarray when I tried to
list them consecutively. I believe that in general, progress in economics has
not been linear. It is certainly true in this sub-discipline. On the other hand,
when I threw all the names and ideas down at random, they quite readily
sorted themselves and formed distinctive groupings. I do not wish to imply
that these groupings are either sacrosanct or unique: another researcher
might toss the cards and find them landing differently. Nor, of course, do I
believe that the categories are watertight and that every author I discuss is a
"pure type". There are, in fact, some people whom I have placed in more
than one category, corresponding to different writings and/or to different
periods in their careers; and several people have been treated *sui generis*.

Part of the reason for this non-linearity may be chance. Much of it has to
do with history. Both the problems economists have tackled and their
method of handling them have varied markedly with the economic and
institutional environment, and hence with "history". Since history often, in
very broad terms, does repeat itself, similar ideas, approaches, methods tend
to reappear. Today our methods are far more sophisticated and elegant than
those of the past, but the similarities and analogies between our present
exploration of international debt, repudiation, and financial stability and

those of the 1930s are too obvious to need belaboring. Many of the same questions are being asked today as were asked then; and many of the answers are surprisingly like. So I shall tell it this way, and hope by the end, at least, to have convinced the reader of the necessity of ordering and of the plausibility, if not the inevitability, of my particular arrangement.

The procedure of classifying writings into groups presents the well-known problem of tidiness. One often finds in the writings of a member of one group or category statements consistent with one or several other classifications. Like all those who struggle with the history of ideas, which is an art, not a science, I face this problem boldly and pass it by. A related but different problem is how to make attributions of "discovery" – to the person who said it first, the one who first realized it was important, or to the one who sold the idea to the world. I believe it was Paul Samuelson who commented once that nobody ever said anything for the first time. Fate is not always fair here; again, I have tried, and where I have failed, I apologize.

### A (partial) cast of characters

I argue that the following broad approaches can be identified, and can be divided into two separable streams.

| STREAM F | STREAM P |
|---|---|
| classical | neoclassical |
| late classical | anti-neoclassical |
| Ohlin | Keynes |
| keynesian | crisis |

THE CONFLUENCE MMM – Metzler, Meade, Mundell

Simplifying heroically, I argue that both streams issued from a common source, a protomodel. Stream F (formal) has to do with long-run equilibrium models, while the stream P (policy-oriented) approaches are concerned with short-run equilibrium, or disequilibrium, systems. The exception to this generalization is the body of keynesian writings, but I include it in stream F because it constitutes an attack on the classical model in the former's own bailiwick. Most of it concentrates on formal, analytical issues. The writings in stream P are about quite different matters.[1] My justification for categorizing

---

[1] A very nice contemporary statement of one of the major distinctions I make, that between the classical model, which is in stream F and the neoclassical approach, in stream P, is to be found in Dornbusch and Frenkel 1984: 243: "The traditional model of the price-specie flow mechanism, originating with David Hume, emphasizes the impact of relative prices on the trade balance and hence on the balance of payments and the international flow of bullion. A deterioration of the external balance due to increased aggregate spending or an adverse development of net exports will lead to bullion export, monetary deflation, declining spending, and price deflation. Both the decline in spending and deflation work to restore external balance.

some writers *sui generis*, I hope will become clearer when I discuss their writings. And as for the distinction between Keynes and the keynesian theories, I shall argue that whatever else Keynes might have been, he was not what I have called a "keynesian".

Chronologically the streams ran almost parallel, but they concerned themselves with different issues, and asked different questions. First, the P group is, as I noted, by and large a treatment of *dis*equilibrium. Secondly, it is policy-oriented, concerned with institutions and their functioning, often with strong normative connotations. I do not mean to deny that the classical economists, for example, dealt with policy issues. But these were, on the whole, questions which incorporated the policy proposals into a long-run equilibrium solution. Tariff policy and various kinds of tax policy, much discussed by Ricardo, Mill *et al.* were of this nature; they had to do with policy actions which affected the structure of the economy at equilibrium. The policy involvement of the P writings is quite different, and it is generally aimed at disequilibrium situations. Furthermore, I would argue that most of the writings of the classicals (and even Marshall) on policy issues in this field were outside of their treatises and formal systems, not an integral part of them. The most outstanding outlier in this respect is Keynes, this being one of the reasons for my treating him individually. When the keynesian research program became broadly accepted, the streams merged, and the Metzler, Meade, Mundell synthesis occurred, in the mid 1950s. Since then, for a variety of reasons, there has been a less sharp division between short- and long-run analysis, between policy-oriented discussion and "pure" model building, but I stop my story here. As the title of this work suggests, I do not attempt to cover the contemporary "new classical" approach, which had its origins in the monetary approach to the balance of payments of the 1960s. And I do not discuss the classical writings in detail, because that has already been done so well by others, most notably Viner (1937) in a manner upon which I could not hope to improve. A quick overview follows; the rest of the book is aimed at fleshing out the details.

"The model we have sketched here, on the contrary, places emphasis on capital flows and banking policy as the main factors in the adjustment process. The two views of the adjustment mechanism are of course complementary, although they may well correspond to different adjustment periods. *In the short run, banking policy and capital flows are likely to be the main factors determining bullion flows, since, in the short run, prices and trade flows do not adjust to the full, possible extent*" (italics mine).

Mundell, on the other hand, seems to suggest that among the classicals there is no long-run balance-of-payments theory. He states that the difference between real trade theory and "the short-run mechanism of balance-of-payments adjustment" is part of the distinction made by the "classical dichotomy between the monetary theory and value theory" (Mundell 1968: 3).

## The protomodel

In the beginning was the PROTOMODEL. In its purest form, it goes back to Gervaise (1720 [1954]). Briefly, it is the generalization that under fixed exchange rates the money supply of any given country is endogenous. From this stems the simple classical doctrine, the Hume price-specie flow mechanism,[2] which in some versions is very much like the protomodel. The latter reemerged phoenix-like, elegantly formalized, over two hundred years later in the monetary theory of the balance of payments (see Frenkel and Johnson 1976, for example). The statement of the adjustment both under fixed and flexible exchange rates, which can be found in the Bullion Report of 1810 (Cannan 1925), is also very much in the spirit of the protomodel.

The protomodel is dazzling in its simplicity, with the following characteristics:

1   It is a stable-equilibrium long-run model.[3]
2   Real disturbances have long-run real effects; monetary disturbances do not.
3   The dynamics of the adjustment *process* are not spelled out but are assumed to take place smoothly. The model is most frequently presented in the form of comparative statics.
4   Factors of production, including capital, are perfectly mobile internally and immobile internationally. Intertemporal exchange does not take place between countries.
5   It is a model of a free market, unencumbered by government interference or market failure. Markets clear.
6   Money plays a central role, but directly through the endogeneity of the money supply in a fixed exchange rate world. The world stock of money is an exogenous variable, but its distribution between countries is not. The role of the central bank and, for that matter, the banking system, is either inessential or non-existent. These statements apply to the analysis of a

---

[2]   This was developed also, at nearly the same time, by Cantillon (see Bordo 1983). However, it can be said to have been stated, succinctly, by a major mercantilist writer, Thomas Mun [1952], a century earlier, c. 1620. Bowley (1973: 16) summarizes it as follows: "It follows, he claims, that if treasure is imported and prices rise, then trade will be lost and the money will disappear again so that nothing is gained by the favourable balance of payment." Bowley's presentation of Mun and others gives credence to Keynes's argument (1936: Chapter 23) that the mercantilists saw the expansionary nature of an increasing money supply, whether on prices, on employment, or both, and the contractionary effect of decreases.

[3]   I trust this interpretation to be non-controversial. It is shared by expositors of the latter-day "monetary approach": "The source of the simplicity of the monetary theory of the gold standard is clear: the monetary theory is an equilibrium model, whereas the alternative theories are to a greater or lesser extent dynamic, disequilibrium, models" (McCloskey and Zecher 1976: 385).

fixed exchange rate regime. Though the model is formally symmetrical and its dual, a world of floating exchange rates, can be analyzed analogously, the protomodel generally deals with fixed exchange rates, usually based on a commodity money.

It follows from the above that there is no need, in the model, for financing of payments imbalances, hence no short-term capital movements of an accommodating type.

Exactly how changes in the money supply or in the demand function for money work their way through the system to cause changes in the balance of payments – this varies with different models. One major variant is the classical price-specie flow mechanism; another is the mid twentieth-century "monetary approach to the balance of payments". There are even, as we shall see, some keynesian versions of it as well; keynesian in the sense that full employment is not taken for granted, but proto- in that the system does not come to rest as long as imbalances of payments persist, and, under fixed exchange rates, the quantity of money is endogenous (see Meade 1951a, 1951b and Mundell 1968). Monetary changes affect expenditure and trade through the rate of interest, investment and the multiplier, so there is generally a stable equilibrium, given time and the absence of sterilization policies.

The classical variant, stated briefly, is as follows. A shock to the basic balance of payments, most often a supply shock such as a crop failure at home, leading to an increase in imports, puts pressure on exchange rates until the gold shipping (export) point is reached. At that point gold flows between countries; this leads to identical changes in the money supply, in a system of metallic currency, or proportional changes in the money supply where there is a well-behaved fractional-reserve banking system. (That last distinction covers a debate which raged in England for at least fifty years during the nineteenth century, and reemerged, slightly muted, in the 1930s. See Chapter 2.) This leads to changes in expenditure which may result in changes in overall price levels or in the prices of non-traded goods in the several countries, which in turn lead to appropriate changes in the trade balance, after which the specie flow stops. This mechanism is generally attributed in the textbooks to David Hume and labeled the "classical", the "gold standard", the "classical gold standard" or the "price-specie flow" mechanism. The term gold standard is often used globally to apply to any metallic, commodity standard, though in scholarly and historical works it is more correctly reserved for reference to situations where that commodity was specifically gold (as distinct, in general, from silver or from a bimetallic standard) (see de Cecco 1987).

Frenkel and Johnson (1976) deny that price changes are required in the classical paradigm, but they define classical much more broadly than I do. I would argue that the classical position certainly involves monetary imbalance as an important element in the mechanism, but some sort of price change is required for a theory to be labeled "classical" in my classification. There are many casual citations and comments about the possibility of adjustment without price changes but not a clearly articulated theory. Ohlin, as we shall see, does discuss adjustment without price changes, but in the context of defining the knife-edge conditions on the elasticities of demand and supply of goods and factors which will elicit appropriate quantity changes at existing prices.

Johnson adopts the same position when he differentiates his own product from the classical:

As we shall see, the new approach to balance-of-payments theory, while basically Humean in spirit, places the emphasis not on relative price changes but on the direct influence of excess demand for or supply of money on the balance between income and expenditure, or more generally between total acquisition and disposal of funds whether through production and consumption or through borrowing and lending, and therefore on the over-all balance of payments. (Johnson 1976: 148)

He thus agrees that the classical mechanism does indeed emphasize price changes, as well as noting that it concentrates on the trade balance "focus[ing] . . . on international transactions in goods, as distinguished from securities, a characteristic that has remained dominant in balance-of-payments theory" (Johnson 1976: 148).

Starting from this prototype, stripped down, my purpose is to explore how other "schools" deviated from, or added to, that mechanism. The progress of the amendments to the model was by no means linear. I suggest that it was strongly influenced both directly by events and indirectly by the response of economics in general (particularly monetary theory) to real world happenings. In the text, I discuss stream P first, and then stream F. It will be helpful to the reader, however, if the introduction reverses that order. Conceptually and chronologically, there is a point to be made for starting with the oldest grouping, the classical, and with the formal rather than the "applied", which is why I present them first in the introduction. However, in the text I have discussed the classical school very little, starting the story, chronologically, with the neoclassical developments of the 1870s; it is therefore convenient to present this discussion first in the main text.

## Stream F

### The classicals

The CLASSICAL model spans a period of more than 100 years, from the middle of the eighteenth until the late nineteenth century. It is represented by Hume and by Mill, Marshall (partly), and some writers less known today, such as Cairnes, Goschen, and Thornton. Thornton is less well known either because fate is cruel or because he did not write a wide spectrum Treatise on Economics. His *Paper credit* (1802 [1965]) is simply brilliant! (see Perlman 1986 for a penetrating analysis and "restoration"; also Hicks 1967: Chapter 10). Ricardo's position in this grouping has been called into question, for example by Iversen (1935: 215). Chronologically, this brings us into the late nineteenth century.

Essentially, what got into the textbooks as the "classical theory" is that branch of the protomodel which focuses attention on the current account and specifies that some sort of price change is required for adjustment. The dual of the classical theory was the theory of the level of flexible exchange rates, which was much discussed throughout the first twenty years of the nineteenth century, when gold exports were suspended. Ricardo's first major work on the subject of international monetary economics, "The high price of bullion," was written in 1809, in the midst of the specie payment suspension, and was about fluctuating exchange rates, as is evident from the title. Exchange fluctuation, in those days, was frequently expressed in terms of changes in the price of gold bullion. The *Report of the Bullion Committee* (Cannan 1925), published the same year, similarly explains the high price both of gold and of foreign exchange in terms of the monetary shock, an increase in the money supply, leading to rising domestic prices of all goods, including traded goods. In keeping with what I said about the distinction between the two streams, however, note that even this part of Ricardo's oeuvre is an equilibrium model: he decries the high price of bullion and the fallacious policy which led to it, but there is no disequilibrium in the analysis, and the sole policy recommendation is to eliminate the disturbance, that is, to restore convertibility. The one concession he makes to "practical policy" and disequilibrium is to state that this should be done at the right time, and not when the currency is at a 30 percent discount. He repeated this admonition often; both Keynes (1923: 153–4) and Hayek (1932 [1984: 121], and 1937: 44) cite him, the sources including a statement in the House of Commons, June 12, 1822, the paper, "Protection to agriculture," and a letter to John Wheatley, 1821. The argument surrounding the bullion report laid the basis for much subsequent debate about monetary theory. It flared up again, not surprisingly, in Germany in the 1920s in the controversy about whether the inflation was a "monetary" or a "balance-of-payments" phenomenon (see Ellis 1934). An interesting, wide-ranging discussion of the behavior of flexible exchange rate episodes, and of early descriptions of and arguments surrounding them is in Bernholz (1982).

The classical model is simple but the classical economists themselves were not simplistic and there was much discussion about detail and timing of adjustment, though as we shall see most of the argument about the monetary aspects of the adjustment was carried on by bankers and men of affairs, and basically not by those whom we now consider to have been the "classical economists". Both O'Brien (1971) and Fetter (1965) note that the "mainstream" economists were not contributing to monetary theory during the nineteenth century.

More recently, another branch of the protomodel became popular and widely accepted. It is referred to as the monetary approach to the balance of payments, sometimes abbreviated to MABP. Since it flowered in a more recent period than I am surveying here, I shall not discuss it at length. Briefly, however, it emphasizes a portfolio, rather than a flow, approach to the balance of payments; it therefore assigns no importance to the distinction between the current and capital accounts. The approach is usually argued by writers who believe not only that the law of one price for traded goods is always satisfied but also that complete purchasing power parity is attained rapidly. Adjustments in international payments take place, therefore, primarily through quantity rather than price changes. An increase in the money supply of a given country (which is the typical shock discussed in most of the examples in this literature, as distinct from the classicals' real shocks) will lead to increased spending on everything, including foreign goods and foreign securities, and this leads directly to balance in international payments and to a restoration of the original distribution of money between countries: the crucial characteristic of the endogeneity of the money supply. "In the monetary theory, the international market short-circuits the effects of domestic policy on American prices, and the expansion of the domestic supply of money spills *directly* into a deficit in the balance of payments" (McCloskey and Zecher 1976: 370, italics mine). For further discussion of the monetary approach to the balance of payments, see Frenkel and Johnson (1976) *passim*, and International Monetary Fund (1977).

When we get beyond the elementary textbooks, we find the classicals in general, and Hume in particular, being accused of neglecting the law of one price. But there is a great deal of evidence that they were not guilty (this includes Hume, according to Viner 1937) and that they were fully aware that commodity arbitrage prevents the prices of internationally traded goods from being different in different countries at the same time. There were indeed varying interpretations of the causes, significance, and meaning of "price differences" and "price changes". There still are. There are models in the contemporary literature in which each country is completely specialized in the production of one good; those in which there are two commodities, with both countries producing both (as in the Heckscher-Ohlin world), and those in which one or more internationally traded goods are produced as well as non-traded goods. In each of these the meaning of price changes is different. Nevertheless the classical school is characterized by the notion that price changes of some sort lead to shifts in production and consumption which result in changes in trade. Price changes are essential and the adjustment is complete (that is, the model was believed to be stable) because the specie flow continues as long as imbalances remain and the system is out of equilibrium.

There have been lively debates about the meaning of the term "equilibrium" in this context. I wish to avoid getting embroiled in that argument here. However, it is common, and useful, to describe as disequilibrium a situation in which, under fixed exchange rates, either the reserve asset is being traded between countries, or substitute financial assets are being traded in a manner induced by the imbalance (this includes a capital inflow induced by a "tight money policy" which is instituted in order to induce such "financing" of an imbalance in payments). Under floating exchange rates, the parallel symptom of disequilibrium would be the observed changes in exchange rates in the absence of a monetary policy specifically designed to prevent them by affecting short-term capital movements[4] (see Nurkse 1945 [1949: 9–12]).

There were arguments about whether or not specie flows preceded or followed the price changes. But the catalyst to the adjustment was the change in the money supply (which might anticipate the specie flow in a fractional reserve banking world) not the disturbance *per se*. In the simple keynesian model, the reduction in income resulting from a decline in exports leads directly to adjustments in trade. In all of the classical models, the monetary effects intervene. There were, as noted above, fierce arguments about the need for specie flows in order to bring about the adjustment. The main proponent of the negative position in this debate was Ricardo. But the reason was that Ricardo was almost always interested in the long-run equilibrium position. He was not concerned with adjustment as a process and appears, like the monetarists of 150 years later, to have believed that adjustment in any case was almost invariably complete and very rapid in terms of real time.[5] Furthermore, he clearly stated the rational expectations argument – in many cases gold would not flow because everybody knew it would have to flow back eventually, so there was no point in going to the expense of shipping it; for the same reason, apparently, there were many cases in which

[4]    This clearly raises problems which I am not entering into here. It suggests that there is a sense indeed in which "there is no such thing as a really clean float." I discussed some of these issues in Flanders (1974).

[5]    This is not suggested as a revisionist interpretation of Ricardo. Sayers, for example, writes: "Like other parts of Ricardo's doctrine, there was an assumption here [in his bullionist views] of instantaneous adjustment to a long-run equilibrium. In later days . . . Ricardo did occasionally concede that, in this as in other respects, there might be some friction in the transition to the long-run effect which alone his intellectual blinkers generally allowed him to see" ("Ricardo's Views on Monetary Questions", in Ashton and Sayers 1953: 81; see also the treatment of Ricardo in Blaug 1985, for example).

prices would not be changed, because people knew that the long-run equilibrium price had not changed and there was no point in undertaking the cost of making temporary changes. "Is it conceivable that money should be sent abroad for the purpose merely of rendering it dear in this country and cheap in another, and by such means to ensure its return to us?" (Ricardo 1811 [1951: 103], appendix to the "High price of bullion").

The classical paradigm generally ignored the role of the interest rate. Not being concerned with short-term capital movements, and not attaching to the rate of interest any importance in determining total expenditure, the doctrine had no important task to assign to the interest rate. The rate of interest determined the allocation between present and future, but that was essentially irrelevant to the question of the balance of payments. As we shall see in the discussion of the late classicals, it could play an important part in determining the level of "autonomous" capital flows, but once that was done, it did not affect the process by which the trade balance was adjusted to those capital flows.

In general the shocks discussed by the classicals were real. This despite the fact that the brief statement by Hume dealt with a monetary shock. The classicals did discuss the transfer problem, but as Laidler puts it:

capital movements tended to be associated with once and for all payments of subsidies to allies, or of reparations to victorious enemies, or to involve the temporary financing of trade imbalances associated with bad harvests. Hence, though capital movements were analysed and discussed in the Classical Economics, they were treated as complicating factors of temporary duration. (Laidler 1987: 28)

I shall not cover the classical writings in detail; I would consider it presumptuous, given Viner's monumental work. In the next chapter we shall meet it briefly in a discussion of the nineteenth-century controversies, as a prelude to the neoclassical view.

### The late classicals

The LATE CLASSICAL school appeared (primarily) in the twentieth century. It consists of Frank Taussig and his students, Harry Dexter White, John Williams, and Jacob Viner. I include James Angell as well, though he would probably have declined the honor. Ohlin referred to them as the Harvard School and considered himself one of them. A potential outlier, both in time and place, is Ricardo, whose co-option into this group has been suggested by several writers, notably Viner (1937) and Iversen (1935).

The late classical is, as the name suggests, very similar to the classical paradigm. At first blush it seems that only time separates the two. It is wholly classical in outlook, an equilibrium system (though at least one member of the school, White, expressed some doubts), in which the moving force is price changes in response to monetary stimuli, and the production and trade shifts which result from these.

However, there are differences:

1   Unlike the classicals the late classicals were trying (clumsily, lacking the tools, but brilliantly) to spell out some of the dynamics of the model.
2   Capital, as a factor of production, is mobile internationally in their work. The studies are a series of explorations of the capital transfers of the nineteenth century, carried out as case studies to test what they considered to be the classical adjustment mechanism, inquiring whether the financial lending got translated into trade surpluses. Since capital as a factor of production is mobile internationally, the door is opened to the contemporary studies of intertemporal optimization in trade, both for the purpose of changing the time path and structure of production and in order to change the time pattern of consumption.[6] Imbalances in payments are a means by which a country can achieve pareto efficient transfers of resources through time. My own view is that Taussig and his students did not set out deliberately to change the assumptions of the classical model. Wanting to test received theory empirically, they were simply looking for particular cases where the disturbance was both large and easily identified.
3   Since there is greater concern with the transfer problem, the possibility of incomplete transfer requires the consideration of short-term capital movements as well, and they do play a role, though not a central one, in most of the late classical works.

The late classicals share with the classicals the concept of the adjustment mechanism as complete and self-equilibrating, without the necessary intervention or even existence of the monetary authorities; the Canada of Viner's study did not have a central bank. They share also, with the classicals and with one another, the view of price changes as an integral, important, indeed essential part of the adjustment mechanism.[7] What is important to

---

[6]   References to the contemporary literature in this area and the intimately related issue of the optimal path of international borrowing include: Helpman (1981); Helpman and Razin (1979); Mosak (1944); Obstfeld and Stockman (1985), an extensive survey, especially 957–71; Persson and Svensson (1985); Sachs (1981), (1982), (1984); Svensson and Razin (1983); and a dissertation in progress by Adam Klug. Some of these are models of exchange rate determination under flexible exchange rates, but the issue of the optimal path of current account imbalances is there.

[7]   It is in this respect that Ohlin cannot be placed squarely in the late classical camp. It is precisely here that he fills the space between the classical and keynesian views. However, before rushing to conclude that Ohlin was wholly keynesian in this respect, we might note that much of Ohlin's rejection of price changes was based on the presumption of quantity adjustments to potential price changes which rendered actual changes in prices unnecessary

them is that an imbalance in the basic balance of payments, by creating an excess demand for foreign exchange, has *immediate* and direct effects, through the banking and monetary system, on expenditures. It is not necessary for the specie shipping point to be reached and for gold to flow in order for an "adjustment" to begin.

An interesting exception to the generalization that transfers tended to get effected was the German Reparations issue and the literature which it inspired, including the famous debate between Keynes (1929a, 1929b, 1929c) and Ohlin (1929a, 1929b). What interests me at this juncture is the implication, not surprising, that the real difficulty with a transfer arises when it constitutes a shock which is exogenous, not only to the trade model, but to the full model of the economy. By this I mean that while an increase in foreign lending can be thought of as a disturbance to the balance of payments, it is an endogenous variable in the context of a full-fledged model of the whole economy. The same cannot be said of reparations (without taking a broader view of "economic variables" than most economists today would be willing to adopt). If one thinks of all the obstacles to a transfer's being effected, the road of reparations must surely be the rockiest one, as compared with private lending or even foreign aid.

Specie movements are not essential to the adjustment, and in fact, in the cases studied, they often occurred after the adjustment had been effected, if at all. Taussig was less emphatic on this point than were his students, but I include him as a "late classical" rather than a latter day "classical" because he was the founder of the Harvard School and because his own agonizing doubts about the correctness of the classical view were presumably a major source of inspiration to his students in their explorations.

At the same time these writers are all classical in the sense that price changes (intersectoral price shifts, or changes in the real exchange rate) play an important, in general, an essential, role. The final adjustment comes about because of a change in intersectoral relative prices. (Here again is an issue on which Ohlin does not fit comfortably into the late classical school.) They are non-classical only in the sense that the banking system (though, to repeat, not the central bank) plays an important role, and any disturbance to the balance of payments results directly in a change in the domestic money supply. Whether this now affects prices more than quantities, purchases of domestic goods more than foreign, tradable more than non-tradable goods – these depend on the viewpoint of the writer and on the events he is analyzing. But, to repeat, it is emphasis on the direct impact of the foreign exchange market on monetary variables and other macro variables which character-

(see Chapter 13). Ricardo sometimes also appears to be an exception, primarily for the opposite reason, his lack of interest in the adjustment *process*; it is for this reason, as much as for the chronological anomaly, that I have not included him fully in this group.

izes this group. Their monetary theory is more complex than the simple, mechanistic quantity theory characteristic of the classical school. The rate of interest, however, is not emphasized as affecting either internal activity and hence the trade balance, or capital movements, which are not important in the adjustment mechanism.

Why the classical model reemerged so robustly when it did I do not know. It may have been in part an accident in the person of Frank Taussig. He was very much a classical economist; in his *Principles of economics* (1915 [1919: 113–224]), he distinguishes between use-value and exchange-value, though he spells out the Marshallian theory of pricing very clearly, elaborating the common metaphor of the scissors of supply and demand, the refinements required because of varying returns to scale, and similar neoclassical concepts. In the later *International trade* (1927), he goes back not only to a real cost theory but to a labor cost theory, attributing international comparative advantage to differences in labor cost, and acknowledging that this "point of departure . . . is that of Ricardo, Mill, and their successors" (Taussig 1927: 4). But the classical paradigm had never died or been rejected; this was not a revival of a corpse. Interest had centered for some years on other issues; many people who were writing about other problems (the neoclassicals primarily) simply took the classical paradigm for granted.

### Ohlin

OHLIN needs to be treated separately. With one foot on the brink of modern macro theory (along with the rest of the Stockholm School) and the other rooted in Heckscher-Ohlin trade theory, he worried about the effects of a disturbance on total spending but at least as much about the price and quantity adjustments of both goods and factors as demand shifted between sectors and between countries. In his emphasis on the essential role of relative price changes in stimulating the required shifts in output, he is thoroughly classical. In his examination of total expenditure decisions in response to what he called "changes in purchasing power" he is almost keynesian.

### The keynesians

I include here writers such as Harrod, Machlup, Neisser and Modigliani (though theirs was an econometric study), and some of Metzler (his work on the transfer problem, for example). These are people who followed Keynes (of the *General theory*) into the realm of disequilibrium, non-market clearing models and applied them, as Keynes did *not*, to an open economy. Metzler, in his "Survey", drew attention to this oft-neglected fact. "It is perhaps unfair to describe the modern theory of adjustment of the balance of payments as 'Keynesian economics', since Keynes himself had little to do with it. The new theory is Keynesian only in the sense that it is a direct outgrowth of the theory of employment" (Metzler 1948 [1973: Chapter 1, 13n]).

The pure keynesian view emphasizes the interrelationship between the balance of trade on the one hand and the levels of income and employment on the other. A disturbance in the trade account engenders responses which lead to changes in the balance of payments, generally in an equilibrating direction, but never (hardly ever) sufficient to restore equilibrium. All the keynesian models are fixprice models. In fact, I would argue that this is a definition of "keynesian" in this context, and it is for this reason that I use the lower case "k". The use of the term "Keynesian" to apply to all models with fixed prices is much debated and I wish to avoid that particular argument. Furthermore, Keynes himself never enunciated the keynesian adjustment mechanism.

Whether to characterize their models as long-run or not is essentially a question of definition of length of run. If long-run means, by definition, long-run equilibrium, then not. They do give a good deal of attention to the possibility of long-run, or permanent, disequilibrium. Structural shifts in an economy, through relative price effects, are non-existent in these models. Monetary effects of payments imbalances are likewise ignored. The incorporation of them into keynesian real models had to await the confluence of the post-keynesian literature (see below).

Like Ohlin, the keynesians are formal model-builders. They operate in the tradition of the classical paradigm: comparative static analysis of market-driven economies responding to exogenous disturbances. They ask the same question that the classicals asked – they reject the classical answers. As in the classical model, neither short- nor long-run capital movements play a role, either in disturbing or restoring equilibrium (although, as we shall see, some of the crisis writers had a decidedly keynesian outlook). In the later keynesian literature there may be policy actions to initiate short-term capital movements to finance a deficit. Again, in the later literature, as noted above, the quantity of money varies with the balance of payments and directly affects the level of expenditures. In the pre-1950 literature there is little of that. See Harrod (1933) for a prescient exception, important because, unique among the keynesian models, it treats money as endogenous and is therefore self-equilibrating. This phenomenon did not recur, I believe, until Tsiang (1961 [1968]). In general there is no serious discussion of specie flows (or reserve changes) and if such do occur, central banks are as likely as not to sterilize them. If monetary changes were unrestricted they would operate in an equilibrating manner by affecting interest rates and therefore investment, not by influencing expenditure directly.

Formally, if the law of one price holds and there is only one commodity produced in each country, there is no room for any sort of "price" change under fixed exchange rates, and only income and expenditure changes can matter. But I would turn this statement around and argue that it was because they assumed a fixprice world that keynesian writers slipped into the assumption of a single good, since with fixed prices and unemployed resources, the elasticity of supply between goods is infinite, so the assumption of a single commodity, or a hicksian composite commodity, is applicable. They thus ignored all intersectoral effects. Non-traded goods were rediscovered in the 1960s (see Salter 1959); they were recognized in all pre-keynesian theories and were crucial to some of them, most notably Ohlin's. How expenditure changes get allocated between home goods and foreign goods is important and interesting, but it is captured fully in the concept of the marginal propensity to import. Relative prices between sectors play no role here. Since income is generally regarded as unconstrained by supply limitations and thus inside the production frontier, elasticities of substitution in production are very high in these models – in general they are infinite, so output can be increased in any category of goods, without reducing it in any other. Most of the models of this group are therefore one-good models, in which aggregate output is treated as a single composite commodity.

Furthermore, in the keynesian model adjustment is generally incomplete (though Metzler, in his treatment of the transfer problem, is able to get complete adjustment in some cases with the help of endogenous investment – Metzler 1942b [1973: Chapter 2]). And since there are no intersectoral relative price changes, the only way of achieving full adjustment is to change the exchange rate. This, to my mind, explains (as much as the historical fact that there were devaluations) the association of the early keynesian writers with the literature on the effects of devaluation. (Here there is of course room for relative price changes between sectors, but it is not necessary. A high enough elasticity of substitution in demand between home and foreign goods is sufficient to assure the success of a devaluation. Supply effects are secondary.) The exchange rate is the only price left which is subject to change and which may have any impact on real variables. These views were particularly prominent during the period when there was topical interest in such models, such as the years following the inconvertibilities and exchange rate changes of the war, the 1920s and the 1930s (Bickerdike 1920, Robinson 1937).

## Stream P

### The neoclassicals

The NEOCLASSICAL view is generally slipped in between the classical and the keynesian. I am arguing, however, that it was an early offshoot into a tradition different from both. The name "neoclassical" is bad, but I continue it because it has been used in this context previously. The problem is that outside the field of international economics, the word "neoclassical" has a fairly precise meaning, which is different from the one used above. Perhaps the "interest rate school" would be better ("banking school" has been appropriated for other uses); Keynes means something very similar when he refers to the "Bank rate school" (Keynes 1930: Volume 1, 186 ff).

It is difficult to name names here. The discussions and arguments leading to it persisted throughout the nineteenth century but we generally think of them as having been integrated into a Doctrine (not a "Research Program") starting with Bagehot and culminating with the Cunliffe Report and working its way into the popular inherited wisdom of what the classical system was about. Here the classical story is augmented with a banking system, not necessarily well-behaved, but now including, importantly, a central bank; and a rate of interest. These together combine to modify the classical story and, significantly, to induce international shifts in short-term financial capital. Commercial banks in the course of their own profit-seeking activity, and the central bank following the famous "rules", will engage in various forms of credit-tightening activity when specie or bullion (or, in a Bretton Woods context, international reserves) flow out, but not before. In some versions this is associated with prescriptive statements to central banks to behave in this fashion – the "rules of the game" story. This term, by the way, is attributed by Moggridge (Keynes 1929–31 [1981: 42]) to Sir Robert Kindersley, in his testimony to the Macmillan Committee February 6, 1930. However, Keynes used it in 1925 in an article in *The Nation and Athenaeum*: "If we must have a gold standard, we had better play the gold standard game according to the recognised rules" (Keynes 1922–29 [1981: 360]). In "The Economic Consequences of Mr Churchill" (1925) we find: "The Bank of England is *compelled* to curtail credit by all the rules of the gold standard game" (Keynes 1931 [1972: 220], italics his).

Superimposed on the classical skeleton is an interest rate which affects not only the domestic economy and hence the balance of trade but also short-term trade in assets, influencing the overall balance of payments, the foreign exchange reserves of the central bank, and hence the endogeneity of the money supply. Harry Johnson, with his usual flair for apt condensation, expresses it as follows, though his terminology is not the same as mine:

The subsequent elaboration of the theory, up to and partly through the 1930s, retained the general notion of automaticity while adding in the complications required by the existence of credit money provided by commercial banks [the late classicals] and of central banking based on partial international reserve holdings, and by the possibility of attraction or otherwise of international short-term capital movements through international interest-rate differentials [part of the neoclassical statement]. (Johnson 1976: 148–9)

One can only speculate on the reasons for the relatively sudden ascendancy of this view of the world in the late nineteenth and early twentieth century. One problem, as we shall see, is the close intertwining of normative with positive statements in this body of thought. A number of people were intrigued by the implausible ease with which adjustment had apparently taken place in the nineteenth century. Keynes, for example, argued that the nineteenth century had never witnessed a real adjustment of the type implied by the "classical theory" and that shifts in the volume of British foreign investment had been sufficient to maintain balance in international payments (see Chapter 6). The expected difficulty of real adjustment, combined with the apparent ease with which payments seemed to be adjusting, troubled Frank Taussig very deeply, and he never succeeded in satisfying his doubts. Similar scepticism about the apparent smoothness of the process also underlies much of the revisionist view of the workings of the gold standard, expressed by people such as Triffin (1964) and Brown (1940), although they were actually attacking the neoclassical position at least as strongly as they were the classical one.

The neoclassical position may well have been based on the assumption that if things were happening too well and too smoothly to be automatic, then, presumably somebody must be in there steering. As Bagehot had noted, "money will not manage itself" (Bagehot 1873: 20). Though the neoclassical position involves a diversion from the classical paradigm, and asks very different questions, it takes the classical view as given and assumes its validity. That is, the long-run equilibrium exists, is stable, and involves the classical kind of price changes leading to the required structural changes. But the issues with which the neoclassicals were concerned involve a short-run system which is not self-equilibrating, and:

1    in which the rate of interest is an important variable, both "externally" and "internally",
2    which emphasizes the dynamics of adjustment,
3    where financing takes place; that is, capital is mobile internationally,
4    where the authorities are interfering in the process.

Whether the monetary authorities played a stabilizing role was a question on which opinions varied, but much of the argument here reads like a preview to the policy debate and the dilemma of internal versus external equilibrium of the 1950s and 1960s. The monetary authorities often were told that their interference was required precisely in order to slow down the adjustment mechanism. In the 1950s, in the Mundell-Fleming literature, we got solutions to this problem which both recognized and internalized the disequilibrium, since they involved incurring sustained capital flows in order to finance permanent current account imbalances.

The neoclassical view is associated frequently with the name of Bagehot, but Marshall figures importantly (in the Gold and Silver Commission testimony). In the twentieth century it flowered in the Cunliffe Committee Report, which is widely cited as the *locus classicus* of the neoclassical doctrine and was the subject of investigation by Keynes in the *Treatise* (where it was named the "Bank rate" school) and in the Macmillan Committee.

### The anti-neoclassicals

There were three forms of objection to the neoclassical position. The first, represented by HAYEK, agreed that it was a fairly accurate description of reality in the pre-World War I period and that this was, in fact, the root of the world's problems. The problem with both the historical gold standard and with the neoclassical prescription was the looseness of the connection between the money supply and the balance of payments. Only a system of fixed exchange rates in which the domestic money supply varies in a one-to-one ratio with the foreign exchange reserves would achieve stability, both external and internal.

The second, HAWTREY, also agreed that the world had been working roughly as the neoclassicals described it, and attributed to this the domestic instability which he observed about him. Excessive concern with the protection of the foreign exchange reserves had made central bankers insensitive to the needs of domestic trade and commerce for a stable supply of credit. Short-term financing through bank-rate induced capital flows was at best useless.

The third, a group I have labelled the REVISIONISTS, Bloomfield (1959) and (1963), Brown (1940), Triffin (1947) and to a lesser extent Whale (1937 [1953]), questioned the historical accuracy of the neoclassical view. Essentially they argued that the apparent smoothness with which the international payments mechanism worked in the pre-World War I period had explanations other than the neoclassical one of the central banks, each following the famous Rules of the Game. The central banks on the whole did not behave that way, they said, and some of them implied that such activity was both unnecessary and insufficient to explain the facts, at least during the latter half of the nineteenth century. The international monetary regime, they argued, was basically that of a sterling standard, much as the period of the 1950s and 1960s is thought by many to have been a dollar standard. In the sense that he emphasizes the hegemony of Britain and the pound sterling, de Cecco (1984) might be classified as a revisionist, but I confess that I do not really understand his rather machiavellian explanation of how the international system functioned; I have therefore not tried to explain it.

### Keynes

KEYNES is an outlier in the sense that he was more solidly placed in the world of affairs than many academic colleagues. He belongs in the P stream, in my view, despite his extensive theoretical writings. He concentrated most of his attention, in this field, on short-run, dynamic issues. The extent of his writings on the subject is one of the reasons I have chosen to deal with him as a separate category. Like the neoclassicals, and like Hawtrey, he was concerned with short-run, disequilibrium situations, with the role of the banks and the central bank, with the history of what had actually happened, and with prescriptions for monetary management. He was a classical in the sense that for him adjustment required price changes. He differed in that he rejected the notion that these would necessarily occur and that the system would converge to long-run equilibrium. In short, if there were an adjustment mechanism, according to Keynes, it would have been a classical one.

### The crisis writers

There is a group of writers (BLOOMFIELD 1950, FANNO 1935 and 1939, KINDLEBERGER 1937, NURKSE 1944) concerned primarily with the problems of shocks, often of a non-economic nature. Like the neoclassicals and others in this stream, they are concerned with short-run, disequilibrium problems, in which management and intervention are prescribed. They differ from the other groups in that they look in general outside the basic balance for the source of disturbances, so their approach is neither one of fundamental disequilibrium in the trade account, nor that of the transfer problem. They are, rather, much concerned (albeit not exclusively) with the destabilizing effects of short-term capital movements, or of domestic monetary shocks. And they worry, variously, about whether the authorities are performing the appropriate stabilizing role, or, in fact, destabilizing and exacerbating disequilibria (if not actually initiating them) themselves.

There is, of course, room for serious question as to whether there should be adjustment to capital movements of this type: short-term flight capital initiated often by political uncertainty. Is it pareto efficient to adjust to hot-money and speculative capital flights by changing internal relative prices and the structure of production, that is, by effecting the transfer? Many, probably most, economists would argue not. Essentially this view underlies much of the argument which Milton Friedman (1953) marshaled in favor of flexible exchange rates: the desirability of isolating an economy from external shocks that did not involve real shifts, such as changes in technology or tastes.

The crisis writers differ from the neoclassicals, however, in that they draw from the keynesian rather than the classical paradigm their view of what the adjustment mechanism would look like if it occurred. Since this generally involved changes in real income and in employment, it was, as a rule, to be avoided rather than encouraged. Like the neoclassical version, it frequently combines normative and positive approaches, which makes it more difficult to summarize.

But they emphasize the effects of monetary changes on expenditure much more than the keynesians – here they are similar to the late classicals. They differ among themselves in their view of how expenditure changes work their way through the domestic and foreign economies, and how their effects are divided between price and quantity changes. But they share the view that such changes are the counterparts of changes in the balance of payments, and that specie flows or reserve shifts are not important to the mechanism.

### MMM: post Keynes

METZLER, MEADE and MUNDELL constitute both a confluence of what preceded and the headwaters of the "modern era". Meade and Mundell, and many others after them, concerned themselves with the interlacing of the problems of balancing international payments with macro models of non-clearing markets and unemployment. The requirement that monetary authorities satisfy some sort of budget constraint on foreign exchange, coupled with their commitments to countering the unpleasant effects of uncleared markets at home was the subject of the discussion. Mundell, in particular, and Meade to a lesser extent, present prescriptive models involving "permanent" short-term capital flows. In this sense, like the earlier keynesian models, they imply long-run disequilibrium. There is very little concern with basic structural adjustment to real shocks, driven by price changes. As distinct from the simpler keynesian models, however, money and the rate of interest have central roles here.

Their models incorporate the real balance effects of changes in the money supply. This marks the "keynesian" movement in the direction back to the protomodel, in which the money supply is endogenous under fixed exchange rates. Thus reserve holdings, or specie, continue to change as long as payments are unbalanced; and as long as reserves, and the money supply, are changing, the system will not come to a stop and will continue to move in the direction of equilibrium in the balance of payments (though not necessarily in domestic income and employment).

Metzler (1960 [1973: Chapter 8]) is somewhat different from the other two, in that his is a full employment, flexible price world. So flexible, in fact, that the dynamics of adjustment to changes (such as taste and technology) enter not at all. I include him in this group because his pinpointing the role of the interest rate (in his model, purely endogenously determined) and the feedback to the balance of payments through capital flows was seminal in the development of this literature. With the development of his model, the money supply is once more endogenous in a fixed exchange rate system (as it ceased to be in the keynesian models) and a function of the rate of interest. It was this which paved the way for the assignment problem literature. Frenkel and Johnson (1976) argue that Meade opened the door to the monetary approach to the balance of payments. In a way this is true, but in fact it was Metzler who did it even more so, and probably earlier; it is precisely the endogeneity of the money supply, for a particular country, that is the cornerstone of his model.

The classification thus far is the one that makes the most sense to me. The reader may be justified in thinking it somewhat idiosyncratic. Other classifications are, of course, possible. Triffin, for example, in 1947, divided the world of ideas or mechanisms into two: those with, and those without, central banks, and, presumably, private banks whose obligations were part of the money supply. In a masterpiece of succinct eclecticism, which is worth quoting in its entirety, he describes the workings of such a system:

International balance, if disturbed, would be restored because of the effects of the ensuing domestic contraction or expansion on relative cost and interest levels at home and abroad and the resulting shifts in trade and capital movements. The automatic monetary contraction produced by gold exports would raise interest rates and attract capital from abroad. It would at the same time exert a downward pressure on domestic prices and costs, thus stimulating exports and discouraging imports. Both of these movements – capital and trade – would tend to correct the balance of payments deficit in which they originated. (Triffin 1947: 48)

This passage is accompanied by the following footnote:

Modern theories of international trade and capital movements would incorporate two further major elements in this analysis. One is the elasticity of supply and demand for imports and exports, the other the direct income effects associated with balance of payments disequilibria. (Triffin 1947: 48)

In this brief paragraph he includes what I have called the classical and the late classical schools, along with many of the salient characteristics of the neoclassical and keynesian approaches. Like Whale, he incorporates interest rate effects into the classical approach, whereas I have allocated them to the realm of the neoclassical. He has also injected the effect of the interest rate on capital flows into the classical mold, whereas in my classification this influence is important only in the neoclassical literature. This creation of a broad supercategory is, of course, entirely legitimate. I simply find it useful to cut with a sharper knife.

Summarizing and generalizing the distinctions I have made, I have suggested that stream P (for policy) has to do with short-run equilibrium, or disequilibrium models, stream F (for "formal") with long-run equilibrium models. What emerges from this is that stream P writers are typically much more likely to be involved with policy issues. Often, at least some of these policy issues involve ways in which the authorities attempt to finance, or to encourage private financing of, imbalances. What then becomes a characteristic of the several models is the way in which they treat short-term financial capital flows. I have therefore chosen to emphasize this aspect relatively heavily in analyzing the several approaches.

The different treatment of trade in financial assets is a symptom, I would argue, of differences between the schools, not a basic element in those differences. From the extreme of the crisis school which views such flows as the main cause of disturbance and problems, through Hawtrey's and Keynes's concern with whether it is desirable to finance imbalances in this way, to the famous neoclassical statement of the rules of the game, passing the late classical inclusion of some factor mobility, and thus to the other extremum of the classical purity of nothing flowing between countries except traded goods and services (including gold), we have the gamut of views as to the automaticity and self-equilibrating notion of the international mechanism.

Think of this chapter as a long annotated table of contents. I begin with a very brief third-hand survey of the classical literature, since, as I noted above, I could not hope to improve on what has been done. As the title suggests, the era between the classical of the nineteenth century and the new classical of the late twentieth century is the period on which I have concentrated my efforts.

# CHAPTER 2

# The classical mainstream and the nineteenth-century monetary controversies

A brief summary of the highlights of the nineteenth century will serve as a background to later developments. I draw heavily on secondary sources, Fetter (1965), O'Brien (in his fascinating introduction to *The correspondence of Lord Overstone*, 1971: 70–82) and Viner (1937). The first two do not concentrate specifically on international considerations, but then the early monetary discussions distinguished less than did later ones between closed and open economy analysis. This justifies the muted distinction made by writers such as Fetter and O'Brien (and even, to a certain extent, Viner). I can think of several reasons for this:

1   The openness of the British economy, which led naturally to the assumption that one was dealing with an open economy model. By contrast, the American economy (whence much of the later discussion issued) was, at least until recently, relatively closed.
2   The institutional differences: throughout most of the nineteenth century, a metallic standard meant that bank notes were convertible into gold (and/or silver) at will, whether internally or externally. Thus, issues of the integrity and convertibility (into metal) of the liabilities of either the central or private banks were essentially independent of who was demanding the specie or bullion and what they planned to do with it. Bagehot indeed did distinguish between internal and external drains, but this came later, towards the end of the nineteenth century.

Most of the literature I shall deal with here is British. This may partially reflect a linguistic bias, but even Schumpeter (1959) admits that the English were predominant in this area at least through most of the nineteenth century.[1]

---

[1]  In the twentieth century, as far as I know, the major contributions were also in English. The important exception is the German monetary controversy thoroughly surveyed by H. S. Ellis (1934). Historical exigencies led to the appearance in English of most of the important writings of the major German and Austrian writers of the first third of the twentieth century and beyond.

## The classicals

To repeat the generalization made in Chapter 1, the dominant feature of the classical view is that it is a long-run equilibrium model. I have argued that price changes are essential to the mechanism. Fetter (1965: 227), *inter alia*, makes the same point, citing Mill (Book III, Chapter 20, Section 3 of his *Principles*): "It is through the prices of commodities that the correction must be administered."

Yet there were lengthy discussions about how essential, in fact, price changes were. Ricardo, in a clear statement of the theory of global monetarism, describes an equilibrium in which the specie stock of the world is distributed (or redistributed after a shock) in proportion to each country's level of economic activity.[2] Such a distribution can take place without any prices changing. All that is required is that payments imbalance lead to monetary changes which in turn affect the balance of payments in an equilibrating direction. He was ever interested in the comparative static equilibrium solutions, less in the adjustment process. He also had the concept of rational expectations,[3] and was, in addition, not greatly interested in highly disaggregated general-equilibrium systems – all of these would make him minimize the importance of price changes in the adjustment process. On the other hand, since he tended almost always to be concerned with the equilibrium solutions it is difficult to tell sometimes whether he has a pure monetary version (the straightforward version of the protomodel) of the balance of payments or whether price changes are lurking in the background, though not spelled out explicitly. What does seem clear is that, like the latter-day monetarists, he thought in terms of long-term adjustment which presumably took place very rapidly in terms of real time.[4]

[2]  Similar statements appear a number of times in Ricardo's writings. One early reference is to be found in Ricardo (1811 [1951]: 53–4): "If the quantity of gold and silver in the world employed as money were exceedingly small, or abundantly great, it would not in the least affect the proportions in which they would be divided among the different nations – the variation in their quantity would have produced no other effect than to make the commodities for which they were exchanged comparatively dear or cheap ... If ... one nation advanced more rapidly than the others, that nation would require and obtain a greater proportion of the money of the world ... While the relative situation of countries continued unaltered, they might have abundant commerce with each other, but their exports and imports would on the whole be equal ... [B]ills of exchange would make the necessary payments, but no money would pass, because it would have the same value in all countries."

[3]  "Is it to be contended that these results would not be foreseen, and the expence and trouble attending these needless operations effectually prevented, in a country where capital is abundant, where every possible economy in trade is practised, and where competition is pushed to its utmost limits? Is it conceivable that money should be sent abroad for the purpose merely of rendering it dear in this country and cheap in another, and by such means to ensure its return to us?" (Ricardo 1811 [1951]: 103]).

[4]  Perlman (1986: 755–7) presents a convincing argument that Ricardo's unblemished monetarist structure was weakened a decade after "The high price of bullion" (first published

Note that the notion of the natural distribution of specie assumes that not only accommodating capital movements, that is, short-term financing, but also autonomous capital movements, are zero. Again, this reinforces the view of Ricardo as one whose interests lay primarily with long-run equilibrium. Except for some of the most recent literature on the sustainability of permanent borrowing, most writers have taken the position that long-term equilibrium is consistent only with balance of trade equality (see Sachs 1984 and Chapter 1, note 5).

Ricardo was not, however, alone in recognizing that changes in the money supply could lead to direct expenditure changes, anticipating the monetary approach to the balance of payments of the 1970s. Viner (1937) devotes a whole section (Chapter VI, Part III) to a discussion of the classicals' awareness of both the "income effect" and of direct effects on expenditures of changes in the money supply, and he joins the names of Wheatley, Bastable, and Nicholson to that of Ricardo as having "denied, or questioned, the necessity of relative price changes for the restoration of equilibrium" (Viner 1937: 303–4). Iversen (1935: 215) goes so far as to categorize Ricardo as non-classical, for precisely the same reason.

A major theme of Viner's argument in the above-mentioned section (perhaps in the whole of Chapter VI) is to defend the classical economists from Ohlin's accusation that they ignored the instrumental role of demand shifts in the adjustment process. Viner recognizes that once the point is made that demand shifts play a part it is obvious, and it is therefore difficult to say how obvious it "should" have been to others. He proceeds to discuss the issue of how important it was in the classical theory, while claiming to "disregard incidental recognition of the relationship between amount of income and extent of demand, which has always been common, even with laymen," and to concentrate on "cases where such recognition is to be found incorporated as an integral part of a more or less formal exposition by nineteenth-century writers of the mechanism of adjustment of international balances" (Viner 1937: 294).

More important than the issue of historical precedence, however, is the interpretation of what Ohlin was in fact arguing. As we shall see below (Chapter 13), Ohlin's emphasis on demand was in part a pre-keynesian insight, but it stemmed also (I would say, primarily) from his detailed, disaggregated general-equilibrium approach, as he emphasized the importance of sectoral demand shifts in inducing structural shifts in output.

in 1810) when, with the publication of the *Principles* (1821) he had developed a real trade theory in which relative prices did and could move in response to real shocks. But Perlman acknowledges as well that Ricardo was indeed interested in long-term equilibrium. Viner (1937: 150) comments, in the course of his discussion on the bullionist controversy: "Here once more Ricardo was applying long-run considerations to a short-run problem."

In his *Studies in the theory of international trade*, a work of great and meticulous scholarship, Viner (1937) details extensively the monetary debates of the nineteenth (and eighteenth) century. The core of the treatment of international monetary issues is imbedded in two central chapters, VI and VII, titled respectively "The International Mechanism under a Simple Specie Currency" and "The International Mechanism in Relation to Modern Banking Processes."

Since there had not been a simple specie currency in Britain for centuries, the distinction implied by these titles is not an historical but rather an analytical one. The first chapter involves the long-run equilibrium, comparative static, classical analysis. The second surveys discussions of issues, some of which found their way into the late classical position, with its concern for the functioning of a fractional-reserve banking system and its role in influencing the stock of money and hence in the adjustment process, while others became the background of the neoclassical interest in disequilibrium and short-term financing. But they are not, in my view, part of the neoclassical system itself. They lack discussion of interest rate changes, either in terms of long- or medium-term effects on the trade balance, or as affecting short-term financing and capital movements.

Keynes (1930) dates the beginning of the "Bank Rate" School (his name for the neoclassical view) to the 1830s. There are two reasons for my choosing a considerably later date (1873 at the earliest – more plausibly 1918): (a) the quasi-frivolous one that the later date is the commonly accepted one, most writers citing the Cunliffe Committee as the source of the position; (b) the important dual role of the interest rate, which was lacking in the literature Keynes refers to as the "Bank-rate Policy" starting after the crisis of 1836.

In Chapter VI Viner invokes the names which are "household words" in the economics profession, whereas Chapter VII is about people whose names are mostly unknown to economists today. The simple theory of the "gold standard" was cut off from the monetary and banking controversy, active and at times surprisingly sophisticated, that was raging at the time. This is consistent with the view that the mainstream economists were concerned primarily with the workings of an equilibrium long-run adjustment mechanism, while the "men of affairs" who wrote the pamphlets and sat on the committees concerned themselves more with immediate policy issues. As noted in the previous chapter, when the mainstream economists (we cannot call them "academic economists"[5]) dealt with policy questions, they were

---

[5] Schumpeter notes that economics was not captured by the universities until the end of the nineteenth century. Maloney's (1985) historical sociology of the British economics profession supports what I have been arguing, both about the establishment of an "insider view of economics" as a profession in the late nineteenth century and about their willingness to abjure dominance in the monetary field. Thus, the "academic economists . . . did [not]

concerned primarily with the effect of various policies (usually fiscal) on the long-run equilibrium structure of an economy, rather than with the design of tools aimed at coping with short-term disequilibrium. And through most of the nineteenth century, from Ricardo to Marshall, when they did deal with current monetary and policy issues this was primarily within the framework of testimony at hearings (the Gold and Silver Commission) or in the form of broadsides ("The high price of bullion," "Proposals for an economical and secure currency"), or at meetings of the Political Economy Club. Presumably monetary theory itself and international monetary theory (which then, as again today, overlapped to a great extent) was thought of by the classicals as being short-term and transitional, for most of the thinking in this area as well was being done by people whose contribution to other branches and other topics in economics was slight or non-existent. Many of them were highly educated bankers and merchants, men of means with a great deal of time to spare. Bagehot (1873: 214–15) argued that if a businessman spent most of his time at his business, this was *prima facie* evidence that he was not doing a good job. It followed that successful businessmen had time available for quasi-public service such as the directorship of the Bank of England, and for thinking and writing about current policy issues.

## The bullionist controversy

Almost from the very beginning the focus of controversy was not over the validity of the classical model as such. As is still true today, the arguments were primarily about the dynamics, the short-term adjustment paths, and, related to all of these, the actual and appropriate role of the monetary and fiscal authorities. (The polished, elegant, and colorful eighteenth- and nineteenth-century English has been exchanged for contemporary mathematical American, but the ideas and arguments being traded are remarkably similar.) The debates centered around events (undoubtedly one reason that men of affairs and of business were so actively involved in them), and the major event of the early nineteenth century was war. During the Napoleonic Wars, the British government suspended specie payments (from 1797 to 1819) and Britain was essentially on flexible exchange rates. But the main thrust of the controversy was not about fixed versus flexible exchange rates. (There were brief but interesting flurries of debate on that subject, to which I shall return below.)

challenge the hegemony of 'practical' men in monetary writings. According to Fay, the Cambridge Tripos in the years before 1914 consisted of 'potted Marshall and sugared sticks of Hartley Withers.' The remark emphasises both the low priority Cambridge gave to teaching monetary economics, and its lack of interest in professionalising it" (Maloney 1985: 231–2).

The issue in what was known as the "bullionist controversy" was the explanation of the behavior of these flexible exchange rates, that is, the cause of the fall in the pound or the premium on gold (in our terms, the rise in the price of foreign exchange). To summarize shamelessly, the bullionists (the monetarists of their day) took the classical position that the increase in the money supply (resulting from deficit financing of the war) led to price increases and a depreciation of sterling, the anti-bullionists arguing that there were other causes of the weakening of sterling, such as the necessity to make large payments abroad. (The arguments in Germany in the 1920s were astonishingly similar. See Ellis 1934, especially Chapter XVI.) Ricardo's pamphlet "The high price of bullion" (1811 [1951]) was the major statement of the bullionist position.

## The banking school and the currency school

The second controversy, the banking versus the currency school debate, grew out of the events following the resumption of specie payments (in the Act of 1819, popularly referred to as Peel's Act).[6] Currency school writings developed as criticism of the Bank of England's behavior, and of the Palmer rule, which was developed in 1831–2 and which specified a tie between Bank of England gold reserves and notes *plus deposits* (see page 33 below). This interest continued into involvement in the hearings of the Committee on Banks of Issue (1840), which led ultimately to the Act of 1844. With the crisis of 1839 and the hearings of 1840 there emerged a group known as the banking school and the battle was joined (O'Brien 1971: 77). The currency school were the direct heirs of the bullionists, but the banking school also accepted the bullionist insistence on a convertible currency (O'Brien 1971: 71).

The theoretical base for . . . both sides in the controversy, was to be found in the Bullion controversy. Starting from the foundations laid by Locke, Hume and Smith, the writers in that debate – Boyd, Thornton, Lord King, Parnell, Foster, Wheatley and Blake – had developed monetary theory in a way that was quite remarkable. Economic theory at that time took one of the longest steps forward that it has ever taken. [Fetter makes a very similar comment.]
     Ricardo's theoretical contribution was very small. (O'Brien 1971: 72)

One of the tenets of the bullionists had been that the very fact of convertibility (if maintained and taken seriously) would guarantee its own success. If currency was convertible into specie, those with convertible liabilities (the commercial banks and/or the central bank) would see to it that

---

[6] The Bank Charter Act of 1844, enacted when Robert Peel was Prime Minister, is also frequently called the Peel Act (see, for example, Schumpeter 1959: 694–5).

their reserves were sufficient relative to those liabilities to assure conversion if required. Following the crisis of 1825, however, which had been characterized by a liquidity crunch, it was no longer to be

taken as axiomatic . . . that convertibility was sufficient to secure itself . . . The principle . . . was that the currency should be varied as an identically circumstanced fully metallic one would have been . . . [T]he whole concept of "metallic" variation of the currency can be seen to stem immediately at least from the peculiar Ricardian definition of excess viz. that the currency was in excess whenever specie was being lost. That this in turn stemmed from Hume and Smith is undeniable: but it was most often to Ricardo that in particular the Currency School turned; even though Ricardo himself seems to have thought that convertibility on its own was a sufficient safeguard. (O'Brien 1971: 72–3)

The main argument was about the relevant definition of money. The position of the currency school was that, in the absence of a metallic currency circulating, it was the duty of the government to provide high-powered money (Bank of England notes) which varied exactly as a full-bodied metallic money would have. Having done this (as was eventually specified by the Act of 1844), the authorities were deemed to have performed their duty, completely and commendably. Variations in the production of near-monies and credit would presumably not be destabilizing or disturbing. If, however, they were, this was unfortunate but unavoidable, and neither the fault nor the responsibility of the authorities.

Since nobody has observed a pure specie currency system in modern history, it is impossible to say how it would function from the point of view of the issues here raised. Would it be permissible under a pure gold standard, for example, to allow the free market to create as many kinds of near-monies and credit instruments and in whatever quantities people wished – permissible in the sense that money would never play a destabilizing or disturbing role? If this is answered in the affirmative, then making the note issue fluctuate precisely with specie holdings is appropriate. If under a pure gold standard, credit instruments need to be regulated (or prohibited), then they certainly need to be so regulated under a fractional-reserve system. I have heard of no argument to the effect that the role of near-monies is in essence different under a partial reserve system from what it would be under a 100 percent reserve, or metallic currency, system. The banking school (or today's free banking) position has, of course, no problem – the optimum supply of total credit, money plus near-money, is the quantity supplied.

From 1819 until 1831, convertibility was presumably considered sufficient to guarantee itself, the Bank of England being obliged, of course, to maintain that convertibility, but free to decide how to effect it. During the recovery of 1825 "the Bank lost metal [gold] but it failed to contract its note issues, while the country banks . . . expanded theirs." When the Bank finally did contract, it caused a panic and a commercial crisis which threatened its own solvency, a threat averted, apparently, only with the help of Rothschild (O'Brien 1971: 71–2).

This crisis led, according to O'Brien (1971: 73) to the beginnings of the currency school writings and debate. Hearings of the Select Committee to consider the renewal of the Charter of the Bank of England heightened the interest, and out of these, in 1831–2, came the "Palmer rule" which is regarded as having originated with G. W. Norman and Horsley Palmer of the Bank of England. This fixed, at the margin, a ratio of one-to-one in changes in the Bank's specie holdings to the combined sum of its *note and deposit* liabilities.[7] When it was agreed (by everybody except the Bank) that the rule had failed, the currency school argument was that what needed to be kept constant was the ratio of specie to *note* fluctuation. Banknotes, that is to say, were money; deposits were not. Varying Bank of England note issue with its specie holdings would duplicate the behavoir of a simple specie currency, which is all that could be asked.

There was widespread commitment to the strict quantity theoretic view, defining money as the money base, or high-powered money (metal or central bank notes); while the ratio of deposits to notes of the Bank of England would adjust itself and so did not need to be controlled directly. Some writers, however, felt that the issues of the country (commercial) banks would not automatically be adjusted to Bank of England note issues and were therefore a potential source of instability; from this it followed, for some at least, that these should be controlled or even prohibited.

The banking school emerged, as noted above, after the crisis of 1839 and the hearings of the Committee on Banks of Issue in 1840. Their argument was that all bank deposits and bills of exchange were money just as were Bank of England notes. Logical consistency would presumably require, then, that the total volume of notes and deposits be regulated, or that nothing be regulated. They came very close to choosing the latter course. The former position, stemming from the recognition that the market would create near-monies as "needed", emerged a century later in Hayek's recommendation that the overall supply of money plus near-money should be made to vary in a one-to-one ratio to changes in foreign exchange (gold) reserves (see Chapter 7).

The banking school argument was that restrictions on the Bank of England were at the very best unnecessary, since the Bank must be allowed to

---

[7] O'Brien's comment on this is instructive. "The Palmer Rule . . . failed to recognise that a drain might fall on deposits, not notes, thus leaving open the possibility that the Bank might be drained of specie with the exchanges uncorrected (unless deposits were *as important* as notes in their effect on prices) and its note circulation undiminished" (O'Brien 1971: 73, italics his). The debate is still not over, and the question of the appropriate definition of the "money stock" rages on in the battle of the M's.

react to and adjust for the behavior of private financial market participants in defending its convertibility. The Bank should be permitted to exercise its discretion, particularly in distinguishing between external and internal drains (O'Brien 1971: 78). Part of the argument, then, involved the persistent rules-versus-authority issue. The banking school position was that a banking system which created credit on the basis of commercial loans (good bills or, as in the Federal Reserve Act, "prime commercial paper") could not expand the money supply excessively and hence could not be responsible for inflation, currency depreciation, or reserve loss.[8] If the banks overissued notes, these would be returned to the banks and retired as loans matured. If there were fluctuations due to monetary and banking considerations, these had to do with credit, not with currency. The optimal quantity of money was the quantity demanded.

Though they shared, according to O'Brien, the currency school's conviction that a convertible currency was the only appropriate regime, they were less monetarist than either the currency school or the deregulation advocates of today (see, for example, Fama 1980 and 1983) since, according to O'Brien, they claimed that "prices were governed by incomes" (O'Brien 1971: 77). If this is so, it would strengthen their argument that the appropriate quantity of money was simply that which would support the current volume of economic activity at the price level exogenously determined. Viner does not make this specific point, but he makes the closely related one that the banking school took the "needs of business" and the willingness of businessmen to borrow to be exogenous, erroneously in his view (Viner 1937: 237–8).

It has recently been argued (White 1984) that there was a third, neglected, group, which he labels Free Banking, the antecedents of today's free banking, or "new monetary" economists (see Fama 1980 and 1983 for a bibliography and clear statements of the position; also Black 1970, Sargent and Wallace 1982 and Smith 1988). They were monetarists (in a way that many of the contemporary free banking people are not, for example Black 1970), in the sense that they believed that the quantity of money does matter and does affect prices, but held that only the absence of a central bank could insure that the quantity of money would not be excessive. "Whereas the Currency School held that any bank could overissue, and the Banking School that no bank could overissue, the Free Banking School held that only a central bank like the Bank of England could overissue" (White 1984: 53). For a radical proposal carrying these views almost to their logical conclusions, see Hayek (1976), to be discussed in Chapter 7.

---

[8] An analogous position, referring to the Bank of England and alleging that it could not overissue if it discounted only commercial paper, was attacked vigorously in the Bullion Report (see Cannan 1925: 46 ff).

The currency school won the debate at the time, in that their views were codified into the Act of 1844. This remained in force for eighty years and formed the institutional foundation on which the neoclassical view was constructed (though the neoclassical assignment of an important role to the rate of interest in determining the level of economic activity is a banking school attribute). It has been argued, most notably by Hayek (1937), that this was precisely what was wrong with the gold standard in practice.[9] Viner takes a similar position in arguing that the currency school should, given their overall views, have favored stabilizing not notes but "aggregate volume of *means of payments*, or taking velocity into account . . . the desired aggregate volume of *payments*" (Viner 1937: 253, italics his).

By the time the United States came to establish a central bank, in 1910, the banking school had gained ground to the extent that the Federal Reserve Act is a strange amalgam of the two positions. The argument has clearly not yet been settled. From the inside-outside money controversy sparked by Gurley and Shaw in the 1950s, to the free banking versus regulation debate currently in swing, it continues.[10]

The Act of 1844 provided for the separation of the Bank of England into an Issue Department and Banking Department. The former was allowed to issue fourteen million pounds sterling in notes against securities (the "fiduciary issue"); the remainder had to be backed by specie so that the bullion flows would be reflected in the note circulation outside not the Banking but the Issue Department. The Banking Department was intended to function as any other bank, holding notes obtained from the Issue Department in exchange for bullion, together with some coin, as its reserve.

[9] "It was the design of the Bank Act of 1844 to make the mixed system of gold and other money behave in such a way that the quantity of money would change exactly as if only gold were in circulation; and for a long time argument proceeded as if this intention had actually been realized. And even when it was gradually realized that deposits subject to cheque were no less money than bank notes, and that since they were left out of the regulation, the purpose of the Act had really been defeated, only a few modifications of the argument were thought necessary. Indeed in general this argument is still presented as it was originally constructed, on the assumption of a purely metallic currency" (Hayek 1937 [1964: 8–9]).

[10] Cowen and Kroszner (1987) place the roots of the current New Monetary Economics rather in the late nineteenth century and early twentieth century, primarily in the United States rather than in England. Their claim that the writers involved have been neglected by the mainstream of the economics profession is irrefutable. The issues raised would take us too far afield from the main line if investigated here, involving monetary theory per se and the role of money in a general equilibrium model. I content myself therefore with an honorable mention of the literature. I note, however, that Cowen and Kroszner fail to distinguish between those contemporary writers who argue for a totally free-market-determined supply of money cum credit on the one hand, and those who argue for government-determined currency, or primary money, allowing the market to determine the volume and types of near-monies. Black (1970) notes that if banking were totally free there would be no money, only various forms of credit. According to White (1984: 85–6), only one Free Banking writer in Britain, Thomas Hodgskin, "was ready to endorse competitive private coinage on principle."

In this position the power of the Bank to act as lender of last resort was, quite deliberately, limited (O'Brien 1971: 79).

While many regarded the panic of 1847 as proof of the failure of the Act of 1844, the currency school insisted that it was no such thing, since panics could occur even under a purely metallic currency. They strengthened their insistence that the Bank of England not be a lender of last resort, "because as the demand for discounts increased during pressure so did the note circulation outside the Bank" (O'Brien 1971: 80). That is, they feared that if the Bank extended credit to its customers during a panic this would unduly endanger its own ability to maintain convertibility.

The Banking School . . . attacked strongly the workings of the Act. Although they came ultimately to accept its continuance they believed that the whole theory underlying the measure was mistaken, and advanced a very different interpretation of its working from that of the Currency School. Although still endorsing the common objective of convertibility they believed that the Act of 1819 had been sufficient to achieve this and that the Act of 1844, far from being a complement to that of 1819 as claimed by the Currency School, was a danger to convertibility. The separation of departments they believed to be fundamentally mistaken. . . It was the only lender of last resort, and the centre of the monetary system. It was the only bank which was able to affect the rate of interest (although only temporarily) and hence the exchanges; and it had a unique moral influence over the level of activity. The stoppage of the Banking Department . . . would paralyse the monetary system and put convertibility in danger . . . yet the Act protected convertibility at the expense of risking the deposits . . . The need to protect [the] . . . Banking reserve . . . led to wide fluctuations in Bank Rate which in turn led to violent fluctuations in confidence and hence in activity.[11] *Regulation of the amount of currency did not affect the level of activity but depended on it*: and in any case there was as much importance attached to credit as to notes proper . . . In sum, denying the crucial connection posited by the Currency School, between the quantity of notes and specie, internal prices, and the balance of payments, they believed the Act to be a dangerous irrelevance. (O'Brien 1971: 81–2, italics mine)

The bullionist position is certainly the classical one, in its emphasis on the relationships between specie, money supply, prices, and trade. Since the Act of 1844 stayed on the books until 1928, one might argue that the establishment branch of the bullionist core, the currency school, formed the underpinnings of the neoclassical position. We shall see, however, that Bagehot in his emphasis on the lender of last resort role of the Bank of England proposed for the Bank a good deal more discretionary power than did the currency school writers; and, as we saw, it was the banking school which emphasized the effect of interest rate changes on domestic activity.

[11] "Bank rate", with an upper case "B" and occasionally an upper case "R" is, for the benefit of American readers who may be unfamiliar with this ancient usage, the rate at which the Bank of England offered to discount bills on the London money market. In these same widely used spelling conventions, the "Bank" when spelled with an upper case "B" refers exclusively to the Bank of England.

The Cunliffe Committee Report sounds on first hearing to be a restatement, with minor variations, of the theme stated in 1844, but the actual behavior of the Bank of England came to be much more discretionary than was implied by either of these.[12]

Is it entirely specious to suggest that the banking school people lacked the courage of their convictions? If it were truly impossible to overissue money based on 'the "needs of trade" and responding to demand, there would presumably be no need for a lender of last resort or for a central bank with broad discretionary powers.

## The role of the rate of interest – capital flows

During the early and late part of the classical period there was very little discussion of the role of the interest rate in affecting domestic spending; in the middle period (with apologies to Egyptologists) there was more.[13] In the theoretical world of the wages fund theory (of early classical economics), when all investment consisted of borrowed circulating capital to finance wage payments, the connection between changes in the money supply and changes in spending becomes very close; so does it in the latter part of the century, in the world of poorly developed domestic securities and equities markets.[14] This is particularly the case if there is fractional-reserve banking and the money supply does not vary in a one-to-one correspondence with the external balance, since the actual volume of credit is more sensitive to demand for credit in that case. In the middle period, when Britain was building up her domestic industrial plant, there seems to have been more concern with the rate of interest as a determinant of spending. As was noted

---

[12] Dornbusch and Frenkel argue that during the panic of October 1847 the Bank behaved in a destabilizing manner by following the rules of the Act of 1844. "The lack of a lender of last resort was emphasized in the 1847 crisis when the Bank of England, in the midst of a banking panic, *sold* consols and *reduced* discounts, thus assuring confidence in deposit convertibility (not gold convertibility) at the expense of devastating financial distress" (Dornbusch and Frenkel 1984: 260, italics theirs). This is rather the inverse of the problem raised by the banking school in the quotation from O'Brien (1971; see page 36 above), namely the incompatibility, given the institutional framework, between the convertibility of Bank of England deposits into notes and the convertibility of Bank of England notes into gold.

[13] The reason the classification sometimes becomes a bit difficult is that, while in the later nineteenth century the importance of the interest rate and of capital movements is clear, and the theory often takes on a normative tone, in the earlier part of the century interest rate and capital movements variations seem to flit in and out of the monetary debate and it is not always obvious how important they are considered to be.

[14] Particularly for the home market. The Macmillan Report observed that domestic British industry had been very poorly served by financial markets and by the big London issuing houses. All the unrivalled skill of the City was directed at facilitating capital export abroad (see Macmillan 1931: 162 and page 105 below). In 1924 Keynes wrote that British practice as well as the law establishing what assets could be held by trust funds biased the choice very heavily in favor of foreign at the expense of domestic investment (Volume XIX [1981: 263 ff]).

in O'Brien's discussion, however, this was generally expressed in terms such as "optimism" and "confidence", rather than in terms of marginal (or even average) rates of return on investment.

Interest rate changes were not in general an integral part of the classical mechanism. Viner's Chapter VI, "The International Mechanism Under a Simple Specie Currency," is 100 pages long and there is no mention there either of short-term capital movements or of interest rates or interest rate changes. Chapter VII, "The International Mechanism in Relation to Modern Banking Processes," does have such a discussion, but it centers on questions of short-term capital movements in response to exchange rate movements (within the gold points) and the temporary equilibrating effects of such movements. In that chapter, the section on "The International Mechanism and Business Cycles" deals with the relationship between international capital movements and domestic capital formation and/or saving, but not with the interest rate (Viner 1937: 432–6).

While the definition of money was debated, the role of international financial capital mobility and its connection with interest rates was taken for granted in this discussion. Everyone seemed aware that a change in interest rates would alter the specie reserves of the Bank of England. Even this effect was played down, however, and not emphasized heavily. There were probably good historical reasons for this. Some of these are:

1   The role of Britain as the center of the world economy was smaller than it was to be later in the century. The "world" was probably smaller, and much of the period was dominated by war.
2   As a result of this, the relative importance of external to internal drains of gold was less in the earlier period than in the later.
3   Keynes (1930: Volume I, 187) attributes it to the low ceiling on Bank Rate (see page 42).

The mechanisms of monetary control and expansion, and the relationship between these and prices, exchange rates, and the trade balance were, however, not universally understood. Most of all, the Bank of England seemed not to understand it.

In appraising the record of the Bank of England . . . the evidence available warrants the verdict that during the period from about 1800 to 1860 the Bank of England almost continuously displayed an inexcusable degree of incompetence or unwilling-ness to fulfill the requirements which could reasonably be demanded of a central bank. During the restriction of cash payments, it not only permitted the paper pound to depreciate, prices to rise, and the exchanges to fluctuate, but *it repeatedly denied that there was any relationship between these phenomena and its own activities*. (Viner 1937: 254, italics mine)

This lack of understanding apparently continued after the decision, in 1819, to resume species payments. It is all the more surprising, Viner notes, in that the public statements of the Governors of the Bank, the advice they received in public, and their own history in the eighteenth century, indicated that they knew better. Horsley Palmer and G. W. Norman[15] are frequently singled out as being notably knowledgeable and sophisticated on these issues. "The growing authority of Horsley Palmer and G. W. Norman in the counsels of the bank in the 1830s brought more enlightened pronouncements to the public, *but does not appear to have improved the practice of the Bank*" (Viner 1937: 255, italics mine).

And Hawtrey, in *The art of central banking* (1932: 135), cites Palmer's testimony to the Parliamentary Committee of 1832: Excessive note issue is "exhibited by a state of prices higher than those in other countries, thereby rendering the foreign exchanges unfavourable" and this should be corrected by monetary contraction.

The first operation is to increase the value of money; with the increased value of money, there is less facility obtained by the commercial public in the discount of their paper; that naturally tends to limit transactions and to the reduction of prices; the reduction of prices will so far alter our situation with foreign countries, that it will be no longer an object to import, but the advantage will rather be upon the export, the gold and silver will then come back into the country and rectify the contraction that previously existed. (Quoted by Hawtrey 1932: 135–6)

Hawtrey continues: "So clear a recognition of the use of Bank rate as an instrument for affecting the price level . . . is remarkable. It is all the more so, considering that only very tentative steps had at that period been taken towards the practical application of the system" (Hawtrey 1932: 136).

This does indeed represent an astonishing level of sophistication and understanding. All that is missing is a statement of why the quantity of loans should be a negative function of the rate of interest. However, there seems to be general agreement by later critics, such as Viner and Hawtrey, that Palmer's statement was out of the ordinary. The domestic effects of changes in the rate of interest were for the most part ignored or not understood. That international integration of capital and loan markets prevailed, hence that specie flows were responsive to interest rate movements, was however widely recognized. Viner comments, for example, that there was very little central bank cooperation during this period, and that central banks either ignored developments in other markets, "or else engaged in *competitive increases of their discount rates and in raids on each other's reserves* at a time of actual or anticipated

[15] George Warde Norman was the grandfather of Montagu Norman, and for many years (1821–72) a Director of the Bank of England, where he was highly influential (though never Governor). A large portion of the Overstone correspondence consists of letters addressed to Norman (*Vide* O'Brien 1971: 5–8).

credit stringency." Generally the discussion of the role of the interest rate, according to Viner, concerned only short-run disturbances. Interest rate changes were related to specie movements through their impact on short-term capital movements, "their effect on relative prices being commonly held to be too slow-working to be an important factor in restoring international equilibrium" (Viner 1937: 274–8).

Those most concerned with the functions of the rate of interest and who came closest to understanding it were those most removed from the classical core analytically. The quantity theoretic, equilibrium approach of the currency school made them resistant to the idea that capital flows, induced by interest rate differentials, could be in any sense desirable.

The role accorded to the rate of interest by the Banking School was far greater than that of their opponents. Tooke [a major figure in the Banking School] in particular divined more correctly than anyone the way in which short-run capital flows could actuate gold flows – yet he never really met Overstone's fundamental objection that such flows were merely palliative if relative international price levels were in disequilibrium. This approach in turn stemmed from a belief in the terminability of drains which could not arise from different quantities of money bringing about different relative price levels, and from a belief that, because of the existence of hoards, *international specie flows could take place without affecting the quantity and value of money in a country.* (O'Brien 1971: 78, italics mine)

The effect on domestic spending was expressed even more vaguely, in terms of ill-defined psychological interactions. Viner's discussion of the role of a modern banking system in the adjustment mechanism highlights this neglect. He separates the issue into two analytical categories, and then adds a third, which he considers not to have been part of the debate at the time:

1 The effect of a specie flow on the means of payments (including both notes and deposits).
2 The effect on interest rates and short-term lending.
3 The longer-run effects of these interest rate changes on output and/or prices.

Viner presents a very detailed and extended discussion of the first point mentioned above. (The second and third figure more strikingly in what I have called the neoclassical views.) He treats at great length his own debate with Angell over interpretation of the Canada story; this is much discussed also in O'Brien (1971). Viner distinguishes carefully between "primary" and "secondary" expansion in money. These could be translated into changes in the money supply which stem from and are equal to changes in the monetary base (the banks' reserves of specie in this case) and the changes due to the multiple expansion or contraction of deposits and notes, pursuant to these reserve changes.

If there were only primary changes the mechanism would be essentially that of the price-specie flow model. (As we shall see in Chapter 7, it was precisely the existence of the secondary changes which exercised Hayek 1937 in his critique of the workings of the historical gold standard. Viner (1937: 396–7) takes pains to refute the argument that early classical writers ignored the importance and even the existence of primary changes and concentrated only on secondary changes. It is the later classical writers and those he calls "modern" writers, of the early twentieth century, who tend, he says, to ignore primary changes. This is the crux of his debate with Angell. We shall return to it below.

Regarding the second two points:

It was common doctrine that the market rate of interest influenced the flow of specie ... [T]here was recognition of the possibility that increases in the Bank rate might act as a deflationary factor not only directly through their influence on the volume of advances to the Bank's own customers, but also indirectly through their psychological influence on the market judgment as to business prospects and therefore on the willingness of private bankers to lend or of businessmen to borrow and on the velocity of circulation. (Viner 1937: 277)

Note that, like the view described by O'Brien, this is an effect expressed in terms of "confidence" and business optimism.

It is not surprising that the classical economists were not closely concerned with the effect of the interest rate on the trade balance. Since the rate of interest was the price which equated savings and investment and did not affect the level of employment and output, or prices, changes in the rate of interest could not affect the current account, except in the short run by altering the structure of spending towards or away from investment goods, with indeterminate effects. In Mill's *Principles* (1849 [1961]), for example, Book III is entitled "Exchange". Chapters XX to XXII are on the determination of exchange rates, the "Distribution of the Precious Metals," and the effects of monetary changes on trade. The rate of interest, private or official, does not enter here. Chapter XXIII, entitled "Of the Rate of Interest," concentrates on the demand and supply of loans in terms of savings and investment functions. Under flexible exchange rates, an increase in the money supply will raise the price of foreign exhange and domestic prices as well, thus lowering real balances and raising interest rates. But this is temporary. "A depreciation of the currency, when it has become an accomplished fact, affects the rate of interest in no manner whatever. It diminishes indeed the power of money to buy commodities, but not the power of money to buy money" (Mill 1849 [1961: 645-6]). Of short-term capital movements, or any other phenomena of interest to the neoclassicals, there is no mention. The only qualification to this I could find is a brief comment that if the money supply doubled suddenly, it would probably result in a rapid increase in lending which would lower the rate of interest and lead to an outflow abroad "before there had been any time for an action on prices." But he clearly regards such a case as pathological and makes no further mention of it (Mill 1849 [1961: 631]). It should be noted, however, that Iversen attributes greater importance to this remark of Mill's than I do and concludes that by "similar reasoning" Mill would argue "that a large capital import is likely to be temporarily offset by equalising credit movements in the opposite direction" (Iversen 1935: 518n).

Although the majority of the writers of the period conceded the efficacy of the central bank discount rate "as a regulator of specie movements through its influence on the international movement of short-term funds and, to a less extent, on the commodity trade balance," some saw problems even with this. Viner cites some writers as noting "that in so far as the movement of short-term funds was concerned what mattered was only the *relative* height of market rates of interest in London and abroad, and that rates were likely to rise and fall simultaneously in the important money markets" (Viner 1937: 279).

Thus, since higher (or lower) interest rates at home than abroad did not necessarily imply a rise or fall in rates, the effect on domestic activity was presumably less predictable. Furthermore, other banks, such as the Bank of France, tended to retaliate, making even the short-term financial effect uncertain. And worse, raising the rate might signal trouble and cause a speculative outflow. And one writer (William Hooley) went so far as to argue that it would discourage exports by raising the cost of credit to finance them (Viner 1937: 279).

Keynes, in a section called "The Modus Operandi of Bank-Rate," gives a somewhat different twist to the neglect of interest rate changes in the early nineteenth century (Keynes 1930: Volume I, 185 ff). He dates the origins of the neoclassical school earlier than I have done, to the "discussions which followed the monetary crisis of 1826–7 and preceded the Bank Act of 1844." The ideas did not exist earlier, he alleges; specifically they are absent in Ricardo and do not appear before 1837. The reason to which he attributes this is that until the Usury Laws were repealed in 1837, the rate of interest was subject to a legal maximum of 5 percent (Keynes 1930: Volume I, 186–7; see Chapter 9, page 175).

What he calls the "traditional doctrine" regarding Bank rate, developed over the ninety years prior to the *Treatise*, combined "three distinct strands of thought, difficult to disentangle, to which different writers attach differing degrees of stress." The first, attributed *inter alia* to Lord Overstone, "regarded Bank-rate as the correct and efficacious method for reducing the demand on the Bank for discounts, and so for contracting the volume of the circulation." The second, the one emphasized by "practical bankers," emphasizes the effect of Bank rate on foreign lending through "the international short-term loan market" (Keynes 1930: Volume I, 187–9).

The use of Bank-rate for this purpose was developed by the Bank of England as a practical expedient in the two decades following 1837. The first clear account of how it worked was given in Goschen's *Foreign Exchanges*, first published in 1861. But Goschen regarded changes in Bank-rate as being in the main a reflection of market conditions rather than as determining them. It was left to Bagehot . . . to complete the story by emphasising the extent of the Bank of England's power . . . to determine what the market conditions should be. (Keynes 1930: Volume I, 189–90)

[I]t is not obvious how [this] . . . is connected with our first strand, and I know of no author who has attempted the synthesis. Moreover – superficially at least – it seems to pull in the opposite direction. It may be objected that the higher Bank-rate can only be made effective if the Central Bank reduces its other assets by more than it increases its stock of gold, so that the effect on balance is to decrease the aggregate of credit. (Keynes 1930: Volume I, 190)

The third strand, in Keynes's view, is a faint prelude to his own concern with the relationship between savings and investment, and a hint of the concept of the marginal efficiency of investment. A higher interest rate "discourages investment relatively to saving, and therefore lowers prices." He attributes to Marshall a view very close to this in the latter's testimony before the Gold and Silver Commission (1887) and the Indian Currency Committee (1898): "Marshall certainly conceived of an additional supply of money as reaching the price-level by means of a stimulation of investment (or speculation) through a lower Bank-rate" (Keynes 1930: Volume I, 190–1). In Chapter 3 I shall argue for a somewhat different reading of Marshall's testimony: it seemed to be speculation rather than investment which he was emphasizing, and then only when pushed by the Committee to do so. Most of his testimony strikes me as quite straightforwardly quantity theoretic. Keynes himself, however, went a good deal further in spelling out the next round: how the primary fall in prices pushes down profits, hence employment, hence wages, hence costs of production (Keynes 1930: Volume I, 201 ff).

Keynes sides with Tooke against Joseph Hume in 1839 that a higher Bank rate will not lower prices by discouraging "speculation" in commodity stocks: the difference in interest rates between 3 percent and 6 percent for three months was too small a part of a price of a bushel (quarter) of wheat to affect speculation (Keynes 1930: Volume I, 195).

### Flexible exchange rates

Finally, a brief note about flexible exchange rates. In the course of the bullionist debate about the reasons for the depreciation of sterling during the suspension, it was generally taken for granted that suspension of specie payments, that is, the flexibility of exchange rates, was temporary.[16] Nevertheless there were some murmurings and suggestions that it might perhaps not be such a bad arrangement after all. Viner comments:

Although all of the prominent members of the classical school were adherents of a fixed metallic standard, I have not been able to find any serious attempt during this period to meet . . . claims that a better currency standard was available. There was then, as there has continued to be since, a marked tendency on the part of the exponents of the fixed gold standard to rely on dogmatic assertions of the injustice of any other system and of the impossibility of devising any system of currency which would have more stability of value than the precious metals . . . As has already been pointed out, James Mill, Ricardo, and their disciples, also tended to minimize both the extent and the evil consequences of changing price levels, and thus to foster the attitude that the metallic standard, variable though it was, met adequately the requirements of a good currency standard. (Viner 1937: 214)[17, 18]

Viner was not greatly impressed by the strength of the arguments on either side of the fixed-versus-flexible exchange rate discussion of the bullionist controversy. That is, he was not persuaded that either side of the debate was really well represented. And though he himself was on the whole in favor of fixed rates, he seems to think the flexible rate side won on points.

The exponents of a *national* paper standard made out a better case for what I am inclined to regard as theoretically a moderately inferior and under ordinary practical

---

[16] And when it was over there was remarkably little controversy about whether "a convertible currency was both necessary and desirable . . . It was accepted by both sides in the Currency and Banking controversy, both having grown, it is probably true to say, out of different aspects of the Bullionist position in the Bullion controversy during the regime of inconvertible paper of 1797–1819" (O'Brien 1971: 71).

[17] Apart from the wording, the argument about fixed versus flexible rates sounds totally contemporary, with quotations such as: " 'The natural order of things will be reversed. Instead of a steady currency and fluctuating exchanges, we shall have steady exchanges, and a fluctuating currency!!!' 'What may be the value of a steady exchange, I shall consider hereafter; but it seems to me it will cost too dear, if the price to be paid for it is a fluctuating currency.' 'After all, what is this mighty evil of an unfavorable exchange, that so much should be lost and hazarded for it.' " (Viner 1937: 215). The references are cited by Viner; they are all from 1819!

[18] Only relatively recently, with work by Elhanan Helpman and Assaf Razin (1979), has it been made clear that the advantage of fixed over flexible exchange rates stems from the fact that under the former system there is automatic financing of imbalances, albeit temporary, since the use of reserves or specie to cover imbalances involves international lending. Whether later adjustment is better than sooner is another matter, which needs to be discussed. This issue also lies at the root of the controversy over use of the discount rate – is a country better off by financing deficits (temporarily) by attracting short-term financial capital? And this in turn is part of the larger and now current topic of intertemporal equilibrium, an awkward name for the concept that long-run equilibrium in the absence of uncertainty is consistent, in general, with changes in production and consumption patterns over time as a result of both technological and taste constellations. The most recent work in this area has dealt with the even more specific question of the dynamics of optimal (international) debt (see references in Chapter 1, note 5).

conditions a seriously inferior cause. They presented valid and novel arguments for the economic advantages of the freedom afforded by an independent monetary standard to escape a deflation (or inflation!) induced by external factors, to cope with a deflation resulting from internal factors and intensified by the prevalence of rigidity downwards in the prices of the factors of production, and, in general, to provide a country with the quantity of means of payments deemed best for it as against having that quantity dictated to it by external factors beyond its control. (Viner 1937: 216–7)

## In brief

In the nineteenth-century British discussions, the main core of the classical mainstream analysis was in the F stream: pure, formal, and long-run equilibrium. This is not to deny that some of the classical economists got involved in contemporary issues but they were on the whole tangential to the argument over what constituted money and the precise role of changes in the several "moneys" in influencing domestic expenditure, prices, and foreign trade (and investment).

The monetary controversies, engaged in by individuals other than the classical "greats", closely paralleled the present day discussions: the early bullionist debate was essentially about the validity of the quantity theory of money, as were the controversies of the 1950s and 1960s. The later banking-versus-currency-school argument was about the role of the banking system and banks' liabilities (whether deposits or notes) in the money supply and hence the desirability and efficacy of controls over the banking system, a debate which is being renewed today in some of the arguments for free (unregulated) banking.

During the first three quarters of the nineteenth century, controversy among the men of affairs centered on definitions of money and the related issue of the effect of changes in the quantity of money (however defined) on spending and on prices. The classical economists were exercised over whether international specie flows preceded or followed domestic monetary, spending and price changes and on whether the gold movements were indeed essential. But except for the famous statement by Horsely Palmer the role of the interest rate in all this was confined to that of short-run capital flows to protect the gold reserves, and even in that capacity it was not heavily emphasized.

In this debate there was little discussion of the interest rate as involved with changes in the money supply, as influencing the level (and to some extent, even the structure) of domestic spending, and of any problems involved in reconciling this line of impact of the rate of interest on international payments with the direct, short-term effect on financial capital flows. These appeared only with the dawn of the neoclassical period in the latter part of the century.

Stream P

# The beginnings of the neoclassical tradition

My interpretation of the neoclassical doctrine is, to refresh the reader's memory, that it is the classical model to which has been added *both* the short-term international capital mobility required to finance imbalances *and* the responsiveness of domestic economic activity, hence the trade balance, to changes in the rate of interest.

I first discuss Bagehot's *Lombard Street*, the origin, or precursor, of the neoclassical position. Secondly, some attention must be given to Marshall's famous statement to the Gold and Silver Commission. This will be followed by a few of the many summary statements of what that position was supposed to have been, and thence to a more detailed analysis of the neoclassical approach, as represented by the Cunliffe Report and subsequent discussions.

## Bagehot

Walter Bagehot's *Lombard Street, A description of the money market*, published in 1873, is a tract, a policy platform, and a "money and banking textbook" combined, and elegantly written besides. Its theme appears early on: "Money will not manage itself, and Lombard street has a great deal of money to manage" (Bagehot 1873: 20). Lombard Street is the financial center of London, London is the financial center of Britain, Britain is the center of the world, and the Bank of England must manage Lombard Street. This is his message. Note the emphasis on the word and the concept "manage". He does not deal exclusively, or even primarily, with foreign drains (nor does he really spell out an adjustment mechanism *vis-à-vis* other countries). But his description of the London money market and the unique and special role therein of the Bank of England makes the book a basic background for almost everything written on the subject subsequently.

The book is a critical response to the view that "the currency manages itself; the entire working is automatic" (Bagehot 1873: 161). This idea took hold, he alleges, during the monetary controversies which he dates from 1793 until 1844 (when Peel's Act was promulgated). In the course of this the remarkable idea developed that the Banking Department of the Bank of England regarded itself, and was generally regarded to be, simply a bank like any other. The central role of London as Britain's intermediary, mobilizing the excess savings of "a county with good land but no manufactures and no trade" and employing these in "discounting the bills of the industrial districts" is emphasized. Lombard Street served to channel funds from "Somersetshire and Hampshire" to "Yorkshire and Lancashire" (Bagehot 1873: 12). The position of the Bank of England within this center is unique: a privately owned company, trying to make profits, having to keep reserves much higher than those of its competitors (40 percent for the Banking Department of the Bank of England, as opposed to about 13 percent for the London and Westminster Bank).

In a delightful speculative history of banking in general, and British banking in particular, he includes an interesting scheme of the development from note issue banking to deposit banking. For many years the Bank of England had monopoly powers (either *de facto* or *de jure*) in banking. The Act of 1742 decreed that no other corporation in London could issue notes, and unincorporated houses stopped issuing them. And it was widely though incorrectly believed that other companies (joint stock companies and corporations) were not allowed to take deposits, so they did not do so (Bagehot 1873: 97 ff).

He emphasizes repeatedly the inherently ambivalent and "unnatural" nature of the relationship between the Bank of England and the private money market. The heart of the market consists of the bill brokers, from whom the Bank, the source of the system's reserves, derives no benefit, since it never deposits any money with them. In fact, it is in competition with the bill brokers for discount business. And yet in time of panic it must bail them out or risk "aggravating incipient demand" and increased pressure on itself (Bagehot 1873: 300). The result is "unnatural."

I have tediously insisted that the natural system of banking is that of many banks keeping their own cash reserve, with the penalty of failure before them if they neglect it. I have shown that our system is that of a single bank keeping the whole reserve under no effectual penalty of failure. (Bagehot 1873: 329)

Nevertheless, he suggests palliatives rather than an overhaul because he is convinced that there is "no manner of use proposing to alter it" (Bagehot 1873: 329).

The Exchequer involved itself too much too early (in history) and too exclusively with the Bank of England. It bailed it out by restrictions on specie convertibility (in 1797, 1847, 1857, 1866), and by 1873 had more responsibility, in Bagehot's view, than it should have (Bagehot 1873: 111). The result was a general consensus that the Bank of England could not fail, or at any rate that the government would not allow it to fail. There had never been a clear statement by government or parliament what its duty was or should be. And yet "[on] the wisdom of the directors of that one Joint Stock Company, it depends whether *England shall be solvent or insolvent*" (Bagehot 1873: 35, italics his).

He is extremely clear (and elucidates in detail) that the financial and monetary system which is Lombard Street cannot be liquid in time of panic unless the Bank of England acts as lender of last resort (though he does not use that expression). The Bank of England is the banker to the country and the world. But it is vulnerable because of the pyramiding of liabilities: the Bank of England's liabilities are the assets of the bill brokers and the London banks; the liabilities of these, in turn, are the assets of the country banks in England, Ireland and Scotland. In addition, foreign individuals and governments keep reserves in London. So the small reserves of the Bank of England are the only reserves "backing" a vast worldwide volume of liabilities (Bagehot 1873: 28 ff). The Bank of England holds the "ultimate cash reserve of the country"; in times of crisis, "it is as the Bankers' Bank that the Bank of England has to pay [the cash], for it is by being so that it becomes the keeper of the final cash reserve" (Bagehot 1873: 315). How large that reserve should be (it cannot be legislated or expressed in a simple formula) and how it should be protected, are the subject of the book.

Since the Bank's notes are fully redeemable in gold specie, its reserves are subject to both domestic (internal) and foreign (external) drains. To meet these the Bank needs, and has, an "effectual instrument" – the rate of interest. Here is the core of his argument and the foundation of what I have labeled the neoclassical position.

If the interest of money be raised, it is proved by experience that money *does* come to Lombard Street, and theory shows that it *ought* to come. . . . [A] rise of the value of money in Lombard Street immediately by a banking operation brings money to Lombard Street. And there is also a slower mercantile operation. The rise in the rate of discount acts immediately on the trade of this country. Prices fall here; in consequence imports are diminished, exports are increased, and, therefore, there is more likelihood of a balance in bullion coming to this country after the rise in the rate than there was before. (Bagehot 1873: 45–6)

Whatever institution holds the reserves of a country, that institution should immediately raise the interest rate when a foreign drain begins, to prevent further bullion losses and to encourage a reflux.

This duty, up to about the year 1860, the Bank of England did not perform at all . . . A more miserable history can hardly be found than that of the attempts of the Bank – if indeed they can be called attempts – to keep a reserve and to manage a foreign drain between the year 1819 (when cash payments were resumed by the Bank, and when our modern Money Market may be said to begin) and the year 1857 . . . The present policy of the Bank is an infinite improvement on the policy before 1857: the two must not be for an instant confounded; but nevertheless, as I shall hereafter show, the present policy is now still most defective, and much discussion and much effort will be wanted before that policy becomes what it ought to be. (Bagehot 1873: 46–7)

Bagehot refers, as noted, to both internal and external drains, but he distinguishes explicitly and at length between them. The appropriate policy in the face of an external drain (a balance of payments deficit), is to tighten up and raise Bank rate. The correct policy to apply to an internal drain, which is usually stimulated by an external problem and a visible decrease in reserves, "is to lend freely" (Bagehot 1873: 48). The problem is that these policies conflict, and if the two kinds of drains occur simultaneously, the Bank must "treat two opposite maladies at once – one requiring stringent remedies, and especially a rapid rise in the rate of interest; and the other, an alleviative treatment with large and ready loans" (Bagehot 1873: 56).

An example of appropriate behavior, he says, is that displayed during the panic of 1866. Citing the *Economist*, he quotes, as they do approvingly, the statement of the Governor of the Bank of England. At the time of the panic (when the news came that the prestigious and important banking house of Overend, Gurney had failed) they lent to everybody, without waiting for approval from the Chancellor of the Exchequer. They advanced 45 million pounds in three months; on the first day, they lent half their reserves (Bagehot 1873: 162 ff). This was entirely appropriate, he argues, since heavy lending at high rates is precisely the policy to be followed when external and internal drains are threatened simultaneously. "But though the rule is clear, the greatest delicacy, the finest and best skilled judgment, are needed to deal at once with such great and contrary evils" (Bagehot 1873: 57).

The power of the Bank of England to affect the rate of interest (the "value of money"), though not absolute, is great but temporary. As I understand him, he took the position that the Bank followed the market in setting its discount rate (Bank rate), at the same time recognizing that it was the largest single seller on the market. This gave it "great sudden power in the Money Market, but no permanent power" (Bagehot 1873: 115–16). This is elaborated; the Bank expands its loans sharply; this leads to a rise in prices, which results in an increase in the nominal demand for loans, raising the [nominal] rate of interest. "[S]udden loans by an issuer of notes, though they may temporarily lower the value of money, do not lower it permanently, because they generate their own counteraction. And this they do whether the notes issued are convertible into coin or not" (Bagehot 1873: 117).

Worse. If the currency is convertible, the price rise increases the current account deficit and requires payment in bullion forcing a rise in the rate of interest in order "to stay the efflux. And the tightness so produced is often greater than, and always equal to, the preceding unnatural laxity" (Bagehot

1873: 118). That is, under fixed exchange rates, an independent monetary policy is not permanently attainable. Throughout, however, he is concerned with the short-run, disequilibrium analysis.

The rate of interest is more volatile than commodity prices, but the better the management on the part of those who "keep the reserve of bullion or of legal tender exchangeable for bullion," the more stable the rate of interest (Bagehot 1873: 121). He spells out an inverse relationship between the rate of interest and price movements, independently of foreign drains. Low interest rates are inflationary.

[H]ere [in England] . . . the excess of savings over investment is deposited in banks; here, and here only, is it made use of so as to affect trade at large; here, and here only, are prices gravely affected. In these circumstances, a low rate of interest, long protracted, is equivalent to a total depreciation of the precious metals . . . "John Bull can stand many things, but he cannot stand two per cent." (Bagehot 1873: 138–9)

He quotes an article in the *Economist* (December 30, 1871) which perhaps he wrote himself, on the causes of inflation. First, in the wake of a commercial crisis, the British call in their debts from abroad, in money (specie), so the bullion holdings of the Bank of England increase (Bagehot 1873: 139 ff). Secondly, people save more than they invest, and deposit their money in banks which have excess reserves and are looking for outlets for new loans. If saving is high and investment low, there will be an accumulation of gold. However, this is not enough. Now a

new channel of demand is required to take off the new money, or that new money will not raise prices. It will lie idle in the banks, as we have often seen it. We should still see the frequent, the common phenomenon of dull trade and cheap money existing side by side. (Bagehot 1873: 145)[1]

An additional requirement is cheap corn (food), which will raise the real income of the workers and thus increase the demand for other goods. (Agricultural distress and high prices would, of course, have the opposite effect.) In a very brief sketch of the germ of the neoclassical view – the internal impact of interest rate changes – Bagehot attributes to the lower agricultural prices the beginning of a boom. Short-term demand by traders for credit is very inelastic, so when the rate of interest begins to rise it will rise steeply. Investors get on the bandwagon, fraudulent operators come into the

---

[1] This theme is strong in his schematic history of the development of banking, which he describes as dealing with the problem of finding outlets for accumulated savings: in most (or many) countries people simply hoard their savings. In Britain in general this has not been the case, but there have been variations over time. He cites Macaulay to the effect that between the Restoration and the Revolution (of 1688), there were not enough good investments available and accumulated savings were increasing, so there was much hoarding (Bagehot 1873: 133). Not at all a mechanical quantity theorist, he is arguing that an increased money supply will not raise prices unless it first raises spending.

market, and there is likely to be a panic. In short, the market is subject to strong fluctuations. This is the reason for "the cardinal importance of always retaining a great banking reserve" (Bagehot 1873: 159).

Unfortunately, according to Bagehot, the Bank's directors did not really understand what they were doing, and their past successes had in many instances been accidental. Being merchants, they understood neither economics nor banking (thus Bagehot).[2] They act by instinct, not always bad. Thus for ten years following the suspension in 1797 they resisted the temptation to over issue notes, and the exchange rate did not depreciate. "But when, in 1810, they came to be examined as to their reasons, they gave answers that have become almost classical by their nonsense" (Bagehot 1873: 175). They denied any connection between the exchange rate and their note issue and denied that this was or should have been a consideration in their decision (compare Viner page 38 above).

And Mr. Harman, another Bank director, expressed his opinion in these terms [in 1810, testifying before the Bullion Committee] – "I must very materially alter my opinions before I can suppose that the exchanges will be influenced by any modifications of our paper currency."

Very few persons perhaps could have managed to commit so many blunders in so few words. (Bagehot 1873: 176)

The reason the Bank directors were successful for a time was that they were guided by a convention which dictated that they should discount only "good" bills and never at less than 5 percent, and, since the number of good bills was not volatile and interest rates were often less than 5 percent, this constrained them to what was, in effect, reasonable policy for a time, even though "the theory upon which they were defended was nonsense." From 1825 till 1857 they made a number of disastrous mistakes, letting their banking reserves fall perilously low. After 1857, he grants, they had been doing much better, although still not understanding why, and not acknowledging, or comprehending, the need for them to keep substantial reserves (Bagehot 1873: 177–80).

They behaved commendably, for example, in the crisis of 1866 and from then until 1870. But in 1870 the Bank of France suspended bullion payments so the Bank of England for the first time constituted the only bullion market. As a result the potential pressures on the Bank of England increased and could materialize more quickly than before. As long as this remained in force, he argued, the Bank of England was the only source of gold for foreign

[2] Bankers were not allowed to be Directors of the Bank of England; these had to be private merchants and businessmen. As such they would be seriously hurt if the Bank failed (Bagehot 1873: 35). They thus had the self-interest, as well as the intelligence and leisure, to do a good job of directing the Bank. See page 30 on the leisure necessarily available to any good businessman.

governments who wanted to increase their gold holdings (Bagehot 1873: 318).[3] The Bank should, therefore, be keeping much more bullion than previously, being Europe's only source of gold, but it seemed unaware of this. He was therefore not at all sanguine about the probability that the Bank would behave the same way during the next panic (Bagehot 1873: 184 ff). Nothing was further from the truth, in his view, than the belief that the Bank could – and should – remain aloof in a panic and that it could emerge unscathed. If the Bank stopped discounting bills, to wait out the panic, its own bills would return unpaid, since the market would not have the cash to give it. Having "no peculiar privilege," it had no choice in time of panic but to "advance freely and vigorously to the public out of the reserve" (Bagehot 1873: 196).

The Bank of England should raise interest rates very early in a panic "so that the fine may be paid early; that no one may borrow out of idle precaution without paying well for it" (Bagehot 1873: 197). At the heightened rates, however, the Bank should meet all demand for loans and lend on all good securities. The point clearly was to assuage the doubts and alarms of the public. Extending loans freely and then stopping, or not lending at all, would bring disaster not only to the market but to the Bank of England as well. "This policy may not save the Bank; but if it do not, nothing will save it" (Bagehot 1873: 199). In the panic of 1825, the Bank hesitated dangerously long, urging the government to issue bonds. Peel, however, was convinced that this would not help and that in any case the Bank would have to provide the liquidity, so the government told the Bank to go ahead and "issue their notes on the security of goods," which they did. They lent extensively, almost without restriction, and saved the situation (Bagehot 1873: 202). O'Brien (1971: 72) had a different interpretation, arguing that it was Rothschild who saved the situation (see page 33 above).

Bagehot gave the Bank fairly high points for having extended sufficient credit in the three subsequent panics, after 1844. Where they were at fault, however, was in not making known in advance what kinds of securities they would accept for such emergency advances. The Bank of England typically confined itself to consols, India securities, and good bills, but this was a mistake, he felt. Railway debentures, for example, were just as good. In fact, the Bank of England should lend on anything that any other banks lend on in ordinary times, because during a panic there is no other lender. If they did not make clear and explicit that in time of panic they would lend freely and on any good security "both our liability to crises and our terror at crises will always be greater than they would otherwise be" (Bagehot 1873: 204–7).

[3] This is highly reminiscent of the position of the United States under Bretton Woods. This point about the strain imposed on the Bank of England by the policy of the Bank of France appears later; we shall meet it in the discussion of the Cunliffe Report.

Bagehot was arguing, essentially, that the Bank of England was in fact the lender of last resort, whether it wanted so to be or not.

It was important that the rise in Bank rate should be adequate. Technically, he proposed (rather, he seconded the proposal of Goschen) that Bank rate should be raised by at least one percentage point when a gold inflow was sought. The typical transaction was a three-month bill, the cost of shipping gold was about 0.5 percent, that is an annual rate of 2 percent. Presumably the additional 1 percent would often be compensated for in the expected appreciation of sterling, since the problem would arise only if sterling were near the bottom of its band – that is, near the gold import point. Adopting this policy enabled the Bank to weather several drains between 1862 and 1865 (Bagehot 1873: 181–2).[4] Though the plea for adequate reserves is incessant, these are not clearly defined. He is emphatic, however, that they should not be a fixed proportion of total liabilities. First, the appropriate level depended on the type of liabilities: call money, for example, should be treated differently from dated acceptances. Secondly, it depends on the concentration of the liabilities among depositors and the predictability of habits of the depositors. One must consider the "quality" and "*intensity*" of the deposits. Thus, because the biggest depositor of the Bank of England is the government, whose pattern of spending is known, the Bank needs smaller reserves than might appear. (In general, since much banking activity involves interbank shifts in deposits, there is an argument for relatively low reserves in the Bank of England.) Furthermore, most government spending consists of dividends on the debt, much of which remains in the banking system. And to the extent that it leaks out, this is predictable. The money multiplier, that is, is stable. Other categories of government spending, on the other hand, such as that of the India Office, are not widely known nor very predictable (Bagehot 1873: 302–5).

On the other hand, he gives two long convoluted examples (Bagehot 1873: 308 ff) of why the Bank of England may need higher reserves than would be indicated by simply computing its deposits. The main point of both of them seems to involve the existence, or threat, of an external drain. But they get involved with internal drains as well, since domestic banks have foreign depositors, often very large, and the Bank of England has no way of ascertaining this. Thus, a large foreign deposit might be placed in a private bank (say by the German Government), which redeposits its reserves at the

---

[4] Sayers (1936 [1970: 54]) notes that in 1907, when the Bank Rate was raised only 0.5 percent, in an attempt to influence the exchange rate, this was "a breach of the tradition dating back to Goschen's 'Foreign Exchanges' of 1863. It had ever since been recognised as axiomatic that the rate must be raised by at least 1 percent to have any noticeable effect on the foreign exchanges." Sayers notes that this move was applauded by the *Economist* as a "commendable innovation, which would be 'appreciated by traders who obtain loans from their bankers on the basis of Bank Rate.'"

Bank of England. The Bank of England cannot know that this deposit is particularly vulnerable to a single large withdrawal and worse, to a single large *foreign* withdrawal. Having a fixed ratio of reserves to bankers' deposits at the Bank of England is not a satisfactory solution. A withdrawal in such a case presents a double problem, since there is both a gold outflow abroad and, in addition, an increased need to make greater advances internally, as bill brokers and bankers at home attempt to restore their liquidity ratios. Thus, through the possibilities of drains abroad, bankers' deposits constitute a very great demand on the Bank of England. "They are the symbol of an indefinite liability: by means of them . . . an amount of money so great that it is impossible to assign a limit to it might be abstracted from the Bank of England" (Bagehot 1873: 313–14). (Remember, "money" is gold.) He distinguishes between the deposits of non-banks at the Bank of England, which are not part of the monetary base, and deposits of bankers, which are. Unlike a modern central bank, of course, the Bank of England had to worry about its own reserves even in the face of internal or "domestic" drains.

In sum, he comes down very hard for management and discretion: discretion with respect to the reserve ratio, which cannot be either fixed or legislated or decreed in advance; and discretion with respect to Bank rate, which cannot simply conform to the market rate, as had been suggested, he noted, by others. The market rate has nothing to do with actual or potential demand upon bullion, whereas Bank rate must have very much to do with this (Bagehot 1873: 318–20).

## Marshall

Marshall is frequently cited as a major, if not "the" enunciator of what I have labeled the neoclassical view. The standard source for his views on the subject is his notes for and evidence to the Gold and Silver Commission in 1887 (Marshall 1887 [1926]). As is obvious from the name of the Commission, much of the questioning concerns the pros and cons of bimetallism, but his views of the workings of the international adjustment mechanism come out, perforce, in the discussion.

### The impact of money flows: interest rates or prices

In the context of response to oral questioning, it is frequently difficult to pinpoint his views. What seems to be the same question evoked apparently disparate replies at different times. But in essence, I would say that his view of the long-run international adjustment and of monetary theory in general is wholly quantity theoretic and, though not spelled out, undoubtedly classical – the Cambridge equation and the demand for cash, $k$, is unmistakable and comes through very clearly.[5] In the short run, he grants a role to the interest rate and/or credit availability as affecting expenditure, sometimes for capital investment, usually short-term inventory investment, which he calls "speculation" (which is, of course, neoclassical). These expenditure changes feed into prices; there is no mention of them having an effect on the current account directly.

The main tenets of his testimony are the following:

1 In the long run the rate of interest is unaffected by the money supply and is the rate of return on capital (or on investment; this is not absolutely clear). In true Marshallian manner he explains to the Commission that both supply and demand mattered. The then current low interest rates, he explained, were due to recent increases in savings, unmatched by expanded investment opportunities, and coupled with expectations of continued decline in prices (Marshall 1887 [1926: 45, 51]).

And ". . . the supply of gold exercises no *permanent* influence over the rate of discount. The average rate of discount *permanently* is determined by the profitableness of business. All that the influx of gold does is to make a sort of ripple on the surface of the water" (Marshall 1887 [1926: 41], italics mine).

When questioned as to why interest rates were currently falling and prices not rising, Marshall answered that in the long run "the rate of interest which can be got for the investment of capital" was falling because of increased saving around the world ("I do not see any necessity at all why interest should be more than 2 percent a century hence.") and "The rate of discount . . . is merely the ripple of a wave on the surface [*He* apparently enjoyed the aquatic reference]" (Marshall 1887 [1926: 49]).

2 In the longer run the quantity of money influences only prices, in accordance with the Cambridge equation, providing $k$ is constant. There are dozens of statements of this in the testimony. Here are two:

I think that, the habits of business being unchanged, a rise of prices requires an increase of the coin in people's pockets to sustain it . . . And what I say with regard to

---

[5]   He was, in terms of the earlier debate, a supporter of the currency school, arguing that it was the quantity of currency which controlled prices, not including demand deposits. In a memorandum which he wrote for the Commission, he stated this explicitly: "According to the older, and, as I believe the juster view, prices in England are determined by the relation in which the amount of business done in England stands to the volume of the currency, account being taken of the methods of business. Thus those purchases which are made by cheques and other instruments of credit are set on one side, and there are left remaining those purchases which are made with currency . . . The precious metals are then so distributed throughout the world, that . . . each country has just that aggregate amount of the two metals which corresponds in value to the volume of that part of her business which the habits of her people cause her to transact by payments in coin, account being taken of the rapidity of circulation of coin, and of the absorption of some quantity of the precious metals to act as the basis of a paper currency" (Marshall 1887 [1926: 176–7]).

the rate of discount is intended to account, *not for the permanent rise of prices, but for those larger supplies of currency in the pockets of the people who sustain the prices permanently*. If a postman [or a helicopter piloted by Milton Friedman?] could go round and distribute to everybody the increased currency straight off, then I think that would in a primitive state of society act upon prices directly. (Marshall 1887 [1926: 45], italics mine)

Asked how an influx of gold would affect prices, he replied that

if there was more gold in circulation than people wanted . . . they would simply send it to the banks. From the banks it would go into the reserve; from the reserve it would go back on to the general market, inflating credit, increasing speculation, enabling people to borrow who could not borrow before, raising prices. When prices had once been raised, say, 10 percent all round, then supposing . . . the habits of business to be exactly the same as before; then people would require 10 percent more cash in their pockets than they did before. (Marshall 1887 [1926: 40–1])

3 In the short run, an inflow of gold can lead to a reduction in the market rate of interest (both because the banks and the Bank of England have a lower discount rate) and because, simply, there is more money available for loan. This leads to an increase in "speculation", which is short-term inventory investment, which generally results in a price rise. This will be reinforced by expectations of price rises engendered by the gold inflow (Marshall 1887 [1926: 131]). Having risen, prices would stay up because there would be more money around to support the higher prices. Here, of course, he is articulating the Cambridge quantity theory: more money and unchanged habits ($k$) yield higher prices (Marshall 1887 [1926: 52 ff]). But since, in the "modern world", increases in the money supply are injected through the money market, they generally result in a decrease in the rate of discount "as well as in prices" (Marshall 1887 [1926: 123]).

Even in the short run an influx of money can affect prices directly. Thus he states that gold

does not always act on prices directly and immediately; that its first action is on Lombard Street, and that it affects prices afterwards through its action on Lombard Street, though of course the holder of the gold may in some cases draw against it, and purchase commodities, and thus act on prices immediately to some extent. (Marshall 1887 [1926: 141])

4 He does concede the "speculation" argument for the short run. An increase in the money supply leads to a reduction in interest rates which causes a price increase through a rise in speculation. The latter is then supported by the increased money stock. In the following quotation, the questioners had been pressing him on the issue of a lower rate of discount (market rate of interest). An influx of gold

would act at once upon Lombard Street, and make people inclined to lend more; it would swell deposits and book credits, and so enable people to increase their speculation with borrowed capital . . . it would, therefore, increase the demand for commodities and so raise prices . . . [T]hat would be only its immediate effect, but it would have the ultimate effect of adding to the volume of the currency required for circulation, as I think; because, prices having risen, a person who had found it answer his purpose to have on the average 17*l*. in currency in his pocket, would now require 18*l*. or 19*l*.; and so on for others. (Marshall 1887 [1926: 38])

5 An additional notion, though not a constantly recurring theme, is that interest rates vary not only because of changes in the money supply, but because of the operation of the law of one price, international arbitrage. With the improvement in communications, financial markets had become highly integrated, he said, and price changes in these markets frequently spread internationally even faster than did commodity price changes. Thus a decline in the British gold stock, raising the market rate of interest, would cause an offsetting capital inflow (from America), reducing the discount rate, faster than a price decline in America would lead to a fall in British prices (Marshall 1887 [1926: 123]). The reason for this seems to be institutional, and

the growing tendency of intercommunication has shown itself in the discount market more than in any other . . . the discount market is becoming international more rapidly even than the wheat market; the tendency, therefore, for a stable rate of discount is growing more fast than the tendency for a stable rate of wheat. (Marshall 1887 [1926: 127–8])

### Monetary and banking policy

When asked about appropriate Bank of England reserve holdings and policy, he answered that large gold reserves were needed for international purposes. The reason, he said, was based on an extension of "the arguments at the end of Bagehot's *Lombard Street*, . . ." (Marshall 1887 [1926: 111]). Like Bagehot, he favored an extremely flexible and discretionary system. The Bank of England should keep large, and variable, gold reserves, which would permit it to exercise discretion in their deployment. Specifically, when the discount rate was very high (10 percent, in his example), the Bank should be able to ignore its reserve requirement. And raising the discount rate when reserves got low was associated with a range of reserves rather than a single number. Raising the discount rate would be "not so much an obligation defined in set legal phrase, as a moral obligation, in which much would be left to their discretion, they acting on their knowledge of the special circumstances of each case" (Marshall 1887 [1926: 111–12]). Flexibility, discretion, and the ability to avoid large and sudden contractions are the desiderata. He approves of the support given by "Mr. Bagehot himself and other economists after his date, writing both in books and in newspapers . . . urging the Bank to avoid the necessity for moving the rate of discount about so much" (Marshall 1887 [1926: 128]).

### Flexible exchange rates: an addendum

In a memorandum to the Commission[6] in response to questions about whether changes (in general, reductions) in the price of silver would give a "bounty" to exporters in India (a silver country), he makes a statement which is often regarded as his view of the functioning of flexible exchange rates, or the effects of a devaluation under a pegged regime. It is not, in my view, quite the same as either of these, though it is related. Nor is it, in my view, a good example of Marshall as a pre-neoclassical. It is, rather, a fairly straightforward piece of classical analysis.

He begins the memorandum with what must be the briefest statement on record of the price-specie flow mechanism, even including some statement about the speed of adjustment. If either purchasing power parity[7] or the law of one price is disturbed (he does not differentiate here between equality of purchasing power of the several countries' currencies, on the one hand, and the equality of traded goods prices on the other), there will be disequilibrium in the market for bills. "Bills drawn in $B$ on $A$ will multiply, and, specie point being reached, gold will go from $A$ to $B$, till prices in $B$ are as high as in $A$. (If $B$ hoards gold this process may be a long one, otherwise it is sure to be short.)" (Marshall 1888 [1926: 191]).

There follows an almost as brief statement of flexible exchange rates – the determinants of the rate of exchange of a single country with "inconvertible currency" vis-à-vis a gold-standard trading partner. "The gold price of the rouble will be fixed by the course of trade just at the ratio which gold prices in [the gold currency] . . . bear to rouble prices in $B$ [the rouble-using country]." A fall in rouble prices (prices denominated in roubles) would give a temporary advantage to $B$'s exporters, until changes in the demand and supply of bills would bring the exchange rate to the new purchasing power parity. Any more permanent "bounty" to any sector implies that a shift in comparative advantage had taken place at the same time, presumably independently of the price level shift (Marshall 1888 [1926: 191–2]).

---

[6] "Memorandum on the relation between a fall of the exchange and trade with countries which have not a gold currency." January 13, 1888 (Marshall 1888 [1926: 191 ff]).

[7] To the best of my knowledge, this expression was used first by Gustav Cassel. Viner (1937: 380) attributes it to him as early as 1916, but his (Viner's) first citation is Cassel (1920). Marshall of course did not use it. It is used extensively in Cassel (1922). But between 1916 and 1918 Cassel published a number of rather short papers in the Economic journal (1916b, 1916c, 1917, 1918) and in the last of these he writes: "I propose to call this parity 'the purchasing power parity'" (1918: 413, italics his). The argument about which prices or price indices to use in interpreting the doctrine continues to this day.

.Now to the third, more interesting case. Country $A$ has a gold currency, and $B$ a silver currency. Here the analysis depends on the fact that there are two very highly arbitrageable commodities, gold and silver, and that "silver is, and roubles are not, an exportable commodity" (Marshall 1888 [1926: 192]). In this case any permanent change in the price ratio of the two metals indicates a shift in either world demand or world supply for them. Perfect commodity arbitrage in the metals assures that their price ratio cannot be different between countries. Purchasing power parity assures that there is no relative advantage accruing from such a change to any specific sector in either country (Marshall 1888 [1926: 193]).

The qualifications to the generalization above are twofold. First, if as in the case of the inconvertible rouble, changes in price levels are accompanied by changes in the structure of comparative advantage, it may seem to observers, and to exporters of the newly competitive commodity, that it is the change in nominal exchange rates which led to the advantage.

The second qualification is more interesting; it involves, not fortuitous simultaneous changes in comparative advantage, but a temporary advantage for one or another sector because of differences, between sectors, in the ratio of fixed to variable costs. Thus, if the price level is falling, those industries with the smallest ratio of fixed to variable costs will develop a temporary comparative advantage and the increase in their exports will mitigate the exchange rate depreciation (Marshall 1888 [1926: 194]).

In conclusion he argues that the temporary effect on the Indian exporter of a fall in the price of silver depends on where that price falls first. If in India, then the Indian price of foreign exchange falls and the British exporter (to India) gets a bounty. If in the rest of the world, the effect is the same as a devaluation of the rupee (not his terminology) and Indian exporters are temporarily stimulated. (In the long run, the price of silver will change throughout the world and there will be no effect.) But if the decline in the price of silver occurred in India first, for local reasons having to do with either demand or supply of silver, this would provide a "bounty" to European exporters to India (Marshall 1888 [1926: 195]).

This in fact sounds very classical. A monetary disturbance, either an increase in the supply of the monetary metal, or a decrease in the demand for money, will lead to a rise in prices in India, resulting in "a bounty to the European exporter," and, for India, a payments deficit which implies an outflow of silver.

## A statement of the neoclassical position: Nurkse

As indicated above, I regard the neoclassical view as two-pronged: a statement of the essentially classical paradigm, with the addition of emphasis on the role of policy, changes in central bank discount rates, with the effect of:

1  attracting foreign capital (or a backflow of domestic capital) and financing an imbalance and
2  influencing domestic spending (generally through investment) and hence feeding back on the trade balance.

There is no single authoritative statement of the neoclassical doctrine (though the Cunliffe Report wins on frequency of citations) by a writer claiming to be propounding that position. Statements of what it was generally believed to be abound, however. Here is one, succinctly stated, which described it retrospectively. It is a description by Nurkse entitled "The Rules of the Game" (Nurkse 1944: 66–105). He added open market operations as a tool to be used by the central bank to change the volume of its domestic assets, but in every other respect his account is very close to that of the Cunliffe Committee (see Chapter 4).

The gold standard, or indeed any system of stable exchange rates, is a system in which the quantity of money in each country is determined primarily by the balance of payments . . .

But the *traditional* view of the operation of the gold bullion standard assigned to central banks more than the passive function of converting domestic into international currency and *vice versa*. Whenever gold flowed in, the central bank was expected to increase the national currency supply not only through the purchase of that gold but also through the acquisition of additional domestic assets . . .

The "rules" were never more than a set of crude signals and signposts . . . Their object, above all, was to secure quick and continuous adjustment of international balances of payments. The expansion of credit in the gold-receiving country were intended to affect prices and incomes in such a way as to close the gap in the balance of payments which had given rise to the transfer of gold; and even before this adjustment through prices and incomes was completed, the changes in money rates which caused or at least accompanied the change in the volume of domestic credit in the two countries could generally be expected to reduce if not to close the gap through transfers of private short-term funds from the gold-receiving to the gold-losing country.

This general picture of the adjustment process and of the central-bank policy in that process was given authoritative expression by the British "Cunliffe Committee" at the very outset of the interwar period; and it was one which during much of that period dominated men's ideas both as to the actual working of the gold standard before 1914 and as to the way the gold standard should be made to work after its restoration. There was a wide belief in the early 'twenties that the monetary upheavals of that time were due to the absence of the equilibrating mechanism enforced by the gold-standard "rules of the game". (Nurkse 1944: 67)

In a detailed discussion of the interwar period, Nurkse argued that in fact there was nothing automatic about the mechanism or the "rules of the game," at any rate during that period, and that there might have been automatic tendencies to neutralize gold movements (Nurkse 1944: 88). As Bloomfield (1959) did for the prewar period, he compared annual changes in central banks' international reserves with their same-year changes in domestic assets and found that they were as often as not perverse (Nurkse 1944: 66 ff). (For a discussion of Bloomfield on this issue see Chapter 7.) He interprets this cautiously, however, referring to lags, central banks reacting only after two or three years perhaps, to a change in their reserves. He is apparently referring to a case in which the central bank reduces its foreign liabilities and assets simultaneously, and only subsequently reduces its domestic liabilities accordingly. This "delayed adjustment" need not, according to Nurkse, imply "a deliberate act of neutralization on the part of that bank. It may well be due to the bank's inaction rather than to its action." Alternatively, it may require the initiative and action of the central bank to prevent "automatic neutralization," which might, in the absence of such initiative, become "the rule rather than the exception." He refers here to an inflow from abroad leading to credit ease domestically which induces borrowers to repay their loans to the banks, automatically sterilizing the inflow. Yet again, the commercial banks may absorb an inflow without expanding credit, since "a maximum limit to the accumulation of cash reserves by commercial banks has nowhere been applied by law" (Nurkse 1944: 70–1). All this is, of course, quite antithetical to the spirit of the Cunliffe Report.

However, Nurkse hits on the inherent conflict in the neoclassical position when he notes that it is precisely the "equilibrating capital flows" induced by discount rate changes intended to follow the "rules" which both made for the inverse changes in domestic and foreign assets of the central banks and "complicated the task of any central bank trying to follow the 'rules of the game' in its internal credit policy . . ." (Nurkse 1944: 72). The United States' neutralization of its gold inflows in the early 1920s, a neutralization which so exercised Keynes in the *Tract* (see Chapter 8), was automatic but it was also deliberate in the sense that the Federal Reserve System decided to let it happen, in the conviction that the gold inflow was temporary and they had to be ready to let it flow out again without causing disruption (Nurkse 1944: 72; see Chapter 11). I know of no other writer who has expressed this particular "inversion". Leaning on short-term equilibrating capital movements as part of the adjustment to the neglect of allowing internal effects to operate is commonplace in the literature. In fact, it much predates what I have labeled the neoclassical view. But to argue that endogenous short-term capital movements get in the way of the proper operation of the system in adjusting internal credit to domestic reserves is unusual.

Again, in the period 1925–31, when Britain had returned to the gold standard, Nurkse cites Gregory's report to the Gold Delegation of the League of Nations to the effect that the Bank of England was explicitly following a policy of stabilizing the volume of domestic credit and sterilizing gold flows. Similarly, when France stabilized the franc and the economy in 1926 large capital inflows were matched by large public purchases of government securities, so the gold inflow did not result in the credit expansion which the "rules" would have required. The Bank of France did lower its discount rate, substantially, but he argues that the money markets were so liquid that this had no effect. "[T]he country had just emerged from a period of inflation and was not in the mood for more." The reverse took place in the period 1935–8 when there were huge capital outflows, gold losses, and a large increase in domestic credit. This was even exacerbated by the fact that the money market was so tight, due to the hot money flight, that the government borrowed from the central bank rather than from the public: this fed the available supply of funds with which to buy gold to export. In general, however, Nurkse argues, clearly approvingly, that most countries took steps to sterilize capital flights during the 1930s. In the early part of the decade this was prevalent in the capital exporting countries; in the late 1930s a number of capital receiving countries generally either offset inflows as long as they were able and took other steps, such as raising reserve requirements, when the central bank ran out of domestic government securities with which to intervene (Nurkse 1944: 75–81).

Nurkse makes a major point of trying to distinguish between "automatic" and voluntary offsetting, but in the context of the neoclassical dictum it is not clear to me that this makes any difference, certainly not qualitatively. For if the market behaves in a way which tends to counteract the gold flow (in its effect on the domestic money supply) the implication of the "rules" is that the central bank will have to tighten up that much more to validate the outflow and the contraction. If it does not do so, this is presumably "voluntary" in any case. An elegantly concise survey of the views discussed above, the adherence or lack of it to the rules both before and after World War I, and extensions to a consideration of problems under the Bretton Woods system, can be found in Bloomfield (1968b).

## Summation

In sum, the neoclassical position, in its full version, has three essential elements: 1) the classical price-specie flow mechanism, on which is superimposed 2) interest-differential-induced capital flows, and 3) interest-rate-change-induced adjustments in domestic expenditure and prices. It was summed up very concisely in the League of Nations *World Economic Survey, 1931/2* (170–1) (cited by Brown 1940: 387–8).

If anything more than temporary disequilibrium developed in the financial relations of any one country with the rest of the world, an outflow of gold brought about a restriction of credit, and therefore rising interest rates, which attracted capital or checked its exportation, and falling prices which encouraged exports and checked imports till equilibrium was restored again. Such a corrective sequence of events was, however, dependent both upon a certain flexibility in the national price-structures and upon a smooth and efficient working of the standard.

I have argued that by these criteria Bagehot qualifies as a neoclassical, since he makes totally explicit the domestic effects of changes in interest rates, as well as the immediate external effects. Note that Bagehot has a "rule" but it is surrounded by a tremendous amount of fine tuning, because everything depends on the circumstance: internal or external drain; who the major customers are at the time; where the drain is to; further, the "desired" or appropriate level of reserves for the Bank of England is a highly discretionary variable, presumably, therefore, subject to change at frequent and irregular intervals.

Marshall, I argue, is still more a classical than not, with a strong link to the quantity theory of money, and a rejection of the notion that the interest rate is affected by the money market (except for very short periods) or affects total spending and hence the trade balance. What he did grant with respect to the effect of changes in the money supply on the rate of interest and on spending was a) rather grudging, and b) confined to short-term "speculation". Like Bagehot, however, he also favored wide discretionary powers for the Bank of England: they should not be required rigidly to maintain a specific reserve ratio, and their response to gold flows should be a function of the circumstances, both domestic and foreign, under which it occurred.

# CHAPTER 4

# The *locus classicus* of the neoclassical position

The neoclassical view is that which is typically regarded as the statement of the "rules of the game" of the gold standard. A widely cited source of this view is the Cunliffe Committee Report, written in 1918, describing the workings of the prewar system. Thirteen years later, the Macmillan Committee gave a drastically different view of how the prewar system had in fact worked. Furthermore (and more interesting), it appears that the Cunliffe Committee described a system that never had existed: the difference between their description of the system and a more detailed analysis of the operations of the Bank of England, Sayers (1936), is striking.

Emphasizing the Bank of England's activities here is, I think, perfectly justified. The revisionists argue that the prewar gold standard was really a sterling standard (see Chapter 7). But even hard line gold standardists would agree that Great Britain was very much at the center of the system and that the Bank of England played a crucial and leading role in its working.

## The Cunliffe Committee and its report

The Cunliffe Committee, the "Committee on Currency and Foreign Exchanges after the War," was appointed by the Treasury, in January 1918 "to consider the various problems which will arise in connection with currency and the foreign exchanges during the period of reconstruction and report upon the steps required to bring about the restoration of normal conditions in due course." Later the following words were added: "and to consider the working of the Bank Act, 1844, and the constitution and functions of the Bank of England with a view to recommending any alterations which may appear to them to be necessary or desirable." The committee of fourteen members was headed by Lord Cunliffe, the Governor of the Bank of England, and was composed of a highly distinguished panel of bankers, plus the Secretary to the Treasury, Sir John Bradbury, and one academic economist, A. C. Pigou (Cunliffe 1918: 2).

What has become known as the Cunliffe Report was their First Interim

Report, published in August 1918. It is this which is known popularly as the Cunliffe Report. The final report, presented in 1919, has not much to add. There they simply noted that they essentially had not changed their minds on any significant detail, and specifically commented that it was unnecessary to elaborate further on the foreign exchanges, it being evident "that a sound system of currency would in itself secure equilibrium in the Foreign Exchanges." Having reviewed the criticisms of the Interim Report, they remained staunchly in support of full convertibility "into gold or other exportable coin" (Cunliffe 1919: 3).

The view of the prewar adjustment mechanism as presented in the Interim Report has been so often referred to and so much discussed that it is worth citing briefly yet once more:

When the exchanges were favourable, gold flowed freely into this country and an increase of legal tender money accompanied the development of trade. When the balance of trade was unfavourable and the exchanges were adverse, it became profitable to export gold. The would-be exporter bought his gold from the Bank of England and paid for it by a cheque on his account. The Bank obtained the gold from the Issue Department in exchange for notes taken out of its banking reserve, with the result that its liabilities to depositors and its banking reserve were reduced by an equal amount, and the ratio of reserve to liabilities consequently fell. If the process was repeated sufficiently often to reduce the ratio in a degree considered dangerous, the Bank raised its rate of discount. The raising of the discount rate had the immediate effect of retaining money here which would otherwise have been remitted abroad and of attracting remittances from abroad to take advantage of the higher rate, thus checking the outflow of gold and even reversing the stream. If the adverse condition of the exchanges was due not merely to seasonal fluctuations, but to circumstances tending to create a permanently adverse trade balance, it is obvious that the procedure above described would not have been sufficient. It would have resulted in the creation of a volume of short-dated indebtedness to foreign countries which would have been in the end disastrous to our credit and the position of London as the financial centre of the world. But the raising of the Bank's discount rate and the *steps taken to make it effective in the market*[1] necessarily led to a general rise of interest rates and a restriction of credit. New enterprises were therefore postponed and the demand for constructional materials and other capital goods was lessened. *The consequent slackening of employment* also diminished the demand for consumable goods, while holders of stocks of commodities carried largely with borrowed money, being confronted with an increase of interest charges, if not with actual difficulty in renewing loans, and with the prospect of falling prices, tended to press their goods on a weak market. The result was a decline in general prices in the home market which, by checking imports and stimulating exports, corrected the adverse trade balances which was the primary cause of the difficulty. (Cunliffe 1918: 3–4, italics mine)

[1] This is an interesting comment, since it implies their recognition of a tremendous amount of activity described in great detail by Sayers (1936 [1970]), which I shall discuss below. Sayers accuses the Committee of having ignored these activities, and, in fact, there is no other mention of them aside from this brief comment.

The dual of the theorem is similarly summarized: how is excessive credit creation at home automatically corrected? It leads to a rise in prices, hence an increased demand for cash and an equal reduction in the Bank of England's reserves and liabilities, that is, a shortfall in its reserves, forcing it to raise its discount rate "and speculative trade activity was similarly restrained. There was therefore *an automatic machinery* by which the volume of purchasing power in this country was continuously adjusted to world prices of commodities in general" (Cunliffe 1918: 4, italics mine).

This analysis fits into the neoclassical category in that there is a banking system and an interest rate, both playing crucially prominent roles. There is even a central bank, but it exercises virtually no discretion (except for the brief and vague mention of "other steps to make bank rate effective"). There is nothing here about the famous "rules of the game," which despite its name, implied some sort of discretionary activity on the part of the central bank. The term itself had not yet been used when the Cunliffe Committee sat. To the best of my knowledge, it was first used by Keynes in 1925 (Keynes 1922–9 [1981: 360]). A reading of Cunliffe (unless, perhaps, one is actively looking for hints to the contrary) leaves one with the impression that a not very sophisticated computer could easily have been a central bank in their sense. Absence of discussion of a discretionary policy of any kind is consistent indeed with our concept of rules. But the "rules of the game" suggested a framework, a set of regulations, within which, however, there was a game being played, a concept necessarily implying some discretion.

Sayers, in his history of the Bank from 1890 until 1914, demonstrates that the Bank of England used many more policies and more tools, with discretion, than Cunliffe implies; one might argue that this was an application of discretion which involved technical tools for effecting the automatically determined policy. See the discussion below.

The rules versus authority discussion is relevant here, but it needs interpreting. Most of the contemporary literature on the subject (see Barro 1986 for an illuminating survey) is expressed in terms of some national goal, such as employment or inflation (the rate of inflation tax). The automatic rule of the gold standard, however, is in a sense more "primitive" than these, since it involves stabilizing what is in effect an instrumental variable rather than a goal variable. It requires, strictly speaking, the stabilization of the *reserves* of the monetary authorities. (This, as we shall see in Chapter 7, is the basis for Hayek's objections to fractional-reserve banking.) In the context of the gold standard, this means stabilizing the overall balance of payments. Price level stability results from this only if world prices are stable and there are no changes in the structural equations for trade and capital movements, such as tastes, technology, and return to capital in the several trading countries.

The institutional framework, as the Cunliffe Committee interpreted it, at any rate, was that of the pre-1914 gold standard, dominated by the Bank Act of 1844. This involved a fixed absolute volume of fiduciary notes issued by the Bank of England (£18,450,000; in 1910 the total note issue was £53 million) plus notes backed 100 percent by gold. While nothing forced the Bank of England to issue notes when it bought gold, it was not allowed to increase its note issue by more than an increase in its gold reserves. Since the reserves of the commercial banks took the form of gold or of Bank of England notes, the monetary base could change only with changes in the banking system's gold holdings. (There is, of course, the question of the role of the Bank's deposits as high-powered money, an issue the Cunliffe Committee did not raise.)

A word, however, is in order about the Bank of England's "Reserve" and the question of the "Proportion" of the "Reserve" to total deposit liabilities.

The so-called "Reserve" consisted not of the gold held by the Bank, but such part of the gold as was not required, under the Act of 1844, to cover the difference between the notes outside the Bank (the "circulation", whether in the banks or elsewhere) and the statutory Fiduciary Issue. This margin was shown in the Bank Return as a cash reserve in the Banking Department, where all the deposits were shown among the liabilities. The Proportion was thus the Banking Department's parallel to the cash ratio of a commercial bank: it was as exposed to public demands for notes or gold for circulation as it was to demands for gold for export. Thus in looking at both the Reserve and the gold, the Governors were apparently as concerned at an internal drain as at an external drain: a confusion entirely proper to anyone brought up to observe the Act of 1844. (Sayers 1976: Volume I, 30)

The famous passage from Cunliffe cited above implies, and the rest of the report spells out explicitly, the view that the quantity of money is endogenous under fixed exchange rates, and to that extent there is a strong resemblance to both the monetary theory of the balance of payments and the pure price-specie flow mechanism. Since the money supply is controlled by the gold reserves, and since the law of one price holds, any disequilibrium must operate temporarily on output and/or (some) prices (they are not entirely clear on this point) to affect the trade balance and restore equilibrium in the money market. This is, of course, the "classical" part of the "neoclassical" theory, with the emphasis on price changes.[2]

The automatic aspect of the adjustment is heavily stressed, and lauded. "Domestic prices were automatically regulated so as to prevent excessive

---

[2]  Sayers (1976: 111) comments briefly that the Cunliffe Report "had taken a view of the power of the Bank over internal prices that might not have been accepted by earlier Governors, . . . The scanty discussions of the question before the war had generally concluded that movements of Bank Rate caused little disturbance of internal economic conditions, unless it went to a really high level, which meant something over 5 percent. That sharp and sustained rises beyond this point could bring prices down was not seriously doubted." The Bank wanted the freedom to raise Bank rate to get prices down after the war and was convinced that this would be effective; the obstacle that concerned them was the large government debt.

imports; and the creation of banking credit was so controlled *that banking could be safely permitted a freedom from State interference which would not have been possible under a less rigid currency system*" (Cunliffe 1918: 4, italics mine). This point is crucial when we compare the Cunliffe and Macmillan Committees; it is almost as if Cunliffe is anticipating and taking issue with the Macmillan arguments. It has been suggested, by Peter Kenen and others (in informal discussion), that this is the crux of the understanding of the Cunliffe position: they were attempting to forestall any attempt to regulate and control the monetary and banking system in general and the Bank of England in particular.

The "received understanding" of the neoclassical approach is that it is an embellished version of the classical. However, whereas the classical paradigm and the protomodel are both perfectly symmetrical, the Cunliffe view is not. Nor is the Bank Act of 1844. According to the Act of 1844 the Bank was not required to increase the issue of Bank notes when it received gold; similarly, the Cunliffe Report did not suggest that the Bank did or should lower Bank rate whenever gold flowed in. The direct effects of gold imports on the domestic money supply were presumed to work their way through the economy into higher prices and greater imports without help from the central bank. On the downside, however, both the Act of 1844 and the Cunliffe Committee Report call for action in case of an outflow, but of a different type. Peel's Act of 1844 refers to the note liabilities of the Bank of England: these must be backed by gold, at the margin with 100 percent reserves, and that was the main instruction. According to the Cunliffe Committee, on the other hand, the Bank could and was supposed to protect its gold reserves by adjusting Bank rate quickly when it began to lose gold, even, presumably, if it were not fully loaned up. The automaticity of the response implied that the Bank should (as it had in the past) respond when the gold outflow began, and not wait until it was forced by a lack of specie to contract its liabilities. As Sayers emphasized, this makes its behavior different from that implied by the Bank Act of 1844.[3]

The Bank Act of 1844 was intended to make a fractional-reserve banking system with a central bank behave like a pure gold standard – with a money supply that varied with the foreign exchange reserve, especially on the downside. The Cunliffe Committee view, while as adamant in its emphasis on automaticity, is different. Both positions rely on monetary changes to produce adjustment in international payments, but the Cunliffe Committee

---

[3] "Had the Bank been prepared to follow the methods intended by the authors of the Act of 1844 ... [it] would ... simply wait until there was a sufficient efflux of gold to send the market into the Bank" (Sayers 1936 [1970: 18]). He refers also to what would have happened "had the Bank followed the strict principles of 1844, waiting for gold to go out or come in before it acted" (Sayers 1936 [1970: 127]). See the discussion below for more detail on Sayers's assessment of the Bank's behavior.

broke new ground. They insisted that the mechanism is automatic and continually acts as a regulator. But they also insisted that the same mechanism operates almost exclusively *through* changes in Bank rate, which is at the same time protecting the gold reserves of the central bank and preventing the automatic reduction in the money supply envisaged by the classical approach (and by the Bank Act of 1844).

From the quantity theoretic nature of both the protomodel and the classical paradigm they have moved into an arena in which the rate of interest plays a much more crucial role, either directly through its influence on spending and hence prices, or through changes in the money supply induced by reduction in the demand for credit in response to higher lending rates. Furthermore, "protecting the Bank's reserves" can mean only aborting the quantity-theoretic adjustment process by preventing or delaying the "automatic" changes in the money supply which characterize the classical process. (As we shall see in Chapter 7, this was precisely the complaint of a super-classical writer, Hayek.)

Whenever before the war the Bank's reserves were being depleted, the rate of discount was raised. This, as we have already explained, by reacting upon the rates for money generally, acted as a check which operated in two ways. On the one hand, raised money rates tended directly to attract gold to this country or to keep here gold that might have left. On the other hand, by lessening the demands for loans for business purposes, they tended to check expenditure and so to lower prices in this country, with the result that imports were discouraged and exports encouraged, and the exchanges thereby turned in our favour ... When the exchanges are adverse and gold is being drawn away, *it is essential that the rate of discount in this country should be raised* relatively to the rates ruling in other countries. (Cunliffe 1918: 6, italics mine)

There should, in short, be no attempt to interfere with the mechanism by which Bank rate changes protected the gold reserves (while the real adjustment which resulted from the Bank rate changes could take place). Thus what is automatic in the classical position is the relationship of the money supply to the gold stock; what is automatic in Cunliffe is the response of Bank rate to threatened changes in the gold stock, with the aim of avoiding or at least postponing them, while yet fostering the internal changes required for adjustment to payments imbalances.

Interestingly enough, there is no suggestion that the Cunliffe Committee felt it was in any way modifying or challenging the classical (or bullionist) position. The insistence on changes in Bank rate as soon as gold began to flow, and appeal to prewar precedence for this policy, was apparently a defense against those who were recommending continuation of a two-tier interest rate system. This recommendation they opposed unequivocally. The idea had been to maintain low interest rates domestically to encourage domestic investment and high rates "for foreign money" to prevent gold outflows.[4] They argue that evasion and arbitrage could be prevented, if at all, "by the maintenance of such stringent restrictions upon the freedom of investment . . . as would . . . be most detrimental to the financial and industrial recovery of this country." And even if possible, it would be undesirable, since the high rate of domestic spending and prices would lead to current account deficits so that gold could be kept at home only at the cost of an ever-increasing debt to foreigners (Cunliffe 1918: 6).

All recommendations involving loosening the ties between gold and the money supply, by easing restrictions on note issues, are rejected. They specifically, and in detail, reject also the proposal to allow the Bank of England to keep reserves of less than 100 percent against new note issues, providing the reserve ratio is fixed. (They are, however, willing to economize on the use of gold by permitting only the Bank of England to hold and to export gold.) Here the analysis is highly reminiscent of Hayek (1937) (see Chapter 7). They argue that if the note issue is much less than the permitted level (if the Bank has excess reserves of gold, that is), then the reserve requirement is totally ineffective. If, on the other hand, the Bank of England is fully loaned up, then any loss of gold requires a multiple credit contraction, and "would thus be likely to cause even greater apprehension than the limitations of the Act of 1844" (Cunliffe 1918: 8).

They emphasize the special position of Britain in the (prewar?) world economy. In an apparent reference to continental, especially French, manipulations designed to protect their gold stocks, they note that other countries

have not in practice maintained the absolutely free gold market which this country, by reason of the vital importance of its position in international finance, is bound to do. It has therefore been open to them to have recourse to devices to steady the rate of discount which, even if successful for this purpose, it would be inexpedient and dangerous for us to attempt [*Noblesse oblige*]. (Cunliffe 1918: 8)

Finally, they come down firmly for maintenance and continuation of the Bank Act of 1844 and most of its basic requirements, particularly, as noted above, the fixed, one-to-one link between changes in gold reserves and in Bank of England note issues.[5] Both the Act as a whole and this aspect of it

---

[4] This idea reemerged in the Macmillan Report. Keynes, in testifying before the Macmillan Committee, supported dual interest rates, through the device of taxing and limiting foreign issues. He carried the idea to its logical conclusion in his pre-Bretton Woods writings; there he expressed constant and ardent advocacy of controls on international capital movements and on the need for international cooperation to effect and enforce them (see Chapter 10).

[5] It is never stated explicitly, but a clear implication of the Report is that the Banking Department of the Bank of England (with liabilities consisting of deposits and reserves consisting of Issue Department notes) is like any other bank, and the role of the central bank in Britain was played exclusively by the Issue Department. Dornbusch and Frenkel (1984), for example, argue that they were mistaken in this, and that the Bank in fact behaved in a

were worth conserving, they argued, even though it meant that occasional suspensions were necessary. They note with pride, however, that there had been no suspensions since 1866. They do not worry about the liquidity of the banking system, since they do recommend that gold be removed both from internal circulation and from the coffers of the commercial banks (Cunliffe 1918: 9).[6]

Though they do not, as the Macmillan Committee later would, recommend widening the gold points, they are aware of the existence of this tool. There is a wry comment (Cunliffe 1918: 5) that it was the German submarines which protected the gold stock during the war, by widening the gold points; this permitted a good deal of exchange depreciation without loss of gold. When the danger was over, gold exports continued to be restricted, this time by licensing (until 1925 and the famous Return to the gold standard).

### A diversion: the facts about the prewar era

The Cunliffe Report invites comparison with another famous Parliamentary Committee report, the Macmillan, more than a decade later. However, before getting into a discussion of it and a comparison of it with Cunliffe, I should like to foray briefly into the description given us by Sayers (1936 [1970]), of the operations of the Bank of England during the high noon of the gold standard, 1890–1914.[7] This is not an historical study, but there are striking differences between:

destabilizing manner by ignoring the high-powered nature of its deposit liabilities. There is a good deal of debate around this point; my concern here is with the fact that the Cunliffe Committee, at any rate, did not recognize this point. They presumably continued not to recognize it when they rejected the proposal to combine the Issue and Banking Departments.

[6] There is an interesting analysis of how to fix the amount of the fiduciary issue, since after the wartime inflation and money supply increase it was clear to them that it needed to be reduced, and they were unwilling to recommend returning to the prewar figure. The money stock, as noted, was considered to be endogenous. Given the behavior of the banking system, this means that the money base is endogenous. All that is left to decide is the division between the legally stated fiduciary component of that base and the residually adjusting gold supply. If you fix the fiduciary issue too high, the country will have no gold; if you fix it too low, there will be an economically wasteful and inefficient excess of gold reserves in the Bank of England. There is a brief discussion of what differences to expect after the war in the demand for cash, efficiencies and economies in the "use of legal tender money" being weighed against the effect of income redistribution in favor of "the wage-earning classes who are the chief users of legal tender money" (Cunliffe 1918: 9). They therefore make a "ball-park" estimate of appropriate gold holdings (essentially the prewar totals of the Bank of England, banks and the public, adjusted downward for the effects of taking gold out of circulation), and suggest that the Bank of England hold this much gold and then reduce the fiduciary issue gradually, year by year, whenever possible, given that constraint (Cunliffe 1918: 9–10).

[7] Sayers had to rely primarily on the excellent financial journalism of London, that is the *Economist* and the *Statist*, a few journal articles, and testimony of Bank officials to the U.S.

1   the Cunliffe Committee's perception of Bank of England operations
    before World War I,
2   the Macmillan Committee's description of the same period, and
3   some historians' interpretation of the events of the same years.

This requires some exploration.

The issues raised by Sayers are, essentially:

1   Whether the Bank of England tried to carry out the policy described by
    Cunliffe, of simply raising Bank rate and thereby protecting its gold stock
    whenever the latter was threatened. This breaks down into the questions:
    a) whether they were able to do this at all, and b) whether they were able
    to do it with the exclusive use of Bank rate.
2   Whether they had any other goals, in addition to protecting their gold
    stock. Two additional goals that suggest themselves are protecting the
    earnings of their stockholders, and showing some concerned "tender-
    ness" towards the home market, that is, recognizing internal balance as
    an additional policy goal.

Very briefly, the institutional setup was one of a very large and well-
developed market for bills and acceptances, the rate in which, known as the
market rate, was that which primarily influenced international flows of
funds. The banks, on the other hand, had by tradition linked their deposit
rates, and hence their lending rates, to Bank rate, the Bank of England's
lending or rediscounting rate. Unless these could be brought together, the
simultaneous adjustment of the capital and current accounts, as described by
the Cunliffe Report, would not take place.

The Bank of England's rate was a penalty rate and had no influence on the
bill market when the latter was easy. The customers of the Bank of England
included London clearing banks, merchant banks, British overseas banks
and some foreign banks (Sayers 1976: Volume I, 5). Tightening up on the
money market enough to get the market and the market rate to respond to
Bank rate was, therefore, a major problem faced by the Bank of England. It
was called "getting control of the market" or "bringing the market into the
Bank." The clearing banks (commercial banks) did not borrow from the
Bank; the bill brokers, the discount market, did, but only when they had to.

National Monetary Commission. Bank records were not available to him: "My greatest
regret is that the material is not so accurate as it might so easily have been. The Bank of
England did not see fit to allow me to inspect its records, the years here studied (as well as
earlier years which I had originally intended to cover) being regarded by the Governor as too
near our own day . . . Is it too much to hope that the Bank will one day turn aside from
exercising the vigour of its maturity to indulge in that privilege of old age, reminiscing of
younger days?" (Sayers 1936: vii–viii). He got access to these records later, for his larger study
(1976), but does not seem to have changed his assessment on the points that interest us here.

"The Bank sold securities, or borrowed from the money market (using consols as collateral), to compel the clearing banks to call funds from the discount houses and force borrowing at Bank rate" (Kenen 1960: 57. Pages 56–63 give an excellent brief overview of "How the System Used to Work"). Clearly, both of these actions reduced the Bank's holdings of interest-earning assets, hence its profits. Executing a policy of controlling the rate of discount on commercial paper consistently with "being rich" and making money for its stockholders exacerbated an already tricky problem. Thus in 1889 the *Economist* commented that the Bank was becoming increasingly weak and "unless there was a rapid collection of Government revenue or a great efflux of gold, Bank Rate was guided by the Market Rate rather than *vice versa*" (Sayers 1936 [1970:5]). Sayers (1976: Volume I, 37–43) gives an historical account, from 1890 and earlier to 1914, of different methods employed by the Bank to "make Bank rate effective". It did not hold bills, so could not sell them, and there were not enough Treasury Bills in existence during that period, so it used varying combinations of selling consols (sometimes selling spot and repurchasing them forward, as the Federal Reserve Banks were later to do), and borrowing in the market to make money tight: lenders were the India Council, private customers, and in the twentieth century, the banks themselves.

It appears, then, that life was a good deal more complicated than a reading of Cunliffe would indicate. We find the barest hint of an awareness of one of these issues in the brief phrase (from the passage Cunliffe 1918: 3–4 that I cited above) about "*steps taken to make . . . [Bank rate] effective in the market*". To the other issues Sayers raises, I can find no reference in the Report. Nor, as we shall see below, could Sayers.

There were frequently times . . . when the Bank wanted to enforce high rates in the City in order to deal with some temporary movement in the balance of international payments, *but did not want to penalise home trade.* In the early 'nineties all too frequently the Bank found that it was penalising home trade without having the desired short-period effect on the balance of international payments. (Sayers 1936 [1970: 6], italics mine)

This quotation supports the view of the historical gold standard as being much closer to that of the short-period financing mechanism induced by Bank rate than that of the Cunliffe Report. In fact, the implication here of the qualification about home trade was to avoid the kind of thoroughgoing adjustment, through a reduction in home spending, which the Cunliffe Report seemed to suggest.

Sayers argues, approvingly, that in the postwar period sterilizing and offsetting gold flows had become much more widespread than it had been in the prewar period. (In this he provided fuel for the ire of those, who like

Hayek thought sterilization a crime.) On the other hand, the Bank "did far more, apart from regulating interest rates, to *hinder* gold movements than it has ever been able to do in the postwar gold standard period" (Sayers 1936 [1970: 130], italics mine).

The sterilization of gold flows was not unknown in the prewar period, but there were difficulties, primarily caused by the need for the Bank of England to show a profit. Here is a colorful description of an apparently appropriate offsetting operation that did not get carried out. The period 1890–5 presented difficulties to the Bank, according to Sayers. Foreign investments fell and trade languished, so there was easy money. At the beginning of 1894 there occurred a tremendous inflow of gold because of (a) South African gold coming in and (b) United States silver purchases under the Sherman Act. Money became even easier, so the Bank had no control over the market because there was no need for rediscounts. According to the spirit of 1844 the Bank should have been "content with the situation, allowing cheap money to have its effect in stimulating trade and the eventual expansion of the credit structure, sending the market once more within its walls" (Sayers 1936 [1970: 14–15]). (This is a reference to the lagged response which presumably was implied by the Act of 1844, discussed above.) But it decided that the influx was being caused primarily not by the South African gold but by the Sherman Act purchases of silver, and that these would be temporary. It wanted, therefore to engage in offsetting operations, but felt itself unable to afford to take this course. In the event, the Bank increased its earning assets, extended credit, enhancing the cheapness of money, and making its "control over the market more remote than ever."

To maintain at once its control *and* its income was to the Bank impossible in the short run.

Had the Bank been prepared to follow the methods intended by the authors of the Act of 1844, none of these problems would have arisen. The Bank would, when the market was independent of it, simply wait until there was a sufficient efflux of gold to send the market into the Bank. The Bank would have been purely passive in its relations with the market. But in fact . . . the Bank was not content to behave in that manner. It wished to take *precautionary* action very often, removing some purely ephemeral ease from the market. For this purpose it had to employ certain devices for acting directly on the open market discount rates, which, to the exclusion of the official Bank Rate, influenced the foreign exchanges. (Sayers 1936 [1970: 16–18], italics his)

This passivity in the face of an inflow, enshrined in the principles of 1844, is in the spirit of the Cunliffe Report. Tightening up in the face of an inflow, in the expectation of a future outflow, is not the type of action one would expect of the Bank based on reading that report. We have here an additional goal, or determinant of policy, for the Bank: not only "tenderness for the home market," not only technical problems of "getting control of the market," not only its own profits, but also anticipations and the need to take "precautionary action." I can think of nothing in the Cunliffe Report to suggest that they were thinking of anything like this.

There appear to be two kinds of automaticity. Waiting for the gold efflux to force the market into the Bank is that which the Bank Act of 1844 prescribed, according to Sayers, and which the Cunliffe Report alleged; it is not, Sayers maintains, the course frequently or typically followed by the Bank. However, another meaning of automaticity implies that the Bank should (and did) respond by changing Bank rate when the gold outflow began, and not wait until it was forced by a lack of specie to contract its liabilities. (The two concepts would lead to the same result only if the Bank behaved perfectly symmetrically on the upside and downside, so that it was always precisely fully loaned up.) On the second criterion, as Sayers emphasized, both the actions of the Bank and the Cunliffe Report differ from the spirit and the terms of the Bank Act of 1844. This difference is, in fact, closely related to the difference between the classical and the neoclassical approaches. The pure classical approach would require, in addition, the absence of fractional-reserve banking in the private sector. This issue will be discussed when we deal with Hayek's critique of the gold standard.

When the Bank did wish to take "precautionary" action, it had to struggle for the power to do so, so that:

in the early nineteen hundreds, [it was] becoming fashionable to urge that there should be more co-operation between the Old Lady, the commercial banks and the bill market . . . The Bank was, by tradition, permitted to take action to force the market to follow Bank Rate as a weapon for the *protection* of its Reserve; but it could not use these weapons to force an *increase* in its gold reserve. (Sayers 1936 [1970: 47], italics mine)

Conventions, even "young" conventions, were very powerful constraints on Bank action. Most of Sayers's study (and much of the later book, 1976) is devoted to a discussion of the tools available to the Bank, and how they were applied, to protect their gold reserves: methods primarily of avoiding gold outflows, secondarily means of offsetting and sterilizing flows that did take place, and devices for "getting control of the market". The major theme, and point of interest, however, is, to repeat, the non-automatic nature of the actual processes.

One set of "devices" must be commented on explicitly: that was a whole bag of tricks which amounted, one way or another, to manipulating exchange rates or moving the gold points. These included interest-free loans to importers of gold (effectively raising the gold import point), paying different prices for gold bars and for gold coins and different for coins from different countries, depending on whom it was hoped to attract gold from.

The Bank of England was not alone in this. The German central bank, for one, had done the same thing (see National Monetary Commission 1910, U.S. Senate Document Number 405).

It was explicitly considered a virtue of these devices that they affected the gold reserves (the exchanges) without harming internal economic activity (precisely the argument of the 1950s and 1960s for flexible exchange rates); it was thus precisely contrary to the Cunliffe story. These manipulations of the gold points came to be recognized as fairly standard operating procedure, according to Sayers, and in the early twentieth century the financial journals, such as the *Statist* and the *Economist*, were ready to include increases in the price the Bank was prepared to pay for gold in the same category as increases in official Bank rate, "and the alternative of manipulating gold prices was shown to have the advantage of leaving home trade unhurt. In this the journals were apparently reflecting correctly the attitude of the London money market"[8] (Sayers 1936 [1970: 93]).

Open market operations were more difficult to execute, and therefore less widespread than they "ought" to have been, in Sayers's view. The problem here was the relatively small volume of government liabilities available for such activities. The need to take other actions, in addition to interest rate changes and, presumably, open market operations is considered by Sayers to be a flaw in the prewar system. More activities were carried out to protect the gold stock, because more were needed. Preventing gold flows, in short, was necessary, because offsetting them was more difficult than it was to become later.

Down to the outbreak of the Great War . . . the Bank continued to control the market when the external situation called for control, mainly by borrowing in the market and securing control of customers' funds previously lent out in the market. But the circumstances of active trade and international alarums were in the Bank's favour to such an extent that, from 1911 onwards, open market operations became increasingly rare. (Sayers 1936 [1970:48])

In the latter half of the period, that is, after about 1900, Sayers argues, the power of the Bank was so respected that the market, and the gold reserves, responded directly to changes in Bank rate, as a signal, so the Bank had presumably to be less concerned than previously with trying to influence the market rate directly (Sayers 1936 [1970: 70]). (This last point is important, since, as we shall see, Sayers uses it as an explanation of the silence of Cunliffe on the question of open market operations.)

---

[8] This comment stands in opposition to Hayek's 1932 suggestion that up until the mid 1920s the gold standard had been allowed to function according to classical prescription. It suggests also that Hayek in 1932 was being unfair when he held Keynes responsible for the idea that the domestic economy should be protected from the discipline of international adjustment (see Chapter 7).

The issue of influencing domestic credit conditions arises frequently in Sayers's discussion. For example he argues that everybody in the City of London, including the Bank, was convinced of the seriousness of the American crisis of 1907. Bank rate was raised only with a lag, however, because of concern for the effect on the domestic economy (Sayers 1936 [1970: 55]).

First and foremost the Bank considered itself obliged to provide for the convertibility of the pound into gold by taking appropriate action to maintain the gold reserve . . . *Yet its actions were by no means automatic.* How far it ignored the principles of 1844 can only be realised by watching the great irregularities, year after year, in the movements of the Proportion, the Gold Stock and the Securities held in the Banking Department . . . [A]part from . . . regular movements, there were many others of which the Bank obviously took no account, even if it did not "offset" them. There are even indications that it sometimes did adopt "offsetting" action. (Sayers 1936 [1970: 116–17])

The Bank of England rarely raised Bank rate when gold was not flowing out, "but the magnitude of flow necessary to make the Bank act varied very much according to the particular circumstances of London and the foreign centres at the time" (Sayers 1936 [1970: 117]). It usually, but not always, lowered rates when gold flowed in (though as we noted, the Cunliffe Report does not specify this as part of its obligation). Conditions in other countries, and expected reactions of their central banks, accounts of foreign governments at the Bank, all these were considered; countries that "mattered" included the U.S., France, Russia, Japan (Sayers 1936 [1970: 118]).

The theme of avoiding action because of the internal effects is a constantly recurring one in Sayers (Sayers 1936 [1970: 125] for example). A piquant side issue here is the envy of the French, voiced primarily on Threadneedle Street, for their ability to maintain a much steadier Bank rate than the British "by employing various devices which made its gold reserve insensitive to the needs of the outside world. Because it was the only free gold market in the world, the entire brunt of any disturbance was liable to fall on the Bank of England" (Sayers 1936 [1970: 126]). Note the quotation from the Cunliffe Report (page 73 above) expressing the same sentiment of envy mixed with self-congratulation.

That this tenderness for home trade was subordinate to the primary object of protecting the gold reserve is undoubtedly true. But it made Bank Rate history in those years very different from what it would have been had the Bank pursued with single-mindedness its primary aim. In the absence of such tenderness for home trade, the account which this book gives of the Bank's operations would have been much shorter and simpler. And had the Bank followed the strict principles of 1844, waiting for gold to go out or come in before it acted, this study would hardly have amounted to a book at all – *or it would have been concerned to show, not how the system worked, but why it failed*. (Sayers 1936 [1970: 127], italics mine)

In the final pages, Sayers raises for the first time the issue which I have been exercised over throughout this survey, the contradiction between his view of the mechanism and that of Cunliffe. He notes that his description of the operations of the Bank "is not, in its details at least, entirely consistent with the broad description given in the First Interim Report of the Cunliffe Committee. The reason is not, I think, difficult to find" (Sayers 1936 [1970: 137]).

Walter (later Lord) Cunliffe became Deputy-Governor of the Bank in 1911 and Governor in 1913.[9] So his ideas and those of his colleagues, Sayers argues, would perforce be influenced primarily by the experience of the years immediately preceding the war. But this was precisely the time that the activities of the Bank had become unusually "standardised and automatic".

The sustained activity of trade, the "record" volume of British overseas lending, the Government's financial operations and the disposition of the great joint-stock banks to help the Bank of England; all these factors helped to facilitate a straightforward Bank Rate policy. The Bank's success in 1907 led it naturally in that direction. Consequently the Bank did not, in those last years, have resort to special devices for influencing gold movements . . . The Bank felt more free than it had in the first decade of the century to raise Bank Rate to high points, and when it did so it more easily took Market Rate up with Bank Rate, and it was this somewhat extraordinary period which had left the most vivid impression on the minds of the Cunliffe Report, *which in its turn has probably helped to shape general post-war thought on the pre-war monetary system*. (Sayers 1936 [1970: 137–8], italics mine)[10]

The Bank continued until the outbreak of World War I to exert control, when necessary, "mainly by borrowing in the market and securing control of customers' funds previously lent out in the market." But after 1911 the use of open market operations became "increasingly rare" (Sayers 1936 [1970: 48]).

---

9   There was a learning problem at the Bank of England. Governors were generally in office for only two years, and non-Governors apparently were barely involved in the technical operations (Sayers 1936 [1970: 135–6]). Cunliffe, however, was a notable exception to this rule. He remained Governor until 1918, an unusually long incumbency, matched and exceeded only, much later, by Montagu Norman (see Sayers 1976, Volume III: 362, for a list of all the Governors).

10  The same idea is expressed in the following passage: "*In the difficult years which immediately preceded the outbreak of the war the Bank appears to have relied entirely on the Bank Rate method*. The rapid fall into disuse of the gold device after the crisis of 1907 was perhaps the result of the success of the Bank Rate method on that occasion . . . The confidence in the Bank Rate methods which the Bank of England expressed to the United States Monetary Commission would have been unthinkable ten years earlier . . . Yet so striking was the success of its action at the end of 1907 that the Bank just before the war was exercising its power with a confidence which pushed the gold devices into the lumber-room as the doubtful expedients of a temporising adolescence" (Sayers 1936 [1970: 100–1], italics mine).

In its endeavour to give a complete analysis of the Bank's operations over the quarter of a century, this book has, I hope, done something to correct the unduly simplified version in the Cunliffe Report . . . In some ways, it is true, the Old Lady of Threadneedle Street had long ago reached years of discretion. That the Bank's Banking Department was little more than an ordinary bank had long ceased to be the fashionable view, although the *Statist* could complain that the Governor of the day was behaving as though the Bank was a purely private institution. But though the Bank had realised its public duties, it had hardly developed a complete and consistent system for carrying out those duties. Old the Old Lady was, yet in her varied technique she showed the ingenuity, and in her divided allegiance the susceptibility, of youth. The mastery of technique which is the mark of maturity had yet to be achieved. (Sayers 1936 [1970: 139])

I find this argument difficult to accept. That such a distinguished group of individuals could be so short-sighted as to view all of history as encapsulated into a three-year period seems strange. However, the Cunliffe Report does not purport to be a history of the Bank of England, nor for that matter, a history of the gold standard, nor of the British monetary system. It is very brief indeed, a set of terse answers to the specific questions put to it in its terms of reference. This makes Sayers's argument a little more plausible.

If the members of the Cunliffe Committee indeed felt that the last prewar years were the apogee of the prewar system, the period in which the learning and struggle and searching for techniques of the nineteenth century had borne its fruit in the form of a smooth-working system, which they could describe as nearly automatic, then they might, I suppose, simply take that as their model for the system which should be striven for in the postwar period. Presumably the learning and the experimentation would not have to be repeated.

Nevertheless, this interpretation implies, when all is said and done, more naivete on the part of the Committee than I am comfortable with. I repeat my disclaimers about writing either a psycho-history or a documentary history of the period: I am interested in the development of the theoretical and analytical framework. Nevertheless, there is an intriguing problem here. The memories of half a dozen very serious bankers and financial experts (and one of the most distinguished economists of his day) cannot have been so short as three years. If Sayers is correct, then, the presumption of these people must have been that the crises and disturbances, not to mention wars (the Cunliffe Report was, of course, written during the final days of the War That Was to End All Wars) of the first decade of the twentieth century were a thing of the past. Perhaps. (The predictions made during the final days of World War II regarding the shape of the postwar world were certainly mistaken along many lines.)

Several scholars with whom I have discussed this issue, among them Peter

Kenen and R. M. Hartwell, have suggested that what was involved was an intense desire on the part of the Committee, as representative members of the British Establishment, to return to the *status quo ante bellum*, as completely and quickly as possible, with a minimum of debate. This desire may have enhanced the glow of the prewar period and convinced people that it had been in fact more tidy and orderly than it in fact was. This latter would have been enhanced, perhaps, by an additional political motive, to show opponents of the old establishment that in fact the system had operated quite automatically and did not require the initiative and intervention of people such as themselves (the banking establishment, heavily represented on the Cunliffe Committee), who might be suspect in the eyes of the emerging political leadership. This is fascinating and provocative speculation; I feel unable to do more than state it. I would note, however, that it is consistent with the tone of the report as well as with its extraordinary brevity. It is difficult to read that report without getting the impression that it was prepared quite quickly by people who knew in advance what they wished to say and wanted to state it as briefly and concisely as possible and get back to business.

It is also notable, furthermore, that the Cunliffe Report finds no grounds for suspected or potential conflict between internal and external balance. The tools which the Bank of England had so painfully developed to try to protect the gold reserves without injuring the domestic economy – these were presumably going to be totally unnecessary. (These are bankers talking, not ivory tower *laissez-faire* economists!) A loss of gold, quite simply, requires a reduction in Bank of England notes. (Sayers says that the day was long since gone that the Banking Department of the Bank of England was thought to be only a private bank, but in the Cunliffe Committee Report the Bank of England's Banking Department does not seem to exist.)

These tools (presumably some of which are the accoutrements of what Sayers, in 1936, called a "modern central bank") included open market operations (on old bills; with a large government debt available on which to operate, these become even easier to execute) designed essentially to "get control of the market," since Bank rate was a penalty rate and would be totally ineffective if the market was liquid enough not to have to come to the Bank. They also tried to perform the Edwardian version of the twist, with very short-term interest rates (to foreigners), guided by the market rate rising while overdraft and commercial rates to domestic "traders", which were believed to be a function of Bank rate, were to be kept constant, or at least were to rise less.[11]

---

[11] "This . . . working on Market Rate in a sense independently of Bank Rate was based on the accepted fact that while Bank Rate ruled the majority of home banking charges, Market Rate was the rate which influenced foreign exchanges. If, therefore, the Bank, in tenderness

There were numerous sophisticated devices for spreading the gold points, and even what in post-World-War-II America came to be called "jawboning" or "moral suasion". All of these are totally ignored in the Cunliffe Report. A comment by Sayers may be helpful here. He is speaking not of the Cunliffe Report as such, but of the postwar attitude of the Bank.

At the outset the Bank had no doubt where it wanted to go, and no doubt what were the lions in its path. In the last years before the war neither the turmoil in Britain's internal politics nor the strains in industrial relations had really troubled the City of London. Much more important to the City had been the extraordinary prosperity of the great export industries and the flood of foreign investment passing through the City's hands . . . The men of 1919 believed that the best monetary system was that of 1913: a world gold standard centred on London, with the Bank of England controlling the system by manipulation of Bank Rate and acting as the watchdog of financial practice. (Sayers 1976: Volume I, 111)

The debate is far from over regarding the role played by the Bank of England in particular (and other central banks in general) in the Game and the extent to which they abided by its Rules. The debate, in fact, is still divisible into at least two sub-arguments. One, explicit, is the assessment of the "facts" of what the Bank of England was actually doing, and the appropriate interpretation of the available data. The second, often submerged, is still the issue of what the Bank was supposed to have done according to the famous "Rules". I shall not delve into this argument, since it would take me too far afield, but the interested reader is enthusiastically referred to Bordo and Schwartz (1984), *passim*, especially Part II, and most particularly Chapters 3 and 4.[12] On one remark, however, I must comment. Moggridge (1984) notes that Dutton (1984) discusses the possibility that the Bank of England pursued a counter-cyclical stabilization policy.

One can see the sense of such a rule in the abstract . . . However, I wonder whether it is . . . appropriate . . . for the pre-1914 international economy given that Bloomfield (1959, p. 38), Morgenstern (1959, chap. 2) and Triffin (1964, chap. 1) have all noted the strong parallelism in movements of economic activity during the period. In such circumstances, nonadherence to the rule might still be consistent with the successful operation of the standard. (Moggridge 1984: 196)

towards the internal situation, wished to act on the foreign exchanges without forcing higher rates on home trade, it could use the devices detailed below to force Market Rate up beyond its normal "effective" relationship with Bank Rate. These devices were (1) the refusal to work at Bank Rate; (2) the raising of the Advances Rate outside its normal relationship with Bank Rate; and (3) the restriction of the eligibility of bills, generally by restricting their currency [length of run], but on one occasion at least by restricting their nature" (Sayers 1936 [1970: 49–50]).

[12]    Part II is entitled "Technical procedures: rules of the game," and Chapters 3 and 4 are by John Dutton and John Pippenger respectively, with comments by Donald Moggridge and Charles Goodhart, and a multilateral discussion from the floor of the conference.

To this I have three comments, all pointing to the conviction that Moggridge has yielded too much on this point:

1 One of the frequent arguments in favor of floating exchange rates or some other form of insulation is precisely to avoid "strong parallelism in movements of economic activity" under some circumstances.

2 Any model of fixed exchange rates in which the money supply is allowed to vary in response to imbalances in international payments (from the "monetary approach to the balance of payments" to the "absorption approach") will yield a close synchronization of economic fluctuations in open economies. In its most pristine form, of course, the monetary approach to the balance of payments holds (along with Ricardo) that nothing can alter the natural distribution of money. McCloskey and Zecher (1976: 361) make this explicit: "The inconsequentiality of the rules of the game may perhaps explain why they were ignored by most central bankers in the period of the gold standard, in deed if not in words, with no dire effects on the stability of the system."

3 I know of no statement of what I have labeled the neoclassical position in which counter-cyclical stabilization is even mooted as one of the central bank's *prescribed* policy targets as part of the game. When, as in Nurkse's discussion, the central bank has felt internal balance to be a constraint on its policy, this is viewed as an infraction of the "rules of the game" and a contribution to an explanation of the breakdown of the system.

### Finally

We have examined in some detail the Cunliffe Committee Report and argued that its very brevity is perhaps indicative of the attitude of its compilers, in that they took for granted the superiority and desirability of what they perceived to be the prewar system. Parts of that report have indeed become the classic statement of what the neoclassical position was, or of how the prewar gold standard functioned, or of what the "rules of the game" were. As a theoretical model of an adjustment mechanism it is incompletely spelled out. As a restatement of the classical mechanism as enshrined in the Act of 1844, it is inaccurate, because it does not really adhere to the rule that the Bank of England have a 100 percent gold reserve at the margin. As a summary of the history of the prewar gold standard and how it worked, it is, according to Sayers and others, highly oversimplified, giving an impression of automaticity which never, apparently, existed. Perhaps it should be read as a normative statement of how the mechanism ought to function: if so, it remains an unexecuted blueprint. I have speculated lightly as to why they painted such a simplified picture of reality. How such an incomplete statement of a major phenomenon got so deeply implanted into the folklore, both of the profession and the public, and became an integral part, foundation even, of Received Doctrine must remain a question for conjecture and further musings.

# CHAPTER 5

# The Macmillan Committee

### The committee

The Committee on Finance and Industry was appointed on November 5, 1929, by the Chancellor of the Exchequer "to inquire into banking, finance and credit, paying regard to the factors both internal and international which govern their operation, and to make recommendations calculated to enable these agencies to promote the development of trade and commerce and the employment of labour" (Macmillan 1931: vi). It thus had a much broader frame of reference than the Cunliffe Committee, and, of course, sat at a very different time in British, and world, history. It convened for a much longer period than the Cunliffe Committee, and we have two large volumes of hearings and testimony, as well as a long and detailed report, which was presented in June 1931. Bradbury, now a Lord, was back. The economists in the group were T. E. Gregory and J. M. Keynes.

The reports are separated by a period of thirteen years, the return to gold, and the beginnings of the greatest depression the world had, and has, ever known. They are distinguished from one another by a number of other characteristics as well: their length, the breadth of their terms of reference and hence the scope of their concerns, their view of the world, of economic adjustments in general and of balance of payments adjustment in particular, their perception of the actual and appropriate behavior of a central bank (or at least of a particular central bank, the Bank of England), and (only partly facetiously do I say this) by John Maynard Keynes.

Though the Macmillan Committee met for much longer and examined a considerably broader set of issues than Cunliffe, what they have in common is a discussion of how the prewar system worked. On this they are obviously comparable and it will be fruitful to engage in this comparison. The differences, I shall argue, are striking. That they should differ on predictions for the future, or even on analysis of the world as they saw it at the time of writing is not the least surprising. That they should so differ regarding history is intriguing.

The report, published, as noted above, in June 1931, constitutes a bridge between the classical and keynesian views of the adjustment mechanism. It is in fact, and not by accident, very closely related to Keynes's *Treatise*. The influence of Keynes in the Macmillan Report is clear. Not only was he a member of the Committee, and not only did he participate in a major way in writing the report, he was also a witness before it. His very extensive testimony there (lasting many hours through a number of sessions) is readily available now and is fascinating reading. His testimony took place just as the *Treatise* was going to press, and he refers to it constantly (Keynes 1929–31 [1981]). In the introduction to this volume of the *Collected writings*, Moggridge notes that "Keynes dominated the proceedings of the Committee, both in examining witnesses and shaping the report. The other active members were Reginald McKenna, T. E. Gregory, R. H. Brand and Ernest Bevin" (Keynes 1929–31 [1981: 38]). Hayek (1932 [1984: 122]) hints at the same degree of influence, disapprovingly.

Throughout the ensuing discussion, it should be remembered that, though the time lapse between the two committees was not much more than a decade, the Macmillan Report was written during the great depression. Furthermore, for good or ill, Macmillan had an additional (fairly disastrous) experience with the gold standard, 1925–31, on which to base its evaluation. Thus the report questions openly the efficiency and desirability of an international gold standard under conditions of sluggish market responses and raises frankly the possible advantages of a system of fluctuating exchange rates (though it does not, in the end, come down in its favor).

The Macmillan Report is substantially longer (200 pages plus addenda) than Cunliffe, and includes detailed discussions of the particulars of the British situation, current and past, as well as extensive discussions of the international mechanism.

## The adjustment mechanism

Macmillan's view of the adjustment mechanism, both normative and positive, is very different from that of the Cunliffe Committee. Gold is a highly convenient and useful asset with which to finance transient and temporary imbalances, both those due to temporary real shocks and those reflecting the desire to transfer long-term capital. But the loss of gold is a signal to action, not part of the mechanism per se. And the appropriate action depends on the cause of the imbalance. In general, we find more discussion in Macmillan of different types of disturbance and a clearer distinction between different kinds of shock than in most of the literature, academic and other.

Thus, whenever gold is lost, the Central Bank is provided with an "automatic" signal of the emergence of conditions which *may* make positive action necessary. The ultimate aim – the restoration of the international value of the currency – is clear, but the action to be taken, and the precise moment at which it should be taken, remain in the sphere of discretion and judgment, in a word with "*management*". That the sphere of "management" in this sense is wide and responsible is beyond doubt. For if the wrong action is taken, the state of disequilibrium which the monetary authority designs to correct may be accentuated or perpetuated. . . *The sense in which the gold standard can be said to be automatic is thus very limited; it is automatic only as an indicator of the need for action and of the end to be achieved.* (Macmillan 1931: 20–1, italics mine)

It would be difficult to be further at odds with the insistence (both positive and normative) on automatic adjustment which characterizes the Cunliffe Committee Report. The emphasis on management and discretion carries over even to the law of one price, and certainly to purchasing power parity, neither of which they take for granted. For, in order for prices to be equalized across countries, "countries which are losing gold must be prepared to act on a policy which will have the effect of lowering prices" and symmetrically for those gaining gold.

In the second place, the economic structure (as distinct from the currency structure) must be sufficiently organic and sufficiently elastic to allow these policies to attain their objective. The first condition concerns central banking policy: the second limiting condition is . . . a question . . . of the actual economic conditions in which such policy has to work. In practice, it may easily happen that where the first condition is present, the second is absent, and vice versa. (Macmillan 1931: 21)[1]

The normative version of the neoclassical position is rejected by the Macmillan Committee on the grounds that adjustment for debtor countries is slow, so that if they cannot borrow to service their debts they are forced to remit gold, which will further reduce their credit-worthiness and may force them off the gold standard. Surplus countries, on the other hand, will accumulate gold and, fearing inflation, sterilize it. Furthermore, the deflation in the debtor countries will have an adverse effect on the surplus countries, which thus suffer both from imported gold and from imported unemployment (Macmillan 1931: 84).

Following a long and detailed discussion of individual behavior (*ad hoc*,

---

[1] That paragraph contains reference to the two salient features of Keynes's testimony to the Macmillan committee (as we shall see in the next chapter) and to what I interpret to be his influence on the committee. The first is his constantly recurrent emphasis on the asymmetry of the system. This conviction on his part persisted, in fact, grew, for the rest of his life. The second is his insistent emphasis on rigidities, particularly of nominal wages, as the crucial characteristic of the system, and as the primary cause of the difficulty of adjustment. I shall discuss this point in more detail when we examine his testimony. I had not in fact thought Keynes to be that much of a "keynesian".

perhaps, but definitely microeconomic), the committee concludes that price reductions are likely to lead to cost (wage) reduction only slowly and with great friction; hence reduction in output and employment is observed. The recent worldwide rise in unemployment they attribute precisely to this phenomenon: price decline rises "unaccompanied by a proportionate reduction of money costs, however brought about" (Macmillan 1931: 88). Keynes's testimony before the committee, discussed in the next chapter, is replete with statements of this sort. This is the closest I have seen to a support of the view that Keynesianism is about rigidities, supporting the interpretation of those whom Joan Robinson labelled the "bastard keynesians" – those interpreters for whom what the Keynes of *The general theory* was about was rigidity in adjustment, particularly of wages (see Coddington 1976).

## The historical workings of the gold standard and prognoses for the future

The major shocks the committee anticipated (in 1931) were a boom in the United States, followed by a "breakdown, after a period of expansion, of the process of international investment." Their fear was that a great deal of direct cooperation between central banks would be required and that American public opinion would not permit this (Macmillan 1931: 78–9). In the postwar world, they alleged, central banks were prone to sterilizing and offsetting gold flows, so that "a policy of stabilising local values has been, implicitly or explicitly, substituted for a policy of maintaining a level of values consistent with international equilibrium." Here the United States is presented as an example of a country sterilizing gold inflows (reminding the reader, not incidentally, as we shall see, of Keynes's fury with the Federal Reserve as expressed in the *Tract*) and the U.K. as an example of a country which tended to offset outflows. These actions are not, however, viewed as equally damnable; I shall argue (in Chapter 10) that Keynes until the end distinguished and discriminated between sterilizing inflows and offsetting (protecting an economy from) outflows. This asymmetry was exacerbated by, and in turn reinforced, the effects of a worldwide shortage of gold. They worry about the inadequacy of new gold supplies, and even a decline in available supply, especially in a period of "expanding trade production and population." If some countries want to increase their reserve ratios and acquire more gold, they will necessarily sterilize the inflow, while the gold-losing countries are likely to contract; the overall effect on the world, then, is deflationary (Macmillan 1931: 22–3).

But, even when central banks are behaving "correctly", "the effect . . . is uncertain when the general economic structure is itself rigid, and more particularly so when the object of that policy is to reduce the price level and income structure." Wholesale prices may fall, but "other prices" may be unchanged, and the adjustment of income and prices "may be interrupted or long delayed or even completely obstructed" (Macmillan 1931: 22). Here it is not entirely obvious whether the problem is that the adjustment will take a long time (or not take place at all) or whether they object to the internal ramifications. I interpret it to be referring to both, with emphasis, in this instance, on the former. Throughout this literature, as I have noted, the line between normative and positive statements and points of view is frequently very faint.

The postwar gold standard, 1925–31, had been beset by difficulties, the committee argued, for two reasons: First, because France and Belgium returned to gold at parities which gave them trade advantages over Britain. And secondly, because France and the United States became the large potential lenders when Britain dropped out of the lending club, having lost a goodly portion of her foreign assets during the war, and having agreed to the settlement of the wartime debt and reparations agreements which left her uncompensated for those losses. But France and the United States failed to follow the practice adopted by Britain in earlier periods, of either increasing imports or engaging in long-term capital exports. "On the contrary, they have required payment of a large part of their annual surplus either in actual gold or in short-term liquid claims. This is a contingency which the *normal working of the international gold standard does not contemplate* and for which it does not provide" (Macmillan 1931: 107, italics mine).

This passage is highly revealing of their view of the historical workings of the mechanism. It rejects the idea that either specie flow or short-term capital movements are part of the "normal working" of the gold standard. Since elsewhere, throughout the report, they do speak of gold flows as part of the mechanism, it is not entirely clear what is involved here. At times there is the implication, which became explicit in Keynes's and other British thought ten years later, that a single country in surplus *vis-à-vis* the rest of the world "should", and did, finance its surplus by lending (or importing, though they don't specify how this got done), whereas individual deficit countries should be permitted to lose gold and only then, if necessary, make what he called the "classical" adjustment.[2]

Note that they are concerned here with the asymmetry in the *activity* of adjusting, not asymmetry in the *burden* of adjustment; the refusal of the

---

[2] Twelve years later Keynes was to argue, first, that there had never been an actual "equilibrating mechanism" and, in his proposals for Bretton Woods, that there must be a mechanism encouraging, or forcing, countries to lend their surpluses. At that juncture he viewed endogenous long-term capital flows to be a thing of the past, so that current account imbalances would constitute the disturbances, with capital flows playing an accommodating role (see especially his "Memorandum" of September 8, 1941, *Collected writings*, 1940–4 [1980: 21 ff]).

surplus countries to expand their demand makes them prey to the deflation and unemployment of the debtors. The deflation and price reduction in the deficit countries, unaccompanied by a decline in money costs, results in unemployment "in every part of the world" (Macmillan 1931: 88). Essentially, this is the inverse of the transfer problem. If one were to treat the transfer model symmetrically, a current account surplus would lead to long-term lending, though it is not at all clear what the mechanism in this direction is supposed to be. (Ohlin discusses this point, arguing that the mechanism is not symmetrical. See Chapter 13 (pages 247–8) and Ohlin 1933a: 384 and 511.) Again, the influence of Keynes is clear here (see 1930: Volume I, 346–50). His later writings, preparing for Bretton Woods, are full of such statements.

This failure to adjust, they argue, is not the fault of the international gold standard as such, but of the specific events of the time, and they hesitantly expect these to be temporary. If not, the gold standard is unlikely to survive. (They were right.) If surplus countries were unwilling to lend their surpluses, under floating exchange rates the rates would fairly quickly reach equilibrating values. The franc and the dollar would have appreciated and "their exporters would have been driven out of business, so that their unlent surplus would have disappeared." The "classical gold standard" will perform the same task, but more slowly. But in the "modern world," where surplus countries sterilize gold inflows and deficit countries are hindered by money-wage rigidity in reducing their costs, "it may be that the whole machine will crack before the reaction back to equilibrium has been brought about" (Macmillan 1931: 108).

This, and the current slump, requiring a round of interest rate reductions on a world-wide basis, led "some people to question the desirability of adhering to an international standard" (Macmillan 1931: 108). Here they are very close to the "revisionist" notions expressed by Whale, Brown, Triffin, and Keynes himself (most strongly expressed in the despairing tone of his pre-Bretton Woods memorandum) about the functioning of the prewar system as an example of a fortuitously favorable constellation of markets rather than the smooth operation of a superb mechanism, quiet, well-lubricated, and ever-ready. So disenchanted are they with the fixed exchange rates regime, in fact, that they are on the verge of proposing floating rates.

The prewar system of fairly automatic central bank responses to gold flows worked primarily because only Britain was at the center, the committee argues. The postwar world is quite different, first because there are now two centers, New York and London, and secondly because international liquid balances are much larger than before the war, so "movements of gold may take place on a considerable scale which are due, not to any fundamental disequilibrium of prices or other deep-seated conditions, but merely to temporary causes for which a change in bank rate may not be a suitable remedy" (Macmillan 1931: 125–6). Presumably they are referring here to destabilizing short-term capital movements. These problems, they argue, were exacerbated by the extension of the gold exchange standard, which raised the ratio of central banks' external liabilities to gold reserves.

A brief discussion of the German situation is instructive. Entering into a subject which has been the ground for much controversy, then and since, they argue that over-borrowing, both long-term and short-, resulted in a decline in exports, an increase in spending, a rise in living standards, and an increase in imports "on such a scale as to affect profoundly the rhythm of German economic life; and the partial cessation of the flow, as well as the uncertainty whether capital could be borrowed or not, which has been the result of events in America and elsewhere since 1929, has had the result of profoundly modifying the economic, and through it, the political situation in Germany." If loans cannot be renewed, Germany will have somehow *"by any reduction in costs necessary,* [*to*] *increase her exports and reduce her imports,* thus affecting the equilibrium of other countries trading with her and her customers" (Macmillan 1931: 81, italics mine). The italicized phrase is particularly piquant if we remember Keynes's position in the *Economic journal* only two years earlier, arguing that Germany could almost surely not restore her credit position with any imaginable reduction in costs.

## The role of the central bank in the adjustment

The gold standard is intended to achieve both exchange and price stability, but "there are 'rules of the game', which, if not observed, will make the standard work with undesirable, rather than beneficial, consequences."[3] I find this difficult to interpret, but it seems to me quite different from what is generally meant by the term. In fact, they basically say just that. Central banks, they argue, are arriving at the recognition that "in many respects the purely traditional and empirical rules by which their conduct was guided in prewar days are no longer adequate as guides of action in present day conditions." It is, however, not easy to define these "rules of the game". "The management of an international standard is an art and not a science" (pace Hawtrey) (Macmillan 1931: 23).

Domestically, the central bank operates on the "volume of purchasing

---

[3] According to Moggridge, Sir Robert Kindersley, in his testimony before the Committee on February 6, 1929, introduced the term "the rules of the game" (Keynes 1929–31 [1981: 42n]). But Keynes predated this by five years: "If we must have a gold standard, we had better play the gold standard game according to the recognised rules." *The Nation and Athenaeum*, May 2, 1925 (Keynes 1931 [1972: 360]).

power," and hence on prices. Perhaps more important, lower interest rates stimulate investment and hence lead to price increases (Macmillan 1931: 24). At this point we have none of the nineteenth-century concern with Bank rate as influencing international capital movements, although elsewhere it is recognized explicitly. It is strictly for its role in influencing prices, apparently through domestic investment, that the central bank is important. The position in fact has a classical quality in the sense that the adjustment mechanism is real and works primarily through price changes; but the central bank is involved in policy which causes, or at least facilitates, these price changes. Whether this is essential or not, in their view, is not clear; I would suppose that it is. To the extent that the central bank fails in this goal, the adjustment is forestalled.

The discussion of international investment (they clearly mean long-term capital movements here) also describes a mechanism very much like the late classical discussion of the transfer problem. A loan to a developing country stimulates imports into the borrowing country both directly and secondarily (through the multiplier effect on income and employment, though clearly they do not use that term). Here, however, the general tone of the discussion, and the absence of concern with price changes, suggests a closer affinity to Ohlin than to the Taussig school (Macmillan 1931: 79–80). (As we shall see, however, in Chapter 6, Keynes specifically cites Taussig as the spokesman of the classical mechanism.) On the whole, despite all the talk of rigidities in adjustment, they still speak primarily of price, not employment and output, changes. Though I shall argue below that the influence of Keynes on Macmillan was powerful, this is Keynes of the *Treatise*, not of the *General theory*. Furthermore, his influence, though large, was apparently somewhat constrained, since some sections of the report emphasize much less heavily than he did the importance of price and wage rigidities and the prevalence of output and employment fluctuation.

They inject an interesting addition to the mechanism: previous loans lead to the need for the borrower to remit interest payments. A temporary export shortfall, caused by a "bad harvest" or a run of bad years, will create problems. Unless financed by new borrowing, interest payments will require the borrower to use up its foreign exchange and gold reserves, and this in turn might force it off the gold standard, at least temporarily[4] (Macmillan 1931:

[4] This is somewhat reminiscent (or prescient) of the later versions of the Mundell-Fleming models which recognized that ever-increasing borrowing created ever-increasing current account deficits, and Domar-type conditions had to be imposed on the magnitudes (see Domar 1950). Willett and Forte (1969) point out the importance of distinguishing between stock adjustments and flow in this analysis. The comment in the report is even more evocative of the public and professional discussions of the "international debt problem" of the present. See Eaton, Gersovitz and Stiglitz (1986) which includes an excellent and useful bibiliography; Eaton and Taylor (1986), a comprehensive survey; Cohen and Sachs, with comment by Nordhaus (1986); and Cohen (1988).

82). Examples of such problems are Latin American countries and Australia, the committee notes; but this is tied in to previous loans which were frequently made on "an undesirable scale," although this does not seem to follow from the earlier discussion. This all has, in 1989, a terribly familiar ring to it.

They seem continually to be torn between their assessment of what the mechanism is, or was, in principle, and the way it in fact functioned. The central bank in its discount rate policy, which includes open market operations, affects first the rate of both long- and short-term foreign lending, though short-term capital movements are the more sensitive. Additionally it affects "enterprise at home and the volume of purchasing power," some of which directly affects imports and exportables and hence the balance of trade. The secondary effect is on prices, directly and indirectly through costs (wages) and thence on the balance of trade (Macmillan 1931: 96).

In one of many paeans of praise of the system, they noted that "it is the peculiar property of bank rate policy that it exercises a pressure in the right direction whether the problem is merely one of momentary short-period adjustment or whether it is of a more fundamental character." For this reason, the committee *seems* to approve of the Bank of England position that the Bank should keep "its eye primarily on the movements of the foreign exchanges" with no need to distinguish between fundamental and transitory shocks. "There can be no doubt, in our judgment, that 'bank rate policy' is an absolute necessity for the sound management of a monetary system, and that it is a most delicate and beautiful instrument for the purpose" (Macmillan 1931: 96–7).

But the "buts" follow fast and hard:

1   Since the market has no way of distinguishing between a change in Bank rate caused by a temporary flurry and one caused by permanent maladjustment, and since great harm may be done by overreaction in the case of the former, the Bank should share its information and its "views of the situation" with the market. A change in Bank rate in order to encourage a temporary capital inflow need then not lead to "unnecessary disturbances to confidence"[5] (Macmillan 1931: 97).

2   The Bank should not wait until gold actually moves before acting. "Such a policy would require definitely to be less automatic and would thus undoubtedly place greater responsibility on the banking authorities" (Macmillan 1931: 97). This is reminiscent of Sayers's description of "precautionary" activities on the part of the Bank of England, discussed above.

[5]   This comment is intriguing in the light of contemporary interest in game theoretic models of policy with asymmetric information. These and other models of credibility (and asymmetry?) are reviewed in Cukierman (1986), and Persson (1988). See also Driffill (1988), and Alesina and Tabellini (1988).

3  Since Bank rate policy is "a *means of maintaining the stability of the exchanges rather than the stability of business*," it makes the home country more vulnerable to external shocks. This raises the twofold question of international cooperation and the issue of attempts to insulate the domestic economy from "international perturbations of a temporary character" (Macmillan 1931: 97–8, italics mine). (Compare page 213 and League of Nations, 1932: 51, sanctioning, even demanding open market sterilization when inflows are temporary.)

4  Perhaps most importantly, when, presumably in a case of fundamental disequilibrium, "substantial changes in the level of our industrial costs are necessary to correspond to substantial changes in the value of money," other tools in addition to Bank rate policy become necessary. The reason proffered is that Bank rate policy by itself works to reduce costs only by reducing profits, forcing output and employment to contract so as to bring wages down. Not only does this hurt the weakest and least protected groups in the economy, but because of this those in charge of policy may be unwilling "to carry through so ruthless a policy to its proper conclusion, with the result that we may continue for a long period in a depressed condition with severe losses and severe unemployment and yet with not enough of both to compel by *force majeure* the necessary readjustment of incomes" (Macmillan 1931: 98). Furthermore, such a depression may become self-perpetuating even without continued monetary tightness. The language is not the contemporary one of time-inconsistent policies, principal-agent games, and overshooting, but the ideas are there. In addition, note again that though there is much talk of employment variation and price rigidities, the mechanism still works, in the committee's view, and it is still, ultimately, the classical one of price adjustment. Price rigidities may make adjustment both more painful and slower, but ultimately it is only to the extent that price changes occur that adjustment takes place.

In "normal times" the effect of Bank rate policy is symmetrical: a tight money policy will discourage, and an easy money policy will encourage, business activity and will "tend to raise prices." They note the argument that in a deep depression monetary ease may by itself be inadequate. They believe, however, "that the monetary authority is not so powerless as is sometimes supposed and that the danger, if any, is rather in the direction of letting loose too strong a force, which it might be difficult to control later" (Macmillan 1931: 103).

### Discretionary versus automatic responses

That the Macmillan Committee is altogether in favor of a more discretionary, less automatic mechanism than the Cunliffe Committee believed to have prevailed earlier is clear. (The Cunliffe discussion was descriptive, not normative, but it carried with it the confident air of approval.) In "the modern world," they argue, "the forces making for disequilibrium are very powerful and . . . any mechanical application of the purely empirical rules derived from prewar experience could easily lead to very grave and unsuspected results" (Macmillan 1931: 78).

Thus, when concerned (Keynes was there!) with worldwide gold shortages, they argued not only that velocity of circulation might increase, thus lowering the need for cash balances, but that central banks could, and should, shift their liabilities from gold-reserve-requiring notes to non-reserve-requiring deposits. They were willing to go further and recommend the elimination of the gold reserve requirement for note issues. And further: "If, as we recommend . . . the principle is adopted that gold reserves should be held, not primarily against note issues, but to meet *temporary* deficiencies in the balance of international payments, there need be no obstacle to the creation of a much increased volume of purchasing power without any increase in the supply of monetary gold." Or, in less formal terms, gold reserves were to be thought of as an umbrella and not as an automatic regulator. This is no longer the endogeneity of the money supply: "The sole practical use of a gold reserve is to serve as a medium of meeting a deficit on the balance of international payments, *until steps are taken to bring it again to equilibrium*" (Macmillan 1931: 66–7, italics mine). Greater flexibility than before the war was now legally possible, since "the provisions of the Act of 1928 permit the expansion of the note issue by an increase of the fiduciary portion."

The "normal" effects of gold movements had ceased to take place, presumably because of French and U.S. sterilization of their inflows. "In recent years it has been impossible to rely on action being taken by both the country losing gold and the country gaining gold to preserve international equilibrium, the one meeting the other half way" (Macmillan 1931: 69). In 1928 and 1929 the stock market boom in the U.S. caused foreign investment to dry up and the French stabilization caused an inflow of gold into that country, much of it from Britain. The Bank of England, including the Banking Department, reduced its liabilities and raised Bank rate by much less than the gold loss would have dictated. In fact, there was offsetting open market activity, "preventing the *full* rigour of the international gold movements from affecting the volume of credit except in so far as it might be directly influenced by rising bank rates" and postponing "the rise in bank rates to a really deterrent level" (Macmillan 1931: 77, italics in original). Their comment on this sterilization of gold flows was made in a positive tone, not a critical one, coupled with an awareness of the heightened sensitivity, in the postwar era, of the domestic market to changes in Bank rate, both directly and "psychologically".

In general, then, the Bank's activity was described as clearly more discretionary and flexible, and was expected so to be, than in the prewar picture painted by the Cunliffe Committee, and even more than in the description offered by Sayers. Direct controls on the capital market and rationing of new issues was one of the policies exercised by the Bank. Brown (1940: 157 ff) indicates that this was the case with foreign issues; Macmillan does not specify whether they are referring to foreign or domestic borrowers, or whether there was any discrimination. (In Keynes's testimony, as we shall see below, it was clear that they were thinking of controls of foreign issues in order to decrease capital outflows when this was considered desirable.) The role of the Bank, after the return to the gold standard in 1925 was, according to the Macmillan Committee, "so far as possible, to stabilise the volume of credit which it placed at the disposal of the banking system, whilst keeping the level of rates sufficiently above those in other centres *to ensure the retention of foreign balances here*" (Macmillan 1931: 77, italics mine). The italicized phrase is an interesting one, since it implies an acceptance of the *status quo* and an elimination of flows of short-term capital in either direction. At the same time, however, it clearly recognizes the influence of Bank policy and interest rates on short-term capital movements.

Monetary policy may have been misguided, they say, but it was probably having to cope with problems it could not possibly handle. Monetary problems set in motion by real phenomena were, they felt, responsible for the world-wide deflation; the overvaluation of sterling and "under-valuation of many other currencies" exacerbated the problem faced by the British. But even if all these difficulties were theoretically solvable, finding that solution may in fact have been beyond the ken of any group or individual, having perhaps "required a degree of knowledge, experience, and prescience which no one in fact possessed or could have been expected to possess." Therefore what was needed was more power to control the price level. This might be difficult, but not impossible. They do not specify, however. "The fact that a motor car is not well-adapted for getting itself out of a ditch once it has fallen in does not prove that it is beyond the powers of good driving to keep it in the middle of the road" (Macmillan 1931: 94–5).

### Money market technicalities and the institutional monetary framework

The flexibility and discretion of the central bank had been increased, as we saw above, by the Act of 1928 permitting an enlarged fiduciary issue. The Macmillan Committee not only approved but had other recommendations to increase the discretionary power of the Bank. Worried, as we saw, about the adequacy of gold, locally and worldwide, they lauded the concept of gold exchange standard and recommended that gold bars and foreign exchange be alternatives to gold coins as assets into which liabilities could be legally convertible (Macmillan 1931: 17–18). Since the Genoa Convention of 1922 intervened between the two committees, this is not surprising. The wide-scale adoption of a gold exchange standard was one of the most notable (and noted) recommendations of that convention.[6]

They agree with Cunliffe on the instability of a minimum reserve ratio, but seem to prefer no legal requirement to a fixed one. A minimum reserve requirement "offers no adequate barrier to a rapid growth of its liabilities in periods of expansion, whilst, at the same time, if it is found necessary subsequently to contract credit, the degree of contraction required, in order to comply with the law, is greater than would have been the case if no fixed relation between cash reserves and liabilities had existed" (Macmillan 1931: 18). Note the similarity between this argument and the almost identical one of Cunliffe (1918: 6) regarding fractional marginal reserves: that they are either ineffective or destabilizing. This is one of the points, as we shall see in Chapter 7, that exercised Hayek in his criticism of the prewar mechanism.

As to the actual reserves of the Bank and their determinants, the spokesman for the Bank, Sir Ernest Harvey, testified that the Bank "do not carry any fixed figure in their mind as at all times an adequate figure of gold. It must be obvious that the sufficiency of the gold held must depend upon the changing circumstances of the moment [seasonal variations]" and other variables. He added, however, that while they tried to accommodate the home money market it was "always, of course, having regard to the external position, the state of our reserve, the position and trend of the exchanges" (Macmillan 1931: 30–40). The perception here is very different from that of the Cunliffe Committee – a point discussed above when I examined the Sayers study.

They recognized, as the Cunliffe Committee apparently had not, the power of the Bank of England to control the supply of credit, and saw that it lay in the Banking, not in the Issue Department (compare Dornbusch and Frenkel 1984). The Issue Department was indeed constrained in issuing

---

[6] This convention was a very shadowy affair. It presumably published no documents of its own (!), and I have been able to trace it through reports of the delegates from Canada and from Great Britain (Great Britain, 1922 and Dominion of Canada, 1923) to their respective parliaments. It is constantly cited as the source of international approval for the adoption of the gold exchange standard, though evidently a large number of other issues were discussed there, notably the Russian debt. An excellent brief but cohesive account can be found in Eichengreen (1985: 147–53). His sources are primarily intergovernmental memoranda, United Kingdom Treasury documents (written by R. G. Hawtrey). He cites a book by Mills (1922) which had escaped my attention and which I have been unable to locate. See also Sayers (1976 Volume I: 153–62). Keynes was there for three weeks, covering the conference for the *Manchester Guardian* and a number of foreign papers. His *Guardian* articles appear in Keynes (1920–2 [1977: 354–425]).

notes to keeping 100 percent reserves (at the margin) of gold; but the Banking Department held these same Issue Department notes as reserves against its deposit liabilities to the government and other banks, both public (in other countries) and private (in Britain and abroad). They recognized that there was no significant difference between the Bank of England's deposits and its notes. Both liabilities were high-powered money and served as the reserves of the commercial banking system. Related to this was the committee's awareness of the power of open market operations by the Banking Department, that is, a change in the composition of the Banking Department's portfolio, which is a powerful tool for sterilizing private gold inflows (Macmillan 1931: 31).

In general they favored open market operations as compared with discount rate policy. (Sayers frequently expresses the same preference.) With it, the Bank of England is "in a position . . . to exercise almost complete control over the amount of bankers' cash in the country and thus . . . over the total volume of deposits within such limits as are set by the existence of the international gold standard" (Macmillan 1931: 33). As a general rule, it is preferable for the Bank to operate on the open market, rather than on Bank rate, thus to affect the prices and returns on existing securities, and to allow this to filter through to rates of interest on new investment and the profitability thereof. (Here there is a nice statement of the Keynesian marginal efficiency of capital.) This would have the advantage of leaving the Bank holding larger volumes of securities with which to attack a future excessive expansion. However, all this is constrained by international considerations, it being unfeasible to be "out of relation" to conditions in other countries. For this reason, again, international cooperation is essential (Macmillan 1931: 105).

### Recommendations

Having made a rather convincing case for flexible exchange rates, they back off. They hope that the prevailing situation is temporary, and refer to an argument (bruited again vociferously, after World War II) about the importance to Britain of "the practice of international banking and associated services." However, it is more than a naive appeal to the importance of the "earnings of the City". They were not recommending the sacrifice of industry to the altar of finance. The problem rather was that

whilst a fluctuating exchange would have undoubted advantages in certain conditions, *it would often be merely substituting one form of instability for another.* It would not be possible for a country so intricately concerned with the outside world as Great Britain is to escape so simply from the repercussions of instability elsewhere. (Macmillan 1931: 109, italics mine)

However, if surplus countries were to persist in their unwillingness to lend their surpluses, floating exchange rates would be preferable. Adjustment would be quick. Had rates been floating, the franc and the dollar would have appreciated and "their exporters would have been driven out of business, so that their unlent surplus would have disappeared." The classical gold standard will perform the same task, but more slowly. (Here, by the way, we can observe a significant change in Keynes's thinking between the Macmillan Report and, ten years later, the plans for the post-World War II institutions; in the later period he totally rejected the possibility of floating rates as a viable system.) Nevertheless, it would be unforgivably selfish of the British to try to cut themselves off, for their own advantage, from the worldwide desideratum of a "sound and scientific monetary system" which can only be achieved "as the result of a process of evolution starting from the historic gold standard" (Macmillan 1931: 108–9). Again, *noblesse oblige*.

They reject also, unequivocally, the suggestion of a devaluation of sterling. Implying that it might have been a good idea in 1925 to return to gold at the par then prevailing, it is nevertheless unthinkable to them at the time of writing that "the Government of the greatest creditor nation were deliberately and by an act of positive policy to announce one morning that it had reduced by law the value of its currency from the par at which it was standing to some lower value." Arguments like this against devaluation were heard well into the post-World War II period, and even in the 1950s, after the sweeping devaluations of 1949. In addition, they pressed a more practical point: that debtor countries might be forgiven for leaving the gold standard, but that Britain was still a major creditor, that the current account was better than was generally believed, and that the terms of trade had moved in Britain's favor, with the sharp reduction in commodity prices, so that there was no excuse for Britain's being the first to disturb the *status quo* (Macmillan 1931: 111–14).

Regarding domestic monetary management, "it *must* be a Managed System." It should not be regarded "as an automatic system, grinding out the right result by the operation of natural forces aided by a few maxims of general application and some well-worn rules of thumb" (Macmillan 1931: 118, italics mine). So much for the Cunliffe Committee. Money must be managed and it must be managed by the Bank of England. In exquisite prose, we have the following panegyric to the Bank as the obvious controller of monetary policy:

independent of political influences, yet functioning solely in the public interest; with long traditions and experience and clothed with vast prestige, yet not distrustful (as we have learnt in evidence) of evolutionary change or hesitant of new responsibilities; entrenched in the centre of the struggle for profit and with access to the arena of the market, yet itself aloof and untinged by the motives of private gain. (Macmillan 1931: 119)

The Bank, in its wisdom, should not wait until gold actually moves before acting. The automaticity which Cunliffe so praised is here again eschewed. There is an interesting progression here. The classical model, and the Bank Act of 1844, suggest that the Bank should wait until gold movements have had their effect on the market. The neoclassical view, and Cunliffe, maintain that Bank rate should be raised as soon as gold starts to flow. And now Macmillan argues that action should precede the gold flows.

The development of open market operations, both in London and New York, they found praiseworthy (Macmillan 1931: 153). The system has proven itself effective. But it is, by its nature, "*the antithesis of an automatic system*" (Macmillan 1931: 126, italics mine). All central banks must face up to the demand on them for more "management" more responsibility, and more cooperation between them. The goals of cooperative central bank policy should be to maintain the gold standard, raise prices (an urgent and top-priority goal), and having raised them, stabilize them. Given the inadequacy of world gold supplies there should be a relaxed gold exchange standard; only foreigners should be able to claim gold or foreign exchange reserves, and central banks should not be bound by specific reserve ratios.

Ever harking on the asymmetry between creditors and debtors, they held it to be of paramount importance that the creditor countries increase their total lending, and thus stop sopping up the world's monetary gold stock. This must be done, however, in consort, otherwise the claims on the lender would be used to pay off the other creditors. Specifically this meant tripartite cooperation between France, Britain, and the U.S. (Macmillan 1931: 134–5). This increased lending need not be to the weaker, more desperate debtors; in fact, it need not necessarily be foreign lending, though this would be preferable. Domestic expansion in the creditor countries is an alternative (another hint of the keynesian approach). "If a creditor country is disinclined to lend its savings to a debtor country, then let it employ these savings at home. It is only to do *neither*, but to accumulate, or endeavour to accumulate, the surplus savings in gold, which serves to embarrass the debtor countries as a whole" (Macmillan 1931: 136, italics in original).

Whereas the Cunliffe Committee's emphasis on the automaticity of the mechanism implied that active coordination among central banks was at best unnecessary, Macmillan strongly endorsed the notion of coordination and consultation with the goal of stabilizing international prices. Remember that this meant avoiding world deflation. Each central bank was to be free, however, to pursue its own internal domestic goals and at the same time, to protect its gold stock. But if, for the sake of internal balance, to combat inflation, a central bank were to raise bank rate and attract gold "unintentionally", it should counteract this by "being prepared to increase its own balances elsewhere." And specifically, central banks should consider both long-term and short-term investment rates "as falling within their purview" (Macmillan 1931: 133). Many of these ideas were to resurface in the literature on defensive versus aggressive (or beggar-my-neighbor) devaluation: Robinson (1937 [1949: Chapter 17, 393–407]), Nurkse (1945 [1949]), in the Bretton Woods agreements, and even, appropriately metamorphosed, into the IMF's 1976 "Guidelines for Floating."

As for technical matters, they argued that the Act of 1844 had become outdated: seasonal changes in note issue tied up enormous percentages of the Bank's gold reserves and threatened its external solvency. If it is considered desirable to put some limits on the Bank of England's discretionary powers, the Committee recommends that the Bank be limited to a maximum note issue and a minimum gold reserve. (Cunliffe's recommendation of an enlarged fiduciary issue, compared with prewar, is analogous.) They recommend that in fact the Bank hold larger gold reserves than it has in the past, but that it have greater discretion in using them (Macmillan 1931: 139–43).

Also technically, they recommend ending the division between the Issue and Banking Departments of the Bank of England (Macmillan 1931:143 ff). This would be good for Britain and for the world as a whole. The adequacy of gold holdings could then be judged, appropriately, in terms of their sufficiency as an umbrella. If it could be accepted that gold should be held only in amounts deemed necessary "to meet temporary deficiencies in the balance of international payments . . . this would be the greatest safeguard we can imagine against the risks of a future shortage in the supplies of gold relative to the natural growth of the world's money-income" (Macmillan 1931: 145).

On the question of short-term capital mobility, the committee distinguishes between movements of residents' capital in and out of the home country on the one hand, and lending and dis-lending on the part of foreigners.[7] This arises in connection with their discussion of how much resources the Bank needed; they note that before the war Britain's short-term international position was roughly balanced, whereas at the time of writing she was a large debtor, the implication being that she had moved from being purely an intermediary to being a credit-creating banker to the world.

This may be expressed by saying that London is now practising international deposit banking, as distinct from international acceptance business and the deposits associated with this, on a larger scale than before the War. (Macmillan 1931: 149)

---

[7] A similar distinction between "home" and "foreign" capital movements appears in Bloomfield (1950) in which he distinguished between gold inflow that resulted from a capital account surplus and "those gold imports that reflected the net influx of domestic capital . . . and the active balance on current account" (Bloomfield 1950: 247). He implied, with some justification for the period, that foreign capital inflows are purely exogenous, hot money flights, while domestic capital inflows are part of the basic balance. See the discussion in Chapter 11.

A rise in discount rates in the pre-war money market functioned mainly by calling in our claims on the rest of the world through the contraction in the volume of our acceptances. A rise in discount rates to-day is more liable to function in part by increasing our liabilities to the rest of the world through the attraction of short-term funds from abroad. (Macmillan 1931: 149)

This historical change, which has to do with where the initiative for a change lies rather than with the accounting sums, may go some way towards explaining Hawtrey's dislike of the Bank rate tool for closing balance of payments gaps (see Chapter 7). Macmillan describes the shift as both "convenient" and "precarious" (Macmillan 1931: 149). This whole discussion is reminiscent, of course, of many of the debates about the U.S. deficit in the early 1960s and the arguments about whether they were simply a manifestation of the necessary short-term liability position of the "world's banker". Even definitions of below-the-line deficits centered on the question of the symmetry or lack of it between increased liabilities to foreigners and decreased claims. In addition, the balance of payments surplus available for long-term foreign lending was getting smaller than it was before the war. Retaining "the precarious foreign funds which we have inadvisedly employed in a non-liquid way" thus became more important than ever, enhancing the conflict between external and internal goals for interest rate policy: concern for the external balance might force keeping interest rates higher than they ought to be for purposes of stimulating the domestic economy (Macmillan 1931: 150).

They favor continued use and refinement of the open market policy tools, primarily to change the composition of the Bank's portfolio and to sterilize gold flows. Many of the devices which Sayers listed as having been used by the Bank for "getting control of the market", and for influencing the exchange rate and gold reserves are recommended, as are open market operations designed to change the term structure of interest rates. Bank rate, on the other hand, is "the traditional instrument, upon which chief emphasis was laid in all pre-war accounts of the Bank's methods." But it should not be used, they think, when there is a long-run problem of lowering "general money-incomes" nor when the problem is one of very temporary balance of payments disequilibrium. It is, however, useful for many cases in between "in particular the control of the Credit Cycle and the regulation of the rate of slow, normal change in the level of money-incomes so as to maintain conformity between money-incomes at home and abroad" (Macmillan 1931: 152–5).

They viewed it outside their terms of reference to discuss domestic policy (and what they have to say on this score is deliberately relegated to their addenda), but proposals "relating to the capital market for home investment" were considered to be legitimately within their permitted framework. Their discussion here is reminiscent of Nurkse's well-known article, much later (1956) on home and foreign investment. For historical reasons, London became the commercial and trading center of England and the center of world-wide commerce, "and it was there that the great private merchant banking houses settled and flourished." But when industry began to grow in the nineteenth century "there was no particular reason why it should look to the London market for its financial requirements." Industry started out with small and family-owned firms, and there were plenty of private investors who wanted to make their own decisions and didn't need banks to do it for them. "Industry therefore, though making full use of the ordinary banking facilities offered by the joint stock banks, maintained its independence of any financial control" (Macmillan 1931: 162).

In Europe, for example, in Germany, industry started later and needed to be bigger to compete with England, so they needed to amass larger resources to get started, and had to have the help of the banks. French banks had more control over industry for a different reason (individual investors were small and needed advice and help from the banks). In the U.S. it was different again. For different reasons it was very much like Germany in the close cooperation between banks and industry. British industry, they argued, must develop closer coordination with banks, as industry gets more "internationalised" [and bigger]. There is tremendous knowledge and expertise in the City and it should be made available to help British industry. The individual investor in Britain gets expert guidance, information, and assistance when investing abroad (and the issuing house will even step in to try to "put matters straight" if there are problems, that is, they stand behind the issue) but not when he wants to invest at home.

This argument is interesting, since it is, in a way, the mirror image, or the inverse, of the arguments heard much later, especially after World War II, regarding the inability of local industry in developing countries to develop because of the incursions of foreign, imperialist capitalists. Here we have the argument that domestic industry was not developing because not only the capital, but the skills in finance and investment, were outward-directed: "imperialism" is evidently costly to the metropolitan area as well as to the colonies!

Finally, Macmillan argues that if international cooperation is not forthcoming to rid the world of its slump, Britain will have to go it alone: in that case "it is of the greatest importance that other domestic action, not of a strictly monetary character, should be taken as an essential condition to the monetary authority being in a position to employ effectively the means of monetary policy" (Macmillan 1931: 185). What these means might be they did not entirely agree among themselves, nor were they certain where they fit into their terms of reference, so they spelled them out in various addenda.

### Peroration

I have argued that two important and well-known statements of the international adjustment mechanism written within a relatively short space of time present widely different, nay, contradictory views of how that mechanism could be expected to work in their own day. This is easy to understand, given the fact that the Macmillan Report appeared just as the rest of the world was getting on board and joining Britain in one of the worst depressions known, while the Cunliffe Committee was writing at the threshold of a new, postwar age, and might be excused for seeing the world in more roseate hues than was retrospectively justified.

What is more interesting, and more difficult to explain, is the striking difference between the two reports in their interpretation of the same past, the 1870 (or 1890) to 1914 Age of Gold. Furthermore, we note that not only was the behavior of central banks during the Golden Age *not* the behavior described by the Cunliffe Committee, but that the only people who thought it had been were apparently those who got their views of the mechanism from that famous and much-cited description. How such a myth was generated and disseminated is, at the moment, something on which one can only speculate.

# CHAPTER 6

# A second diversion: Keynes and the Macmillan Committee

## Keynes the neoclassical

As I noted above, the Keynesian influence in the Macmillan Report is clear when one examines the report. In fact, Keynes was not only a member of the committee, and not only played a large role in writing the report, he was also a major witness before it. His very extensive testimony there (lasting many hours through a number of sessions) is readily available now and it makes fascinating reading (Keynes 1929–31 [1981: 38–312]). Throughout the testimony, Keynes frequently reminds his interlocutors that they will shortly be able to read a "technical" version of his ideas, since his *Treatise on money* is about to be published, and did in fact appear during the prolonged course of the committee's hearings.

On the first occasion on which he testified (February 20, 1930), Keynes presented his view of the historic role of Bank rate policy. "Bank rate" here includes all the means at the disposal of the Bank of England to influence the terms of lending.

The great historic virtue of Bank rate policy is . . . that it works on both . . . [the current and capital accounts] and on both in the right direction . . . But the way it works on the two factors is very materially different. Its influence on lending is rapid, but not permanent . . . The Bank rate could not restore permanent equilibrium, if it merely affected the short-loan situation. On the other hand, its immediate efficacy on the short position is very great. Its influence on the price factor is much slower, in fact it may be intolerably slow, but when it has produced its final effect on price levels this effect is much more lasting. It is the real change which, in some circumstances, is necessary for the restoration of real equilibrium. So the Bank rate sets in motion rapid forces to diminish the calls on us to lend abroad, and slow forces which will have the effect of increasing our ability to lend abroad by reducing our price level to a more competitive level with the outside world . . . It is the traditional doctrine, I think, that Bank rate not only diminishes lending, but also affects price level in a downward direction, but *what the reason is, what the conditions are for doing it rapidly is another matter.* (Keynes 1929–31 [1981: 41–2], italics mine)

This is the neoclassical position, elegantly stated with the explicit presentation of an export surplus as foreign lending and hence intimately involved – in some way – with the rate of interest.

Internally, higher Bank rate makes it "less attractive to embark on new enterprises" so inventories accumulate or are sold off at lower prices than were anticipated. Credit is reduced because there is less demand for loans, not because banks are refusing borrowers. For Keynes there were many lags in real adjustments; even unemployment came slowly, because firms are reluctant to sack workers. "I do not think we have yet got the whole of the unemployment due to what happened in 1925" (Keynes 1929–31 [1981: 46–8]). I remind the reader that these words were uttered in February 1930!

## Keynes the pre-keynesian

Now, only one year after the *Economic journal* controversy with Ohlin, in which he argued exclusively in terms of the elasticities approach to the transfer problem, we get a statement of current account adjustment working through expenditure changes. A decline in home demand leads to reduced demand for imported inputs. The reduction in home demand leads to a "willingness of manufacturers to sell at cut prices [which] means a stimulus to export . . . Thus the Bank rate helps us both on capital account and on income account. There are one or two very good examples of that in the recent history of Germany" (Keynes 1929–31 [1981: 48]).

The next step, after the immediate expenditures effect, and the reason for "the historical approval of Bank rate policy" is the secondary downward pressure on money wages; if this is not possible, the entrepreneurs will "withdraw from the business." The reduction in money wages is crucial to the adjustment mechanism. "*There is no way by which Bank rate brings down prices except through the increase of unemployment*" (Keynes 1929–31 [1981: 48–9], italics mine). Later in the testimony he says something different, though I interpret the spirit to be the same. He is to argue that prices fall instantly and unemployment causes the wage reduction necessary to restore profits and establish the lower prices as the equilibrium levels.

Foreign lending depends on relative interest rates at home and abroad.[1] If these are such as to make it profitable for us to invest abroad, we must have an export surplus and this may require our having lower real wages than otherwise. So the lower real wages are not to be laid at the door of the Bank rate policy as such. "*[A]ssuming fluidity in the economic system*," Bank rate, and hence the market interest rate, allocates labor appropriately and allocates

---

[1]  At one point he distinguishes between foreign investment (the current account surplus) and foreign lending (which is the purchase of foreign assets), the difference being gold movements, but he is not consistent in this distinction (Keynes 1929–31 [1981: 141–2]). At a later stage in the testimony he even, fairly wickedly, teased Lord Bradbury, who was questioning him, with this distinction (see page 116 below).

capital between domestic and foreign uses, all of which is commendable, and with no adverse effects "on labour and real wages" (Keynes 1929–31 [1981: 52–3], italics mine). This argument he labels the classical theory and attributes it most particularly to Taussig; he seems quite clearly to be referring to real trade theory at this juncture. Within this framework, Bank rate helps achieve the optimum allocation of world investment and production.

And furthermore, the Bank of England can play this beneficial, capital-allocating role with the greatest of ease. It has merely to watch its gold movements, which are a "barometer" informing it when to make the required changes in Bank rate. Once it has done that, "the economic system will then automatically grind out the proper levels of price and of wages at which everyone can be employed, at which business men can get normal profits and which furnishes the most advantageous division of the country's savings between investment at home and investment abroad, all owing to the fact that the Bank rate has this double influence." This argument, he says, is "the beginning and the end of traditional sound finance in this country . . . I have told you the whole story of how the traditionally sound financier thinks that he can make the adjustments required . . . and . . . there is no need to wonder why two generations, both of theorists and of practical men, should have been entranced by it" (Keynes 1929–31 [1981: 53]).

He laid the groundwork for the Macmillan Committee's distinction between very short-, medium-, and long-run disturbances and the importance of applying different policies to each. The first kind of disturbance he discusses is a temporary external shock. "The use of Bank rate to tide over a mere temporary disturbance is, I think, an example of Bank rate operation at its best." Before the War, "probably four out of five changes of Bank rate would be of this character" (Keynes 1929–31 [1981: 54–5]). These may include cyclical disturbances in the price level, but they do not require changes in income domestically and involve, at worst, "transitory" unemployment.

The second is a "permanent change in the value of gold in the outside world," by which he obviously means the "long swings" of the nineteenth century (Keynes 1929–31 [1981: 55])

The third is the case in which the goal is to discourage foreign investment in order to encourage domestic investment, especially if the investment abroad is apparently due not primarily to better returns abroad, such as in the nineteenth century, but "to a feeling of discouragement at home" (Keynes 1929–31 [1981: 63]). In this situation, with pessimism rife at home and, in his later terminology, the marginal efficiency of capital low, the system may be unstable, with a higher interest rate at home leading to *more* lending abroad as domestic investment declines.

He continually emphasized the macroeconomic identities of trade surplus with an excess of savings over investment, so that an increase in foreign lending has to be matched by a reduction in domestic investment. (This is, as we shall see, at the heart of the model developed in the *Treatise*.) It has to be matched also, however, by a rise in the trade surplus, so that price competitiveness and cost flexibility are of paramount importance. And here, precisely, lies the difficulty. The downward rigidity of money wages as an empirical fact of life is a phenomenon he stressed heavily throughout his testimony (and in the report). This does not seem to have anything directly to do with immediate institutional considerations, such as strong labor unions; it seems rather a political, psychological, and historical fact.

## Keynes's view of the disequilibrium system

The reason Keynes praised Bank rate as a tool for the prewar period and pinned so little hope on it for the future lay in his analysis of history. His point was not that rigidity had increased; it was, rather, that downward flexibility had generally, in the past, been unnecessary. Except for the period of slump, 1885–95, when unemployment was high, Bank rate had never had to force a reduction of wages in the prewar period; simply decelerating the rise in wages was sufficient (Keynes 1929–31 [1981: 55–6]). He argued that "apart from . . . cyclical fluctuations, there has never been in modern or ancient history a community that has been prepared to accept without immense struggle a reduction in the general level of money income." Throughout history there had been large price decreases (and at that with great difficulty) only twice: after the Napoleonic wars and in the middle ages before the influx of American gold and silver. "Many of our monarchs rest under unjust imputations of depreciating the currency for their own personal advantage, I am sure they only did it to avoid what they regarded as intolerable wage adjustments" (Keynes 1929–31 [1981: 64–5]).

(Lord Bradbury): The previous history was that adjustments of money wages were comparatively easy both before the War and after.
[Keynes]: You cannot quote any case in which they had gone down. (Keynes 1929–31 [1981: 59])

Again, we have here an intimation of the later (1941) statement that there never had been an international adjustment mechanism (see Chapter 10), in the sense of something like the classical adjustment mechanism, requiring downward movement in nominal variables.

Arguing that the return to the prewar parity in 1925 implied a commitment to using Bank rate policy to force wages down by 10 percent (Keynes 1929–31 [1981: 56]), he continued that in 1925 we put on the Bank rate policy a task of greater magnitude than it had ever been asked to perform before and which it proved to be incapable of performing. If we make the usual assumptions about perfect markets and absence of friction, Bank rate policy must always be capable of doing the work asked of it; but humanly and politically it was impossible. The result is that we are left jammed in a position of what I described as spurious equilibrium without applying any alternative policy to Bank rate policy; and that spurious equilibrium may be gradually ruining us.

One can put it another way by saying that we have a currency policy and a wages policy which are incompatible with one another. (Keynes 1929–31 [1981: 68])

He stated explicitly that there are two exogenous variables, the money wage rate and the exchange rate (the "currency"), whereas the "system" assumes that there is only one fixed point, the exchange rate, and that "wages will always sooner or later follow business receipts." The result is unemployment, though often with a lag; and a government budget deficit, as transfer payments and wages are high and receipts fall off. This requires a tax increase, which further exacerbates the problem (Keynes 1929–31 [1981: 68–9]).

Keynes's model at this juncture was one with traded and non-traded goods (sheltered and unsheltered, in his terminology). Wages in the sheltered industries can resist a decline better than in the traded, but these sheltered industries provide inputs to the unsheltered (as railways, for example, provide inputs for the steel industry) so wages in the traded goods industries have to fall even further in order to reduce average costs by a given percentage (Keynes 1929–31 [1981: 70–1]). (This is a nice short piece of general-equilibrium trade analysis in the Heckscher-Ohlin-Samuelson-Jones tradition.)

## Internal versus external balance

As a result of this rigidity, exclusive reliance on Bank rate policy to restore equilibrium implies permitting (in fact, welcoming) the resulting unemployment. Otherwise you "hamper without hitting . . . injure without killing, and so . . . get the worst of both worlds" (Keynes 1929–31 [1981: 71]). This last represents a recurrent theme. Both in the testimony and in the report, one of the frequently raised objections to the use of Bank rate as a major policy tool is that the authorities (including the Bank of England) are certain to back off and reverse a tight money policy when they see the unemployment it creates, and not persist long enough for the policy to work. The weakness of the Bank rate mechanism is "not that it is ineffective, but that the desired result is only brought about as a sort of by-product, so to speak, of a process which affects credit facilities for all sorts of internal purposes" (Keynes 1929–31 [1981: 182]).

A great deal of time was spent trying to explain to the committee who seem to have been remarkably open-minded, despite some occasional difficulties accepting everything he said, what happens when savings and investment are not equal. He explained that this was part of the need to discuss disequilibrium situations and tried to simplify for them the model that was about to appear in the *Treatise*. In fact, his explanation was awkward, since he neither used an explicit Swedish-type analysis, nor did he emphasize that he was dealing with functional relationships rather than accounting ones. He contented himself with arguing (in an attempt to explain the paradox of thrift) that an excess of savings over investment was necessarily equal to business losses; to make the case more vivid, he assumed that output consisted of a single perishable good – bananas. In this example, real investment can be changed not at all, or with a lag, so in the short-run an increase in intended savings implies that some bananas rot and some businesses incur losses. The committee seems to have digested that, but had somewhat more difficulty with the notion that an autonomous increase in investment, in more banana plantations, could have an expansionary effect.

The effects here are on profits, prices, and only finally on employment. (Ultimately, as we saw in Chapter 5 in the discussion of the Macmillan Report, the unemployment leads to reductions in costs, that is wages, and the lower prices finally become equilibrium prices.) The *General theory* was as yet six years away (Keynes 1929–31 [1981: 75–80]). Keynes was still in a flexprice world. "As soon as savings exceed investment, whatever is the level of wages, prices must fall below the equilibrium, because business men can only get rid of the goods they have made by making concessions in price" (Keynes 1929–31 [1981: 136]).

Time and again (and this is his main point here) Keynes stresses the open economy dilemma. In a closed economy one can always solve the problem by making the interest rate low enough (and here there is a very clear explanation of the marginal efficiency of capital) but in an open economy this may encourage the export of capital greater than "our available balance of exports." Increasing exports to match the increased foreign lending caused by a low domestic interest rate, however, may be blocked: if "our wage system is rigid the amount of our foreign investment is rigid also" (Keynes 1929–31 [1981: 79–80]).

Alternatively, an increase in savings should lead to a rise in investment as interest falls "but as the rate of interest cannot fall for foreign reasons, our savings can only flow into investments if it takes the form of increased exports" (Keynes 1929–31 [1981: 80]). Not only do rigid wages and world interest rates prevent equilibrium, but the transfer of capital abroad is more difficult than it had been in the nineteenth century. Then there had often been a close relationship between foreign lending and exports, with orders directly resulting from foreign loans (as in the nineteenth-century railroad loans); this mechanism is now less widespread, he argues. In addition, tariff barriers in other countries are often variable and increase with our exports to them. In some of Britain's major export sectors, such as coal, worldwide surplus and inelastic demand are hampering improvement (Keynes 1929–31 [1981: 85–6]).

He states the policy dilemma, not in terms of the absence of capital mobility, as it was expressed in the early days after World War II, but in terms of the absence of a keynesian fiscal policy. He describes a world of one tool (monetary or Bank rate policy) and two goals: internal and external balance. Thus the problem is:

> that relative costs of production at home and abroad, taken in conjunction with the relative demand for loans at home and abroad for investment purposes, are such that a Bank rate which is high enough to prevent us from lending too much abroad [relative to our ability to export, given the level of domestic costs] is too high to enable us to have the right amount of enterprise at home. (Keynes 1929–31 [1981: 94])

This is essentially the Mundell-Fleming model without fiscal policy, rather than the pre-Mundell-Fleming dilemma, because it recognizes the inter-relationship between the capital and current accounts, which the "naive keynesian" models of the dilemma literature did not.

### Possible remedies

Having rejected the exclusive use of monetary policy (Bank rate) as a remedy, he considers others and discusses them seriatim. One is devaluation, and he seems to be of two minds about it. He felt there would be a great deal of opposition, both at home and abroad. Britain had missed her chance in 1925 when a change in parities could have been carried out with relative ease. (This assertion is reinforced by his argument that France and Belgium went back on gold at undervalued exchange rates.) It would probably still pay to devalue, even if they had to compensate holders of short-term sterling funds. However, he was sure (and confident that the committee agreed with him) that it would be so unpopular a move that it did not merit further discussion[2] (Keynes 1929–31 [1981: 100]).

A second would be a kind of social contract, "an agreed reduction of the level of money incomes in this country." Agreeing reluctantly that it was not

---

[2] In Addendum I to the report, he wrote: "Precisely the same effects as those produced by a devaluation of sterling by a given percentage could be brought about by a tariff of the same percentage on all imports together with an equal subsidy on all exports, except that this measure *would leave sterling international obligations unchanged in terms of gold.* This proposal would avoid the injury to the national credit and to our receipts from foreign loans fixed in terms of sterling which would ensue on devaluation" (Keynes 1929–31 [1981: 296], italics his).

currently practicable, he nevertheless considered it to be "the ideal remedy," and "one that this Committee ought to ponder to a certain extent before they reject it." What he had in mind here was a 10 percent cut in wages, and a 10 percent tax on unearned income[3] (Keynes 1929–31 [1981: 102]).

The third solution, theoretically sound but practically not important (thus Keynes) would be subsidies (bounties) to all or some industries. Here is an interesting incursion into the theory of the second best: "It may be that our social feelings have caused us to fix wages at a higher level than the economic machine grinds out. If we were to balance that by a bounty that would be the public subscribing to meet the difference out of the common purse" (Keynes 1929–31 [1981: 108]).

The fourth solution would be an increase in productivity, but he did not regard this as practical, knowing no way to effect it. All these remedies, he notes, are "ways of being able to produce at lower costs in terms of gold" (Keynes 1929–31 [1981: 113]).

In addition, he had three other ideas. The first of these (the fifth proposal in the longer list) was an increase in protectionism. This presumably diminishes imports and hence increases foreign investment, that is, the export surplus. In that respect he thought it like Bank rate.[4] When it came to drafting the report he also wrote favorably of tariffs, arguing that since there was at the time unemployment a tariff would be likely to have the effect of increasing employment and "national productivity". It need not feed back to reduced demand abroad and reduced demand for British exports, if they used the opportunity to increase domestic investment and output and imports (Keynes 1929–31 [1981: 298–9]). But he appears to have been trying here to have things both ways: to the extent that tariffs led to increased output and imports, they would presumably not improve the balance of trade.

All the proposals to this point involve ways of increasing the export surplus, that is, increasing foreign investment (to make it equal to home savings). The sixth idea was the one he preferred: to increase domestic investment. There are two subsets of this, depending on whether or not

---

[3] As R. M. Hartwell has pointed out, this was in fact done (at any rate, partially) in Australia in January, 1931. There wages were actually cut by 10 percent across the board, twice: first, in accordance with cost of living index clauses in wage contracts, following price level declines, and then again to effect a real wage decline (see Butlin, Barnard and Pincus 1982: 105).

[4] "Free trade tries to . . . [increase our foreign investment] by increasing exports. Protection tries to do it by diminishing our imports. If it is essential for equilibrium that we should invest abroad on a larger scale than at present, the protectionist way of doing it may be the method of least resistance, because it does not require reduction of money wage and it has less effect . . . in turning the terms of trade against us. It is easier to produce things ourselves than to reduce wages to a point where we can get over the foreign tariffs! . . . The upshot would be that with protection we should have lower real wages but less unemployment; with free trade, *if it works*, we should have no unemployment" (Keynes 1929–31 [1981: 117], italics mine).

government interference is needed (Keynes 1929–31 [1981: 126]). The argument against an expansionary policy "results from following too obediently the teaching of the doctrine of the economics of equilibrium." The "Treasury view" "demonstrates that home investment is not a cure for unemployment, by first of all assuming – in effect – that there is no unemployment to cure" (Keynes 1929–31 [1981: 130]). He accuses those who take this position of viewing unemployment as a purely transitory phenomenon and concluding therefrom that to base policy on the presumption that it was a continuing problem would be "unsound".

One might say, perhaps, that the view in question is the natural result of standing half-way between common sense and sound theory; it is the result of having abandoned the one without having reached the other. (Keynes 1929–31 [1981: 130])

Economists spend most of their time describing and discussing what happens in a position of equilibrium, and they usually affirm that a position of disequilibrium is merely transitory. *I want to study what happens during the process of disequilibrium*, – one which lasts long enough to observe it. (Keynes 1929–31 [1981: 72], italics mine)

In order to stimulate domestic investment there would need to be a separation between the international and the domestic loan market. "The degree of interconnection which exists in this country exists in hardly any other country; our conditions are abnormal in that respect." He suggested numerous technical devices for separating the markets. One idea, which he himself particularly favored, was a tax on foreign issues, which he says was highly successful in France (and which the United States imposed in the 1960s)[5] (Keynes 1929–31 [1981: 139–40]). His justification was that Britain had decided, as a matter of social policy, on wages which were higher relative to efficiency than those of many other countries. The result was that "this wages policy of ours . . . is definitely incompatible with the policy of *laissez-faire* towards foreign investment" (Keynes 1929–31 [1981: 147–8]). His point here is essentially the same as that of Sayers, that if domestic demand for credit is sluggish, then "even when the Bank of England does lower Bank rate it still remains an ineffective rate and the foreigner is tempted to borrow at a [market] rate which may be under 4 per cent." A lower Bank rate, if domestic investment is depressed, will result only in capital outflow. Domestic borrowing, on the other hand, will keep the market rate of interest up and so not tempt foreigners to borrow; an expansionary policy, by raising interest rates at home, discourages a capital outflow, "crowding out" the foreigners. "Domestic borrowing would absorb sufficient funds to make the Bank rate effective" (Keynes 1929–31 [1981: 150]). Nevertheless, he was aware of the danger and ease of evasion. Preventing new issues being sold on

[5] Brown (1940: 1,130 ff) and *passim*, gives a very interesting account of how Britain came, late, reluctant, but finally solidly, to join the camp of the restrictionists in this regard.

the London market was useless if it diverted English funds to the buying of existing securities. The only effect of that is that the London issue houses lose the commission on the flotations. He suggested an extra income tax of 5 percent to 10 percent on the coupon to put a wedge between foreign and domestic rates (Keynes 1929–31 [1981: 232–3]).

"[Lord Bradbury] You do not want to restrict the volume of foreign investment at all? [Keynes] Why should I? Our volume of foreign lending is always equal to our favourable balance of trade" (Keynes 1929–31 [1981: 237]). He seems to have been playing games with Bradbury here, using his earlier definition of foreign investment as the current account surplus, and distinguishing it (as Bradbury was not, here) from the desire to buy foreign securities. After a brief exchange, he agrees that "I have to prevent . . . [the British investor] buying too many [foreign securities] otherwise I lose gold" (Keynes 1929–31 [1981: 238]).

Keynes's seventh "remedy" is one he cherished until the end of his life: international cooperation, specifically cooperation between the "leading central banks . . . to raise prices to a parity with the international level of money costs of production . . . I think it is clear that in nearly all parts of the world money incomes are too high in relation to the international raw commodity index numbers at the moment." Particularly needed was a consortium between the U.S., the U.K. and France. Its tasks would be, first, to lower central bank discount rates and secondly, to reduce legal reserve requirements all round. He was referring here to the legal reserve holdings of gold imposed by law on the central banks. Next, there would be an extension and expansion of the gold exchange standard (by utilizing deposits at the Bank for International Settlements), beyond that envisioned by the Genoa agreement. Finally (and this sounds rather tame for Keynes), he wanted international agreement "that a world-wide encouragement of investment and of capital development generally would help" (Keynes 1929–31 [1981: 151–3]). The world's problem was underdemand and not, as some argued, overproduction.

In the meetings to discuss and draft the report,[6] Keynes expressed strongly the view that there should be adjustment to short-term changes in the world outside as long as Britain remains an open economy, but not to long-term changes. "[I]t must be our object to reconcile the fluctuating character of capital movements in the international loan market with the relatively steady character of our income surplus available for foreign investment." He

---

[6]  Moggridge (Keynes 1929–31 [1981: 309]) notes that it is clear from his papers that Keynes drafted the following sections as published: paras. 118–23, 155–8, 160–74 (The Sequence of Events since 1925), 205–21 (part of The Influence of Monetary Policy on the Price Level), 243–65 (The Gold Standard), 308–16 (Proposals to Meet the Present Emergency), 320–74, 405–25.

was clearly assuming that Britain would continue to be a net long-term lender, requiring an export surplus unattainable without draconian measures (and unemployment) at home. This was the major root of the problems he anticipated. The kinds of long-term changes he worries about are those involving either "change in the level of money incomes relatively to efficiency" either at home or abroad or both, or a change in the relationship between these at home and abroad; or "the new feature of the tendency of our foreign lending on long term to exceed over a period our income surplus" (Keynes 1929–31 [1981: 180–91]).

Driving a wedge between domestic and international fluctuations might involve a good deal more direct intervention than had been considered heretofore. Predating his later suggestion of Schachtian devices and bilateral balancing he suggested the possibilities of soviet-type controls on the economy. While ten years later he had rejected the notion of state trading (unless there was no acceptable alternative), this dirigiste tendency remained fairly strong in him[7] (see Chapter 10).

If we wish to have our money incomes move differently from the rest of the world, but nevertheless remain on an international standard, we may be able to do it by handling our foreign trade on the Russian model. The Russian model has immense theoretical interest for me from that point of view, and it may be that some day we shall come much nearer to the Russian model than we think probable at this moment. (Keynes 1929–31 [1981: 184])

Anticipating somewhat the position of Nurkse and others in the crisis school he alleged that short-term lending is much more volatile than either income or the balance on current account, so that capital movements are often destabilizing rather than financing. He argued that in no other country were international transactions so large relative to domestic ones, and in no other country were the bill rate and other short-term interest rates as important as in London. Nevertheless, when there is a long-term disturbance, "then it is necessary to take steps to produce a new domestic equilibrium" (Keynes 1929–31 [1981: 183]). (This seems to contradict his overall desire to insulate the domestic economy as much as possible from foreign shocks.)

Sometimes, he argued, the Bank would want to influence both the short-term loan markets (domestic and foreign), but when the problem is clearly a

---

[7] We have a system which "is incompatible with large changes in the value of money in an upward direction." The reason is that that works only by creating unemployment and the Bank necessarily gets soft-hearted when it sees this happening and reverses its policy. "We must therefore avoid large changes of money in an upward direction or have quite a different system, which would involve some departure from individualist capitalism . . . because we have no instrument to bring about the necessary readjustment" (Keynes 1929–31 [1981: 223]).

temporary one, it would be preferable to be able to deal with it without upsetting internal balance. "If you want to upset the domestic system whenever you have an international disequilibrium the present system is admirable for the purpose, and I have no improvement to suggest" (Keynes 1929–31 [1981: 260]). Related to his desire to drive a wedge between the domestic economy and foreign shocks is his concern about the resources available to the Bank of England for meeting short-term fluctuation. He felt that this problem was being ignored by the Bank itself, among others.

They are relying on pre-War practices and while they have managed to use them . . . with remarkable success, it has been, in my judgement, at the cost of a great deal of interference with the domestic market, which everyone would have wished to have avoided if possible. I do not say the resources are inadequate for the safety of the Bank . . . But I think that *its reserves are inadequate to allow the bank to attend as much as it ought to the internal position with an unpreoccupied mind* . . . Nothing is worse for our credit in the world at large than this constant appearance, and indeed reality, of some measure of anxiety. . . We are getting the name of being very near on our beam ends (Keynes 1929–31 [1981: 192], italics mine)

Keynes's recommendations to strengthen the Bank of England were that the Bank should hold large gold and foreign exchange reserves and allow them to fluctuate (Marshall, we remember, had similar leanings) and the joint stock banks should hold smaller reserves of Bank of England notes than formerly, since these tie up gold in the Bank of England.

Other techniques would be to widen the gold points (Keynes 1929–31 [1981: 217]) and to allow the Bank to play more with the difference between spot and forward exchange (see Hawtrey's discussion of this in Chapter 7). The Bank should enter the forward market itself, selling forward dollars at an attractive rate when it wants to strengthen the spot rate (Keynes 1929–31 [1981: 214]). If the spot rate at the end of the three months had not risen, the Bank would have borne an exchange risk, but this is exactly the cost which other participants in the market would have borne had the Bank changed Bank rate in order to defend the rate in the first place. He suggested a number of other technical devices, involving the Bank, the bill brokers, and the joint stock banks, all aimed at keeping rates high enough to attract foreign capital (or prevent outflows), while not discouraging domestic borrowing: some of these would simply involve "consultations" among the banks and between them and the Bank of England. The banks might refrain from buying bills (keeping the rate up, but forgoing some profits), manipulating deposit rates to the public, offsetting gold movements by varying reserve requirements of the banks at the Bank of England, and varying the time profile of its own portfolio as needed to affect the interest rate structure (Keynes 1929–31 [1981: 224–8]).

## Summary

Keynes has been accused of having proposed scores of ideas and plans –
simultaneously. There is much justification in that. His view of the nature of
the problem was not, I think, subject to much variability, even over his
lifetime. But in his ceaseless search for cures, solutions, palliatives he lit out in
many directions. This can be seen as a virtue: looking for the cure (a) that will
work and (b) that the patient will take. However, I am not here to judge;
only to report.

What to me is very clear here and in the Macmillan Report itself, is a deep
concern for the conflict between external balance in payments and internal
balance in the labor market. It is still a highly classical view of the adjustment
mechanism, with price changes, rather than keynesian effective demand,
playing the major role in adjustment, but with market rigidities, especially in
factor markets, leading to a continual problem of getting those prices down
while maintaining satisfactorily full employment. And particularly keen in
the testimony, and the writing of the report, is his awareness of the presence
and importance of an active money market and short-term financial
transactions, which can be either benevolent or destructive. It is not an
accident, I think, that it was Keynes and Hawtrey, both of whom spent much
of their time out of academe, who participated in a controversy about the
technicalities of covered interest arbitrage.

## Postscript

A charming divertimento is provided by the reprinting of a paper which
Moggridge found among Keynes's personal papers at King's College. It has
to do with a secret correspondence with Reginald McKenna and a memo
written at McKenna's request. The subject was a secret process, to which
McKenna claimed to have access, for producing gold at one shilling per
ounce. The memo was a fanciful flight on Keynes's part as to what the world
would look like under such circumstances, and particularly what international monetary arrangements would be like. It is a fine statement of the
commodity theory of money and concludes with a prediction that, when the
secret is finally out, the gold standard will be finished and the world will have
to move to an "international managed currency" and an "international
bank." "[I]n fact there would be a managed international currency run from
London, and if Paris or Washington or any other place showed an inclination
to absorb a quantity of gold, there would be no difficulty in obliging them."
The memo is something like a combination of his own earlier statements in
the *Tract* about the desirability of an internationally managed fixed
exchange rate system and the article in *The Economist*, written, I presume by

Fred Hirsch, in a spirit of year-end jocularity, quoting the putative diary of Per Jacobsson describing what happened "The Year We Demonetized Gold".[8] Moggridge concludes that "[s]cientific enquiries in Cambridge lead us to believe that the scheme was a hoax" (Keynes 1929–31 [1981: 162–5]).

## Appendix: Keynes on methodology

Finally just for amusement, I give the reader the following:

My belief is that in the near future economics will become increasingly technical and difficult for the outsider, because the economists will be settling a number of matters among themselves and will have to discuss them in their own way, but a point may come when over a certain part of the field there will be much wider agreement. They will settle their quarrels among themselves and come to an agreement. When they have done that, they will be able to expound that part of the subject which is settled in very much simpler language, and then it will rest with the world whether it understands them. Very likely they will themselves get still more advanced on a part which is again in the technical realm, but at present the difficulty is that parts of the subject which one feels ought to be elementary are still in this disputed condition. (Keynes 1929–31 [1981: 269])

---

[8]  *The Economist*, "Where the rainbow ended," December 24, 1960, 1325–6.

# The anti-neoclassicals

I have categorized both Hayek and Hawtrey as anti-neoclassicals, in the sense that both of them accept as fact, but decry, the proposition that the world is operated very much as the neoclassicists describe it. What Hayek and Hawtrey share is a severely critical attitude toward the neoclassical position in its normative version. Both emphasize the negative effects of Bank rate policy, albeit for different reasons. While Hayek (1932 [1984]) blamed first some central banks and some economists, including Hawtrey, and later (1937) the very institution of the modern banking system, Hawtrey lays the responsibility at the door of benighted central bankers too concerned with issues which should not command their attention – namely, the level of their own reserves.

## Hayek

Hayek is perhaps best described as a super-classical writer. Though he changed his views over time regarding the historical workings of the gold standard, he consistently held the position as to what the equilibrium mechanism was and how it should be allowed to function: the model was that of a full-bodied commodity currency. His model of the adjustment mechanism is one in which stable equilibrium exists and would be achieved in a fairly straightforward way if meddlesome institutions did not intercede.

The classical paradigm is clearly present throughout. In addition, he comes very close to an explicit statement of the kind of intertemporal optimization model of the balance of payments which has recently gained widespread popularity (see Chapter I, note 6). His approach is highly monetary, but not based on simple quantity-theoretic maxims: he places more emphasis on changes in the demand for money as a result of a change in money receipts and expenditures than as a cause.

Indeed, he comes out very strongly in an attack on what he labels the "mechanistic Quantity theory of Money" and its "representatives," Irving Fisher and Gustav Cassel. Their fault lay in proposing and furthering the notion of "price [level] stabilization as the objective of monetary policy" and elevating it "into a virtually unassailable dogma" (Hayek 1932 [1984: 119]). Even for a closed economy, as we shall see, he argued that price stabilization is an inappropriate policy goal. For an open economy it is simply disastrous. Fisher, and still more Cassel, in his view, apparently did almost as much harm as Keynes and Hawtrey. Hawtrey, in his official capacity as a Treasury official, adopted the concept of stabilization as the appropriate goal of monetary policy. In this vein he formulated and propagated the conclusion of the Genoa Conference of 1922 that price stabilization was being threatened by a worldwide shortage of gold. (See Davis 1981 for a biography of Hawtrey and an account of his activities in the Treasury and involvement in the Genoa Conference.) Later Hayek (1937) switched his attack and focused more intently on Harrod (1933), but for fundamentally the same reason. Refusal to accept the prescription of the classical mechanism in Harrod's case meant the espousal of flexible, or at any rate adjustable, exchange rates, that is, abjuration of the pure classical adjustment mechanism.[1]

In the 1932 paper he emphasized that the goal of price stabilization was cited by the British in the early 1930s (having suffered through the wrenching deflation required by the return to gold in 1925)[2] as a motivation for later sterilization of gold outflows. It had been used as a justification on the part of the United States for not allowing prices to fall in the 1920s. In a passing anticipation of Hicks's Inaugural Lecture (1953) he asserts that technological progress since 1925 was faster in the United States than in Britain, so that with fixed exchange rates, especially under a gold standard,

[1] This theme is emphasized most strongly in the 1932 [1984] paper, but it is totally consistent with the views expressed in the longer, more analytical, less strident lectures of 1937. This short book consists of five lectures which Hayek (then a Professor at the London School of Economics) gave at the Graduate Institute of International Studies at Geneva. They constitute a fascinating *normative* statement of the monetary approach to the balance of payments, undeservedly neglected.

[2] He cites Ricardo as support for his contention that the return to sterling in 1925, at a then overvalued rate, was a mistake. "More than a hundred years previously . . . [Ricardo] wrote that he would never recommend a government to ease back to par a currency whose value had declined by 30 percent" (1932 [1984: 121] and 1937: 44). He cites "a letter to John Wheatley, dated September 18, 1821, reprinted in *Letters of David Ricardo to Hutches Trower and Others*, edited by J. Bonar and J. Hollander, Oxford, 1899, p. 160." Keynes cites the same idea and attributes it to a speech in the House of Commons and to "Protection to Agriculture", *Works*, p. 468 (Keynes 1923: 153–4). The letter to Wheatley appears in the Sraffa Edition of Ricardo 1821–3 [1952], which states "I never should advise a government to restore a currency, which was depreciated 30 pc$^t$, to par; I should recommend, as you propose, but not in the same manner, that the currency should be fixed at the depreciated value by [lowerin]g the standard, and that no further deviations should [take] place. It was without any legislation that the c[urrency] from 1813 to 1819, became of an increased value, and within 5 pc$^t$ of the value of gold, – it was in this state of things, and not with a currency depreciated 30 pc$^t$, that I advised a recurrence to the old standard" ([] indicates that the manuscript was torn, Ricardo, 1821–3 [1952: 73]).

there must be a chronic flow of gold from Britain to the United States, even if they started from equilibrium. The fall in costs in the United States should have been allowed to lead to a fall in prices. This would then have "forced the ultimately unavoidable reduction in costs in Europe by absorbing Europe's gold" (Hayek 1932 [1984: 123]). He attacked the view that there could be no harm done by the United States stabilizing its price level "even if it was simply a question of the domestic price level within that member of an international system whose productivity was rising most rapidly." This is dismissed as being as preposterous as the notion of stabilizing the price of "that commodity whose cost of production was declining most rapidly." This notion of stabilization permitted "an expansion of credit . . . which would not have been possible under the automatic gold standard of the pre-war years" (Hayek 1932 [1984: 124–5]).

The French, on the other hand, got it right. They were accused of hoarding gold, and it seemed that they were guilty, because they did not allow the domestic money supply to expand proportionately to the gold inflow. But by allowing domestic money to expand "by the very same amount as that of the gold inflow" they did exactly the appropriate thing "for the gold standard to function" (Hayek 1932 [1984: 125], italics mine).

The link between the ideas developed here and those of the 1937 lectures are to found in the explanation of why the ideas of price stabilization had recently been allowed to prevail, sabotaging the international mechanism. The Bank of England was not the only central bank to violate the rules, though the British, he noted, were the only ones to justify the violation theoretically. The reason these violations had occurred recently was the widespread disappearance of gold from circulation. When gold had circulated freely, the export of gold had come primarily from gold coin, market interest rates had risen, and eventually Bank rate had had to follow. When gold for export comes from bullion held by the central bank, the temptation to sterilize the outflow is great (Hayek 1932 [1984: 128]). The rule that gold reserves are there to be used is correct, but it should not be interpreted to mean that they are there to be used and sterilized. He here states the rule that he was to emphasize strongly in 1937, that the money supply should vary in one-to-one correspondence with changes in reserves.

He dismisses the notion that the world is suffering from a shortage of gold (in 1932). Britain did indeed have a chronic gold shortage, but that was due to overspending. He aims a pointed sociopolitical barb:

If Britain had not been the country from which the rest of the world had been accustomed to draw its views on monetary policy for over a century, it would hardly have come about that the existence of a gold shortage in Britain would readily have been accepted throughout the whole world as sufficient proof of the need for a policy to combat the gold shortage. (Hayek 1932 [1984: 126])

His main theme throughout is that the classical mechanism had worked, could work, and would work again if permitted to. Permitting it to work, however, meant allowing or forcing (depending on the institutional environment) the domestic money supply to vary identically with the change in the foreign exchange reserves, that is, with the balance of payments. This means that sterilization of gold flows, allowing gold flows to occur without affecting the domestic money supply at all, is ruled out.

> It was not in vain that the great monetary theorists of the classical period from Ricardo onwards always insisted that a non-metallic circulation of money ought always to be so controlled that the total volume of all money in circulation changes in just the same way as would happen if gold alone were in circulation. (Hayek 1932 [1984: 129])

In 1932 he was evidently persuaded that the prewar system had functioned satisfactorily and that most of the problems of adjustment had developed only after sterling's return to gold in 1925 (Hayek 1932 [1984: 121]). The Federal Reserve System in the late 1920s and the Bank of England in the early 1930s (as well as Keynes and the Macmillan Committee) are the butts of his polemic. They had returned to ideas which had been definitively refuted "by the classical economists more than a hundred years ago." Policy led theory here. The Bank of England had been violating "the traditional rules of the gold standard" for the past six years. Then the *Treatise* ("a grandiose attempt to justify this policy") and the Macmillan Report ("predominately influenced" by Keynes) served "merely to elevate to the status of principle" these violations of the rules (Hayek 1932 [1984: 127–8]).

> It was not a big step from the desire to be released from the unpleasant necessity of adapting the general standard of living to the lower level of national income by reductions in wages and prices, to a theoretical justification of a monetary policy which rendered inoperative the tendencies of the gold standard in that direction . . . The most important error is the distinction drawn between temporary movements of gold, which cannot be attributed to deep-rooted causes . . . and hence should not be allowed to bring about any changes in the domestic volume of credit, and "genuine" movements of capital which should provide the only occasion for effecting changes in the rate of interest. What is left unexplained in this is why movements of gold should under any circumstances represent movements of capital which are not genuine. Nor is it explained why a country which is unable to cover its current obligations from current output . . . should nevertheless still be in a position . . . to make just as much capital available to domestic industry for investment purposes as previously. These theories are neither new nor do their advocates take the trouble to show that the refutation of them provided by the classical economists more than a hundred years ago, a refutation which was finally held to be definitive, is unfounded. (Hayek 1932 [1984: 127])

However, while sterilization and offsetting are contrary to the classical doctrine so, at the other extreme, are multiple expansion and contraction of domestic credit. By 1937 he had come to identify this type of response with the "prewar system", and criticized the latter for its violation of the classical prescription, its unfaithfulness to the principles by which fixed exchange rate regimes are to be operated. Thus, whereas in 1932 he attributes the failure of the system to behave correctly to the wrong-headedness of various economists and central bankers, by 1937 he finds the "system" lacking. The institution of fractional reserve banking created serious difficulties which could be overcome only with great difficulty – and with the aid of very finely orchestrated central bank policy.

The reality, according to Hayek, was that that which was called the "gold standard" was in fact a "mixed system". It did not function at all like a true gold standard; this inadequacy it was that led to the flaws in the world order that stimulated demands for reform and for "Monetary Nationalism". What was really needed, he contended, was a truly homogeneous international world system, with absolutely fixed exchange rates. Thus, though a classical par excellence, he is by implication a critic from within of the classicals and especially the late classicals. They are accused of yielding to the notion of multiple credit expansion and contraction with a modern banking system. The neoclassicals are dealt with even more severely for proposing as a virtue what he views to be the cardinal vice of the system. The later piece includes that position, but it is more concertedly directed against proposals for flexible exchange rates. His main argument is that the prevailing objections to a fixed exchange rate regime are misplaced. They are aimed at the historical gold standard, widely but quite mistakenly considered to be the ideal type of a fixed exchange rate standard.

There are three "types" of monetary system in Hayek's schema:

1 A "truly international monetary system", that is, perfectly fixed exchange rates.
2 "Monetary nationalism", characterized by flexible rates, not necessarily freely floating, which are determined one way or another by the several monetary authorities.
3 The "mixed system" which had prevailed under what had been misnomered the "gold standard".

The "truly International Monetary System" would consist of a single homogeneous currency in circulation in all countries; movement of this currency between countries and regions would be a function solely of the "action of all individuals". This is the system which the "classical writers" assumed in their analysis. They thought it had been achieved by the Bank Act of 1844, which decreed that, at the margin, changes in the note issue must precisely equal changes in the gold reserves (Hayek 1937: 4–6). The point of the act had indeed been to make the quantity of money behave as it would have had it consisted entirely of specie. As was apparent in the discussion in Chapter 2, the question of whether the relevant money supply was being made to vary with the stock of specie was at the heart of the major nineteenth-century controversies; the battle lines then were drawn at the issue of defining the relevant money stock, that is, at the debate over whether demand deposits were part of the money supply. But Hayek maintains that the issue was never settled satisfactorily – never pursued to its conclusion. The role of the banking system in determining the amount of money "was only imperfectly grafted upon, and never really integrated with, the theory of the purely metalic currency" (Hayek 1937: 6), and when people did come to realize that demand deposits were money just as much as banknotes were, so that the intentions of the Act of 1844 had been circumvented, they still thought that what was needed was only a "few modifications of the argument" (Hayek 1937: 8–9).

A constant theme – his major point, in fact – is that the core of the problem is the heterogeneity, not of the monies of different countries, but of the different assets used as money *within* individual countries. The high but finite elasticity of substitution between these, between banknotes and deposits, for example, is the cause of the problem and is that which "constitutes the real difference between different monetary systems." Modern countries have three kinds of money: that which is held by the public (deposits), that which banks use for settlements among themselves, and ultimate reserves for paying out abroad. The difference between a system of a perfectly homogeneous currency throughout the world and that of "national reserve systems" is greater and has a greater effect on the international mechanism than is generally thought (Hayek 1937: 9–14).

In the event of a real shock, it is necessary to redistribute the world's money supply in line with the Ricardian criterion (though he does not invoke Ricardo's name here) of conforming to the "share in the world income which different countries can claim." The important difference between the different kinds of international system lies in the way they carry out these redistributions. Under perfectly fixed rates, a "homogeneous international currency," this redistribution is effected by "actual transfers of the corresponding amounts of money from country to country." Under the mixed system, the engine of adjustment is likewise the change in the quantity of money in each country, though how these changes occur is different. Under "independent currencies," that is, flexible exchange rates, the relative values of the two currencies are changed, and "whatever redistribution of money between persons may be involved by the redistribution between countries has to be brought about by corresponding changes inside each country" (Hayek 1937: 17–18). We shall return to this later. For the nonce, let us examine the difference, as he sees it, between the homogeneous and the mixed systems.

### An international monetary system

Consider the homogeneous, perfectly-fixed-exchange rate system. The adjustment mechanism is not spelled out. But, by allusion and hint, we can deduce it. It is, as I noted, monetary but not mechanistically quantity theoretic. A real shock, generally a decline in demand for one of a country's export goods, will lead in the first instance to a flow of money balances from the deficit to the surplus country. Various changes will take place in the incomes of different individuals in the two economies, resulting, *inter alia*, in changes in the desired holdings of money. Whereas this occurs in both directions, there is an asymmetry which temporarily absorbs some of the shock and injects a lag into the system.

People who find their income increasing will generally *at first* take out part of the increased money income in the form of a *permanent* increase in their cash balances, while people whose incomes decrease will tend to postpone *for a while* a reduction of their expenditure to the full extent, prefering [sic] to reduce their cash balances. [He cites Hawtrey, *Currency and credit*.] (Hayek 1937: 18, italics mine)

I interpret "at first" to mean "right away" and not to imply reversibility as it does in idiomatic English. (Hayek was not, of course, speaking his native language.) Thus, the response to an increase in income is an immediate increase in cash balances to their new permanent level, while the response to a decrease is a lagged decline in expenditure, money holdings falling below their final equilibrium level to absorb part of the shock. The final adjustment mechanism, he argues, became known precisely only recently. The writers he cites are Paish (1936), Whale (1937), and K. F. Maier (*Goldwanderungen*, Jena 1935). In discussing Paish (see Chapter 14 below) he specifically refers, though not by name, to the marginal propensity to import: how long the adjustment takes depends on how much of the initial impact falls on imports.

He does not spell out a specific dynamic model, but he is clearly interested in the micro adjustments that are taking place. It is superficial, he argues, to talk about "*the* prices and *the* incomes of the country . . . [rather than] prices and incomes of particular individuals and particular industries" (Hayek 1937: 23, italics his). He sees no reason for prices to overshoot their new equilibrium values. Nor should the macroeconomic aggregates respond in any predictable way. He sees no reason for changes in the money supply in an open economy to cause temporary changes in relative prices. "Nor does there seem to exist any reason why, to use a more modern yet already obsolete [in

1937!] terminology, saving and investment should be made to be equal within any particular area which is part of a larger economic system." On this last point, he cites Keynes's *Treatise*, with its explicit and oft-repeated awareness of the macro identities, the savings-investment gap being equal to the current account. Most important, there is absolutely no presumption, he insists, as to which way, or whether, interest rates will move when money flows from one region of a homogeneous currency system to another. For example, when money income falls individuals may reduce both consumption and cash balances and simultaneously increase their investment; in this case the rate of interest would fall (Hayek 1937: 24–5).

Thus, in sum, neither the general neoclassical presumption of rising interest rates nor the frequent allegation that prices overshoot their long-term equilibrium is a necessary characteristic of the classical adjustment model. These are rather attributes of the "existing mixed systems" than the results of fundamental causes (Hayek 1937: 25).

### The mixed system

The most significant difference between the pure and the mixed system is that in the latter money is not actually transferred in the course of an adjustment but is expanded in one country and contracted in the other by the respective banking systems. Here Hayek's interest in disaggregation emerges again. His discussion is somewhat reminiscent of Paish's comments (discussed in Chapter 14) to the effect that when bankers retrench this leads to rising interest rates which are in effect arbitrarily discriminatory among customers. Hayek extends this to whole sectors, noting that

there is no reason to assume that [the banks] can take the money to be extinguished exactly from those persons where it would in the course of time be released if there were no banking system ... There are ... strong grounds for believing that the burden of the change will fall entirely, and to an extent which is no way justified by the underlying change in the real situation, on investment activity in both countries. (Hayek 1937: 26)

Thus there will be highly undesirable real adjustments to monetary shocks, a continual refrain of Hayek's. The root of the problem is the institution of fractional-reserve banking. One dilemma of the central bank is how on the one hand to limit expansion on the part of individual banks by threatening not to bail them out if they become overextended – to regulate, in brief – and on the other to come in and save them if they do get into trouble – to be a lender of last resort (Hayek 1937: 13). The other side of this is that the central bank cannot let the outflow of high-powered money continue to run its course without endangering its own reserves, so it must "indiscriminately . . . bring pressure on those who have borrowed from it to repay their loans" (Hayek 1937: 27). In this way it is possible to reduce the adjustment period "to almost any extent." The problem with this, however, is that those whose expenditure will be reduced in the process of adjustment are not necessarily those whose expenditure would have declined under "a homogeneous international currency system, and that the equilibrium so reached will be of its nature only temporary." Specifically, this means that the burden of adjustment falls primarily on investment. The adjustment mechanism necessarily involves a rise in interest rates and a contraction of credit in the deficit country (which we noted was not true in the pure gold standard). The system works by raising the market rate of interest above the "equilibrium or 'natural' rate" (Hayek 1937: 28–9).

But to a considerable extent its effect will be that international transfers of money which would have taken the place of a transfer of goods and would in this sense have been a final payment for a temporary excess of imports will be intercepted, so that consequently actual transfers of goods will have to take place. The transfer of only a fraction of the amount of money which would have been transferred under a purely metallic system . . . *deprives the individuals in the country concerned of the possibility of delaying the adaptation by temporarily paying for an excess of imports in cash.* (Hayek 1937: 29, italics mine)

Again, there is the emphasis, noted before, on intertemporal optimization and balancing of payments over time. In the face of a one-time shock, optimum response would involve borrowing in order to smooth consumption expenditures over time. This a fixed exchange rate system would permit; the mixed system, he is arguing, imposes a bias, relative to the pure fixed rate system, in favor of "adjustment" as opposed to financing of temporary imbalances. As we shall see in Chapter 8 a constant theme of Keynes's was in a sense very similar: that real adjustment was being forced in situations where monetary adjustments would be more appropriate. Keynes meant that the surplus countries should, as an entity, lend abroad to the extent of their surplus. Hayek, on the other hand, is arguing for the right of individuals in the deficit country to borrow.

Furthermore, in contrast to the homogeneous currency case, the adjustment process in the mixed system will not stop when it is complete – there will be overadjustment and a surplus.

It seems to me impossible to doubt that there is indeed a very considerable difference between the case where a country, whose inhabitants are induced to decrease their share in the world's stock of money by ten percent, does so by actually giving up this ten percent in gold, and the case where, in order to preserve the accustomed reserve proportions, it pays out only one per cent in gold and contracts the credit superstructure in proportion to the reduction of reserves. It is as if all balances of international payments had to be squeezed through a narrow bottle neck as special pressure has to be brought on people, who would otherwise not have been affected by the change, to give up money which they would have invested productively. (Hayek 1937: 30–1)

But worse is yet to come, since the changes that take place under a mixed system are purely "monetary" in the sense that they must "be reversed because they are not based on any corresponding change in the underlying real facts" so that disappointment of plans, unemployment, and readjustment of production take place in one direction and subsequently need to be undone (Hayek 1937: 31). Unless one holds to the quantity theory in its most "mechanistic" interpretation the changes in income following a disturbance to the balance of payments will give rise to changes in the demand for money on the part of people first affected. So a part of the adjustment is purely monetary, and to this extent real adjustment is avoided. In a mixed system part of this shift from real to monetary adjustment is sacrificed. (Compare with this the discussion (page 127 above) of the built-in lags provided by slow and asymmetrical adjustments of the demand for money.) The damaging effect of all this is exacerbated when the money multiplier is different between countries, which means that every flow of gold from one country to another will be inflationary or deflationary from the world point of view (Hayek 1937: 32–3).

Hayek is emphatic in his insistence that the problem here is institutional and has nothing to do with individual central banks or particular policies. Nor is he arguing against specific ways of "protecting the reserves" but rather with the need to protect them at all. On the contrary, to attempt to avoid the effects of gold movements by offsetting policies, "replacing the gold lost by the central bank by securities bought from the market, is of course not to correct the defects of the mixed system, but to make the international standard altogether ineffective." Here he cites Harvey's testimony to the Macmillan Committee, attesting to the Bank's frequent use of such policy (see Chapter 5). The only solution would be for the Act of 1844 to apply to all forms of money, including deposits, so reserves could "vary by the full amount by which the total circulation of the country might possibly change" (Hayek 1937: 33–4). As we shall see below, he gives a great deal of attention to the problem of so organizing the economy as to achieve this result.

### Flexible exchange rates: independent currencies

To sum up thus far: according to Hayek, the flaw in the fixed exchange rate system is that rates have not been sufficiently fixed. The instability observed, the conversion of real into monetary shocks with the subsequent real effects of these, the overshooting in adjustment and the resulting fluctuations in income and employment, all these stem not from the institution of fixed exchange rates, but from the fact that variations in the money supply of the several countries have not occurred in one-to-one correspondence with changes in international reserves.

Now what of flexible exchange rates, that is, "independent currencies" or "monetary nationalism"? We note first of all that Hayek does not discuss the possibility of free market floating; he is dealing rather with individually managed currencies, exchange rates being determined by the monetary authorities through the use of exchange equalization accounts and the like; this was indeed the prevailing view of variable exchange rates in the 1930s. He is insistent on demonstrating that it is not true that a change in exchange rates is a substitute for all other changes, specifically for changes in relative prices within the individual countries. In this he is, of course, absolutely correct. A country faced with a decline in world demand for one of its export goods will have to experience a relative decline in the price of that good and a shift of production to other exportables, to import substitutes, or to non-tradables.

Assume there is a real shock, a shift in demand between countries. Assume all demands are elastic. The currency of the "deficit" country depreciates and relative prices inside the country are changed. In fact, this is essential for the mechanism to work. Here Hayek is attacking the position that flexible exchange rates operate only on the exchange rate, leaving relative prices inside each country unchanged.[3] The argument for depreciation "seems to be based on the assumption (underlying much of the classical analysis of these problems) that relative prices within each country are uniquely determined by (constant) relative cost" (Hayek 1937: 39). In this case a depreciation of the currency, that is, a uniform reduction of all prices in one country relatively to those in the rest of the world, would be adequate.

But this is not, he argues, the case in either regime. If a specific export industry is faced with declining world demand its relative price will, and must, fall. Under flexible exchange rates, the price of foreign exchange rises, leading to a rise in the domestic price of imported goods and of other exportables, and the required relative price change instead of being "brought about by a reduction of prices in the industry immediately affected is now being brought about largely by a corresponding rise of all other prices" (Hayek 1937: 40). (Here is another example of the classical awareness of the traded-non-traded goods distinction, which got lost during

---

[3] One's immediate response to this is that he was beating a dead horse here. On the other hand, even later arguments in favor of floating rates, such as Milton Friedman's "A case for flexible exchange rates" (Friedman 1953), emphasize heavily the apparent ease with which adjustments can take place if only the relative prices of the currencies are allowed to change, and relegate to footnotes disclaimers to the effect that real changes must of course lead to changes in relative prices and shifts in the allocation of productive resources between sectors within each of the several countries.

the period of high keynesianism and rediscovered later. The earliest rediscovery of it, to my knowledge, is Salter 1959.)

His attack on arguments for flexible exchange rates is directed primarily against Harrod (1933). The theoretical argument in that attack is as follows. If under a pure gold standard money gets redistributed between countries because of real disturbances that is a good thing and will not lead to overall inflation or deflation in either country or to a temporary, unsustainable, boom or bust. If in the face of real changes between two countries, however, the money supply in each of the countries is stabilized, this is equivalent to inflation and deflation respectively, relative to the appropriate money supply. This forces real changes in both economies, changes which are unsustainable and which are not movements toward equilibrium in response to the original real disturbance. The exchange rate change implies that

the relative value of the total amounts of money in each country is changed and ... the process of internal redistribution takes places [sic] in a manner different from that which would occur with an international monetary standard. We have seen before that the variation of exchange rates will in itself bring about a redistribution of spending power in the country, but a redistribution which is no way based on a corresponding change in the underlying real position. There will be a temporary stimulus to particular industries to expand, although there are no grounds which would make a lasting increase in output possible. In short, the successive changes in individual expenditure and the corresponding changes of particular prices will not occur in an order which will direct industry from the old to the new equilibrium position. Or, in other words, the effects of keeping the quantity of money in a region or country constant when under an international monetary system it would decrease are essentially inflationary, while to keep it constant if under an international system it would increase at the expense of other countries would have effects similar to an absolute deflation. (Hayek 1937: 51)

This is very close to the argument discussed (page 123) in his earlier paper (Hayek 1932 [1984]). At this juncture he is discussing "unequal economic progress in different countries" (Hayek 1937: 49) and he is arguing, in opposition to Harrod, that relative monetary contraction and expansion, and relative inflation and deflation (of wages) is part of the adjustment to this phenomenon, not an addition to it. In the case of reduced demand for a country's exports (Hayek 1937: 38 ff), devaluation, unlike the mechanism under the 100 percent gold standard, induces unsustainable changes during the transition. He enumerates two such.

The first case is one in which there is a temporary increase in the profitability of some industries as a result of the devaluation. Eventually rises in cost will eliminate this advantage, so one gets first an expansion and then an unravelling. The resource cost of such unsustainable shifts of resources is a constant theme of his. With a permanent change in world demand, there must be shift of production away from the now less-profitable export which has been initially affected, since the shock was a real one, so some other sector(s) must become permanently more profitable. His argument implies that these are not necessarily those made more profitable by the devaluation. The other temporary, monetary change comes from the monetary ease which results from the decline in imports. This "releases" cash, which the banks will rush to relend, at more favorable terms than prevailed before, causing inflation (which is presumably what is leading to the cost rise making the new investment mentioned above unsustainable).

On the political economy of flexible (independently fixed) exchange rates, he is outspoken and unambiguous. First, he argues that the gold standard, and fixed exchange rates, got an unfairly bad press from the 1925 experience.

It was not a case where with given exchange rates the national price or cost structure of a country as a whole had got out of equilibrium with the rest of the world, but rather that the change in the parities had suddenly upset the relations between all prices inside and outside the country. (Hayek 1937: 45)

That is, the relative price structure within Britain was satisfactory, compatible with equilibrium with respect to the rest of the world; the exchange rate, translating levels of prices domestic and foreign, was out of kilter. Wage rigidities, he argues, serve to put the price *structure* out of line; this is not correctable by exchange rate changes. But the effect of the experience after 1925 was to give

many British economists a curious prepossession with the relations between national price- and cost- and particularly wage-levels . . . And this tendency has received considerable support from the fashionable pseudo-quantitative economics of averages with its argument running in terms of national "price levels", "purchasing power parities", "terms of trade", the "Multiplier", and what not. (Hayek 1937: 45)

The preoccupation of "anglo-saxons" with price levels and wage levels as national phenomena he blames on Irving Fisher. It took a "non-anglo-saxon", Ohlin (1929a), to point out against his English opponents in the reparations debate, "that what mainly mattered was not so much effects on total price levels but rather the effects on the position of particular industries" (Hayek 1937: 46n).

He describes the political problem involved in applying individual national monetary policies to stabilization in the face of a "given" nominal wage, arguing that the money wage is endogenous under these circumstances. Furthermore, he does not believe that it is possible to continue to reduce real wages by devaluation: the workers will catch on and "the belief that it is easier to reduce by the round-about method of depreciation the wages of all workers in a country than directly to reduce the money wages of those who are affected by a given change, will soon prove illusory" (Hayek 1937: 53).

At the same time, if the authorities are determined to avoid having to force down sticky wages by unemployment, and they increase the money supply, they are likely to generate a cycle of overspending, misdirection and mistaken allocation of resources which then has to be reversed. He frequently and specifically refers to Harrod's *International economics* as representative of the fallacy he is speaking of.

### International capital movements

In a truly international system, with fixed exchange rates, changes in short-term capital movements will occur

concurrently with normal fluctuations in international trade; and only certain remaining balances will be settled by a flow of funds, largely of an inter-bank character, induced by differences in interest rates to be earned ... [A]part from ... special cases, it is difficult to see how under a homogeneous international standard, capital movements, and particularly short term capital movements, should be a source of instability or lead to any changes in productive activity which are not justified by corresponding changes in the real conditions. (Hayek 1937: 60)

In this instance again, the problem is not that an international system exists, but that it is flawed. The trouble starts when the central banks react to gold flows by changing their discount rates, and it is this which makes for "frequent and violent" changes in short-term international capital flows (Hayek 1937: 61). (On the other hand, he does not specify the cause of the interest-rate differentials referred to in the quotation above.) Departing from his 1932 position, however, he does not find fault here with the central banks or their managers, but rather with

the differentiation between moneys of different degrees of acceptability or liquidity, the existence of a structure consisting of superimposed layers of reserves of different degrees of liquidity, which makes the movement of short term money rates, and in consequence the movement of short term funds, much more dependent on the liquidity position of the different financial institutions than on changes in the demand for capital for real investment. It is because with "mixed" national monetary systems the movements of short term funds are frequently due, not to changes in the demand for capital for investment, but to changes in the demand for cash as liquidity reserves, that short term international capital movements have their bad reputation as causes of monetary disturbances. And this reputation is not altogether undeserved. (Hayek 1937: 62)

The solution, however, is not flexible exchange rates. Hayek is convinced that short-term capital movements would be greater under flexible rates than under a fixed or an imperfect mixed-fixed system. Under fixed rates, when the rate moves away from par, this raises the expectation that it will return, so that speculation is stabilizing; under flexible rates this does not happen. Still aiming his darts specifically at Harrod, he disputes the position that flexible exchange rates would permit a country to insulate itself from monetary conditions abroad, specifically from "dear money." The idea was not new, he noted, but Harrod had carried it to new lengths by insisting that exchange stabilization must always be sacrificed if it meant raising domestic interest rates. He suggests acidly that Harrod's position implies an unrealistic assessment of the authorities' ability to prevent capital outflows or to offset their effects on the domestic money markets (Hayek 1937: 65–6).

Not so, he says. The effects of a capital outflow on the exchange rate would be inflationary; the export surplus required to offset the capital outflow would increase apparent profits and the demand for capital and put upward pressure on interest rates (Hayek 1937: 66). His point here is that the goal of maintaining permanently lower interest rates at home, while permitting free movement of capital internationally, is unattainable. We have, in short, a clear statement of the integration of current and capital accounts and the lack of independence under floating rates when there is capital mobility; in the 1980s a highly uncontroversial position.

The logic of the position of the "advocates of Monetary Nationalism" would lead them to "demand that monetary policy proper should be supplemented by a strict control of the export of capital." As we shall see in Chapter 10, Keynes, for one, did exactly that, and precisely for that reason. He proposed what Hayek called "a full-fledged system of foreign exchange control" (Hayek 1937: 67). Hayek, however, goes farther than Keynes in arguing the incompatibility of controls on exports of capital with free convertibility on current account; leads and lags in payments would constitute capital transfers unless these were also subject to tight controls. Experience in recent decades will have convinced many economists that Hayek was correct on that one.

Furthermore, even in the absence of international capital transactions, commodity markets serve to link interest rates in the several countries of the world. A rise in interest rates leads to a fall in the price of capital goods. If there is relatively free trade, this will eventually get transmitted to the country whose interest rate was not permitted to rise. Falling prices of capital goods there, with low interest rates, will put tremendous pressure on demand for credit for investment, so the central bank will have to allow interest rates to rise after all or to "allow an indefinite expansion of credit." This is undoubtedly a much longer run view than that envisaged by any of the proponents of floating rates whom he was attacking. At any rate, the logical conclusion of all this is that you must retreat into autarky if you want an independent monetary system. "[T]he ideology of Monetary Nationalism ... will prove ... to be one of the main forces destroying what remnants of an international economic system we still have"[4] (Hayek 1937: 70–1).

The other side of this story is that capital mobility and interest rate changes serve, by transmitting shocks, to dampen them in the originating country, and this will be lost if there is retreat into Monetary Nationalism. (We find, as we shall see in Chapter 14, the same idea clearly expressed by Haberler.) In defense of the "monetary nationalists," however, I think it only fair to point out that this was precisely their point: that countries should have to bear the consequences of their own – and only their own – mistakes. Hayek, as might be expected, went on to point out the loss of world welfare stemming from the implied restriction of long-term capital movements, the lessening of the "international division of labour," the "intensification of the differences in the standard of life between different countries to which it would lead," and the political consequences of all of this (Hayek 1937: 71–2). Again, people such as Keynes and Harrod were quite clearly aware of these arguments in favor of free trade. The issue was over the assessment and evaluation of alternatives: the social welfare function and not the tradeoff curve was the subject of disputation.

### Can the system be made truly international?

What, after all this, does Hayek recommend? On purely economic considerations, the international standard should not be based on gold, because of the "absurd" expenditure of resources in extracting it out of the ground. For practical reasons, however, he declared that as long as there are sovereign states, the standard must be gold.

The major problem, however, remains the existence of fractional-reserve monetary systems in the individual countries, which has destroyed "[t]he homogeneity of the circulating medium of different countries." The alternatives, both pure and idealized, are free banking on the one hand (see the discussion in Chapter 2) which leaves private banks free to choose the volume of their note issue and reserves, as well as the specific market they wish to serve, irrespective of political boundaries; and, on the other hand, a world central bank. These are, as noted, the pure types, and presumably some compromise is inevitable, but the existing one, he submits, "that of national central banks which have no direct power over the bulk of the national circulation but which hold as the sole ultimate reserve a

---

[4] Again, reading Keynes's writings before Bretton Woods and some correspondence of the same period between him and Joan Robinson (see Chapter 10) for example, we see that Hayek's prediction was not far off, in the sense that these writers were willing to go to very considerable lengths on the road away from free and unregulated international trade.

comparatively small amount of gold is . . . one of the most unstable arrangements imaginable" (Hayek 1937: 76–7).

His view of the demand for money is that individuals want to hold a certain level of "liquidity" and allocate this among a number of assets in accordance with their rates of return and people's expectations about how easy it will be to convert them into bank deposits. Thus a rise in uncertainty will lead to an increased demand for bank deposits and cash and a reduction in the supply of deposits. Once more, the root of the problem is the existence of heterogeneous monetary assets. Furthermore, shifts in preferences between assets are "probably a much more potent cause of disturbances" than shifts in the overall preference for money over goods "which have played such a great role in recent refinements of theory" (Hayek 1937: 78–80).

It is the job of the central bank to provide cash when demanded, and also to provide the most liquid money, that which is internationally acceptable. Thus, precisely when there is pressure and uncertainty, the central bank will be called upon to supply more both of its own money and of international money. But it can constrain the demand for the international money only by restricting the supply of its own liabilities. Furthermore, the central bank has been powerless to prevent this situation from arising, since though it is the ultimate provider of cash, it has "little power to prevent the expansion leading to an increased demand for cash" (Hayek 1937: 78–9).

"All this is of course only the familiar phenomenon which Mr. R. G. Hawtrey has so well described as the 'inherent instability of credit'" (Hayek 1937: 80). Where Hayek feels he has added emphasis to Hawtrey's dictum is in highlighting the instability of the demand to substitute different kinds of monetary assets for one another and to suggest that the problem is exacerbated when the banking of a country is centralized, "since the effect of any change in liquidity preference will generally be confined to the group of people who directly or indirectly rely on the same reserve of more liquid assets" (Hayek 1937: 80, italics his). This conjures up the kind of imagery we noted in Bagehot's *Lombard Street*.

In looking for solutions, he comes first to the "so-called Chicago or 100 per-cent plan" (Simons 1936 and Lutz 1936). This is in effect, he says, "an extension of the principles of Peel's Act of 1844 to bank deposits . . . But there is no reason why it should not equally be used to create a homogeneous international currency" (Hayek 1937: 81). One way would be to raise the price of gold enough so every country could have 100 percent backing immediately, and then to start operating the 100 percent rule.

Such a plan would *clearly* require as an essential complement an international control of the production of gold, since the increase in the value of gold would otherwise bring about an enormous increase in the supply of gold. But this would only provide a safety valve probably necessary in any case to prevent the system from becoming all too rigid. (Hayek 1937: 82, italics mine)

This last passage is, to me, ambiguous. It begins as an un-Hayekian demand for controls, which is surprising. Halfway through he observes that this is, in fact, not necessary, and that the rise in the production of gold consequent upon an increase in its price is probably a good thing. Given that a 100 percent reserve plan for gold internationally would require large and growing stocks of gold, it is surprising that he thought otherwise even briefly.

To critics who might object to the 100 percent reserve plan because it amounts to the "abolition of deposit banking as we know it" Hayek would reply that this is precisely its attraction. However, Simons abandoned it, and Hayek rejects it for the same reason, namely the resilience and inventiveness of the market: just as deposit banking developed after 1844 in response to the limitation on note issue, so other forms of bank liabilities, near-monies, would take on increased importance and new ones would emerge. Furthermore, these new forms might be even more difficult to control than demand deposits (Hayek 1937: 82–4). (We encountered this point in Chapter 2 in the discussion of the nineteenth-century debates over the definition of "money".)

There is thus not a great deal left by way of reform possibilities. The major goal is to make the various kinds of money as highly substitutable for one another as possible, so that shifts between them should leave the quantity of money unchanged (Hayek 1937: 84). For international money the implication is, of course, the opposite of that of the monetary nationalists; exchange rates should be made still more fixed by "a system of international par clearance" so that they could not fluctuate even inside the gold points. This would require

an international gold settlement fund on the lines of that operated by the Federal Reserve System . . . The main aim here would of course be rather to remove one of the main causes of international movements of short term funds than to prevent such movements or to offset their effects by means which will only increase the inducement to such movements. (Hayek 1937: 84–5)

Like the crisis writers (see Chapter 11) Hayek is concerned about short-term capital movements, particularly when they result from speculative responses to movements of exchange rates within the gold points. His remedy for that is to eliminate the gold points by narrowing the band to a point. Exchange rates should be fixed and "secured by a system of international par clearance" (Hayek 1937: 84).

Invariability of exchange rates is only one part of the solution, however. The second branch is to decrease the heterogeneity of different kinds of money within countries. Here the similarity between Hayek and his latter-day disciples of the new classical school dwindles, since he comes down firmly for very powerful central banks which engage in extraordinarily fine tuning. First, the central banks must hold gold reserves large enough so that a change in their reserves will not force them to undertake multiple contraction. The point is that there be no "'secondary' contractions and expansions of the credit superstructure of the countries concerned" (Hayek 1937: 85–6). The world gold supply was large enough, he felt, to accomplish this, but it was badly distributed. The countries holding large stocks of gold should

reduce the price of gold in order to direct the stream of gold to those countries which are not yet in a position to resume gold payments. Only when the price of gold had fallen sufficiently to enable those countries to acquire sufficient reserves should a general and simultaneous return to a free gold standard be attempted. (Hayek 1937: 86)

He had nothing like 100 percent reserves in mind. If the central banks started off with gold reserves equal to "one third of the total monetary circulation" he felt this would be adequate. Again, under a stable system such as the one he was proposing, he was convinced that gold losses would be much less frequent and of smaller magnitude than in the past. The large fluctuations in countries' gold holdings in the past were due to the combination of fractional-reserve banking, which injected lags into the mechanism, and the attempts of central banks to offset or sterilize the flows (Hayek 1937: 87–8). The task of central banks would be much more difficult under his proposal. The recommendation is not that they should change their liabilities in any fixed proportion to changes in their reserves, even unity. It is, rather, to influence "the total volume of money in their countries in such a way that this total would change by the same absolute amounts as their reserves."

[A]s the amount of ordinary bank deposits and other forms of common means of exchange based on a given volume of central bank money will be different at different times, this means that the central bank . . . would frequently have to change the amount of central bank money independently of changes in its reserves and occasionally even in a direction opposite to that in which its reserves may change. (Hayek 1937: 89)

It would indeed require the greatest art and discernment for a central bank to succeed in making the credit money provided by the private banks behave as a purely metallic circulation would behave under similar circumstances. (Hayek 1937: 90)

Given these requirements, it is not surprising that he does not end on a highly optimistic note, noting that the difficulties of fine tuning, the "impossibility of prescribing any fixed rule," and the exposure to political pressure "certainly justify grave doubts." The alternative, however, he viewed as being wholly impractical politically. If banking were more competitive, if there were more banks, the solution would be to let the Bank of England Issue Department issue notes in a one-to-one ratio with gold, "while the duty of holding appropriate reserves is left to individual banks," though the central bank could be lurking in the background for ultimate suspension of note limitation and issues of emergency currency in case of a run (Hayek 1937: 91–2). In short, he is suggesting, presumably as a second- or third-best solution, unregulated "free banking" coupled with a strict relationship (unity) between changes in the volume of the monetary base and the balance of payments. It is interesting that he saw the major obstacle to this to be the oligopolistic nature of British banking. It is astonishing, to me, that he inserted the final qualification that the central bank should, after all is said and done, be ready to provide "last resort" facilities to the system "in case of a run."

Forty years later Hayek (1976) had changed his mind: he both despaired of getting any government or central bank to behave "responsibly" and had accepted a solution which previously he had rejected: free banking and free money. He would allow banks to issue paper money competitively – not perfectly competitively, because each money would have a patent on its name, so the issuer would be responsible for it. And he would allow perfectly free international trade both in banking and in currency. He had changed his mind, he said, only with regard to technical problems, not to his basic outlook. Referring to Hayek (1937) as "a series of lectures hastily and badly written" (Hayek 1976: 81n) he remained faithful to the view that nationally managed flexible exchange rates was a very poor arrangement, and that, if governments persisted in controlling and managing money, a gold standard was the (second) best solution (Hayek 1976: 99). But better by far would be totally free trade in money. His argument here was that gold was "a wobbly anchor" and worldwide acceptance of a gold standard would probably lead once more to a gold exchange standard. Paper money was a bad thing when it was imposed by force on the public, by the government, with the power of enforcing its legal tender quality. When issued freely and competitively by issuers who would have to stand behind their commitment to convert their notes (to a foreign currency or to a bundle of commodities), there was nothing wrong with paper as such. The main point, in 1976 as in 1937, is that the crucial role of prices in an economy is that of relative prices. Just as moving a country's price level relative to the world's under flexible exchange rates blocked the necessary adjustment in relative prices inside the country, so stabilizing a country's price level in a trading world is likely to "disturb and . . . not assist the functioning of the market." Citing Adam Smith he insists that private enterprise, serving its own self interest, and staking its existence on giving the public "what currency it liked best" is the only institutional body capable of providing good money (Hayek 1976: 83–100).

In terms of the subject of this study, Hayek can be interpreted to say, in essence, that the subject does not, or should not, exist, that trade between national units is an irrelevant and uninteresting magnitude to study, to stabilize, or to be concerned with in any way. Prices move, output shifts, and trade flows, between regions or between areas, but not, presumably, in any important way, between countries. A true internationalist.

## Hawtrey

Hawtrey's *bête noire* is the powerful effect of Bank rate policy. He is a near-keynesian, and he is at least related to the crisis school line of thought, in his interest in the issue of short-term capital movements and their generally undesirable effects. The crisis writers (Chapter 11), however, were exercised over capital movements going upstream, "abnormal" in Marco Fanno's (1939) terminology. Hawtrey devotes a good deal of attention to capital movements which are endogenous (in the sense that they are elicited by central bank policy), financing (that is, accommodating), and a Bad Thing. They are not adjusting, as in the neoclassical view, nor are they, as in the crisis school, exogenous shocks requiring adjustment in the rest of the balance of payments. In this sense he is similar to Hayek.

He is emphatic about the role of money in influencing real variables. In *The art of central banking*, he makes some very clear statements about the effects of money and monetary policy on both domestic spending and the balance of trade, and the role of the central bank, through interest rate policy, in affecting both short-term capital movements and internal spending on non-traded goods – the neoclassical mechanism. But he views it as a problem, exacerbated by the fact that in a modern banking system changes induced by the central bank are multiplied in their effects on the supply of money and credit.

A major theme in his writings was internal-external balance tradeoffs. He emphasizes the destabilizing domestic effects of policy designed to maintain (short-run) external balance, that is, to protect the gold reserves of the central bank. In a sense, however, he does not even think of it as a *tradeoff*, since the traditional policy directed at maintaining external balance generally failed, in his view, to achieve even that end.

### The importance of money in domestic activity

His primary concern, to repeat, was the real impact of monetary events. Money matters. And credit matters. And the interest rate matters. And benighted central bankers, less perceptive than some of their nineteenth-century predecessors, were likely to aggravate rather than moderate any problems or crises. A few quotations will give the reader a flavor of the intensity of his disapproval, the tenor of his beliefs, and the charm of his writing.

Perhaps motives of caution suggested the conservation of the gold reserves. That is the kind of caution that spares water during a conflagration. (Hawtrey 1932: 238)

When under a gold standard a central bank contracts credit . . . the problem of adjustment put before the industry of the country is no more than the accommodation of the level of wages to the international price level. If the international price level is stable, the extent of the requisite adjustment is limited.

But when the central banks of the gold standard countries are, between them, taking measures which are calculated to reduce the world price level, the adjustment involved is limited only by the severity of the measures taken. (Hawtrey 1932: 281–2)

While concerted wisdom may be necessary to preserve stability, the calamities of the past three years have been caused not by the mere absence of co-operation, but by a disastrously synchronised unwisdom. (Hawtrey 1932: 248)

On the specific subject of the importance of interest rate policy to the level of domestic activity and its consequent effect on the current account (which we met in the Cunliffe Committee), Hawtrey cites with approval the testimony of Horsely Palmer, then Governor of the Bank of England, testifying to the Parliamentary Committee of 1832. Surprisingly, in his testimony Palmer did not even mention the effect on short-term capital inflow. Hawtrey implies (see below) that this idea gained currency in the years after Palmer's tenure as Governor.

"By the term excessive issues," says Palmer (Qn. 925), "I have intended to refer to such excess as has been exhibited by a state of prices higher than those in other countries, thereby rendering the foreign exchanges unfavourable and causing a return of notes upon the Bank for bullion." Asked "What is the process by which the Bank would calculate upon rectifying the exchange by means of a reduction of its issues" (Qn. 678) he replied: "The first operation is to increase the value of money; with the increased value of money, there is less facility obtained by the commercial public in the discount of their paper; that naturally tends to limit transactions and to the reduction of prices; the reduction of prices will so far alter our situation with foreign countries, that it will be no longer an object to import, but the advantage will rather be upon the export, the gold and silver will then come back into the country and rectify the contraction that previously existed." By the "value of money" was meant, of course, the short-term rate of interest.

So clear a recognition of the use of Bank rate as an instrument for affecting the price level formulated a hundred years ago, is remarkable. It is all the more so, considering that only very tentative steps had at that period been taken towards the practical application of the system. (Hawtrey 1932: 135–6)

Hawtrey's own view of the mechanism, Palmer's understanding of which so impressed him, can be found neatly stated in his discussion of Keynes's

*Treatise.* Reading it reveals his reason for the approbation he heaps on Palmer. (As I read Hawtrey, it seems that the differences between him and Keynes were less sharp than a reading of what each said about the other might suggest.)

But Hawtrey adds a pre-keynesian twist to the Palmer position. Inadequate credit, he argues, resulted in general in unemployment. The unemployment problem, as it presented itself to industry throughout the world in the century preceding 1914, was a product of the trade cycle. Compression of consumers' income and outlay meant a shrinkage of demand for all goods. For non-traded goods the result is both a decline in prices and a decline in industrial activity. The result was unemployment. Unemployment might be avoided by a drastic reduction of wages, but that too often meant friction and labor disputes. At the same time shrinkage of demand meant a decline in profits, or the conversion of profit into loss, and a writing down of assets which often threatened insolvency (Hawtrey 1932: 207). For traded goods, there is also a reduction of demand, some of which involves reduced imports, but some of which is a decline in domestic purchases of traded goods (Hawtrey 1932: 403).

### The importance of money in international adjustment

What should, in his view, be done to bring about equilibrium in international payments, is not absolutely clear. Since he viewed most disturbances as monetary in origin, a stable money supply would eliminate the need for serious counter-cyclical action, and long-term lending would tend to finance balance of trade surpluses. I do not remember, however, that he has spelled this out. "What has led in the past to monetary contraction has been a *preceding excessive monetary expansion*" (Hawtrey 1950: 428, italics his). The implication is that fundamental, structural disequilibrium is not a problem; much of Keynes's writing on this subject gives the same impression.

Hayek's acerbic criticism of him notwithstanding, I would argue that Hawtrey shared Hayek's view that the amount of fluctuation in activity and/ or prices engendered by a full-fledged gold standard is appropriate, but that the disturbance caused by fractional reserve banking and the importance of credit in a modern economy exacerbate the variations and make the economy unstable. A central bank following a policy of stabilizing the exchanges enhances this instability. In this sense, Hawtrey deserves the title anti-neoclassical.

In the Ricardian theory of foreign trade, he argues, the money supply varied one-to-one with the gold stock. "The practice of the Bank of England, as explained to the Parliamentary Committee of 1832, was intended to make the currency system behave as if that were so." The Act of 1844 enshrined this precept into law. "And in fact the currency did behave substantially as a purely metallic currency would have behaved." But as the superstructure of credit grew, the system diverged from the Ricardian theory, "for it [credit] furnished the principal medium of payment of the community. *Instead of a gain or loss of gold automatically modifying the value of the currency unit, it became no more than a signal* which prompted the Bank of England to relax or restrict credit" (Hawtrey 1932: 195, italics mine).

His bottom line, therefore, is similar to Hayek's, but he arrives at it by a different route. According to work now being done by Adam Klug, Hayek's conclusion was driven by his commitment to the framework of intertemporal equilibrium. Hawtrey was much more concerned with the destabilizing effect on "trade", that is wholesale and retail commerce, of monetary swings caused by the Bank's misapplying the Act of 1844. Hawtrey's view of the real adjustments involves both the long and the short run. The decline in domestic relative to "external" prices causes, in the short run, a reduced demand for traded goods, especially imports.

On the other hand *ultimate* equilibrium requires the adjustment of wages to the internal price level, and this when it occurs gives rise to a windfall gain or loss to the producers of foreign trade products, and therefore in the long run to increased or reduced productive power being applied to those products. (Hawtrey 1932: 404, italics his)

This sounds much more like the late classical analysis, including Ohlin.

### The role of short-term capital movements

Horsely Palmer's alertness to the effect of Bank rate on domestic activity was forgotten, Hawtrey argues, and central bank policy, including that of the Bank of England, did not follow his prescriptions. Instead the (neoclassical) doctrine developed that the Bank of England should raise interest rates in order to attract short-term capital. He argues that in 1930 it was denied that this would intensify the depression – though, Hawtrey says, if it did not do so then it could not work. Furthermore, improving the exchanges by attracting short-term capital inflows is futile, "utterly precarious and delusive. And when credit is restricted for that purpose, the deadly effects of deflation are not the less operative because they are not designed" (Hawtrey 1932: 219). Short-term capital movements are not only not equilibrating in that they fail to restore long-term equilibrium, but they are disturbing in and of themselves because "the progressive accumulation of short-term indebtedness becomes itself an independent threat to equilibrium" (Hawtrey 1932: 413).

The theme is repeated in *The gold standard in theory and practice*. High interest rates, "dear money," deters "traders" from borrowing and buying goods, so demand and income shrink. Foreign money enters temporarily, but this is "transitory and precarious . . . The contraction of the consumers' income is the only substantial corrective" (Hawtrey 1933: 42–3). In the fourth edition of *Currency and credit*, published in 1950, Hawtrey still maintained the same view, expressed in very similar terms. Short-term capital inflows were "counter-productive," and the employment and depression generated by high interest rates constituted "an uncomfortable and, what is more, a dangerous procedure" (Hawtrey 1950: 166). Most balances are not highly mobile with respect to short-term interest rates. Those that are will move quickly, at once, when there is a change in rates, which will drive the spot rate up and the forward rate in the opposite direction. There will be instant, and instantaneous, portfolio adjustment, and then pressure on spot and forward rates will stop. In any case, "it is essentially a *transitory* phase" (Hawtrey 1932: 409–10, italics his). Even if the interest rate differentials persist, the flows will end. And when the difference in rates is closed, the balances that flowed before will reverse direction. It is thus a mistake both to raise Bank rate in order to attract inflows and to keep it up in order to prevent outflows. Encouraging foreigners to hold a portfolio of one's short-term debt is dangerous, since it is "the equivalent of a negative gold reserve" (Hawtrey 1932: 410).

### The debate with Keynes over remedies

Hawtrey included in his testimony to the Macmillan Committee a detailed discussion of Keynes's proposals which appeared both in the *Treatise* and in testimony to the committee, in which Keynes argued in favor of trying to insulate domestic interest rates by activities on the forward market or by changing the gold points. Hawtrey's critique was prepared for the Macmillan Committee, and published as Chapter VII of *The art of central banking*. Keynes's proposals appear in Chapter 36, Volume II, of the *Treatise*, aptly entitled "The Problem of National Autonomy." Hawtrey interprets Keynes's proposals regarding appropriate central bank behavior to be directed at the danger "that the continuance of the discrepancy between the foreign balance and the *long-term* foreign lending may be made possible by an offsetting movement of *short-term* foreign lending" (Hawtrey 1932: 413, italics his). The generally accepted policy, according to Keynes, is to raise Bank rate, which causes a capital inflow "which restores apparent equilibrium, at a stage at which the rise of Bank rate is still quite insufficient to re-establish underlying equilibrium. The country is therefore placed in the position of borrowing short and lending long." In keeping with the statements quoted above, he argues that the capital inflow simply delays the contractionary effect of the tight money and "becomes itself an independent threat to equilibrium. We must distinguish here between the *apparent* equilibrium, which depends upon a flow of short-term investments, and *underlying* equilibrium, which means equality between the items other than short-term investment" (Hawtrey 1932: 413, italics his).

Thus far, Keynes and Hawtrey are in agreement: the scenario described above is an undesirable one and to be avoided. With this end in mind, Keynes proposed that the central bank should be in a position to affect the forward premium or discount on the exchange rate (and, to avoid a loss to itself, offset this with an equal spot transaction in the opposite direction, as a hedge). The point would be to close the interest arbitrage gap and allow the central bank to use Bank rate as a tool to control the basic balance of payments and achieve "underlying" equilibrium without the temporary offsetting short-term capital flows which both men viewed with displeasure. With him neoclassicism has come full circle, from the use of Bank rate to achieve temporary financing, to the addition of domestic equilibrating effects, and finally to the attempt to avoid the very short-term financing with which the approach began. (Later, in the case of Keynes, the point was to free Bank rate as a tool, not for payments equilibrium, but for domestic stabilization policy.)

Under the gold standard, however, the forward discount or premium cannot be very high, since they are constrained by the gold shipping points; hence Keynes's second proposal, to widen the gold points to 1 percent in each direction. Keynes associated the two proposals; Hawtrey says that the second is not dependent on the first: a wider spread between the gold points, without any intervention in the forward markets, "would allow more room for the natural obstacle provided by exchange risk against the migration of money" (Hawtrey 1932: 415). The first, however, would seem to be dependent on the second in order to be effective.

Suppose there is a deficit in the overall [basic] balance. Bank rate is raised and a short-term capital inflow ensues. "The Central Bank is likely to make a more moderate rise in Bank rate than would otherwise be necessary, and so to protract the process of returning to equilibrium." Once all the mobile capital has come in, if equilibrium has not been restored, Bank rate must be kept up, but gold will flow out "till underlying equilibrium has been secured." Or underlying equilibrium may be reached by the time the portfolio adjustment has been finished. "In either event the reduction of Bank rate to the international level will lead to an outflow of the foreign money temporarily attracted by the high rate" (Hawtrey 1932: 415–16). This is dangerous, according to Hawtrey, and he attributes to Keynes awareness of the same danger. Note that the short-term capital movements here are a stock adjustment response rather than the flow phenomenon which they became in the early Mundell-Fleming literature (see Chapter 16).

The problem Hawtrey perceived was that when equilibrium has been restored, the subsequent return of the short-term capital will be wholly in gold and "an embarrassment". To avoid said embarrassment, "the Central Bank is likely to continue the credit contraction, thereby carrying deflation further than international equilibrium by itself would require. Considering the difficulties and distresses anyhow involved in deflation, this may be highly injurious." At this juncture, Hawtrey notes, intervening in forward markets will not help. He may be slightly unfair to Keynes here, since I do not have the impression that the latter was suggesting it would. The problem is that, as is often the case, the effects are not symmetrical. The forward premium has to be raised to avoid the capital inflow when Bank rate is raised; inducing a forward discount to prevent repatriation of foreign funds later is, however, useless. Maintaining a discount on forward exchange may prevent covered arbitrage. But a person "who has already invested abroad, and who can no longer make any net gain from the rate of interest, is not likely to be induced to *leave* his money abroad a little longer by the opportunity of selling it forward in the foreign exchange market on more favorable terms" (Hawtrey 1932: 416, italics his).

There are two points here worthy of note. The first is the implied criticism of Keynes, though there is no reason to suppose that Keynes was oblivious to this point. The second is the implication in this whole discussion that the capital flow one is talking about is foreign capital coming in, and leaving, rather than home country residents repatriating their short-term assets when interest rates rise. Formally this distinction is unimportant, but the passage cited above suggests a (reasonable) asymmetry in asset preferences, and in this case it does make a difference. (We saw a similar distinction in Bloomfield, for somewhat analogous reasons.)

However, Hawtrey (in contrast, evidently, to Keynes) is not opposed to all short-term capital inflow during an adjustment. The reason for this is that if you allow no capital inflow, as in the Keynes proposals, gold continues to flow out until underlying equilibrium has been restored, so that when equilibrium has been achieved the gold reserves are too low and the central bank has to have "a further spell of credit contraction." This seems to me to be a mistake. If there has been a basic shift in conditions, the new equilibrium money supply, hence the reserves of the central bank, should remain lower than they were before the disturbance. In this case it would be a mistake for the central bank to "maintain its reserves up to a normal standard" as Hawtrey suggests it ought (Hawtrey 1932: 417).

Hawtrey argues that if there is a capital inflow, the country finds itself with debts when equilibrium is restored, though there has been no gold loss. As soon as Bank rate is returned to the world level, gold is lost. Alternatively, he considers a second situation, in which Keynes's plan has been adopted, and the capital inflow has been prevented; the outflow of gold continued until equilibrium was restored, by which time gold has been lost to the same extent as in the first case. In short, he is arguing that regardless of what policy is followed with respect to short-term balance of payments equilibrium, the ultimate loss of reserves depends on how long it takes to achieve *fundamental* equilibrium, because during that time either gold flows out or you accrue short-term debt. "The only substantial harm that the inflow of foreign money might do is to *delay* the credit contraction, so that the period over which foreign balances are accumulating exceeds that over which, in the alternative, gold would be flowing out" (Hawtrey 1932: 417, italics his).

I think the disagreement with Keynes (I am not aware of an answer by Keynes to this point) is buried in the question of what is involved in achieving fundamental equilibrium. To return to the point I made above, if there has been a fundamental disequilibrium requiring a permanently lower level of money income, the new equilibrium gold stock of the central bank should have been lowered as well, so the loss of gold during the adjustment process is appropriate. Hawtrey is right, I think, in suggesting that it makes no difference whether you lose the gold directly or by repaying short-term capital borrowings. His point seems to be that you want to prevent importing more short-term capital than the gold you will lose if you do not import any capital at all (Hawtrey 1932: 418). This converts the problem into one solely of timing.

The short-term capital inflow could be more than enough to offset the gold flows, so that the country would accumulate even greater debts. Further-more, "the inflow of gold would tend to make Bank rate ineffective, but that tendency could be counteracted by sales of securities in the open market." (However, since the object is to avoid domestic contraction, "making bank rate ineffective," it seems to me, is precisely what the policy is intended to achieve.) The optimal policy, therefore, is not to prevent capital inflows during the adjustment (since this makes no difference), "but to prevent the inflow from reaching such proportions as to cause an actual inflow of gold" (Hawtrey 1932: 418). In sum, Hawtrey shares with Keynes the view that raising Bank rate in order to attract short-term foreign capital is a mistake, and that the main purpose of higher interest rates in periods of deficit is "a compression of the consumers' income." The benefit to be expected and hoped for from Keynes's proposals, in Hawtrey's view, is not an immediate practical one but rather a "change of attitude" on this issue on the part of "people practically concerned in finance" (Hawtrey 1932: 424).

## The revisionists

Hayek and Hawtrey attacked the neoclassical position normatively. That is, they were opposed to having the central bank do what the Cunliffe Committee had both described and prescribed. The revisionists, on the other hand, Bloomfield (1959) and (1963), Brown (1940), Triffin (1947) and Whale (1937 [1953]), questioned the historical accuracy of the neoclassical view; it is not always clear whether or not they thought it would have been a good idea, but they are quite convinced that the world did not function as Cunliffe described it. I shall try to present the flavor of their message. A detailed report would be lengthy indeed and would lead us further into the realm of economic history than I should like to venture.

Brown (1940) has written a highly detailed and ambitious two-volume study of the gold standard from 1914 to 1934. The story is intertwined, however, with comparisons with the prewar period. He makes the point, frequently, that the pre-World War I system was a sterling system, dominated in every way by and from and in London (just as the post-World War II system was a dollar standard). Thus he argues "that the relatively successful functioning of . . . [the gold] standard before the war was due to the attainment by London of a central clearing position in the world's international financial system, and to the manner in which the responsibilities of that position were carried out" (Brown 1940: x). One of the effects of the dominance of London was that "the key to the world's foreign exchange mechanism lay in the sterling balances of foreign bankers kept in London" (Brown 1940: xv). This he contrasts with the postwar period, when there was no "focal point" (Brown 1940: xxiii) and it was never clear whether life centered on London, New York, or Paris – or on all three; the situation was analogous to that of "a local clearing house with three members of nearly equal importance, each pursuing an independent policy in the extension of credit" (Brown 1940: 790). As Keynes argued, the United States (the Federal Reserve Board) did not know how to manage an international system (Keynes 1923: 168–9). London did not have a well-developed foreign exchange market (just as the United States did not under the Bretton Woods system), since sterling was the currency dealt in, and London did not need a special market in which to buy and sell sterling (Brown 1940: 637–41).

What I find interesting here is the persistence and ubiquity of the notion that there never was the kind of multilateralism and symmetry implied by all the formal models and even by the Cunliffe Committee Report: the international monetary system apparently always had an active major center or it had serious problems, even with fixed exchange rates and a putatively unyielding metallic standard. The implications for the present situation are intriguing, to say the least.

Triffin (1947) and (1964) goes further and argues that a crucial role in the actual system before World War I was performed by the integration, not only of markets for short-term financial assets, but also of the commodity and labor markets of the major countries of the center. Discussing what he takes to be the received doctrine, he describes, in a masterpiece of succinct eclecticism (1947), the workings of a fairly pure gold standard with neither a central bank nor, presumably, private banks whose obligations were part of the money supply.

International balance, if disturbed, would be restored because of the effects of the ensuing domestic contraction or expansion on relative cost and interest levels at home and abroad and the resulting shifts in trade and capital movements. The automatic monetary contraction produced by gold exports would raise interest rates and attract capital from abroad. It would at the same time exert a downward pressure on domestic prices and costs, thus stimulating exports and discouraging imports. Both of these movements – capital and trade – would tend to correct the balance of payments deficit in which they originated.

Modern theories of international trade and capital movements would incorporate two further major elements in this analysis. One is the elasticity of supply and demand for imports and exports, the other the direct income effects associated with balance of payments disequilibria. (Triffin 1947: 48, 48n)

In 1947 he viewed the existence of a central banking system as necessitating a major revision in this theory. "Little attention is usually paid . . . to the latent antinomy between central banking and the classical gold standard" (Triffin 1947: 49). But in 1964 he accepted the neoclassical story, arguing that the problem was that there were too many departures from the script. "These 'automatic' adjustment forces were strengthened and speeded up by central banks through the so-called 'rules of the game'" (Triffin 1964: 2) before World War I, but in the postwar period the rules were "widely violated" by the central banks with their policies of sterilization and offsetting reserve flows.

But he then exposes the theory to factual "testing", looking at Europe from 1880–1960. Here he does not seriously distinguish between the gold-standard-rules-of-the-game era before World War I and the deviations of the interwar period. His generalization is that trade and income and prices in the several countries moved in tandem rather than countervailing fashion. Wage rate reductions, he agrees with Keynes (see Chapter 6, page 110), never were significant, even in the prewar period, and would have been no easier to effect in that period than later. On the contrary, the only really sizable reductions in money wages occurred after World War I, in 1920–2 and in the early 1930s (Triffin 1964: 3–9).

As to central bank behavior, he cites Bloomfield to the effect that it was no better before World War I than after. Bloomfield is more cautious, however, than Triffin suggests, though he does cast serious doubt on the textbook functioning of the mechanism. In (1959) he concluded that though central banks did not deliberately offset reserve movements, and a majority (but not all) of them moved their discount rates in the right direction, their holdings of domestic assets generally moved the wrong way; that is, all the central banks studied more often than not (and most of them, much more often) experienced changes in their holdings of domestic credit instruments in the opposite direction to changes in their international assets. The rules of the game required them to move in the same direction, reinforcing foreign reserve outflows with credit contraction. However, as I noted, Bloomfield is somewhat cautious in interpreting these data, particularly since they are annual and he is well aware of the problems involved in using annual data for a problem like this one (Bloomfield 1959: 47–51). For this reason I have grouped his name with that of Triffin and the others with a good deal of hesitation and reservation.

The central role of Britain had some effects which enhanced the responses to imbalances and others which dampened them. The automatic response was suppressed to the extent that many of Britain's trading partners kept their foreign exchange reserves in the form of sterling bank accounts, so the total of these was unchanged when the U.K. balance of payments fluctuated, eliminating the need both for gold flows and for credit contraction (Triffin 1964: 6). Presumably the effect of the shift in ownership of claims on banks is important in that it made *multiple* credit contraction unnecessary. But the purchasing power in the hands of the British public was nevertheless reduced in such a case. Aiding the adjustment was the impact of a tightening in the British money market on the cost of financing international trade in raw materials, causing a liquidation of stocks and a decline in price of primary products, a major item in British imports. The effect on the prices of British industrial exports was much smaller and slower, so the British terms of trade improved in the interim, leading to direct improvement in her balance of payments.

According to Triffin, financing, accommodating capital flows in response to interest rate changes seem to have been important only for the pivotal country, the United Kingdom (Triffin 1964: 5). However, there was a good deal of smoothing and financing going on by way of variations in long-term capital movements – more than was suggested by most of the theories in which long-term capital flows are basically taken as exogenous in a model of the balance of payments. This was argued by Keynes repeatedly, in his insistence on surplus countries' making their surpluses available to the deficit countries, both as historical fact and as institutional desideratum (Keynes 1940–4 [1980: 31, 179–80]; Chapter 10, page 192 ff) and at one point going so far as to argue that capital movements should be *restricted* to cases in which capital was flowing from surplus to deficit countries (1940–4 [1980: 16–17]). It was a major point in Nurkse (1956) and was supported, according to Triffin, by a number of historical studies, which he cites. Not adjustment of trade fluctuations, but the financing of them, was the predominant phenomenon. But these cyclical fluctuations in capital movements, Triffin argues, played a stabilizing role for the industrialized capital exporters only, and not for the developing capital importers. "The exchange-rate instability of most underdeveloped countries – other than those of colonial or semi-colonial areas tightly linked to their metropolitan country's currency and banking system – finds here one of its many explanations" (Triffin 1964: 7–8).

Though specifically questioning and attacking the notion of the gold standard as a highly automatic, smoothly functioning system, Triffin drops a heavy hint of the monetary approach, when he argues that one of the major reasons for the apparent smoothness of the prewar mechanism was that, with fixed exchange rates, "national *export* prices remained strongly bound together among all competing countries" and "[i]nflationary pressures . . . spilled out *directly* . . . into balance-of-payments deficits rather than into uncontrolled rises of internal prices, costs, and wage levels" (Triffin 1964: 10, italics his). Additionally, in sharp contrast to writers such as Bagehot, Triffin argued that *internal* drain of specie from the central reserves had a stabilizing effect in that it limited the ability of the central bank to expand credit "very much as commercial banks' credit and deposit expansion may be limited today by the drain on their paper-currency reserves" (Triffin 1964: 11).

Whale's somewhat idiosyncratic revision of the "classical gold standard mechanism" is different from the Bloomfield-Triffin stance. The quantity theory of money combined with the fact of full-bodied money with no fractional-reserve banking would generate the classical model. But in a world of fractional reserve banking, he argued, the classical mechanism necessarily involved changes in the rate of interest. However, as a statement of history, he alleged that, at least for Britain, France, and Belgium, the central banks before World War I did not observe "'the rules of the game'; and yet the system worked" (Whale 1937 [1953: 154]). The question then, of course, is why it worked. What happened, in his view, was that a reduction in demand for a country's exports, for example, would lead to reduced income and *hence* to a decrease in the demand for money and *hence* to a reduction in the rate of interest and *hence* to an outflow of capital and often a resulting outflow of gold. The causality is essentially reversed. This makes a difference because the effect on the structure of the economy, and on the structure of saving and investment, is different in the two cases. "I think there is a difference between a change in the demand for loans due to a change in the aggregate demand for products, and one due to a change in the relationship between the Market Rate of interest and the marginal productivity of capital schedule." If interest rates fall when the productivity of capital is unchanged, there will be an increase in investment of the capital deepening type (not his terminology) and "an immediate distortion, in the Austrian terminology, of the structure of production" (Whale 1937 [1953: 157]). Even without his specific mention of the Austrians we can recognize here an argument very reminiscent of that of Hayek, discussed above. He is less stern in his disapproval of the monetary authorities and condemnation of the system, but he shares with Hayek the sense of an external shock being converted into a real structural shift in the domestic economy through a monetary process.

He offers an alternative explanation of historical facts: A decline in the demand for exports of a country leads to a fall in output in the export industry and then in other industries and these declines in themselves cause a shrinking of the money (credit) supply, which need not have been caused by a rise in the rate of interest. But if the money supply is inelastic, interest rates may rise and it is this which will induce international capital and gold flows. The desirability of making the money supply more elastic by something like the banking school recommendations is one of the implications Whale draws from this analysis.

## Summary

We have examined here the writings of a number of people who, often for widely different reasons, addressed themselves to the neoclassical paradigm, examined it, and found it wanting.

Hayek on the whole agreed that the system had worked the way the neoclassical generalization said it had. This it was that had led to instability and given fixed exchange rates and an international monetary standard a bad name. Only rigidly fixed exchange rates and a money supply that varied, at the margin, one-to-one with the imbalance of payments could lead to worldwide stability. The problem was how to achieve this end, and here Hayek moved from detailed intervention and fine tuning on the part of the central bank to advocacy of (almost) wholly free and private banking and money creation.

Hawtrey also accepted the facts as spelled out by the neoclassicals, but disapproved of the resulting instability in money and short-term credit markets. He argued, furthermore, that the so-called financing achieved by short-term capital flows was at best useless and at worst exacerbated the instability; these monetary effects heightened the depressing effects of the high interest rates beyond that needed to restore basic balance of payments equilibrium, so that monetary disturbances were turned into unnecessary real ones.

The revisionists, in contrast, argued that the system historically had never worked in the neoclassical manner. On the one hand, it was much less automatic, in that central banks were regularly breaking the famous rules. On the other hand, it was in a sense much less deliberate, in that historical accident had a great deal to do with making the system viable: the centrality of London to every kind of international market that mattered, the key currency role of sterling, and the general close linkage between the major economies of the center – all these explained the smooth working and apparent success of the system before World War I, and their absence, in the minds of most of these writers, similarly accounted for its breakdown in the interwar period.

# Indian currency and finance; a tract on monetary reform

I shall concentrate primarily on Keynes's formal writings and leave aside his letters, newspaper articles, and memoranda, with two important exceptions. I felt that I must devote attention to the letters and memoranda issuing from his preparations for the Bretton Woods meetings (which, by the way, take up a whole volume of his *Collected writings*). And I have incorporated, in the discussion of the Macmillan Committee Report (Chapter 6), Keynes's own testimony to that committee, of which he was a member.

Somebody has commented (may I be forgiven the churlishness of not referring to the person by name? I do not remember where I read it) that Keynes's writings moved monotonically from openness to closedness over his lifetime. His first book, *Indian currency and finance* (1913), described the functioning of an economy on the gold reserve standard, specifically a sterling standard, with India holding its reserves in sterling and Britain holding its in gold. It was written at a time when the continued existence of the international gold standard (or at least the gold exchange standard) was not seriously open to doubt.

The next work, the *Tract on monetary reform*, was about the world monetary system. It appeared in 1923, when Britons in particular were asking what kind of regime, and what exchange rates, would be appropriate to the postwar world. *A treatise on money* (1930) can be described as the macroeconomics of an open economy, written while Britain was, in the event temporarily, back on gold; the *General theory* (1936) is a macroeconomic model of a closed economy.

As we shall see, the model behind the *Tract* and that of the *Treatise* are virtually the same, but the emphasis in the former is on the problems of the management of money in a world in which pegged and floating exchange rates coexisted. Some countries, with Britain still at the hub, had more or less floating exchange rates both *vis-à-vis* one another and with respect to the gold bloc, of which the U.S. formed the center. By the time of the *Treatise* Keynes was concerned with the question of protecting Britain from all of the rest of the world and not only from the United States.

When the *General theory* appeared, world trade and payments were at their nadir; Keynes, among others, felt that problems of domestic stabilization were not only more pressing than, but independent of, the international monetary system. A brief discussion at the end, the "Notes on Mercantilism," bearing some reference to openness, appears to come as an afterthought. The application of the formal model of the *General theory* to an open economy was left to others, such as Machlup, Harrod, and Metzler (see Chapters 14 and 15).

In my estimation Keynes was constant in his underlying view of how the world economy worked. He has been accused of having taken every possible position, both serially and simultaneously, but these presumed contradictions had more to do with his search for the accoutrements of institutional change to achieve various solutions than with his basic interpretation of how things did, or did not, work.

I shall deal briefly but separately with *Indian currency and finance*, since it is somewhat eccentric *vis-à-vis* the others. I shall try to emphasize those aspects of the *Tract* that were specific to it and incorporate most of his views of the adjustment mechanism into the discussion of the *Treatise*. On the *General theory* I have nothing to add to the few words above. It is significant by its silence on the subject. And I shall deal separately with the pre-Bretton Woods discussions, since they are so specifically policy oriented. They share, however, the *Tract's* concern with the role of Britain in the world economy. The testimony to the Macmillan Committee, a spinoff from the *Treatise*, was discussed in connection with the comparison of the Cunliffe and Macmillan Committees, in Chapter 6.

## Indian currency and finance

In the context of this study, the most interesting and important aspect of the book is Keynes's interpretation of the history and functioning of the gold exchange standard, as distinct from both the idealized gold standard and the peculiarly British version of it. The theoretical heart of the book is Chapter 2, "The Gold-Exchange Standard." Here he sets out to show that the British currency and monetary system is, appropriately, nearly unique, since the British system is suited to the "peculiar" British conditions (Keynes 1913 [1971: 11]).

In a thumbnail history of British money, Keynes notes that Britain alone had a fully gold-based currency as early as the second quarter of the nineteenth century. However, bank notes became more widely used and threatened the exclusiveness of gold; in response the Bank Act of 1844 was passed to "encourage the use of gold as the medium of exchange as well as the standard of value." The result (legislators take note and beware) was a rapid and dramatic expansion in the use of checks. As noted in Chapter 7, Hayek refers to the same phenomenon, the market's ability to circumvent restrictions on money by creating its own. Except for certain traditional types of payment, particularly wages, gold coins were being used relatively little in domestic transactions. "Our gold reserve policy is mainly dictated, therefore, by considerations arising out of the possible demand for export" (Keynes 1913 [1971: 11–12]). This theme, that the function of gold is to make payments abroad, not to regulate the domestic money supply, is one of his leitmotifs. The gold standard ought not to have been, in Keynes's view, the kind of automatic mechanism we get in the prototypical classical enunciation of it.

Another important theme, and Keynes will ring the changes on it for the rest of his life, as we shall see, is the asymmetry between debtors and creditors. There is a difference, however. While in his later writings, especially in the pre-Bretton Woods memoranda, his emphasis was on the difference between countries with balance of payments deficits and surpluses, with differences in flows, here he is distinguishing between existing asset positions, arguing that the adjustment to a deficit of a given size will be different for creditor than for debtor countries. A country such as Great Britain, a creditor, can adjust by reducing its lending. This is very different, he argues, from the position of a debtor which must borrow still more. The policy mechanism for achieving the first "may be ill suited for action of the second. *Partly as a consequence of this . . . the 'bank rate' policy for regulating the outflow of gold has been admirably successful in this country, and yet cannot stand elsewhere unaided by other devices*" (Keynes 1913 [1971: 13], italics mine). That is, the neoclassical mechanism is one particularly suited to the British situation, in his view. One implication of this is that countries other than Britain have had to take pains to develop short-term assets abroad, ensuring them some realizable holding in case of need. This is the reason for central banks holding foreign exchange reserves; otherwise they would have to have "a much larger reserve of gold, the expense of which would be nearly intolerable. The new method combines safety with economy" (Keynes 1913 [1971: 18]). As noted in the previous chapter in the discussion of Brown (1940), Britain before World War I, like the United States after World War II, did not hold foreign exchange reserves to any significant extent. This, in both cases, reflects their respective positions as the reserve center.

When other countries adopted the gold standard in the last quarter of the nineteenth century, they emulated Britain, but the system did not work for them, and they in effect were "led to imitate the form rather than the substance." As a result, though most of the countries of Europe have gold currencies and official bank rates, "in none of them is gold the principal medium of exchange, and in none of them is the bank rate their only habitual support against an outward drain of gold" (Keynes 1913 [1971: 14]). What do these countries have that Britain does not have?

1    large gold reserves,
2    partial suspension of convertibility when necessary (a tool Britain used fairly liberally in the nineteenth century, at least up to 1866, see Cunliffe 1918: 8, and
3    reserves of foreign bills and deposits, that is, foreign exchange reserves.

The remark about other countries not having gold currency in circulation, however, strikes me as inappropriate in the sense that it seems to imply that Britain does (or did) have gold currency in widespread use. But a little later, Keynes announces that no country, with the possible exception of Egypt, currently had a situation in which gold was even a major medium of exchange. "Gold is an international, but not a local currency" (Keynes 1913 [1971: 21]).

The gold-exchange standard was adopted first by India (in 1898, under the Lindsay scheme). When Lindsay, the deputy secretary of the Bank of Bengal, suggested it in 1876, 1878, 1885, 1892, and finally in 1898 (he was nothing if not persistent!) it was attacked by government and bankers, including the Rothschilds and the Montagus. The argument against it was that one could not have a gold standard without physical gold backing all the currency (Keynes 1913 [1971: 24]). There had been some earlier approximations to the system. The first attempt to have a cheap-material local currency (with gold backing) was made by Holland in and after 1877. The Bank of Holland kept reserves in gold and foreign bills, and managed the standard very successfully. But it did not keep "standing credit in any foreign financial centre." That idea was apparently first developed by Count Witte in Russia in 1892, when they were moving from inconvertible paper to a gold standard; the Austro-Hungarians followed suit after 1896. The Russians continued to be net short-term creditors until 1914, despite the heavy indebtedness of the commercial banks, because of these official balances abroad (see Bloomfield 1963: 80). It had subsequently been adopted by and for a number of colonies and small dependent economies.[1] And "it is also closely related to the prevailing tendencies in Europe." The idea had been suggested by Ricardo during the bullionist controversy, on the grounds that it would save gold for use for export, and Marshall revived the idea in 1887. Keynes, like Ricardo, was attracted by the efficiency of using a cheap local material to tie the value of the currency to whatever the international standard of value might be; this would be a characteristic feature of the "ideal currency of the future" (Keynes 1913 [1971: 22–5]).

[1]  The United States established or encouraged the system for the Philippines, Mexico and Panama; it was adopted in Siam, French Indo-China, Dutch Java, Japan, the British Straits Settlements and West Africa (Keynes 1913 [1971: 23–5]).

The Indian reserves had been growing more liquid, as the use of bank-notes spread, and fewer notes were being converted into gold. The bullion reserves were therefore available "[to] support in times of depression and maintain at par the gold value of the rupee" (Keynes 1913 [1971: 35]). I do not wish to delve into the intricacies of the Indian currency system, which are legion and have long been infamous.[2] The knowledge of institutional facts and grasp of their importance which Keynes demonstrates here is indeed impressive. The problems of a state without a central bank which must juggle convertibility from silver coins (which involves stocks of silver to be newly coined) to local notes to gold sovereigns to bills on London – all of this in a huge country with transport and communication problems, different local institutions, and large seasonal variations in activity – this is all cogently set forth. He concludes that

in her gold-exchange standard, and in the mechanism by which this is supported, India . . . is in the forefront of monetary progress. But in her banking arrangements, in the management of her note issue, and in the relations of her government to the money market, her position *is* anomalous; and she has much to learn from what is done elsewhere. (Keynes 1913 [1971: 182], italics his)

Note, however, the following, which is directly relevant to our broader theme:

The Indian currency is internally (i.e. apart from the import of funds from foreign countries) absolutely inelastic. . . Additional currency, whether notes or rupees, can be obtained in two ways only – by buying council bills in London or by bringing in sovereigns . . . The fact that a temporary increase in the media of exchange can only be obtained by bringing in funds from abroad partly explains the high rate of discount in India during the busy season. . . [I]f funds are to be attracted from abroad for a short period . . . the rate of interest must be high enough to repay the cost of remittance *both* ways, which in the case of places so remote from one another as India and London is considerable. If there were some authority which could create credit money in India during the busy season, it would not be necessary for the rate of discount to rise so high. (Keynes 1913 [1971: 40–1], italics his)

Here, of course, the short-term capital movements are serving an equilibrating function, according to Keynes, and yet he deplores them, because of the transactions costs involved. They were not destabilizing (as he was to argue later they were, or might be, in the British case) – they were simply expensive. His point here, evidently, was that the phenomenon he described was not that of short-term capital flows financing temporary imbalances in payments; rather it is, quite literally, a matter of importing currency for

---

[2] *Vide*, e.g. Oscar Wilde, *The Importance of Being Ernest*, Act II, Boni and Liveright, Inc, New York, 1919: 80. "Miss Prism: Cecily, you will read your Political Economy in my absence. The chapter on the Fall of the Rupee you may omit. It is somewhat too sensational. Even these metallic problems have their melodramatic side."

domestic circulation, and reexporting it when seasonal requirements ebb. The transaction cost, in the form of the higher interest rate, is negative seigniorage. India would be better off if it could supply its own currency in response to seasonal changes in demand for it.[3] Keynes's recommendations for improving this situation involve the use of open market operations (though he does not use that term) to enhance the seasonal elasticity of the domestic credit supply. Permanent increases in the note supply can and should be provided only in exchange for gold (sovereigns) or foreign exchange (council bills in London) (Keynes 1913 [1971: 42–3]).

## A tract on monetary reform

The gap between *Indian currency and finance* and the *Tract* is the intervening period of ten years – and World War I. Keynes was writing about a very different world, and he was keenly aware of this: the *Tract* is, in fact, an attempt to describe the world as it appeared after Armageddon. The time was 1923, and the international monetary system was in disarray. Britain was "off" gold. Exchange rates were "unregulated and left to look after themselves." They fluctuated seasonally and in other ways irregularly. In the long run they depended on relative price levels, which were influenced by domestic monetary policies in the several countries. But while there was de facto floating, this was not "as yet, the avowed or consistent policy of the responsible authorities." The authorities were still aiming at a restoration to prewar parities *vis-à-vis* the dollar, and Bank rate might still be used in a manner counter to the interests of domestic price and credit considerations in order to influence the exchange rate (Keynes 1923: 184–5).

The first third of the book is fairly general monetary theory: Keynes describes vividly the evils of both inflation and deflation and the role of the government in causing one or the other, or choosing between them and other policy tools. The remainder of the book is devoted to the "foreign exchanges" and, in particular, the aims of monetary policy and its effects on the exchange rate.

### The adjustment mechanism

The quantity theory of money, Keynes alleges, is incontestably correct. The question is how stable the Cambridge $k$ is in the short and medium runs, since "*In the long run* we are all dead" (Keynes 1923: 80, italics his). A painstaking analysis of the purchasing power parity doctrine, augmented by non-traded goods and capital movements, leads to the conclusion that exchange rates

---

[3] This is reminiscent of Ricardo's attitude toward reversible short-term capital movements. The difference, of course, is that while Keynes deplored them, Ricardo denied they would exist, since they were totally irrational (see Chapter 2, note 3).

under a floating rate regime will be volatile. This brings him to the issue of the forward rate and its sensitivity both to expectations regarding future spot rates and to interest rate differentials between countries. His well-known discussion of interest parity and the role of the forward exchanges in establishing it is first to be found here.

### Floating exchange rates

He sets forth the two prongs of the neoclassical position, and adds that under floating exchange rates interest rates are a poor tool for influencing exchange rates. Neither private nor central banks should try to distinguish and discriminate between forward exchange dealings which are "speculative" and those which are "hedging," he insists; in the first place, this is an impossible task, and in the second place, speculation may be stabilizing. Interest parity, however, leads to stabilizing short-term capital movements only under fixed rates, when the extent of fluctuation of forward and expected future spot rates is highly restricted; this constrains the difference between spot and forward rates. The relation between spot and forward exchange rates is important and often improperly understood, thereby leading to inappropriate policy. "Dear money" has the indirect effect of diminishing the supply of bank credit. And money which is dearer in one place than in another used to have the effect of drawing gold. "But nowadays the only immediate effect is to cause a new adjustment of the difference between the spot and forward rates of exchange between the two centres" (Keynes 1923: 136–7).

The reasons given for the maintenance of a close relationship between the Bank of England's rate and that of the American Federal Reserve Board sometimes show confusion. The eventual influence of an effective high bank-rate on the general situation is undisputed; but the belief that a moderate difference between bank-rates in London and New York reacts directly on the sterling-dollar exchange, as it used to do under a régime of convertibility, is a misapprehension. . . [T]his difference . . . cannot much affect the absolute level of the spot rate unless the change in relative money-rates is comparable in magnitude (as it used to be but no longer is) with the possible range of exchange fluctuations. (Keynes 1923: 138–9)

Here follows a discussion of appropriate actions for various European countries, which were choosing between deflation and devaluation, with Keynes arguing that many of them could, or should, do neither. Italy wanted to try (presumably by deflation) to appreciate the lira to its former value. "Fortunately for the Italian taxpayer and Italian business, the lira does not listen even to a dictator and cannot be given castor oil."[4] Czechoslovakia

---

[4] It may be necessary to point out to younger readers that this was a commonly used instrument of torture in Fascist Italy.

borrowed abroad to appreciate the crown, and got "an industrial crisis and serious unemployment . . . Pursuing a misguided policy in a spirit of stern virtue, she preferred the stagnation of her industries and a still fluctuating standard" (Keynes 1923: 145–7).

Keynes defends the justice of devaluation at that point in history (he was to deny that justice in 1930) on the grounds that current prices were not very different from what they had been when most of the then existing contracts were made; comparison with 1913 might not be the appropriate point of departure. A country with an exchange rate near its prewar parity might try to aim for that parity, but the "right policy for countries of which the currency has suffered a prolonged and severe depreciation is to *devaluate,* and to fix the value of the currency at that figure in the neighbourhood of the existing value to which commerce and wages are adjusted" (Keynes 1923: 151, italics his).

On the argument over fixed versus flexible exchange rates, Keynes said it must depend in part on the degree of openness of the economy. There is, however, a presumption in favor of price stability, that is, fixed exchange rates. The fixed rate system forced the domestic price level to adjust, and it was therefore "too slow and insensitive in its mode of operation." In the postwar fluctuating rate regime, the price level is a function of domestic monetary policy and credit policy "and the rates of exchange with the outside world have to adjust themselves thereto." That system "is too rapid in its effect and over-sensitive, with the result that it may act violently for merely transitory causes." In the postwar period, however, shocks have been large and sudden and quick responses are necessary, so the prewar system is "inapplicable" (Keynes 1923: 159).

Discount rate policy played a different role under the two systems. In a fixed exchange rate regime it is "a vital part of the process" of equalizing foreign and domestic prices. Under floating rates it is less essential and works primarily through its effect on domestic prices and *hence* on the exchange rate (Keynes 1923: 163). This reinforces the statement quoted above and reiterates the argument that Bank rate policy can affect only the spot-forward relationship in the several countries and not induce capital flows, under floating rates. Interest rate policy therefore affects only domestic prices and, *through the current account,* the exchange rate. This apparently leaves no room for a situation analogous to that prevailing in the mid 1980s in which, it is often argued, the causality runs from interest rates to capital flows to the spot rate to the current account. This is, incidentally, part of the early Mundell-Fleming story, generally believed to be "keynesian".

I think what Keynes has omitted here (incredibly) is expected future exchange rates. Covered interest arbitrage determines the relationship (as Keynes has taught us) between the spot and forward rates. But this relationship can change without affecting the spot rate only if we assume that the forward rate is unconstrained by expectations regarding future spot rates. Granted, under floating rates, the monetary authorities are not committed to support the spot rate, so that fluctuations in future spot rates are potentially of much greater amplitude under floating than under pegged exchange rates. But it is a far cry from that to the assumption that there is no constraining expectation at all. I find support for my interpretation here in that elsewhere in the *Tract*, Keynes recommends the idea, developed more fully in the *Treatise*, that the Bank of England should quote a price on forward exchange, which would facilitate short-term capital movements (between London and New York) without inducing gold flows (Keynes 1923: 192). This is consistent with the proposition that, without such interference, expectations are that the future spot rate can be any value and there is no constraint on it at all.

### Fixed exchange rates

How did the prewar method work?

If gold flowed out of the country's central reserves, this modified discount policy and creation of credit, thus affecting the demand for, and hence the price of, the class of goods most sensitive to the ease of credit, and gradually, through the price of these goods, spreading its influence to the prices of goods generally, including those which enter into international trade, until at the new level of price foreign goods began to look dear at home and domestic goods cheap abroad, and the adverse balance was redressed. But this process might take months to work itself out. Nowadays, the gold reserves might be dangerously depleted before the compensating forces had time to operate. *Moreover, the movement of the rate of interest up or down sometimes had more effect in attracting foreign capital or encouraging investment abroad than in influencing home prices.* Where the disequilibrium was purely seasonal, this was an unqualified advantage ... But where it was due to more permanent causes, the adjustment even before the war might be imperfect; for the stimulus to foreign loans, whilst restoring the balance for the time being, *might obscure the real seriousness of the situation, and enable a country to live beyond its resources for a considerable time at the risk of ultimate default.* (Keynes 1923: 159–60, italics mine)

The adjustment mechanism under fixed exchange rates, then, is the neoclassical one, with non-traded goods. Keynes is already concerned about the destabilizing influence of short-term capital movements in response to central bank action. And he emphasizes the slow working of the real adjustment compared with the rapidity of capital account response, so that a country can continue to overspend and borrow short while the internal economy is adjusting more slowly. I find it intriguing, by the way, that Keynes's estimate of the long run in this context seems to be measured in months.

Under flexible exchange rates prices of traded goods change instantly when the exchange rate moves, and prices are subject to

the most fleeting influences of politics and of sentiment, and by the periodic pressure of seasonal trades. But it also means that the post-war method is a most rapid and powerful corrective of real disequilibria in the balance of international payments arising from whatever causes, and a wonderful preventive in the way of countries which are inclined to spend abroad beyond their resources. (Keynes 1923: 161)

This quotation represents a relatively rare statement of a price mechanism (flexible exchange rates in this case) working, quickly and fairly effectively, to redress an imbalance caused by basic or structural disequilibrium or by what has since been called overspending. The same kind of structural disequilibrium is mentioned briefly (as we shall see in Chapter 10) in his plans for Bretton Woods and there too he recognized the need for a fundamental adjustment under such circumstances.

The gold standard system was stable, in the sense that adjustment would come about eventually, but it might be very slow and difficult if gold and silver outflows led to a reduction in the money supply "faster than social and business arrangements allow prices to fall" (Keynes 1923: 162).

We shall look on Edward III's debasements of sterling money with a more tolerant eye if we regard them as a method of carrying into effect a preference for stability of internal prices over stability of external exchanges, celebrating that monarch as an enlightened forerunner of Professor Irving Fisher in advocacy of the "compensated dollar," only more happy than the latter in his opportunities to carry theory into practice. (Keynes 1923: 163)

### Predictions and recommendations

What then, Keynes muses, of the future? Should the world return to a gold standard? The world supply of gold had always been erratic and serendipitous. Stability had been attained in spite of this, in the past, by variations in the ratio of reserves to liabilities for countries, banks, and individuals, generally acting independently. But "gold now stands at an 'artificial' value, the future course of which almost entirely depends on the policy of the Federal Reserve Board of the United States" (Keynes 1923: 167). If everybody kept reserves of gold, there would be a shortage; if the gold exchange standard is adopted, the "actual value of gold will depend . . . on the policy of three or four of the most powerful Central Banks, whether they act independently or in unison." (He is surely referring here to the central banks of Britain, France and the United States. What the fourth would be I am not quite sure.) Furthermore, there is the danger that the U.S. will demonetize gold, since it seemed irrational for it to continue to receive and store gold and yet "maintain the value of the dollar which is irrespective of the inflow or outflow of gold." "Confidence in the future stability of the value of gold depends therefore on the United States being foolish enough to go on accepting gold which it does not want, and wise enough, having accepted it, to maintain it at a fixed value" (Keynes 1923: 168–9).

Restoration of the old system of a fixed ratio of central bank liabilities to gold reserves (the "proportion") was not a feasible alternative. In fact, even before the war, "the system was becoming precarious by reason of its artificiality. The 'proportion' was by the lapse of time losing its relation to the facts and had become largely conventional. Some other figure, greater or less, would have done just as well" (Keynes 1923: 171). He maintained this position strongly through the Macmillan sittings. See, for example, Keynes 1929–31 [1981]: 152.)

Note, however, that Keynes is not saying here that the fixed proportion between reserves and domestic money (or high-powered money) did not exist before the war; what he is saying is that the multiplier was an arbitrary one. I fail to see anything in the "standard" description of the gold standard mechanism that contradicts that; unless we accept Hayek's argument that the multiplier should be unity as in a gold coin standard, it is indeed completely arbitrary.

He also made the point, frequently, that the fixed proportion is a bad idea. He argued very explicitly (for example, Keynes 1923: 193–4) that there should be no relationship between the gold stocks of the central bank and the domestic money supply, since domestic contraction is the wrong way to go about defending the exchange rate, and since the fixed reserve both immobilizes the gold stock and makes it unusable; furthermore it forces adjustment too late, after the disequilibrium has already led to a movement of gold.

The note issue should be separated completely from the gold reserves. The money supply should be adjusted to maintain internal balance, and the gold reserves should be used by the Bank of England "for the purpose of avoiding short-period fluctuations in the exchange" (Keynes 1923: 196). The idea of a fixed proportion of reserves having been abandoned, interest rate policy had been turned to purely domestic goals, "to regulate the expansion and deflation of credit in the interests of business stability and the steadiness of prices. In so far as it is employed to procure stability of the dollar exchange . . . we have a relic of pre-war policy and a compromise between discrepant aims" (Keynes 1923: 172).

In truth, the gold standard is already a barbarious relic. All of us, from the Governor of the Bank of England downwards, are now primarily interested in preserving the stability of business, prices, and employment, and are not likely . . . deliberately to sacrifice these to the outworn dogma, which had its value once, of £3:17:10 ½ per ounce . . . A regulated non-metallic standard has slipped in unnoticed. *It exists*. Whilst the economists dozed, the academic dream of a hundred years, doffing its cap and gown, clad in paper rags, has crept into the real world by means of the bad fairies – always so much more potent than the good – the wicked Ministers of Finance. (Keynes 1923: 172–3, italics his)

Even the advocates of a return to gold, such as Mr. Hawtrey, Keynes notes, view the future gold standard as necessarily a managed one, with central bank cooperation directed at maintaining the purchasing power of gold. If this is not achievable, it is preferable, Hawtrey says, to stabilize the value of sterling in terms of commodities. Keynes objects, however, to "reinstating gold in the pious hope that international co-operation will keep it in order." On the one hand, hope of cooperation between the Bank of England and the Federal Reserve Board is unrealistic because of the preponderant strength and power of the latter. On the other, the Federal Reserve Board cannot be trusted to run the international monetary system alone; it is too new and inexperienced, and too much subject to sectional and political interests (Keynes 1923: 174–6).

What is needed is a scheme which will permit the supply of money and credit to be regulated to maintain stability of the internal price level and avoid changes in the supply of foreign exchange as a result of seasonal or temporary disturbances. Domestic price stability should be announced as the primary goal of the Bank of England. If the Americans behave, and avoid deflation, Britain can have fixed exchange rates *vis-à-vis* the dollar as well as stable prices. If not, she (Britain) must choose domestic price stability over exchange rate stability (Keynes 1923: 186).

Given the prevailing situation of more or less floating exchange rates, this should be codified and the authorities "should adopt the stability of sterling prices as their *primary* objective." If the Federal Reserve maintains dollar prices steady, this is consistent with a policy of stabilizing the exchange rate. What Keynes very specifically wishes to avoid is to let "sterling prices . . . plunge with [dollar prices] merely for the sake of maintaining a fixed parity of exchange" (Keynes 1923: 186). This fear of American deflationary proclivities continued to be a theme of his for the next twenty years.

Objecting to the gold standard's tyranny of control over domestic goals, Keynes yet coveted the short-run stability he felt it proffered. Seeking a criterion for stabilizing internal prices, he is in favor of stabilizing the price of a composite bundle of commodities, but wants a number of additional countercyclical policy objectives added. He rejected Fisher's proposal of a "compensated dollar" on the grounds that it was too mechanical and that it was an ex post rather than ex ante policy. On this he cites Hawtrey approvingly: "It is not the *past* rise in prices but the *future* rise that has to be counteracted" (quoted from *Monetary reconstruction*, 105. Keynes 1923: 187).

Intervention for short-term smoothing was desirable, and should be carried out publicly. He suggests that the Bank of England be free to "regulate" the price of gold and announce a weekly buy and sell price just as it announces Bank rate. The spread between its buying and selling price should be somewhat wider than the prewar spread. If gold flowed out for seasonal or temporary reasons, it should be allowed to continue unchecked. If it "seemed to be due to a tendency of sterling to depreciate in terms of commodities, the correct remedy would be to raise the bank rate"[5] (Keynes 1923: 191). This last sentence suggests a reasonably strong faith in the workings of the neoclassical mechanism.

Keynes emphasized even more than I have done the importance of the changes in attitudes (on his part and that of others) since the prewar and wartime days. This is most clearly spelled out in his critique of the Cunliffe Report. This was published, as he notes, in 1918,

three months before the Armistice. It was compiled long before the unpegging of sterling and the great break in the European exchanges in 1919, before the tremendous boom and crash of 1920–21, before the vast piling up of the world's gold in America, and without experience of the Federal Reserve policy in 1922–23 of burying this gold at Washington, withdrawing it from the exercise of its full effect on price, and thereby, in effect, demonetising the metal. The Cunliffe Report is an unadulterated pre-war prescription – inevitably so considering that it was written after four years' interregnum of war, before Peace was in sight, and without knowledge of the revolutionary and unforeseeable experiences of the past five years.

Of all the omission from the Cunliffe Report the most noteworthy is the complete absence of any mention of the problem of the stability of the price-level; and it cheerfully explains how the pre-war system, which it aims at restoring, operated to bring back equilibrium by deliberately causing a "consequent slackening of employment." The Cunliffe Report belongs to an extinct and an almost forgotten order of ideas. Few think on these lines now; yet the Report remains the authorised declaration of our policy, and the Bank of England and the Treasury are said still to regard it as their marching orders. (Keynes 1923: 194–5)

Gold should be held only by the Bank of England and used only as a "war-chest" in case of a temporary adverse balance of payments, in order to smooth day-to-day fluctuations in exchange rates (Keynes 1923: 195). Thus it was possible to benefit from having and using gold, "without irrevocably binding our legal-tender money to follow blindly all the vagaries of gold and future unforeseeable fluctuations in its real purchasing power" (Keynes

---

[5] The authorities should also try to mitigate the destabilizing influence of their own activities. "The service of the American debt will make it necessary for the British Treasury to buy nearly $500,000 every working day. It is clear that the particular method adopted for purchasing these huge sums will greatly affect the short-period fluctuations of the exchange. I suggest that this duty should be entrusted to the Bank of England to be carried out by them with the express object of minimising those fluctuations in the exchange which are due to the daily and seasonal ebb and flow of the ordinary trade demand. In particular the proper distribution of these purchases through the year might be so arranged as greatly to mitigate the normal seasonal fluctuation" (Keynes 1923: 191–2).

1923: 197, italics mine). His main objection to gold was, evidently, the threat to the world supply of it and the danger, perhaps, of the Americans again adopting the benighted policy of sterilizing gold inflows, as in 1920–1, rather than a conviction that a government should avoid policies leading to balance-of-payments adjustment. However, here as elsewhere, my reading is that Keynes vacillated between, on the one hand, thinking that balance-of-payments adjustment was impossible and, on the other, feeling sanguine that it was not so difficult to attain and did not constitute a problem on its own.

The United States, Keynes is pleased to note, has started in the same direction: it is demonetizing gold. The evidence of this is that the Federal Reserve Board seemed to be motivated primarily by considerations of internal stability in establishing its interest rate policy. In fact, the economists of the United States, he argued, were far ahead of their British counterparts in developing the theory of the business and credit cycle and it would be more difficult even for the Federal Reserve Board than it was for the Bank of England to ignore such considerations, even if it was not entirely conscious of their influence. Thus, regarding the Federal Reserve System: "Out of convention and conservatism it accepts gold. Out of prudence and understanding it buries it" (Keynes 1923: 197–8). The United States, he said, has "*pretended* to maintain a gold standard. *In fact* it has established a dollar standard; and, instead of ensuring that the value of the dollar shall conform to that of gold, it makes provision, at great expense, that the value of gold shall conform to that of the dollar" (Keynes 1923: 198, italics his).

But Keynes thinks that the fiction may be dropped some day. Some Senator may "read and understand this book. Sooner or later the fiction will lose its value . . . The economists of Harvard know more than those of Washington, and it will be well that in due course their surreptitious victory should swell into public triumph." The British should consider the possibility "that some day soon the Mints of the United States may be closed to the acceptance of gold at a fixed dollar price" (Keynes 1923: 199–200).

However, the United States cannot get rid of its gold by lending it, unless it inflates. Approaching the keen awareness of the accounting identities and economic forces that link the current and capital account, an awareness that, we shall see, informs the *Treatise* throughout, he argues that an increase in foreign lending by the United States, if matched by an increase in savings, "will no more denude the United States of her gold than they denude Great Britain of hers." Only foreign lending which is an addition to purchasing power, that is, inflationary, will do that, by depreciating the dollar (Keynes 1923: 202–3). Managed currency was essential and inevitable, but there was no single authority available to manage it. The best alternative then, was to "have *two* managed currencies, sterling and dollars," with as much cooperation between the managers as possible (Keynes 1923: 204, italics his).

## Summary

The early writings of Keynes present a picture of adherence to the neoclassical view of the adjustment mechanism. *Indian Currency and Finance* is concerned heavily with the mechanics of fixed exchange rates under a gold exchange standard. The resource costs of importing one's currency (both in terms of world dead weight loss of transport and similar costs and in terms of the temporary transfers implied by balance of payments surpluses required in order to attain more cash) bothered him, specifically in regard to a country with highly variable seasonal needs for cash, a country where at best the resource costs of maintaining a centralized monetary system were high. The idea of a system which economized the use of gold, however, appealed to him, a theme to which he returned often, particularly in the *Tract*.

The *Tract*, written while Britain was off gold, describes adjustment under floating exchange rates. The notion of the conflict between internal and external balance pervades the book, with the clear preference for domestic stability. Large and variable reserves of gold should be used to protect a country from the need to sacrifice domestic price and employment stability to the dictates of foreign balance as imposed by an excessively deflationary United States. He was in favor, it appears, of more or less fixed exchange rates – certainly not advocating totally free floating – but the "gold standard" in terms of rigid ties between domestic money and the foreign balance was already, he declared, a "barbarous relic."

The arithmetic of national income accounting, and the equivalence of the foreign balance to the difference between domestic expenditure and income make their appearance here, though much less well-developed than in the *Treatise*. And the famous Keynesian discussion of covered interest rate arbitrage appears here; it is brought in in connection with the policy goal of driving a wedge between domestic and world interest rates, so a country could pursue its own monetary policy.

# CHAPTER 9

# A treatise on money

## The mechanism of adjustment

Keynes's view, as expressed in the *Treatise*, of the international adjustment mechanism under fixed exchange rates stems from the neoclassical preoccupation with the importance of the rate of interest and its impact on both the capital and current accounts. And it is Keynesian in its emphasis on the macroeconomic relationships. The inherited wisdom is difficult, he argues, to define and delineate.

No systematic treatment of the subject exists in the English language, so far as I am aware. You will search in vain the works of Marshall, Pigou, Taussig or Irving Fisher. Even Professor Cassel's treatment, which is somewhat fuller, does not examine the train of causation in any detail. Mr. Hawtrey has a little more to say; but he is somewhat unorthodox on this matter and cannot be quoted as an exponent of the accepted doctrine. There remains, however, one outstanding attempt at a systematic treatment, namely Knut Wicksell's *Geldzins und Güterpreise*, published in German in 1898, a book which deserves more fame and much more attention than it has received from English-speaking economists. (Keynes 1930: Volume I, 186)

I think his position can best be classified as a Wicksellian macroeconomic theory combined with a Marshall-Lerner type of analysis, involving real adjustments, relative price changes, elasticities, and non-traded goods. Since the current account of the balance of payments depends heavily on relative prices and the capital account on relative interest rates, a disturbance may come from either side and *may* require adjustment in *both* interest rates and prices. May but not must. Keynes was keenly aware of the general-equilibrium interdependencies and feedbacks. But the impact of interest rates on prices (through the demand for investment) is stronger, he argued, than the reverse effect. So an imbalance in the current account may be eliminated by changes only in prices, whereas disequilibrium due to interest rates "falling out of gear" is likely to require a permanent change both in income- and price-levels "*due to a change in the demand for investment abroad relatively to the demand at home*" (Keynes 1930: Volume I, 327, italics his).

If the shock is a current account deficit, gold flows out, Bank rate is raised, and prices and money incomes fall as a result; when this has been completed, Bank rate can be lowered again and the capital account can be restored to its previous position. That is to say, the equilibrium capital flow is unchanged, therefore the equilibrium level of trade imbalance is the same as it was; the price changes are required to clear world commodity markets at that level of trade balance. As we shall see in Chapter 16, this anticipates Metzler's treatment. Implicit here is the assumption that the gold outflow plus the higher Bank rate have resulted in a permanently reduced money supply. (Compare the discussion in Chapter 7, pages 146 ff, on Hawtrey's debate with Keynes over the latter's gold points proposal.) Provided, he says, that there is no change in relative factor prices within the country, nothing real will have changed (Keynes 1930: Volume I, 327). (As noted in Chapter 6, Keynes was less sanguine about the possibility of flexibility of prices and money incomes with no real effects when he was testifying before the Macmillan Committee at roughly the same time the passage above was being written.)

If, on the other hand, the disturbance consists of a higher interest rate abroad, gold will flow out because of the deficit on capital account. The final equilibrium depends on many considerations; this is, of course, the transfer problem, which exercised the Harvard School and Ohlin, among others. Keynes's views here are consistent with his frequent statement that this is a more difficult adjustment, since historically the capital account has more frequently adjusted to the current account than conversely (Keynes 1930: Volume I, 327 ff; also 1929a [1949: 167]). In this discussion, a disturbance in the trade account leads directly to an adjustment in the trade balance, whereas a shock to the capital account also leads to a change in the current account (compare Metzler 1960 [1973]).

[A]t the new point of equilibrium, the prices of all home-produced goods will have fallen relatively to the prices of all foreign-produced goods. The *amount* of this relative fall will depend . . . on the change in the terms of trade resulting from the physical characteristics of the productive forces at home and abroad. (Keynes 1930: Volume I, 328, italics his)

What is Wicksellian is that the link between gold movements and prices, through the quantity of money, is the interest rate. Thus the transfer mechanism works, presumably exclusively, through the effect of an imbalance on the transfer of gold, hence on Bank rate, hence on domestic interest rates and investment in both countries, leading to the required changes in relative prices, in both countries (Keynes 1930: Volume I, 329).

He sets out to mediate between what he sees as two opposing doctrines regarding the adjustment mechanism. The first he attributes to Ricardo and

Taussig, and it is a version of the price-specie flow mechanism. The second he attributes to Ohlin and some earlier, unspecified

traditional doctrine which was widely held in Great Britain, mainly on empirical grounds, during the nineteenth century, and is still held to-day. According to this view foreign lending stimulates the foreign balance directly and almost automatically, and the actual movement of gold plays quite a minor part. This conclusion was, I think, based much more on British experience during the nineteenth century than on *a priori* reasoning. But recently . . . it has been supported by argument also, notably by Professor Ohlin. (Keynes 1930: Volume I, 330)

It is not clear to me what literature he is referring to in general here. The reference to Ohlin is obviously to the latter's debate with Keynes in the *Economic Journal* the previous year, in which Ohlin (1929a, 1929b) was arguing that the changes in buying power associated with a transfer would in themselves have a direct influence, in an equilibrating direction, on trade flows. Surprisingly, Keynes never seemed to have grasped what Ohlin was driving at in that debate (see Keynes 1929a, 1929b).

The final equilibrium terms of trade will depend on the elasticities of demand and supply (including the supply of output), that is, on the Marshall-Lerner conditions. The change in the terms of trade "is independent of the character of the transition and of the means by which it is brought about." It depends on the real determinants of supply, factor endowments and techniques, and on the elasticities of demand in the several countries. Thus, the British lending for railway construction in North America in the nineteenth century resulted in a very small deterioration in Britain's terms of trade because Britain "was herself the only efficient producer of much of the materials required for these new investments . . ." and not because the act of lending conferred a bias in favor of exports (Keynes 1930: Volume I, 334–5).

The terms of trade are likely to deteriorate more if the borrowing country imposes a high tariff or if the capital movement is sudden, such as capital flights and hot money flows. Here follows an aside which is, in fact, a strong attack on the purchasing power parity doctrine. "For this not only upsets the validity of [Prof. Cassel's] conclusions over the long period, but renders them even more deceptive over the short period, whenever the short period is characterised by a sharp change in the attractions of foreign lending" (Keynes 1930: Volume I, 336). As for the tariff, however, it seems that he is here stating the optimal tariff argument, which has nothing conceptually to do with the transfer problem.

Part of the mechanism he describes (which does not arise in the simplest, aggregative versions of the analysis) involves the lending country's having to slide down the ranking of comparative advantage in order to generate an export surplus and suffering a deterioration in the terms of trade as a result of this. This was implicit in the debate with Ohlin on the German reparations as well (Keynes 1929a). What is new, and Keynesian in spirit, is the idea that the distribution of the burden of changing the relative levels of money wages between the two countries depends on the attitudes of the several countries (the central banks, actually, and their respective credit policies) toward gold flows. This kind of argument is very similar to much of the analysis in the seminal paper by Metzler (1960 [1973: Chapter 8]), discussed in Chapter 16. Metzler's argument about the distribution of the burden, however, is more involved and sophisticated than this (see also Eaton and Flanders 1987).

In his criticism of Ohlin (here as in the *Economic journal* debate Keynes 1929a and 1929b and Ohlin 1929a and 1929b) it is quite clear there is no sense of income effects in the mechanism, to the point where he evidently does not understand what Ohlin is trying to say. One might argue that this effect would be more relevant and obvious in the reparations case, where each country's permanent income has changed, than in the foreign lending case, where it has not, except for the interest differentials.[1]

Actually, Keynes comes very close to this last point (Keynes 1930: Volume I, 345) when he notes that in general a lending country experiences a loss because of deterioration in the terms of trade and a countervailing gain from the additional interest income, whereas in the case of reparations there is "no set-off corresponding to the higher rate of interest earned or to the subsequent improvement in the terms of trade" when the interest is paid. He does not take the additional crucial step of connecting the income loss of the transfer to a direct change in the balance of trade, that is, of injecting the income effect into the demand function for foreign and home goods, thus lessening the terms of trade deterioration required to effect the transfer, which was Ohlin's point.

In the transfer problem discussion, he gets into the issue of the internal-external balance dilemma. This provides a justification, in Keynes's view, for interfering with short-term capital movements. Thus, maintaining equilibrium becomes a matter of being passive to large changes in gold flows. If both foreign capital movements and domestic investment are highly elastic with respect to the rate of interest, demand for exports inelastic, and domestic wage rates inflexible, "then the transition from one position of internal equilibrium to another required by the necessity for preserving external equilibrium may be difficult, dilatory and painful" (Keynes 1930: Volume I, 349–50).

He has a fully developed view, as noted, of the general-equilibrium

---

[1] There has long been some discomfort attached to treating all transfers the same in the literature: it was clear that lending is not the same as giving aid or paying forced reparations. The recent literature which handles international trade as a problem of intertemporal optimization implies the distinction, since a transfer lowers permanent income, whereas a loan does not. In defense of Ohlin (who is discussed in detail in Chapter 13) I should note that he spoke of changes in "buying power" or "purchasing power" and not in income.

interactions, and of the national income accounting identities of the balance of payments. He notes that for every level of the interest rate there is always a price level at which the balance of payments is zero, and there is always an interest rate at which savings and investment are equal. "Consequently there is always a pair of values of bank-rate and of $P$ at which both $I = S$ and $B = L$ [the current and capital accounts are equal, and opposite in sign]" (Keynes 1930: Volume I, 215).

As an example, he cites the automatic gold standard mechanism in which the money supply is uniquely related to the gold stock and interest rates are market determined. Then there will always be equality between $S$ and $I$ and between $L$ and $B$ "(assuming an absence of economic frictions and of time-lag, and in particular that the rates of money-earnings are free to move in response to the competition of entrepreneurs for the services of the factors of production)" (Keynes 1930: Volume I, 216).

## Short-term capital flows and the policy dilemma

Bank rate should be a powerful instrument in restoring external equilibrium, according to Keynes, since it demonstrates "extraordinary efficacy . . . for effecting" equilibrium internally and externally. The reason is that it operates on both $L$, the capital account, and $B$, the current account, in the right direction. "Thus Bank-rate is both an expedient and a solution. It supplies both the temporary pick-me-up and the permanent cure – provided we ignore the malaise which may intervene between the pick-me-up and the cure" (Keynes 1930: Volume I, 214).

The causes and the role of short-term capital movements in the balance-of-payments adjustment process are discussed more fully in the *Treatise* (1930: Chapter 13, "The Modus Operandi of Bank-Rate") than in any of Keynes's other writings. His survey of the theories regarding the working of the Bank rate in the mechanism is instructive:

1. The first of these regards Bank-rate merely as a means of regulating the *quantity* of bank-money . . . Lord Overstone, for example . . . regarded Bank-rate as the correct and efficacious method for reducing the demand on the Bank for discounts, and so for contracting the volume of the circulation. (Keynes 1930: Volume I, 186–7, italics his)

The association of a higher Bank rate with a lower quantity of money Keynes attributes also to Marshall (1887 [1926], 1888 [1926]), Sir Robert Giffen, Pigou, and Hawtrey (1919, 1927, 1950) (Keynes 1930: Volume I, 188). The second path of influence is to attract short-term loans from abroad. Keynes says that Bank rate was thus used by the Bank of England for twenty years following 1837, and notes that the first "clear account" of the mechanism was presented by Goschen (1861). But Goschen, he said, argued that Bank rate changes followed the market and did not influence it. "It was left to Bagehot . . . to complete the story by emphasising the extent of the Bank of England's power . . . to determine what the market conditions should be" (Keynes 1930: Volume I, 189–90), and he states the dilemma which has confronted every attempt to formalize the neoclassical position.

[I]t is by no means obvious how [this] . . . is connected with our first strand, and I know of no author who has attempted the synthesis. Moreover – superficially at least – *it seems to pull in the opposite direction* . . . It may be objected that the higher Bank-rate can only be made effective if the Central Bank reduces its other assets by more than it increases its stock of gold, so that the effect on balance is to decrease the aggregate of credit. (Keynes 1930: Volume I, 190, italics mine)

A third potential influence of Bank rate policy is to reduce "foreign lending" (long-run investment as distinct from the short-term loans discussed above). But this can lead to a permanent change only if there is finally a change in the rate of return on investment (Keynes 1930: Volume I, 208).

## The domestic impact of the interest rate

The major theme of the *Treatise* in the international arena, as noted, is the dual role of Bank rate in influencing domestic spending and hence the balance of trade and in encouraging short-term accommodating capital movements (we saw this distinction already very clearly in the *Tract*; see Chapter 8); and he emphasizes also the distinction between the effect of Bank rate on the quantity of money and on the level and composition of domestic spending, that is, on investment decisions.

"Bank-rate Policy", in the modern sense, was originated in the discussions which followed the monetary crisis of 1836–7 and preceded the Bank Act of 1844. Before 1837 such ideas did not exist – in the works of Ricardo, for example, nothing of the sort is to be found; and the explanation is not far to seek. For throughout the life of Ricardo, and up to the repeal of the Usury Laws in 1837, the rate of interest was subject to a legal maximum of 5 percent . . . The traditional doctrine, which has been developed in the ninety years which have since elapsed, has been woven of three distinct strands of thought, difficult to disentangle, to which different writers attach differing degrees of stress. All of them have been obscurely present from the beginnings of the discussion. (Keynes 1930: Volume I, 186–7)

These strands are the effect of changes in interest rates directly on the money supply; the effect on short-term capital flows; and, third, the effect on investment. The last, according to Keynes, is the heart of the matter. The argument is that the rate of interest influences "in some way the rate of investment, or at least the rate of some kinds of investment, and, perhaps in the case of Wicksell and Cassel . . . the rate of investment relatively to that of savings" (Keynes 1930: Volume I, 190).

A higher interest rate "discourages investment relatively to saving, and therefore lowers prices." This pushes down profits, hence employment, hence wages, hence costs of production. He argues that most previous writers treated the price decline as the end of the story, without carrying on to the reduction in costs (read "money wages"); this point is emphasized, as we noted, in the Macmillan testimony. "But how far previous writers have perceived that to discourage investment relatively to saving is *in itself* calculated to reduce prices is more difficult to say" (Keynes 1930: Volume I, 191, italics his). This is, of course, the Wicksell/*Treatise* point of view emerging.

Even short-lived changes in interest rates to preserve equilibrium can do a lot of damage by affecting domestic lending and investment, therefore employment and output, in a period too short for wages to fall. Thus, the use of Bank rate to decrease foreign lending is not really a virtue; it has been proposed as a substitute for lengthy and painful adjustment in costs and prices, to be avoided whenever the imbalance is expected to be temporary. "Since the influence of Bank-rate on foreign lending is both quick in taking effect and easy to understand, whereas its influence on the internal situation is slower in operation and difficult to analyse, the awkwardness of handling such a double-edged weapon is being but slowly realised" (Keynes 1930: Volume I, 350). Thus, maintaining domestic equilibrium may involve being indifferent to or passive with respect to fairly considerable gold movements, that is, ignoring and absorbing them.

He notes that Hawtrey's early ideas were similar to his own, but takes issue with Hawtrey's emphasis on the enormous sensitivity of short-term commercial credit to changes in Bank rate, a sensitivity "which certainly does not exist in fact" (Keynes 1930: Volume I, 193). Quoting at length from *Good and bad trade*, Keynes concludes that Hawtrey's account is "very incomplete." It is based on the assumption that higher interest rates affect the costs of commercial traders significantly, though they do not have a similar impact on manufacturers. Keynes alleges, in an equally *a priori* manner, that the difference between 5 and 6 percent on bank loans will affect the dealer "very little more" than it will the manufacturer relative to the present and expected rate of profit based on "prospective price-movements." Keynes goes back a hundred years and sides with Tooke (against Joseph Hume), in 1839, that a higher Bank rate will not lower prices by discouraging "speculation" in commodity stocks; he quotes Tooke to the effect that the difference in interest rates between 3 percent and 6 percent for three months is too small a part of a price of a quarter of wheat to affect speculation (Keynes 1930: Volume I, 194–6).

In his own survey of the literature, Keynes attributes to Marshall (in his testimony before the Gold and Silver Commission) the idea "of an additional supply of money . . . reaching the price-level by means of a stimulation of investment (or speculation) through a lower Bank-rate" (Keynes 1930: Volume I, 191). Keynes argues however against excessive emphasis on the word and idea "speculation." He is convinced that Marshall's main point was "the idea that what raises prices is the creation of additional purchasing power, but that in the modern economic world the organisation of the credit system is such that the 'speculators' are the people into whose hands new money is most likely to find its way in the first instance, Bank-rate playing an obvious part in this causal train" (Keynes 1930: Volume I, 192-3). As I interpret this, it is consistent with my reading of Marshall, as discussed in Chapter 3, that he seemed not altogether comfortable with the role of the discount rate or Bank rate in the mechanism, solid in his adherence to the quantity theory; it almost seemed that he ceded the effect of the rate of interest on "speculation" only when pressed quite hard by his interlocutors.

Hawtrey, according to Keynes, emphasized the effect of Bank rate on one kind of investment only. Wicksell, on the other hand, despite the distortion injected by Cassel's interpretation, and despite the fact that his presentation was, to Keynes, "obscurely presented", nevertheless "was closer to the fundamental conception of Bank-rate as affecting the relationship between investment and saving" (Keynes 1930: Volume I, 196). Keynes reports Wicksell's distinction between the natural and market rates of interest; whenever they differ, even if the difference is constant, there will be cumulative, unbounded movements of prices. This, says Keynes, is very close to his own analysis. For, he says, if Wicksell's natural rate of interest is defined as that which equalizes saving and investment, then so long as the money rate of interest is such as to induce investment in excess of saving, prices will rise, entrepreneurs will bid up wages, "earnings," and the process will continue as long as the money rate is less than the natural rate. In any case, Wicksell, Keynes argues, was the first to emphasize the importance of investment as the avenue through which the rate of interest reaches the price level, and to be aware "that *Investment* in this context means *Investment* and not speculation" (Keynes 1930: Volume I, 197-8, italics his).[2]

The effect of a change in interest rates on domestic èxpenditure is spelled out in some detail. Savings are supposed to increase, slightly, and investment to decrease more. The investment theory is a prologue to that of the *General*

---

[2] Of great historical interest is Keynes's approving citation here of a new school of thought expressing ideas, he says, very close to his own, the Austrian and German writers of what he calls the "neo-Wicksell school": Ludwig Mises, Hans Neisser, and Friedrich Hayek. They are cited only in passing because they are recent, having appeared as the *Treatise* was going to press, and because "in German I can only clearly understand what I know already! – so that *new* ideas are apt to be veiled from me by the difficulties of language" (Keynes 1930 I: 199 and 199n). Neisser's early work (1936) is discussed briefly along with that of Neisser and Modigliani (1953) in Chapter 15 below.

*theory*. Short-term interest rates affect long-term ("bond-rate") and the demand for capital goods responds to this promptly and elastically. Anticipations of future government policy play a role, as do expectations in general. And availability of funds at existing rates is here as well. So the initial and *"primary"* effect of a rise in Bank rate is a decline in the price of capital goods, and a rise in saving "of which the former is more likely to be quantitatively important than the latter" (Keynes 1930: Volume I, 204, italics his). The secondary effects are a fall in the output of capital goods and, to the extent that saving increases, a decrease in the demand for and output of consumption goods. The tertiary effect is a further decline in prices of consumer goods due to the reduced income of the producers of capital goods.

Thus far, then, we have reductions in the prices of all types of goods, losses to all classes of entrepreneurs, and a reduction in employment. This unemployment will continue either until there is a decline in Bank rate or, fortuitously, there is a change (a rise) in the natural rate of interest (Keynes 1930: Volume I, 206). The unemployment may actually increase, since initially employers may try to avoid laying off workers if they expect their losses to be temporary. In addition, the prospects of losses lowers the natural rate of interest below its normal level and widens the gap between the natural and the market rate.

Eventually wages will fall, and this is the "consummation of the whole process of pressure," but if they do not, unemployment will continue. There is a tendency to view with satisfaction the decline in prices, which improves the balance of trade, and the decline in the demand for money. This is unjustified, however. The lower prices involve losses to entrepreneurs, as indicated by the existence of unemployment: wages have not yet fallen. As long as this situation continues, unemployment continues to grow. If the monetary pressure can be alleviated only by reduced employment and output, "then monetary equilibrium will continue to require the indefinite prolongation of chronic unemployment" (Keynes 1930: Volume I, 207–8).

Here Keynes has left completely the mechanical quantity theory. In his avowedly Wicksellian approach, it is the initial deficiency of investment, resulting from higher interest rates, which causes prices to fall. The subsequent process is that which brings costs (wages) down "at which point a new position of equilibrium can be established" (Keynes 1930: Volume I, 191). The issue of the importance of reducing "costs" (wages) is a theme which pervades Keynes's discussion of the international mechanism throughout the *Treatise* and the Macmillan Committee testimony.

## The dilemma and what to do about it

Keynes emphasized heavily and discussed extensively a problem close to that which later became known as the "policy dilemma", the conflict between internal and external equilibrium. But not quite. Keynes is not really worried here about the difficulties of achieving structural equilibrium in the balance of payments. He is more concerned, in general, with the question of short-term equilibrium and short-term capital mobility.

A particularly clear and explicit statement of the problem is embedded in his discussion of the reasons that though business cycles are highly concurrent between countries the world nevertheless does not behave exactly like a single country on a gold standard. This account is combined with an intense questioning of the desirability of a gold standard in particular or fixed exchange rates in general.[3] The major villain in the piece (then as now!) is the high degree of capital mobility. International capital flows are highly elastic with respect to the rate of interest (specifically, to interest rate differentials). The trade account, as noted above, responds more sluggishly; thence the problem.

This high degree of short-period mobility of international lending, combined with a low degree of short-period mobility of international trade, means . . . that even a small and temporary divergence in the local rate of interest from the international rate may be dangerous. In this way adherence to an international standard tends to limit unduly the power of a Central Bank to deal with its own domestic situation so as to maintain internal stability and the optimum of employment. (Keynes 1930: Volume II, 309)

The implication of this is that given enough time, the basic balance of payments (the current account and long-term capital flows) would recover its equilibrium, even if the country maintained an independent monetary policy. But the rate of interest which keeps the overall capital account in balance (since the current account responds more slowly [his constant theme]) may well not be "the optimum rate for maintaining the equilibrium of domestic industry" (Keynes 1930: Volume II, 318). Stated alternatively, under a fixed exchange rate regime a country participating heavily in international capital markets will be hard put to maintain an independent monetary policy, one designed to influence domestic expenditure.

The belief in an extreme mobility of international lending and a policy of unmitigated *laissez-faire* towards foreign loans, on which most Englishmen have been brought up, has been based, as I have repeatedly urged above, on too simple a view of the causal relations between foreign lending [the capital account] and foreign investment [the current account]. Because – apart from gold movements – *net* foreign lending and *net* foreign investment must always exactly balance, it has been assumed that no serious problem presents itself . . . All this, however, neglects the painful, and perhaps violent,

---

[3] It would take me too far afield to cite or discuss the passage, but Keynes's brief section on the history, mythology, and psycho-analytic aspects of the gold standard is a sheer delight. The reader is urged to peruse it in the original (Keynes 1930: Volume II, Chapter 35, (i) Auri Sacra Fames, 289–92).

reactions of the mechanism which has to be brought into play in order to force *net* foreign lending and *net* foreign investment into equality.

I do not know why this should not be considered obvious. If English investors, not liking the outlook at home, fearing labour disputes or nervous about a change of government, begin to buy more American securities than before, why should it be supposed that this will be naturally balanced by increased British exports? For, of course, it will not . . .

If it were as easy to put wages up and down as it is to put bank-rate up and down, well and good. But this is not the actual situation. A change in international financial conditions or in the wind and weather of speculative sentiment may alter the volume of foreign lending, if nothing is done to counteract it, by tens of millions in a few weeks. Yet there is no possibility of rapidly altering the balance of imports and exports to correspond. (Keynes 1930: Volume II, 335–6)

A solution, therefore, is to make capital movements costly, widening the permissible spread between domestic and foreign interest rates, and giving the authorities at least some leeway in setting domestic rates, at least temporarily. If capital movements were totally costless they would be large and frequent, and interest rates would always be identical everywhere. "If, therefore, a country adopts an international standard, it is a question just how international it wishes to be " (Keynes 1930: Volume II, 319).

One way of discouraging capital movements was to widen the gold points. This should be coupled with forward market intervention, Hawtrey's critique of which we have already discussed. The point of the proposals is to increase the cost and the uncertainty associated with short-term capital movements, thus reducing their elasticity with respect to interest rates, making interest arbitrage imperfect. This is, of course, the precise opposite of Hayek's recommendation, which was to narrow the band to zero, making the par value unique and equal to the gold export and import points. This difference is fitting, since their goals were precisely opposite: in Keynes's case, to enhance the power of the monetary authorities to pursue what Hayek would call a "nationalistic" policy, and in Hayek's case to lessen or eliminate it (see Chapter 7). Keynes made this explicit, recognizing that costless capital movements would lead to complete equalization of interest rates across countries. An independent monetary policy to achieve national income goals involved making a country less "international" and one way to do this was to make capital movements more costly.

Historically, the spread between buying and selling prices for gold originated, Keynes said, from transport costs and as a measure of convenience of getting notes from the Bank of England on demand *vis-à-vis* the cost of taking gold to the Mint and waiting for it to be coined. This option was eliminated with the Currency Act of 1928, since when this reason for a spread between the Bank's buying and selling prices had been simply "an historical survival" (Keynes 1930: Volume II, 322). "The present system of an international gold standard, in combination with separate national systems of Central Banks and domestic money, would be unworkable if the gold points coincided (as they do, in practice, within a country)." Having established the principle, one was now haggling over the price, and he argued that the "degree of . . . separation [of the gold prices] should not be a matter of material costs of transport or historical survivals" (Keynes 1930: Volume II, 331).

The possible objections to adjusting the gold points as a policy tool are twofold. First, that the discretion thus granted the central bank could be abused

and become the occasion and the excuse for a Central Bank to omit to take measures to remedy what was not a passing phase but a cause of persisting disequilibrium. It is true, of course, that every increase in the discretion allowed to a Central Bank, so as to increase its power of intelligent management, is liable to abuse. (Keynes 1930: Volume II, 329)

The second reservation would be that for a financial center (such as London) to function well, the gold point spread should be as narrow as possible, ideally zero. But he feels this objection is covered by his recommendation that the Bank of England be permitted to quote forward rates at which it would trade and could offer foreigners as much certainty of short-term transactions into and out of sterling as it, the central bank, felt they should have (Keynes 1930: Volume II, 330). Again, the idea of having different conditions for residents and for foreigners, rejected by the Cunliffe Committee, was one that cropped up on numerous occasions in the ensuing decades.

Giving specific examples of the kind of situation he has in mind, he cites the conditions that prevailed in the fall of 1928 when on domestic considerations the Federal Reserve Board wanted higher short-term interest rates, the Bank of England wanted rates to be as low as possible, and neither was interested in encouraging capital movements. Under Keynes's plan, the Federal Reserve Banks could have lowered their buying price for gold and the Bank of England could have raised its selling price. Forward market intervention could have helped strengthen the effects of this increased spread. In the event, the only policy the Bank of England had at its disposal in 1928–9, Keynes argues, was moral suasion. In September 1929, on the other hand, the Canadians successfully insulated the domestic economy from the effects of abnormally high interest rates on Wall Street by informally widening the gold points. They were vindicated, *inter alia*, by the brief duration of the high rates in New York (Keynes 1930: Volume II, 329).

Other proposals involved selective taxation of short-term financial capital movements. Abandoning his previous sharp distinction between debtor and creditor countries, Keynes notes that contemporary major financial centers, such as London and New York, probably had small net positions, since short-term debits were very high. Since the balance sheet totals were also large, this meant that such a market was "very much at the mercy of the initiative of its foreign clients" who make portfolio adjustments between long- and short-term assets, gold and paper, or moving their holdings between various international centers (Keynes 1930: Volume II, 316).

Regarding restrictions on foreign lending, Keynes has a number of ideas regarding both the long run and the short. In the long run, he argued, British banking and capital institutions were biased toward lending abroad, and habits and institutions were geared to foreign investment.[4] Discriminatory taxation (as in France) might be necessary. It might be necessary also for another, more fundamental, reason, apart from discouraging short-term capital mobility. With capital mobile and labor not, real efficiency wages could not remain different in different countries. Thus workers in rich old countries could not enjoy the fruits of the country's wealth in the form of higher wages unless foreign lending were restricted, and foreign lending postpones

the day at which the workers in the country can enjoy, in the shape of higher wages, the advantages of this growing accumulation of capital.[5] Nineteenth-century philosophy was wont to assume that the future is always to be preferred to the present. But modern communities are more inclined to claim the right to decide for themselves in what measure they shall subscribe to this austere doctrine. (Keynes 1930: Volume II, 313)

This is an interesting precursor of the literature of the 1960s on the optimal rate of taxation of capital export (Kemp 1966, Jones 1967), as well as of much of the contemporary literature on the theory of international trade as a problem in intertemporal optimization (see Chapter 1, note 5). His

[4] Brown (1940: Volume I, 158–60) discusses the change in attitude after World War I, in Britain, toward control over capital flows. "The prevailing attitude [in Britain before the war] was that new capital issues stimulated trade in general, and, therefore, British trade as a whole." If they had imposed restrictions, like the French, they would have challenged the primacy of the London money and capital market, which was characterized by "the lack of restriction imposed by the London market upon the utilization of sterling as a world medium of exchange. The war ended with a victory in Great Britain of the principle that the proceeds of foreign loans should be spent in the lender's country."

[5] This is reminiscent of some much later arguments to the effect that a number of countries would have been better off (with higher incomes and higher rates of growth) if they had restricted their foreign lending. One hears this argued particularly with respect to Great Britain in the nineteenth century and the United States in the post-World War II period. Harrod (1933: 128–9) wrote, for example: "It is arguable that in the post-war decade . . . [Britain] clung too tenaciously to her lending habit in a period when for various reasons her . . . [traded goods] output was checked in its normal rate of expansion, and that unemployment and depression in the country would have been less, had she lent less." White made a very similar point about fin-de-siècle France (see Chapter 12, page 236).

restrictionism with respect to capital movements came to full flower, as we shall see below, in the memoranda of the 1940s leading up to Bretton Woods.

What also came to light in those papers, and we see it in the *Treatise* as well, is Keynes's persistent belief in international cooperation and organization. Thus, as early as the *Treatise*, he developed an early version of what became his proposed Clearing Union and presented it as the ideal solution: a Supernational Bank, with every country announcing its "obligation to buy and sell its local money on prescribed terms in exchange for balances" at that Bank. Gold movements would then occur only between each country and the Supernational Bank, never between pairs of countries (Keynes 1930: Volume II, 330–1; also Chapter 38). Essentially the advantage of this is to help central banks mobilize the resources they need to sterilize capital flows when they deem it desirable. Again, he stresses the asymmetry between debtors and creditors, since "it is easier to lend less in an emergency than to borrow more" (Keynes 1930: Volume II, 309–10).

## On the choice of an exchange rate regime

Keynes presents an overview (or his view) of the ideal type of international system ("Should Standards of Value be International?") which is an interesting coupling of elegant logic and (to me) incomprehensible acceptance of popular wisdom.

He notes that for traders (in commodities) fixed exchange rates are highly convenient and useful but not essential if there are well-developed forward markets. For lending, however, certainty is more desirable, but this is more true of short-term than of long-term lending. The reason for this, evidently, is that, since he never considers a completely free float, long-run fluctuations in exchange rates will be small. He assumes that the limit to fluctuation of the exchange rate has been set, say, at 5 percent. Fluctuation within such a range would not discourage long-term lending; it would discourage the short-, but this is certainly not a disadvantage in his view.

A major practical difficulty in achieving an international standard is the differences in the overall policy stance of the world's several major central banks; he refers to the difference in the "attitude toward gold on the part of the Bank of England or of the Reichsbank . . . from that of the Bank of France or of the Bank of Spain" and the position of the United States, combining immense holdings of gold and being "exceedingly jealous of surrendering any of her own autonomous powers to an international body" (Keynes 1930: Volume II, 336). If these could be overcome, there would still be the question of what is best for an individual country, a standard based on the "Purchasing Power of Money or Consumption Standard" (price stabiliza-tion?); one based on "the Earnings Standard" (wage stabilization?); or "some version of the International Standard, *i.e.* a standard based on the prices of the principal commodities which enter into international trade weighted in proportion to their importance in world commerce, which in practice might not be very different from a wholesale standard of raw materials" (Keynes 1930: Volume II, 337). In the long run all three of these standards would probably move the same way, he argues. Nevertheless, before the return to gold (1925) it seemed

that there were better prospects for the management of a national currency on progressive lines, if it were to be freed from the inconvenient and sometimes dangerous obligation of being tied to an unmanaged international system; that the evolution of independent national systems with fluctuating exchange rates would be the next step to work for; and that the linking up of these again into a *managed* international system would probably come as the last stage of all. (Keynes 1930: Volume II, 338, italics mine)

To-day the reasons seem stronger – in spite of the disastrous inefficiency which the international gold standard has worked since its restoration five years ago (fulfilling the worst fears and gloomiest prognostications of its opponents), and the economic losses, second only in amount to those of a great war, which it has brought upon the world – to reverse the order of procedure; to accept, substantially, the *fait accompli* of an international standard; and to hope for progress from that starting-point towards a scientific management of the central controls – for that is what our monetary system surely is – of our economic life. For to seek the ultimate good *viâ* an autonomous national system would mean not only a frontal attack on the forces of conservatism, entrenched with all the advantages of possession, but it would divide the forces of intelligence and goodwill and separate the interests of nations. (Keynes 1930: Volume II, 338)

He concludes that the best solution open for the time is "the management of the value of gold by a Supernational authority, with a number of national monetary systems clustering round it, each with a discretion to vary the value of its local money in terms of gold within a range of (say) 2 percent" (Keynes 1930: Volume II, 338).

This was to come, of course, formally at any rate, fifteen years later, with the establishment of the IMF.[6] It seems to me, however, that Keynes was never able satisfactorily to reconcile his passion for national autonomy of economic policy which, given his life-long advocacy of capital controls, might have been at least partially achievable with flexible exchange rates, with his (aesthetic?) distaste for floating rates. As will become apparent in the next chapter, he persisted in this until the end of his life. In his plans for the post-World War II institutions, leading up to the Bretton Woods meetings, he took the rejection of floating rates as axiomatic.

[6] I would argue that this was a formal victory only, and that the famous Bretton Woods system was no less a dollar standard than the pre-World War I system was a sterling standard.

## Summary

The *Treatise* is the most formal of Keynes's writings discussed here. And yet, even in Volume I, subtitled *The pure theory of money*, as contrasted with Volume II, *The applied theory of money*, he never loses sight of the real world and its problems.

His description of the international adjustment mechanism under fixed exchange rates starts with the neoclassical emphasis on the rate of interest and its dual role in influencing both the capital and current accounts. Strongly Wicksellian in its macroeconomic theory, combined with the Marshall-Lerner price elasticities conditions, it is formally a two-country model with non-traded goods. It is a general-equilibrium model, and he emphasizes continually the national income accounting identities of the balance of payments. Savings and investment being functions of the rate of interest, there is a gap between them associated with every level of the rate of interest. Some combination of price level and interest rate will yield zero on both accounts. The problem is that achieving the required price level for the rate of interest that is determined by international capital market conditions may be very unpleasant and may require a high rate of unemployment for an unacceptably long period of time. His constant theme is the dual role of the central bank's discount rate in influencing both the capital account on the one hand, and, on the other hand, the current account, via investment, employment, and ultimately prices.

Since the major villain is the inordinately high mobility of financial capital, one solution is to make capital movements costly. For this he recommends a number of techniques which enable the authorities to maintain a wider spread between interest rates in the several countries; most notable of these is intervention in forward exchange markets to reduce the advantage of covered interest arbitrage. But this is not likely to suffice. The problem of the conflict between internal and external balance, and the resulting conflicts of interest between various central banks cause him to question seriously the desirability of fixed exchange rates. But the alternative of floating rates he considers to be worse. He is left therefore (as we shall see more clearly in Chapter 10) with the desirable (and he believes feasible) establishment of some sort of world central bank, that is, a very high degree of cooperation and integration internationally, and the much less attractive path of a good deal of restriction, particularly on capital movements and also on trade.

# Late Keynes: towards Bretton Woods

What became known as the keynesian theory of international payments was not, to my knowledge, ever spelled out by Keynes. The marginal propensity to import, and then the multiplier, began to appear in the late 1930s and early 1940s, associated with the names of Harrod (1933), Machlup (1939, 1943), Metzler (1942a, 1942b), Neisser and Modigliani (1953), Paish (1936), and others. A detailed account of these is presented in Chapters 14 and 15 on "the keynesians." The full-blown integration of keynesian macroeconomic theory with endogenous capital mobility, monetary changes, and some notion of balance of payments equilibrium (even of a short- or medium-run nature) did not appear until the 1950s, with Meade, Mundell, Fleming, and, with great qualification, Metzler, whom I discuss in Chapter 16.

Keynes himself, after the *Treatise* and the Macmillan Committee testimony, which were roughly coeval, wrote nothing of importance on international economics except for the proposals and correspondence regarding the postwar monetary plans. These, however, constitute a major body of work expressing his views on the international monetary system and the problems he thought were likely to arise in the postwar period. While they are less formally expressed, more diffuse, and more "politically" oriented than the earlier writings I have discussed, they do reveal an analytical stance which is highly recognizable and worth exploring.

In the letters and drafts (and redrafts) of plans for the postwar monetary system (Keynes 1940–4 [1980]) several themes are prevalent throughout. These are the non-existence, or extreme weakness of an international adjustment mechanism and the destabilizing influence of capital movements.[1]

---

[1] For discussion of the meetings, preparations, and evaluation of the events since Bretton Woods, see Thirlwall (1976) *passim*, especially the contributions of Lords Kahn and Balogh. I have tried to concentrate primarily on what Keynes's own writings leading up to the meetings tell us about his views of the adjustment mechanism, rather than on either his success in persuading the world to accept his views or on their vindication by subsequent events.

## The mechanism of adjustment (or lack thereof)

His view of the adjustment mechanism, throughout, including the *Economic journal* debate with Ohlin (1929a, 1929b) and until the end of his life, was that if it existed at all it was basically a classical one. "Keynesian" in its emphasis on disequilibrium, his mechanism is nevertheless unrepentantly classical in the sense that it operates through the price and terms of trade effects. This may involve a good deal of painful contraction and deflation on the part of a deficit country, which is the basis for Keynes's concern with the asymmetry between deficit and surplus countries. But I can find no statement of a "keynesian" foreign-trade multiplier, of the type which Machlup exposited (Machlup 1943) and which made its way into the textbooks for a period of about thirty years.

However, since this was the only mechanism available, and since it functioned so haltingly, even if the Marshall-Lerner conditions held and elasticities were appropriate, because of the downward stickiness of incomes, he came to despair, by the fall of 1941, of the possibility of a viable adjustment mechanism at all. (There are strong hints of this in his testimony before the Macmillan Committee, discussed in Chapter 6.) He subsequently recovered his optimism slightly and went on to try to create the institutional environment in which a mechanism might function, however imperfectly and unautomatically.

In a memorandum accompanying his first draft of a proposal for an International Clearing Union, he spelled out his then current views of the past, present, and future state of the international adjustment mechanism. It is breathtaking in its condemnation of the notion of a stable equilibrium, attainable by a mechanism which would be socially and politically acceptable.

[T]he problem of maintaining equilibrium in the balance of payments between countries has never been solved, since methods of barter gave way to the use of money and bills of exchange . . . [T]he failure to solve this problem has been a major cause of impoverishment and social discontent and even of wars and revolutions. In the past five hundred years there have been only two periods of about fifty years each (the ages of Elizabeth and Victoria in English chronology) when the use of money for the conduct of international trade can be said to have "worked", first whilst the prodigious augmentation of the supply of silver from the new world was substituting the features of inflation for those of deflation (bringing a different sort of evil with it), and again in the second half of the nineteenth century when . . . the system of international investment pivoting on London transferred the onus of adjustment from the debtor to the creditor position. (Memorandum of September 8, 1941, Keynes 1940–4 [1980: 21])

This theme of the asymmetry between debtor and creditor countries is, of course, one of Keynes's major leitmotifs.

A third period during which he grudgingly admits there may have been a successful international system occurred during "the vast development of trade and prosperity throughout the Mediterranean countries and beyond which followed the dispersal of the temple hoards of Persia by Alexander the Great" (Keynes 1940–4 [1980: 30]).

To suppose that there exists some smoothly functioning automatic mechanism of adjustment which preserves equilibrium if only we trust to methods of *laissez-faire* is a doctrinaire delusion which disregards the lessons of historical experience without having behind it the support of sound theory. So far from currency *laissez-faire* having promoted the international division of labour, which is the avowed goal of *laissez-faire*, it has been a fruitful source of all those clumsy hindrances to trade which suffering communities have devised in their perplexity as being better than nothing in protecting them from the intolerable burdens flowing from currency disorders. Until quite recently, nearly all departures from international *laissez-faire* have tackled the symptoms instead of the cause. (Keynes 1940–4 [1980: 21–2])

In short, the golden age of the gold standard, which in the twentieth century became the paradigm for the classical (actually, what I have labeled the neoclassical) model of international monetary economics was, Keynes is arguing here, an outlier, an exception, an isolated event, and not the prototype it was thought to have been.[2]

While exogenous changes in expenditures certainly affect the trade balance, he averred, and hence have an impact on other countries' trade and income, changes in expenditures are not a significant part of the adjustment mechanism. Nor, as we noted, are changes in capital movements, which were viewed as both destabilizing and an obstacle to a country's pursuit of its own independent interest rate policy.

And floating exchange rates are no palliative, as far as Keynes is concerned. That a freely floating exchange rate "would discover for itself a position of equilibrium" seems to him so obviously misguided that he does not trouble to spell out why it is wrong (Keynes 1940–4 [1980: 22]).

In the interwar period almost every solution was tried and found wanting, he argued. The period was "a laboratory experiment [in] all the alternative false approaches to the solution":

1   freely fluctuating exchange rates;
2   "liberal credit and loan arrangements between the creditor and the debtor countries . . . [based] on the false analogy of superficially similar

---

[2]   This is clearly the "revisionist" view of the Golden Age discussed in Chapter 7. Analogously, there are those who argue, correctly in my view, that the Bretton Woods System functioned relatively smoothly in the 1950s and part of the 1960s because it was really a dollar standard in whch the basic balance deficit of the United States was financed, to the satisfaction of almost everybody, by the U.S. serving as the world's banker, borrowing short, and supplying the rest of the world with the means of payment it demanded.

nineteenth-century transactions between old-established and newly developing countries where the loans were self-liquidating because they themselves created new sources of payment";

3 "the theory that the unlimited free flow of gold would automatically bring about adjustments of price-levels and activity in the recipient country which would reverse the pressure";

4 deflation and, even worse, "*competitive* deflations" to force wage and price adjustments "which would force or attract trade into new channels";

5 devaluations, and still worse, competitive devaluations, to the same end;

6 tariffs, and other impediments to trade, "to restore the balance of international commerce by restriction and discrimination" (Keynes 1940–4 [1980: 22–3], italics his).

He thus set about considering the postwar prospects in a mood of extreme pessimism, which stemmed from three roots.

One is this conviction of the absence of an automatic adjustment mechanism.

Another is his view that most capital flows – those that occurred between the first and second World Wars, those that he feared would occur after World War II, and presumably also those, if any, that took place between the reigns of the Two Queens (Elizabeth I and Victoria) – are destabilizing. Of his conviction that this was the case in the interwar period and was highly likely to be the case after the war there can be no doubt.

The third is his belief that whatever mechanism there was was asymmetrical; he was concerned throughout with the tendency of surplus countries (read: the United States) persistently to sterilize inflows and the difficulty for deficit countries (sometimes Britain, sometimes the rest of the world, other than the United States) to contract. He is obviously very angry at, and distrustful of, the Americans from this point of view. (This view was strongly expressed as far back as the *Tract*. See Chapter 8.)

I find his argument here slightly ambiguous; it is not always clear how he allocated his skepticism and aggravation between the several faults of the system: whether he thought that there did not exist any automatic adjustment mechanism at all, or whether he thought that there was a chronic, built-in tendency to thwart adjustment by sterilizing the monetary effects of imbalance, especially on the part of surplus countries. The failure of adjustment to occur down the centuries (with the above-noted exceptions) could hardly have been the fault of the benighted Governors of the Federal Reserve System. As we have seen, there is at times a similar ambiguity in both the Macmillan Report and in Keynes's testimony before the Macmillan Committee.

I have emphasized here the persistence, over time, of Keynes's view of the inadequacy of the international adjustment mechanism. I consider this to be consistent, rather than at odds, with Moggridge's statement that by the time we are dealing with here, the early 1940s, Keynes "had at one time or another recommended almost every exchange rate regime known to modern analysts except completely freely floating exchange rates" (Moggridge 1986: 66–7). Continuing dissatisfaction with the way things worked, currently or, with few exceptions, in the past, led to continued searching for ameliorating institutional arrangements.

## The asymmetry of adjustment

The asymmetry between deficit and surplus countries is his constant refrain and has long been associated with Keynes, and with the Keynes as opposed to the White Plan at Bretton Woods. He argues eloquently that debtor countries are forced to adjust while creditors have the choice – the view again is one of the widespread practice of sterilization and of offsetting the monetary effects of imbalances.

On the deficit side, the description of the adjustment is no different from that in the Macmillan Committee, for example; thus the early Memorandum of September 8, 1941 (Keynes 1940–4 [1980: 21 ff]), like the Ohlin debate, dwells at some length on the terms of trade changes required to effect a transfer (to eliminate a deficit). It is the most simple form of Marshall-Lerner analysis, combined with concern about the inelastic demand for primary products. Money income effects will work, if at all, only through this mechanism; thus, using language very similar to that of his testimony to the Macmillan Committee, he speaks of deflation "to force an adjustment of wage- and price-levels which would force or attract trade into new channels" (Keynes 1940–4 [1980: 23]).

To repeat, he is still basically "classical" (or "anti-classical") and un-"keynesian" in his discussion of the mechanism. That is, he worries about a price-adjustment mechanism plagued by rigidities and frictions; he is not explicitly substituting the keynesian mechanism in its place. It is true that the formal pure "keynesian" adjustment mechanism also gives incomplete adjustment to a disturbance; that is, it does not substitute an automatic stable system for the classical one; thus price adjustments are never irrelevant. (I shall deal with this in greater detail in Chapter 15.)

Clearly, if the mechanism of adjustment is viewed as working through a change in relative prices, and if prices are not perfectly flexible, then the system is indeed not symmetrical. The welfare cost of achieving any given change in relative prices between two countries is very different if the deficit country has to contract income and employment in order to reduce its prices than it is if the surplus country is expanding. (This is the basis for what became known in the 1970s, among financial journalists, at any rate, as the "locomotive theory".)

However, he adds that there is a further asymmetry in that when "small" countries adjust they have to experience a real income loss, a deterioration in the terms of trade, whereas this is not true for large countries. I can make sense of this only by assuming that what he meant by a "small" country was, as distinct from the contemporary meaning of a country unable to affect the terms on which it trades, a debtor country; a not small country was a creditor. He names both Germany (paying reparations) and Brazil as "small" here. A "large", that is to say creditor, country with a deficit could reduce its foreign lending and thus achieve overall balance. A "small", debtor, country would have to do something to earn more revenue in trade, and this in general would imply a deterioration in the terms of trade. He does not even mention the possible symmetrical situation of a surplus/creditor country which reduces its purchases from abroad (by domestic inflation) and thereby improves its terms of trade, thus causing the same deterioration in the terms of trade of the debtor/deficit country. Presumably that would never occur (Keynes 1940–4 [1980: 28–30]).

Thus the main reason the adjustment mechanism neither could, nor should be expected to, work is "that it throws the main burden of adjustment on the country which is in the *debtor* position on the international balance of payments, – that is on the country which is (in this context) by hypothesis the *weaker* and above all the *smaller* in comparison with the other side of the scales which (for this purpose) is the rest of the world." Social strain, he argued, is greater on the downside than on the upside. Furthermore, the creditor can choose whether or not to adjust; the debtor cannot (Keynes 1940–4 [1980: 27–8], italics his). It might be argued by some that this would make the adjustment more inequitable, but it is not clear to me why it should render it more *difficult*.

At this juncture Keynes was evidently thinking not of price adjustment after all, which would involve price increases in the surplus countries, causing a decrease in their exports or stimulating their imports, but rather of expenditure increases which would shift their offer curves out. Here, as noted above, it matters to the several countries which one does the "adjusting"; this affects world income, and symmetry goes by the board.

Later, in 1942, he argued that income and employment can be exogenous factors affecting the balance of payments: if the United States succeeds in maintaining a high level of employment after the war, as it is promising to try to do, he wrote, this will go a long way toward making the world livable, according to Keynes; but he is not optimistic about this happening. The mechanism he described is the keynesian one: any increase in demand in a country decreases available output for exports and increases imports (Keynes 1940–4 [1980: 155]).

If a country is too poor to live the way it would like, it must reduce its standard of living.[3] But

if, possessing the productive capacity, it lacks markets because of restrictive policies throughout the world, then the remedy lies in expanding its opportunities for export by removal of the restrictive pressure . . . It used to be supposed, without sufficient reason, that effective demand is always properly adjusted throughout the world; we tend to assume, equally without sufficient reason that it never can be. On the contrary, there is great force in the contention that, if active employment and ample purchasing power can be sustained in the main centres of the world trade, the problem of surpluses and unwanted exports will largely disappear. (Keynes 1940–4 [1980: 180])

By 1942, then, he seems to have had his faith in the existence of an adjustment mechanism somewhat restored, in the sense that full employment equilibrium in international payments is readily achievable, if only the world economy can be kept buoyant enough. This buoyancy, however, he certainly did not take for granted. Past successes had been both episodic and, by implication, accidents of fate. Thus, adjustment had occurred during the Elizabethan period because the Spanish silver raised prices in the creditor countries, so they took the initiative in the adjustment. And in the age of the other Queen, Victoria, the specific gestalt of markets, in London and in Paris, was such that gold movements immediately resulted in changes in the outflow of investment from the creditor countries, rather than in pressure for price and wage changes, so that "the burden . . . [was] carried by the stronger shoulders." The new system must once more demand that initiative come from the creditors, "whilst maintaining enough discipline in the debtor countries to prevent them from exploiting the new ease allowed them in living profligately beyond their means" (Keynes 1940–4 [1980: 30]).

This kind of comment about the need for restraint on the part of the deficit countries appears rarely in these writings; perhaps Keynes took them to be too obvious to need emphasizing, whereas the idea of exerting pressures on surplus countries was (rightly) considered to be an innovation which he perceived it necessary to emphasize and to market.

## Devices for pressuring the recalcitrant

The proposals for the International Clearing Union (which started in September 1941 and went through numerous drafts and changes) are wildly

---

[3] This seems to be in contradiction to many other statements, including the resolution which had been inserted to "satisfy Mr. Bevin" (Keynes 1940–4 [1980: 143]; see below).

optimistic compared to the memorandum which had preceded them. They deal extensively with technical problems and exhibit concern for the real world issues that were expected (in some cases, such as that of the overhang of sterling balances, correctly) to prevail in the postwar period. Much more aggressive than the final agreement,[4] they are buoyant, in the sense that he seemed to feel that a multilateral clearing system would and could function satisfactorily. In sharp contrast is his very bleak and gloomy view of the situation that could be expected to prevail in the absence of such a system.

Most of the sanctions against and pressures on deficit countries which are employed by the IMF in its standby agreements do not appear on Keynes's list. His suggested weapons seem gentle by current standards. A central bank whose debt for more than a year has been more than half its quota is a "Supervised Bank" and may be *required* (his italics) to devalue by not more than 5 percent in any one year; required to pay in any free gold it or its government may have in order to reduce the deficit; required to institute capital controls. Finally, in extremis, it is subject to expulsion from the system.

So, while the international organization could get tough about results, it was not to be excessively demanding with respect to what policies to propose. In 1942, to placate Mr. Bevin, Keynes went so far as to proffer the following amendment to his proposals, which was approved by the War Cabinet. "[T]he measures [for a country] 'to improve its position', if it has a substantial debit balance, do *not* include a deflationary policy, enforced by dear money and similar measures, having the effect of causing unemployment; for this would amount to restoring . . . the evils of the old automatic gold standard" (Keynes 1940–4 [1980: 143]). The possibility that both controls on capital movements and devaluation might together be inadequate even if the creditor countries were doing their bit is not considered.

As to the creditors, initially he proposed that there should be no limit to the size of a credit balance. The fear of a contraction forced on the world by a single large creditor was clearly expressed. A country with a net overall credit must (should) not be allowed to force the whole world and ultimately, therefore, itself as well, into contraction (Keynes 1940–4 [1980: 178]). A central bank which has been in credit for more than a year by more than a quarter of its quota is a "Surplus Bank". It may appreciate by no more than 5

---

[4] Somewhere along the line, as is the case in any successful negotiation, the sharp distinction between the original Keynes plan and the American plan, from the point of view of their expansionism, faded considerably. Keynes's original plan for the Clearing Union proposed an institution which behaved like a central bank and created credit. The American scheme was much more a mechanism for clearing balances. But by the end of the debate Keynes had stopped emphasizing this point, apparently accepting the American refusal to go along with anything as open-ended as his original scheme. Instead, he was emphasizing technical differences between the two schemes.

percent within any one year; it must permit foreign-owned assets to be withdrawn, if necessary by relaxing its exchange controls and encouraging non-resident convertibility, even of capital assets; and it may extend loans to countries declared to be in "Deficiency" (Keynes 1940–4 [1980: 36]). If pressures on the surplus countries did not avail, the world would either retreat into bilateralism (see below) or would need to establish a sufficiently expansionary institution so that the deficit countries did not have to contract as much; in other words, it would be necessary to establish a world central bank which would force a transfer from surplus to deficit areas by imposing an inflation tax. At one point he referred not to an inflation tax, but to *outright confiscation* of credit balances. "If at the end of any year the credit balance on the Clearing Account of any central bank exceeds the *full amount* of its index quota, the excess shall be transferred to the Reserve Fund of the Clearing Bank" (Keynes 1940–4 [1980: 36], italics his). In a later draft he indicated that he had never meant this seriously. The point of including it was "to make sure that some other way could be found. The main point is that the creditor should not be allowed to remain passive. For if he is, an impossible task is laid on the debtor country, which is for that very reason in the weaker position" (Keynes 1940–4 [1980: 49]).

In a similar vein he was to argue, two years later, that the Americans' acceptance of (nay, initiative in proposing) extremely strong sanctions against "scarce currencies" indicated their determination that such a situation would never be allowed to develop. He was right, as we know, but for the wrong reason. The scarce currency clause was never invoked, *inter alia*, because the dollar, for which it was intended, was never really "scarce".

Pressure on surpluses was to be immediate, after the war, and multilateral. Postwar relief and reconstruction, as well as commodity stabilization, is to be financed "in the first instance by those countries having credit balances on their Clearing Accounts for which they have no immediate use and are voluntarily leaving idle, and in the long run by those countries which have a chronic international surplus for which they have no beneficial employment" (Keynes 1940–4 [1980: 39]). This is very Keynesian in that it emphasizes (by implication) the notion that shortage and scarcity are not likely to be *the* postwar problems, and that aid for relief and reconstruction would be "free" to the donors, in the sense of bearing zero opportunity costs.[5]

Throughout these wartime discussions (Keynes 1940–4 [1980: 177], for example), one thing that comes through very clearly is the extent to which Keynes's view of the world was still colored by his perception of the United

---

[5] When the Marshall Plan was announced after World War II, it was widely hailed as an incredibly unselfish (I think the term was used by Winston Churchill) act: the idea of a country giving aid to foreigners during a time of full employment and inflationary pressure was astounding.

States' sterilization policy of the 1920s, the problem that so exercised him in the *Tract*. This was the major cause of the "contractionism" of the old gold standard. At that point he had expressed concern about the adequacy of the world's gold stock and had advocated the gold exchange standard. Now he was advocating a more deliberately expansionist monetary institution. What he really wanted was a world with only inside money, the quantity of which could change as needed, presumably when it passed from a low to high $k$.[6] He considered it, therefore, a major virtue of his plan that under it, if a country had a surplus and accumulated international reserve assets, this

would not involve, as would the importation of gold, the withdrawal of this purchasing power from circulation or the exercise of a deflationary and contractionist pressure on the whole world, including in the end the creditor country itself . . . Just as the development of national banking systems served to offset a deflationary pressure which would have prevented otherwise the development of modern industry, so . . . we may hope to offset the contractionist pressure which might otherwise overwhelm in social disorder and disappointment the good hopes of our modern world. The substitution of a credit mechanism in place of hoarding would have repeated in the international field the same miracle, already performed in the domestic field, of turning a stone into bread. (Keynes 1940–4 [1980: 177])

Again, when there are underemployed resources, there is, fairly clearly, a free lunch. This was written to White in August 1942. By then, though he was apparently still convinced that worldwide expansionism would be the first-best solution, he had toned down his demands upon creditors to advocacy of having the creditor share the onus and "responsibility for adjustment" with the debtor. Again, he views this as a partial return to the Victorian era when foreign investment was the shock absorber in the system. Paris and London played the game properly; New York has inherited their mantle but is not wearing it properly. The difference was the failure of gold to have the effect it was supposed to, the "breakdown of international borrowing" and the frequent hot money flights. But the creditor must be forced to participate and not remain "entirely passive" (Keynes 1940–4 [1980: 179–80]).

When Keynes came to defend the Bretton Woods agreement to the House of Lords, he stressed once more the sharing of responsibility for adjustment between deficit and surplus countries. But by that time all that was left of surplus countries' responsibility was the scarce currency clause.[7]

---

6 I argued essentially from the same position, positively rather than normatively, that such was the implication of the demands during the late 1950s and 1960s for more "international liquidity" (Flanders 1969).

7 There are numerous references in the correspondence to the scarce currency clause, generally expressing amused astonishment that the Americans had volunteered an arrangement which was likely to be used almost exclusively to their disadvantage. The hint frequently was

## The destabilizing effects of capital movements

Keynes was emphatic in all these papers on the need for restrictions on capital movements. Long-term capital mobility was a Good Thing, but was not likely to be very large. It should, for reasons unspecified, flow from countries with balance of payments [current account] surpluses to countries with deficits. That is the only configuration consistent with equilibrium in the basic balance of payments, which may have been what Keynes had in mind when he wrote that. (The League of Nations Gold Delegation had proposed essentially the same thing in 1932. For a discussion of Viner's criticism of the idea see Chapter 12, pages 230–1). During the nineteenth century, he argued, capital flowed from rich to poor, for development. After World War I, it first flowed from creditor to debtor but much of it was not for productive investment. Then things went from bad to perverse. In what he calls "the second phase preceding the present war," capital moved in the wrong direction, from countries with balance of trade deficits to those with surpluses. In brief, they were destabilizing. If the only problem in the interwar years had been the United States' trade surplus, it could have been financed by the output of new gold in the rest of the world. The addition of the speculative and "refugee" funds on top of this "brought the whole system to ruin." This could happen again. There might be speculative and refugee capital flights at any time, and in any direction, after the war. "Loose funds may sweep round the world disorganising all steady business. Nothing is more certain than that the movement of capital funds must be regulated; – which in itself will involve far-reaching departures from *laissez-faire* arrangements" (Keynes 1940–4 [1980: 31]).

The argument for multilateral trade and unrestricted payments was valid only for commodities and perhaps long-term capital "on the basis of exchanging *goods for goods*" (Keynes 1940–4 [1980: 12], italics mine). International investment for loan purposes should be revitalized and encouraged. Genuine new investment should be encouraged as should the movement of funds from surplus to deficit countries. But movements of

dropped that it was best not to draw this to their attention, since they were apparently a bit dim-witted and did not realize what they were recommending. This came up in correspondence with Robertson and also with Viner (see, for example, Keynes 1940–4 [1980: 320 ff]). But despite his pleasure at the Americans' willingness to go along with the scarce currency clause, Keynes, later in the war, expressed some lack of certainty about the emergence of a dollar shortage. "Everyone seems to me to be assuming, without sufficient reason, that the United States is going to run after the war an enormous credit balance *after having allowed for long-term capital movements*. I regard this as quite uncertain" (Keynes 1940–4 [1980: 324–5] italics mine). Viner also gets high points for clairvoyance on this issue, writing in 1943: "Over the long pull . . . I think the U.S. is as likely to be short as to be long of foreign short-term funds . . . I put no stock in a 'chronic scarcity of dollars'" (Keynes 1940–4 [1980: 330–1]).

"floating funds", based on the fears of political refugees, tax evasion, and similar flights of funds must not be allowed. Therefore, "[f]loating and liquid funds" other than trade acceptances and other funds involved in current banking business "shall only be lent and borrowed between central banks" (Keynes 1940–4 [1980: 54]). Capital controls need to be made a permanent part of the postwar institutions. "If this is to be effective, it involves the *machinery* of exchange control for *all* transactions, even though a general open licence is given for all remittances in respect of current trade" (Keynes 1940–4 [1980: 52], italics his). (On this latter point he was, incidentally, agreeing with the position of the Bank of England.) Since exchange controls are easier to enforce the more countries impose them, Britain should urge the United States and others to adopt controls as well. In fact, one reason for having an international organization, according to Keynes, was to insure that all countries had capital controls, since it was impossible for a single country to have them *without opening mail* [!], and this he would prefer not to have to advocate. Indeed, one of the main themes of his arguments with the Americans in the pre-Bretton Woods discussions was his insistence that they cooperate by imposing exchange controls on their residents, making the task of other exchange control authorities easier.

[I]nternational capital movements would be restricted so that they would only be allowed in the event of the country from which capital was moving having a *favourable balance with the country to which they were being remitted* . . . In the pre-war system they were unrestricted and we then had to take what steps we could . . . *to adjust other items in the account* so as to restore the balance. (Keynes 1940–4 [1980: 16–17], italics mine)

The italics in the above quotation, which are mine, emphasize another second theme, to be discussed below: the bilateralism in Keynes's *Weltanschauung* at this time.

At one point, the Americans seemed astonishingly receptive to the universality of exchange controls. In 1942 Keynes wrote a memorandum on the then current White proposals, and commented on a "useful proposal" not to allow capital inflow from a country that did not want the outflow; and even to return capital on request to the originating country! He quotes the American proposal to the effect that opposition, in principle, to control over trade in goods, capital, and gold "are hangovers from a Nineteenth Century economic creed, which held that international economic adjustments, if left alone, would work themselves out toward an 'equilibrium' with a minimum of harm to world trade and prosperity" (Keynes 1940–4 [1980: 164–6]).

The major reason for advocating controls on capital movements was to maintain control over domestic monetary policy. Monetary policy was a major tool of domestic management and "[c]apital control is a corollary to this" (Keynes 1940–4 [1980: 149]). Keeping control over the domestic interest rate involved limiting foreign investment to the amount of the trade surplus (Keynes 1940–4 [1980: 275]). Keynes had, incidentally, favored capital controls earlier, though for somewhat different reasons. Already in the Macmillan Report and his testimony before the committee we noted the concern expressed over destabilizing speculative capital movements. The adjustable peg system planned for the postwar era could only exacerbate this problem by adding another motive for speculative capital flights, or floods. This was actually on Keynes's mind as early as 1936 when he wrote to L. F. Giblin, in Australia, that Australia, Britain, and probably most countries, would eventually need control over all movements other than current account transactions. And the reason was, not interest rate autonomy directly, but exchange rate autonomy: the ability to undertake "from time to time . . . an alteration in the exchange rate as a part of the technique of monetary management." The response of speculative capital movements to past or expected (further) devaluation, would, if not prevented, "tend to aggravate a delicate position" (cited by Moggridge 1986: 58–9).

## Multi- versus bilateralism

The only useful innovation of recent times, in Keynes's view, was that of Hjalmar Schacht in the years just before the war. For discussions and descriptions of the German prewar arrangements, involving bilateral trade agreements, multiple exchange rates, frozen balances, counterpart funds and the like, see Nurkse (1944: 177–83) and Ellis (1941, especially Chapter IV). The fact that the purpose was evil and that the Germans exploited their trading partners, Keynes contended, "must not blind us to its possible technical advantage in the service of a good cause." In his early memorandum (Keynes 1940–4 [1980: 19]) he indicated that the ideal solution for the world was a clearing union, the proposed details of which he spelled out. Failing agreement on that, Britain should draw up a set of bilateral agreements, and agree to purchase only from those countries who were willing to buy her goods! The idea was to restore barter of goods between economies (not between individuals) "to return to the essential character and original purpose of trade whilst discarding the apparatus which had been supposed to facilitate, but was in fact strangling it." The world would enter the postwar era in severe disequilibrium. This would be particularly true for Britain, which never really restored equilibrium after World War I. Britain would have to export a lot more and would need markets. Here the opportunity for bilateralism came in, as, for example, Argentina would not be able to sell its wheat and corn to the United States so Britain could agree to buy these from her on condition that Argentina be "prepared to expend the proceeds on taking textiles and engineering products from us" (Keynes 1940–4 [1980: 23–6]).

The tone of this early memorandum, dated September 8, 1941 (Keynes 1940–4 [1980: 21 ff]) was, to repeat, gloomy. It was, even for Keynes, rather astonishingly interventionist. The reading I give it is that Keynes was arguing that if a multilateral system could be established that would probably be a good idea. If, as was likely, it could not, then bilateral balancing of a Schachtian type was essential. Even when he came to propose the International Clearing Union, he commented that for Britain a Schachtian bilateral program would probably be better in the immediate postwar period "whilst we were expanding our exports to the level we shall require in future" (Keynes 1940–4 [1980: 32]). This was based on *need* for exports, not on "conventional" mercantilist notions, or even what might be labeled keynesian-crypto-mercantilist ideas, perhaps of the kind that one might derive from Chapter 23 of the *General theory*, "Notes on Mercantilism." He did not, however, pursue the idea with much determination, and devoted his considerable energies to propagating the plan for the Clearing Union that later came to be known as the Keynes Plan.

While eschewing armchair psychoanalysis, I must note that the correspondence and drafts for a Clearing Union are considerably more optimistic than the first Memorandum of 1941. Whether the London blitz had depressed him, or whether as he got involved in working out the details of the Clearing Union he became more sanguine as to its feasibility, I do not know. But we find not only cogent arguments in favor of the scheme, but also severe – and apt – attacks on the evils of bilateralism, protectionism, quantitative restrictions and regulation, and the like.

By the second draft of the proposal for the Clearing Union, Keynes was vigorously opposing administrative restriction of imports as a response to balance of payments tightness. This would be, he argued, the worst policy. He demanded a general commitment against high tariffs, or any quotas or prohibitions of imports, export subsidies, barter agreements, or "restrictions on the disposal of receipts arising out of current trade" (Keynes 1940–4 [1980: 48–51]).

As the drafts and correspondence continue, the objections to bilateralism persist and, in fact, become more vocal and emphatic. Throughout, there is the concept of a multilateral scheme as an *alternative*, perhaps the only alternative, to restrictive bilateral balancing achieved through controls. Keynes rejected completely (perhaps correctly) the notion that the postwar world could conceivably be characterized by free multilateral payments, even if only on current account, without the help of an international organization. By May 18, 1943, in his maiden speech to the House of Lords, he was emphasizing multilateral clearing as perhaps the main point of the scheme and averring that "we may hope to get rid of the varied and complicated devices for blocking currencies and diverting or restricting trade which before the war were forced on many countries as a superimposed obstacle to commerce and prosperity" (Keynes 1940–4 [1980: 270]). An additional argument for multilateralism was the preservation of the role of the City as a financial center, which would be jeopardized by bilateralism (Keynes 1940–4 [1980: 94]).

The institution Keynes was promoting continued to be a frankly expansionist, money-creating one. His model was of that which he labeled the banking system in a "closed system" (Keynes 1940–4 [1980: 44]). "The plan aims at the substitution of an expansionist, in place of a contractionist, pressure on world trade, especially in the first years" (Keynes 1940–4 [1980: 46]). His concern was that the majority of countries would be concerned about paying for imports and would therefore try to stimulate exports and reduce non-essential imports and this would redound to the disadvantage of all. To avoid this kind of pressure, it would be required that the creditor countries not exercise contractionary pressure. As was noted above (p. 195) he felt that the advantage of the mobility of short-term funds which prevailed in the nineteenth century had been lost when "New York succeeded to the position of main creditor" and the system was subject to "the flight of loose funds from one depository to another." As usual, the villains' roles are played, each in its own way, by the Federal Reserve Board and the owners of flight capital (Keynes 1940–4 [1980: 179–80]).

In the second draft of the proposal, in December 1941, he specified that each member state would get a stated overdraft facility. Since the system is multilateral, "the overdraft facilities, whilst a relief to some, are not a real burden to others." A credit balance is to a country like importing gold: command over resources which it chooses not to spend just now, but can at any time. But the overdraft means that "the fact that the creditor country is not choosing to employ this purchasing power would not mean, as it does at present, that it is withdrawn from circulation and exerts a deflationary and contractionist pressure on the whole world including the creditor country itself." In short, he wanted a central organization to behave like a central bank stabilizing the volume of the world's transactions balances; the overdrafts would have constituted, however temporarily, increases in world money supply. This is the expansionism which I referred to above, and which Keynes explicitly advocates. It makes his views very closely akin to that of the nineteenth-century Banking School: the money supply is the correct one so long as it satisfies the "needs of trade". The political unacceptability of this arrangement is too obvious to dwell upon, in my view. We need only look at how long and difficult a process it was to implement the SDR scheme in the IMF, a much more modest undertaking. Of course, no country would have been forced to hold a credit balance and it could be cashed in at will. The overdrafts, he argued, are obviously no long-run solution to any country's problem; they are merely a way of buying time while adjustments are being made. What was needed was a machinery to effect such adjustments (Keynes 1940–4 [1980: 44–8]). I have already noted my difficulty in ascertaining just what Keynes thought this machinery was going to be.

In fairness to Keynes, it should be pointed out that bilateral clearings, pressure on surplus countries to "help" in the adjustment, to the point of forfeiting their surpluses, and similar departures from free multilateral exchange were either directly proposed or, by default, implicit in many of the schemes proposed for postwar institutions. Kindleberger (1943) presents an excellent survey and critique of many of these.

## Exchange rate adjustability

Keynes was very strongly in favor of fixed exchange rates, though, as I have noted, he barely elaborated on his reasons. Remember Moggridge's statement, cited page 190, to the effect that a flexible exchange rate regime was the only system not advocated by Keynes at one point or another. He dismissed the notion of flexible exchange rates summarily with one or two comments. Fixed "settled" exchange rates were important to stability and "if we can find a level, though not necessarily the optimum, which we and our markets and our competitors have settled down to, it is only in exceptional circumstances that we could gain much by disturbing it" (Keynes 1940–4 [1980: 106–7]). At the same time, he supported the commitment to an adjustable peg on the grounds, *inter alia*, that if there were mistakes in setting postwar exchange rates, a difficult and uncertain task, they ought to be amenable to correction without undue fuss (Keynes 1940–4 [1980: 439]).

He was convinced that it would be easier to settle on the correct rates of exchange after the war than it had been after World War I because wages were not yet, at least, so much out of line. The depreciations after World War I had not been successful. "Even such advantage as used to exist in depreciating the exchange has been greatly diminished by the growing practice of linking money wage rates to the cost of living" (Keynes 1940–4 [1980: 106–7]). He expressed, furthermore, the old concerns about the size of the relevant elasticities. On the other side of the coin, the permitted exchange rate changes (up to 5 percent) were not, in his view, great enough to encourage speculative capital movements in expectation of them. I find it interesting, and a bit of a puzzle, that although Keynes advocated his plan on the grounds that, unlike the gold standard, it did not require rigid exchange rates, he was thinking in terms of very small changes: 5 percent, without consultation, up to 10 percent *cumulatively* in case of real disequilibrium. And this in the face of his severe elasticity pessimism.

The most important aspect of the postwar arrangement was to be its expansionary nature. Again and again he emphasized the elasticity of supply of the international money he wanted the Clearing Union to create, bancor. His proposals were thus the opposite of the Bank Act of 1844. He stressed also that his plan "substituted bank money for gold, which would not in future limit the amount of money there would be." Throughout it is clear that the major objection to the gold standard was the inelasticity of the stock of gold (rather than the fixity of exchange rates). To get "good trade and full employment" it was necessary to "dethrone gold and creat[e] . . . a system of international credits so that trade was not limited by the amount of gold available" (Keynes 1940–4 [1980: 141]). But as he made clear elsewhere, it is not only the global inelasticity of gold supply which troubled him, but the mechanism for inducing such supply increases. No commodity money, no matter how elastic its supply might be, could be expected to increase specifically to serve the convenience of the debtors; increases would occur only consequent upon painful world deflation which was needed to encourage additions to the stock of the monetary commodity.

At other junctures, however, he worried that permanently fixed exchange rates imposed unnecessary and undesirable restrictions on a country. In defending the Bretton Woods Agreement before the House of Lords, he made this clear, almost in defiance of the Agreement he was so staunchly defending:

We are determined that, in future, the external value of sterling shall conform to its internal value as set by our own domestic policies, and not the other way round. Secondly, we intend to retain control of our domestic rate of interest, so that we can keep it as low as suits our own purposes, without interference from the ebb and flow of international capital movements or flights of hot money. Thirdly, whilst we intend to prevent inflation at home, we will not accept deflation at the dictate of influences from outside. In other words, we abjure the instruments of Bank rate and credit contraction operating through the increase of unemployment as a means of forcing our domestic economy into line with external factors. (Keynes 1941–6 [1980: 16])

This plan, he said, is the exact opposite of the gold standard.

The gold standard, as I understand it, means a system under which the external value of a national currency is rigidly tied to a fixed quantity of gold which can only honourably be broken under *force majeure*; and it involves a financial policy which compels the internal value of the domestic currency to conform to this external value as fixed in terms of gold. On the other hand, the use of gold merely as a convenient common denominator by means of which the relative values of national currencies – these being free to change – are expressed from time to time, is obviously quite another matter. (Keynes 1941–6 [1980: 17–18]).

These two quotations together can be interpreted only as an expression of faith in the potential stability of the postwar system and confidence both in the efficacy of exchange rate variation – and relatively slight variation at that

– as a restorer of balance and in the willingness of governments, including the British government, to use it. By the time of Bretton Woods, the terms under which exchange rates could be changed had been eased slightly, relatively to the initial proposals. Thus it would be incumbent on the Fund to approve changes which would make the value of a currency "conform to whatever *de facto* internal value results from domestic policies, which themselves shall be immune from criticism by the Fund . . . That is why I say that these proposals are the exact opposite of the gold standard" (Keynes 1941–6 [1980: 18–19], from a speech in the House of Lords Debate on Bretton Woods, May 23, 1944). Fairly fixed exchange rates was what he wanted: an adjustable peg.

By 1943 he seems to have resigned himself to accepting a clearing arrangement rather than a supernational credit-*creating* central bank and even making a virtue of necessity. His argument in defense of this was that while a world central bank creating bancor would produce an elastic quantity of international money, a well-functioning clearing union would produce all the flexibility needed in the velocity of that international money, so that the quantity would be unimportant (*Economic journal*, June–September, 1943. Keynes 1941–6 [1980: 31]).

And yet, he continued to ponder the problems facing a world living within the constraints imposed by a fixed exchange rate system. The gold standard had been rejected because the "world, after a good try, has decided to discard" a system in which only the deliberate creation of unemployment can "confine the natural tendency of wages to rise beyond the limits set by the volume of money." But the "new standard which aims at providing the quantity of money appropriate to stable prices" may be vulnerable to question or rejection on the same ground (Keynes 1941–6 [1980: 31–2]). The international currency scheme would have to deal not only with the problem of chronic creditors soaking up all the gold but also the more difficult matter of

members getting out of step in their domestic wage and credit policies. [They] . . . may be asked in the first instance to reconsider their policies. But, if necessary . . . exchange rates will have to be altered so as to reconcile a particular national policy to the average pace. *If the initial exchange rates are fixed correctly, this is likely to be the only important disequilibrium for which a change in exchange rates is the appropriate remedy.* (Keynes 1941–6 [1980: 32–3], italics mine).

The problem is that of an individual country getting out of line. If prices and wages throughout the world double, "international exchange equilibrium is undisturbed. If efficiency wages in a particular country rise ten percent more than the norm, then it is that there is trouble which needs attention." And in reply to Hayek's argument for commodity money, he argued that "[c]ommodity standards which try to impose [internal price stability] from without will break down just as surely as the rigid gold-standard" (Keynes 1941–6 [1980: 33]). To Frank Graham he wrote: "How much otherwise avoidable unemployment do you propose to bring about in order to keep the Trade Unions in order? Do you think it will be politically possible when they understand what you are up to?" (December 31, 1943. Keynes 1941–6 [1980: 36]).

By formalizing exchange rate changes one: (a) forces creditor countries to appreciate, and (b) prevents changes from being neutralized by competitive devaluations. This latter point he considered important; I can only speculate that the reason he suggested relatively small devaluations (5 percent to 10 percent) was that he was indeed assuming that only one or a few countries would attempt to devalue at any one time. He also deemed it important, thinking obviously of the 1920s, that the system of prescribed and limited devaluations would permit any individual country, more particularly Britain, to correct any mistakes made in establishing the initial value of sterling after the war (Keynes 1940–4 [1980: 93]).[8]

### Hubert Henderson

Keynes was an outstanding figure in his time. But he was not alone. And many of his ideas were echoed in similar voices by some of his contemporaries. One of these, a friend and colleague, was Hubert Henderson. His views were closely allied to those of Keynes; whether these were two people responding to the same past and the same stimuli, or whether there was interaction and direct exchange and influence of opinions, I do not know. But in Henderson (1943 [1955]) for example we meet many of the notions encountered in this chapter:

1   The attribution of the failure of the 1920s to the unavailability of increased lending by the creditors to finance their current account surpluses. As a result, "when the flow of American lending ceased, most countries in central and eastern Europe and Central and South America became unable to meet their financial obligations to the outside world" (Henderson 1943 [1955: 245]). They had been borrowing heavily to support imbalances (which were in turn caused by reparations or repayment of previous debts). This led to speculation against their currencies, by their own and foreign residents.

2   The justification of capital controls to protect foreign exchange reserves and prevent them from being "dissipated on unnecessary imports"

---

[8]   It is of interest that most of the discussions in 1925, including Keynes's, of the extent to which sterling was out of line, relative presumably to its purchasing power parity, homed in on the figure of 5 percent (see Moggridge 1972).

(Henderson 1943 [1955: 241]). This is even stronger and more judgmental than Keynes's language.

3  The internal-external policy conflict is explicit. In his description of the 1920s, Henderson argues that the debtors, in the late 1920s, had two alternatives: floating exchange rates or trade and payments restrictions. They were, however, afraid of floating exchange rates because they associated this with inflation. "In Central European eyes . . . inflation and exchange depreciation had become virtually synonymous terms of terrible significance." Henderson accepts the interpretation that in the hyperinflations of the twenties the exchange rate had led to internal price inflation (Henderson 1943 [1955: 246]). This is reminiscent of many of the German debates of the 1920s over the engine of inflation (see Ellis (1934) Part III, especially Chapter XVI: 264–95).

The same type of policy conflict, he argues, motivated the refusal of the British authorities to return to gold in the 1930s, allowing changes in the reserves to regulate the economy. In fact, he argues, the creation of the Exchange Equalization Fund, the agency responsible for exchange market intervention, had broken "the link between internal currency and the gold reserve." This was a new idea: the "essence of the old gold-standard system [was] that money rates, and the abundance or scarcity of credit, were determined by the movement of the exchange rates and the inflow or outflow of gold. The system was praised as being essentially 'automatic' . . . [I]t is certain that the old regulator has been removed for good" (Henderson 1943 [1955: 263–4]). "Few countries would be willing in future to make the volume of their internal purchasing power depend on the magnitude of their gold reserves" (Henderson 1943 [1955: 291]). The maintenance of full employment made yielding to "blind external forces unthinkable . . . In this respect there can be no return to the automatism of the gold-standard system" (Henderson 1943 [1955: 264]). This would necessitate and justify control of capital movement. And if capital controls were acceptable, why is it forbidden to control other variables, presumably trade? (Henderson 1943 [1955: 290–1]).

On exchange rate policy, Henderson strongly rejected floating on the one hand and too-frequent adjustments on the other. He was less sanguine about the efficacy of some exchange rate changes than was Keynes, and yet he insisted on the availability of adjustability as a policy tool. It was, after all, preferable by far to deflation. But it could not become "an efficient substitute for deflation as the regulator of a quasi-automatic system," nor should it be countenanced for a moment that

the alterations of exchange rates which are to serve this critical purpose might be made the subject of amicable international decision . . . Once it is granted that deflation must be thrown on the scrap-heap, the self-adjusting international system is destroyed, and it may become necessary for the individual country to regulate its balance of payments by deliberate action. Moreover, this may be necessary, not only in occasional emergencies, but as a continuing policy, so that equilibrium, once re-established, may be maintained. (Henderson 1943 [1955: 291–2])

Less hopeful than Keynes that international cooperation would be both attainable and efficacious, he is left with not much more than a panoply of direct controls of various kinds, since he has rejected all other alternatives. During the grim and regulated years of World War II this undoubtedly sounded less radical than it does to many of us today.

## Summary

Keynes's memoranda and letters from the early 1940s until the Bretton Woods Conference and beyond on the future of the world monetary order show a progression from what can only be called despair to a good deal of buoyancy. Despair because he pictured a world in which there had never been international adjustment except by accident, and there was no reason to expect that another such accident was near. The only solution immediately in sight for him was state trading, bilateral barter and, perhaps at best, some sort of quasi-multilateral trading with multiple exchange rates. He explicitly named Schacht and the system which prevailed in Germany in the late 1930s as an example.

As time went on he became more optimistic, opting for a world central bank with money-creating powers and a system of managed fixed exchange rates. Some of his early plans for a clearing union were extremely harsh on creditor nations, to the point of expropriating their unspent surpluses. This may have been a ploy to draw attention to the issue of the difficulties of adjustment when some countries are chronically in surplus.

Ever the realist politically, he bowed gracefully to the American insistence that the plan be a true clearing union with no power actually to create money, or international liquidity, as it came to be called. He insisted to the end, and alleged that the IMF as established permitted, that gold and foreign exchange be used as a temporary means of financing deficits, not as a trigger to the price-specie flow mechanism. Exchange rates were to be adjustable, and he seemed confident that temporary financing plus relatively small corrections, approximately 5 percent, plus any once-for-all corrections of mistakes made in setting exchange rates immediately after the war – that these together would be sufficient to maintain equilibrium in the current account. As for the capital account, there seemed no question in his mind that extensive and tight control would remain a necessity for a long time, if not indefinitely.

# The crisis writers

The neoclassicals viewed short-term capital movements as a phenomenon that resulted from central bank policy and performed the role of financing imbalances. The anti-neoclassicals either denied that this was the way the world functioned or, more often, argued that it ought not to work that way. Hawtrey challenged the neoclassical concept of short-term capital movements as playing a benevolent role: adjusting and financing imbalances. Hayek argued that short-term financial capital movements should not be thought of or treated differently from any other kind of trade in assets (including goods), and should not be deliberately elicited by central bank policy (see Chapter 7). The late classicals used long-term capital movements as a starting point for analyzing the classical adjustment mechanism. That is, capital flows constituted the disturbance they chose in exploring empirically ("inductively") the process of adjustment; short-term capital movements were often, in their work, important components of the adjustment, substituting for gold movements, and offering temporary financing.

The group of writers I am discussing now fixed their attention on capital movements, primarily short-term capital movements, with the aim of sorting out when they were endogenous and when exogenous, when financing, when destabilizing. They emphasized monetary and money market phenomena, and the possibly stabilizing or destabilizing effects of these, through internal, domestic monetary repercussions. I am thinking here of people such as Bloomfield (1950), Kindleberger (1937), Nurkse (1944). Predating most of these is the Italian, Marco Fanno (1935 and 1939). Parts of Keynes's writing, particularly in the *Tract*, have a similar flavor; in fact the theme of the destabilizing effects of capital movements runs through most of Keynes's writing, as we have seen. The role of the central bank, for good or ill, is important in all of these. In a certain sense this group can be thought of as successors to Bagehot, parallel to the neoclassical stream. They have much in common with him, and with one another. This includes a strong involvement in policy issues. But they differ from all the writers of the nineteenth and early twentieth centuries in their frequent emphasis on capital movements, especially short-term financial capital movements, as the *disturbing* phenomenon in international monetary affairs. That this reflects and was influenced by the events they were describing, or which were taking place around them, in the 1920s and 1930s is evident, but not the less interesting for that.

## Marco Fanno

Marco Fanno, to the best of my knowledge, invented the terminological distinction between normal and abnormal ("anormali") capital movements and was much concerned with the association of the latter with instability and crises. The 1939 book, according to the preface, is a translation and updating of the 1935 Italian work, and it is this which I refer to here.

"Abnormal" transfers are defined as those resulting from causes other than differences in the rate of interest. Essentially these are reparations and capital flight (Fanno 1939: 31). They create problems primarily because they do not lead to the kinds of adjustment spelled out by the price-specie flow mechanism. Capital exporting countries do not reduce their credit and importing countries do not increase theirs. This sterilization (Fanno has a concluding chapter emphasizing this point) disturbs the Ricardian equilibrium distribution of the precious metals. He refers eloquently to the "paralysis of the Ricardian law of the international circulation of the precious metals" (Fanno 1939: 109). This concern with the sterilization of flows, particularly on the part of the receiving country, is a point we have met often in the writings of Keynes, *inter alia*, starting with the *Tract* (Fanno 1939: 70, 106). The shortage of international reserves – he refers almost exclusively to gold – is exacerbated, as Fanno puts it, since "there is created in the world a mass of unutilized gold which moves, as in a void, from one country to another, exerting on the world economy a depressive effect" (Fanno 1939: 71).

The effects are real, because as debt and financial crises disturb the several money markets, finance for commodity trade becomes unattainable and "international trade remains paralyzed, thus transforming the monetary crisis of the financing country into a general world crisis." Furthermore, when the financial crisis is brought to a quick resolution, this generally occurs at the expense of movement of goods and services or of normal capital movements. Thus, for example, he argues that the London money market recouped quickly after the crisis of 1931, but the cost was considerable British disinvestment abroad, which exacerbated the world crisis (Fanno 1939: 97–102).

## Nurkse

Chronologically Nurkse is last in the list. He is, however, the prototypical crisis writer, at any rate in his classic *International currency experience*, published semi-anonymously under the imprimatur of the League of Nations (Nurkse 1944). His later writings, and even parts of this work, were keynesian, with heavy emphasis on income effects (in both directions) and the policy dilemma, the beginning of the assignment problem (see Chapter 14). In his early (1933) study he presents an essentially real, general-equilibrium discussion of capital movements (including reparations) their causes and their effects on the terms of trade, taking into account the internal shifts in the structure of production in the several countries required to make the adjustment. It is more than slightly reminiscent of Ohlin (1933).

The 1944 book is the story of the period between the two World Wars. But it is more than that. It is a blend of analysis and history which is almost impossible to separate out, since his views of the adjustment mechanism and the way the system worked, and was supposed to work, are inextricably intertwined in the account. As is the notion of the size, importance, and destabilizing nature of short-term capital movements, which appears every few pages, in virtually every context.

Before World War I, according to Nurkse, short-term capital movements had functioned effectively as financing, endogenous, "equilibrating" flows. In the 1920s long-term capital movements had generally taken place in an equilibrating direction, whereas in the 1930s they had stopped. Short-term movements had not stopped, however, but they were perverse and generally exogenous (see the discussion of Kindleberger below for a further discussion of the terminology). A fall in the exchange rate would arouse expectations of a further fall; "a rise in the bank rate would be taken as a danger signal," short-term capital would move, in the "wrong" direction, and with it gold. At times it even served as a substitute for private gold hoarding: the French, for example, were allowed to buy dollars, but not gold, so gold moved from France to the United States: the United States held the gold, the Frenchmen held the dollars (Nurkse 1944: 15–16).

In a sense, the same problem existed at a "higher" level, that is, in the holding of reserves under the gold exchange standard. One of the reasons that regime broke down was the large and sudden shifts of reserve holdings from one of the centers (New York, London, Paris) to another. Among other things, the need for the centers to hold reserves covering themselves against such withdrawals tied up larger gold stocks than otherwise would be needed and hence vitiated the supposed anti-deflationary advantages of the gold exchange standard, which had been based on the idea that the world could function with less gold, in toto, than under a full-fledged gold standard (Nurkse 1944: 46).

Nurkse's view of the adjustment mechanism and the operation of the "rules of the game" was discussed in Chapter 3. It too is laced with references to the counter-equilibrating direction of capital and, hence, gold movements. This made it both defensible and desirable for the authorities to break the "rules", to neutralize the gold flows, automatically, as he put it, or deliberately. He quotes an American official to the effect that the United States regarded the gold inflows of the 1920s as temporary and was reluctant to expand credit on this base, since it was expected that the gold would shortly flow out again and force the United States into a credit contraction (Nurkse 1944: 74). Whatever one's position about allowing the inflation and deflation required to adjust to changes in the basic balance of payments (which is the internal/external policy dilemma), Nurkse takes it as given and obvious that no country should be asked to make such adjustment to hot money and speculative capital flows. "The desire of both losing and receiving countries to offset the effects of international currency transfers arising from 'hot money' movements needs no explanation." Nevertheless, he recognizes and cites, without accepting, arguments that the rules ought not be infracted, under any circumstances. Interestingly, when he states this in its strongest version, that even hot money flights should not be sterilized, he does not indicate who it is who is taking that position. It is not, of course, far from Hayek's view (Nurkse 1944: 80–7). His own opinion, essentially like that of Keynes and of Hawtrey, is that gold (or foreign exchange) reserves should be available as a shock absorber, permitting countries to avoid immediate adjustment to changes in their payments balances. This implies, of necessity, specifically not adjusting or responding to all changes in the external accounts. In this connection, Nurkse discusses both the optimum worldwide distribution of gold (or other foreign exchange reserves) and the optimum reserve requirements for central banks; he predates the debates and research of the 1950s and 1960s on the optimal level of international liquidity, its distribution, and methods of increasing and allocating it (Nurkse 1944: 88–98).

On the adjustment mechanism of the balance of payments, he scrutinizes the late classical literature, points out that gold flows were small because short-term capital movements were frequent substitutes for them, and asks what the long-term adjustment to, as distinct from this short-term financing of, capital flows might be. Here he offers, as in much of his later writing, a keynesian multiplier view (see page 273). When applied to long-term foreign lending, foreign investment, he finds no problem with the analysis; short-term equilibrating capital flows are just that, and serve as stopgaps while the income effects bring about adjustment to the imbalance which induced those flows. A good example of rapid adjustment to a decline in capital inflows, through income reductions, he avers, is Germany in 1926. All monetary and price changes were counter to the classical scenario, and yet imports fell sharply following the decline in "expenditure financed by foreign loans", although he goes on to speculate that a recession in Germany may have caused the simultaneous decline in imports of goods and of capital, which is a somewhat different story (Nurkse 1944: 102–3).

But what of the disequilibrating flows with which he is so concerned? Since these involve liquid "money capital" which do not enter the income stream, since as he has been telling us, they are typically sterilized, "instead of acting as stop-gaps they create new gaps or widen those existing" (Nurkse 1944: 102). Throughout the 1930s there were large disequilibrating capital movements, which were typically neutralized both by the capital-exporting and -importing countries. When exchange rates were flexible (to greater or lesser degrees during the 1930s) speculation regarding exchange rates added a strong motive to those already existing for hot money flights. Fortunately, Nurkse says, gold continued to be used to effect some of these movements; fortunately, because to the extent that it was not so used, trade changed and goods moved to accommodate the capital flows (Nurkse 1944: 123–4).

He offers no nostrums. In general, he seemed convinced that what was needed in the postwar period was stability of exchange rates and commitment on the part of the major countries to maintain full or "good" levels of employment. If necessary they should engage in policy coordination among them to achieve that (reminding us of the various G summits of our day). These, with the political stability that everybody hoped would accompany the end of the war, would presumably minimize the incentive for hot money flights. If exchange rates remained out of equilibrium, this would encourage speculative capital movements: the cure is to change the exchange rates when needed. If one country is perpetually in surplus, rationing of its currency by an international agency on a multilateral basis would be far preferable to individual exchange control regimes in the separate countries. This is, of course, basically the "scarce currency" clause of the IMF Charter, discussed in Chapter 10.

### Bloomfield

Bloomfield (1950) was also writing about the interwar experience, particularly the late 1930s, the period of perhaps greatest instability as far as hot money and destabilizing capital movements were concerned. The book was published in 1950, but Professor Bloomfield has informed me that most of the work on the dissertation on which it is based was carried out in 1938–41, at the height of the disruptions of the 1930s, and the work places a heavy emphasis on the destabilizing, exogenous, "abnormal" nature of capital movements. Nevertheless, he recognized the possibility that capital movements could under certain circumstances play a financing and even an adjusting role. The conclusions of the "classical" analysis, he said, "would be essentially unaffected if 'induced' short-term capital movements were substituted for gold movement" (Bloomfield 1950: 254n). At the same time, he did make distinctions, because a few pages later he writes that it was more justifiable [on the part of the American monetary authorities] to sterilize the gold inflow that resulted from a capital account surplus but not "those gold imports that reflected the net influx of domestic capital . . . and the active balance on current account . . . In theory, at least, those gold imports might seem to have called for some degree of credit expansion to help facilitate a readjustment in the balance on current account" (Bloomfield 1950: 247). This implies that foreign capital inflows are purely exogenous, hot money flights, while domestic capital inflows are part of the basic balance.[1] It seems to me that Bloomfield's distinction between capital movements which cover the "active balance" (surplus) in the balance of payments and those that do not is the more apt, since banks and individuals can repatriate their capital because of fear of political unrest abroad or large exchange rate changes, at least as easily, and often more legally, than foreigners do. This does not make it any the less "hot money".

Like Kindleberger and Nurkse, Bloomfield discusses the various categories and groupings of capital flows:

1  normal/abnormal, conventionally, though not wholly accurately, defined in terms of whether the movement is positively or negatively related to the interest rate differential involved;
2  equilibrating/disequilibrating, which follows Nurkse's definition and which we discussed above. Nurkse considers definition (1) but prefers (2) because it is a distinction based on function, though he grants that for the interwar period they probably would yield the same classification of actual cases (Nurkse 1944: 72n). Here the direction of the flow is related to the sign of the basic balance of payments. If the sign of the capital flow is the same as that of the basic balance of payments it is disequilibrating, exacerbating a surplus on current account and long-term capital combined, by adding a short-term capital inflow. By this definition, the capital inflow to the United States in the period Bloomfield deals with, 1934–9 was primarily disequilibrating;
3  induced/autonomous, the distinction which survived the longest, which is based on motive. Difficult as it is to pin down empirically, it distinguishes between capital flows that occur *because* the rest of the

---

[1]  This is reminiscent of the debate which raged for a number of years over the insistence of the United States Department of Commerce in defining the liquidity balance of payments by putting changes in United States short-term assets abroad, in foreign banks, above the line, and changes in United States banks' liabilities to foreigners below the line, that is, as part of the measure of the deficit. The battle ended with the appointment of a committee of distinguished economists, which suggested dropping the liquidity definition of the balance altogether (see Review Committee 1965).

balance of payments is unbalanced, and those which take place independently of the state of the balance, though not independently of other economic considerations. This is not easy to define precisely and empirically, even more difficult to measure, but it has some analytical usefulness (Bloomfield 1950: 33–5).

Analytically, Bloomfield starts from the keynesian position. In a concise history of doctrine he distinguishes between classical (including late classical, in my terminology) and "modern" (keynesian) analysis.[2] Analyzing the United States experience, primarily in the second half of the 1930s, Bloomfield applies the keynesian approach to autonomous capital movements. The question is, what is the adjustment mechanism like under these circumstances. He notes that in this case, and most particularly when the autonomous capital inflow is of the hot money, capital flight variety, problems arise instantly. Almost any kind of financial capital inflow (short-term, bank balances, repatriation of foreign direct investment, portfolio investment in the United States) is likely to miss the first step of the process, the increase in the multiplicand of keynesian multiplier analysis. There is an exception only "perhaps to the extent that interest rates are thereby lower or . . . stock prices raised." Where the capital inflow consists of increases in foreign holdings of domestic bank deposits, such as occur when there is capital flight, speculation regarding exchange rate changes, or "an unusually large forward exchange premium", there can be "no primary income disbursements as long as they remain idle in the hands of foreigners" and no adjustment will take place (Bloomfield 1950: 261). Given that these flows are volatile and probably will soon be reversed, the banking system is unlikely to expand credit on the basis of the increased reserves. The weakness of the adjustment mechanism in this kind of case was noted, he points out, both by Nurkse (1944) and Metzler (1948, [1973: Chapter 1]).

In the paying country, again, the story will depend heavily on who is investing abroad, at the expense of which, if any, alternative expenditure, and the effects of these on bank balances, savings, investment, and the rate of interest. Given the "real" foreign trade multiplier, adjustment in either one of the countries involved will bring about income changes in both in the direction of equilibrium, however (Bloomfield 1950: 262–3). Note that

---

[2] He puts Ohlin more squarely into the ranks of the keynesians than I have done, albeit as an early formulator of the keynesian view and constituting an "incomplete emancipation from 'classical' preconceptions." Ohlin's analysis suffered, according to Bloomfield, in that it assumed full employment, "lacked an appropriate theory of income generation and employment," concentrated excessively on changes in the supply of money, and lacked dynamic specification (Bloomfield 1950: 256–7). I agree with almost all of these points; but I have argued that these are precisely what separated Ohlin from the keynesian camp. I have argued also that he has a much stronger micro orientation than the keynesian position (see Chapter 13).

despite his interest in the "modern" approach, Bloomfield is much more aware of and interested in monetary and interest rate effects than the builders of the early keynesian models were.

In principle, all capital movements were potentially endogenous, in Bloomfield's view, and "at times long-term capital movements may also act as 'adjusting' items to external disturbances . . . One writer [Meade] has, in fact, explicitly incorporated the balance of such long-term capital movements into his models" (Bloomfield 1950: 264n). In Meade's case, as we shall see, this is the result of policy directed to that end. But endogenous changes in long-term capital flows, associated with business cycle behavior, and particularly differences between countries in cyclical patterns, is also possible. However, it is also true that cyclical fluctuations might generate flows of both capital and goods in the same direction, maintaining overall payments equilibrium; he argues that this is a good description of the United States balance of payments between 1919 and 1929: cyclical upswings leading to simultaneous reductions in the export surplus and in capital outflows (Bloomfield 1950: 264–5).

Empirical ("inductive") studies of balance of payments adjustment have always been difficult and inconclusive, perhaps because most of them applied the "discredited 'classical' theory", perhaps because at least in some instances what appeared to be adjustment was simply "the influence of a common causal force . . . working simultaneously on both the current account and capital balances" (Bloomfield 1950: 268). Nevertheless, examining the United States data for 1934 to 1939 he concludes that there was no adjustment to the very large capital inflows (Bloomfield 1950: 268 ff). Net capital inflow cumulated over the six years to just under six billion dollars. In fact, it was probably a good deal more, since the errors and omissions item totaled $2.4 billion and was positive in every one of the six years. The cumulated current account surplus was $2.6 billion, and gold inflows almost $10 billion. Bloomfield insists that the low propensities to import and the small share of trade in United States income are not enough to explain the results. More important is the "nonincome-generating" nature of the capital flows. They simply did not, Bloomfield argues, enter the income stream. Interest rates did decline as a result of the capital and gold inflows, but investment proved inelastic with respect to the rate of interest. Gross, but not net, investment did rise, but Bloomfield accepts the argument attributed to Alvin Hansen that this was induced investment, stimulated by the income and consumption increases which resulted from expansionary fiscal policy. He considers the wealth effect of the interest rate decline, but is unable to measure it.

There was some deterioration in the merchandise trade balance of the United States during this period, but Bloomfield attributes this to a general world-wide improvement in activity, with United States income rising faster than that of its trading partners, leading to an increase in imports larger than that in exports. He goes further and explores the question of whether the slower growth of income abroad was the result of their capital exports; if it were, there could be said to have been an adjustment process at work. He examines the data and concludes that the evidence for the United Kingdom does not support this argument; for France, the Netherlands, and Switzerland (part of the Gold Bloc), on the other hand, there may have been some effect: retardation of domestic expansion because of higher interest rates resulting from the capital and gold outflows. He concludes, however, that this was too small to have had a major effect on United States exports, even allowing for multilateral feedbacks. In 1937, with the sharp drop in activity in the United States, and again in 1938 there was a large increase in the current account surplus, again an income effect; this was financed by capital outflow, reducing the net capital inflow for the period. This, however, he characterizes as an "induced" not autonomous capital movement (Bloomfield 1950: 283). The proceeds of the capital imports, he concludes, were to a significant extent hoarded; the quantity of money increased by 2.5 times the gold inflow (which is a very small money multiplier) indicating that the secondary expansion was weak. Banks, individuals and foreigners held large liquid balances.

The conclusion of Bloomfield's analysis is not that the "modern" theory of adjustment is invalid or rejected, but that the period constitutes "an egregious example of the failure of the mechanism-of-adjustment process, because of a number of special factors, to operate at all." Large capital inflows did not result in a corresponding commodity flow because the funds were liquidity seeking hot money, or United States banks' repatriation of foreign deposits, presumably for similar reasons; interest rates fell somewhat but seem not to have affected private spending; the capital outflow from most of the exporting countries came from idle balances and did not cause contractions there. And though there is no indication of deliberate sterilization of the inflow, Bloomfield quietly reprimands the "authorities" for not taking steps toward "a more aggressive expansionist fiscal policy" which would have, *inter alia*, caused the required deterioration in the trade balance as well as increasing domestic income and employment (Bloomfield 1950: 290–1).

## Kindleberger

I have reversed chronology in this chapter. Kindleberger was Angell's student. His thesis (1937) was surely begun no later than 1935, and probably earlier. He starts his analysis from the late classical position. (Later writings –

Kindleberger's Middle Period? – I have classified as keynesian; they are discussed in Chapter 15.) Like Angell, he places heavy emphasis on the role of monetary changes, consequent upon gold (or capital) flows, in the adjustment process. Although he does devote a chapter to "'Abnormal' Capital Movements," and his main focus is on short-term capital movements, he is not a full-fledged crisis writer, which is why I have put him last in this chapter, despite the chronology. In his description of the adjustment mechanism, which he calls the transfer problem, he argues that many (or most) short-term capital movements are equilibrating, endogenous, and essentially substitutes for gold movements, as we saw them to be in Viner's schema in the previous chapter.

He sees his work as a step in the direction of "rewrit[ing] the theory of international trade in terms of the national money income." To this end, he suggests defining "equilibrium . . . in terms of the effects of the balance of payments on the national money income." The balance of payments is thus defined as being in equilibrium when it puts no pressure on the domestic money supply in either direction (Kindleberger 1937: 237–8). He thus proposes an amended version of Angell's recommendation to define balance of payments equilibrium in terms of short-term capital flows, but argues that gold plus net short-term capital flows would be better (Kindleberger 1937: 234).

He insists that he is in no way challenging or even revising "the body of analysis that has been developing continuously from generation to generation from the days of Smith and Ricardo down to Taussig, Viner, Angell, Williams, and the other outstanding contributors to the field . . . It would be more in the way of a translation of that body of analysis from 'real' terms to money terms." He states this goal modestly but considers it of primary importance. However, by "monetary" he means something approaching the latterday macroeconomic concepts because he refers specifically to improving the understanding of the international implications of the business cycle, and even suggests that such a monetary translation might show benefits of such tools as tariffs in "reliev[ing] a country of deflationary pressure from abroad which is likely to become cumulative" and may justify the resource cost of protection (Kindleberger 1937: 237–8).

His treatment is much more nearly symmetrical than most as between fixed and fluctuating exchange rates. To my knowledge he is the first to discuss a regime of pegged non-convertible exchange rates (though Keynes approached it closely in the *Tract* and again in the *Treatise* 1930 II, especially Chapter 38 and discussed in Chapter 9, page 183), and devotes a whole chapter to "The Paper Standard with Fixed Exchanges". He persists in the general notion, undoubtedly empirically valid for the time, that there is something at least slightly pathological about floating exchange rates, since countries will not adopt a paper standard unless they are forced to do so. He treats the two cases fairly symmetrically though he recognizes, as do other writers, the importance of the wider fluctuations in exchange rates under floating rates and is concerned about the global stability of the system. He considers three institutional cases: pegged exchange rates, gold standard, and floating rates. With respect to the first, he concludes that a transfer "can be accomplished . . . through the medium of short-term capital movements. In the limiting case, when shifts in the exchange rate and movements of gold are not operating, short-term funds are capable of achieving the desired results by themselves" (Kindleberger 1937: 77). These short-term capital movements are tied in with interest rate changes – the central bank changes the discount rate (in either the receiving or the paying country or both) in response to exchange rate changes.

He distinguishes between four types of short-term capital flow, by motivation:

1  equilibrating "which arises directly out of an independent change in an item in the balance of payments or in response to it";
2  speculative, born of exchange rate expectations;
3  income, stemming from interest rate differentials; and
4  autonomous, hot money capital flight (Kindleberger 1937: 16).

He does not emphasize heavily the exogenous, destabilizing nature of short-term capital movements. In his preface he comments that, at the time of writing, crisis and autonomous and abnormal capital movements were more important than they had been (Kindleberger 1937: vii). He devotes a chapter to these, which will be discussed below. Considering why the emphasis in theory seemed to shift away from consideration of short-term capital movements, he argues that, particularly in the postwar period, movements of gold had more of an impact on credit policy and received more attention than did short-term capital flows. Noting that the period prior to World War I was primarily a sterling standard, he says that the Bank of England anxiously defended its small gold stock against change, so that what was watched for and conspicuous were the gold movements. This tendency was less marked in the postwar era. As I understand him, he is arguing that before the war, the industrial countries were very sensitive to small changes, actual or expected, in their gold stocks, and adjusted domestic credit policy quickly. Thus, large capital movements were possible with very small gold flows: the elasticity of the balance of payments to changes in gold reserves was high. This was not true to the same extent of changes in short-term foreign assets, however; that is, "few persons sufficiently understood the nature of short-term capital shifts to make the practice general in industrially mature countries of deflating when net short-term foreign assets fell and of inflating when they rose." He expresses a hope that in the future if and when the gold standard is restored, it will be understood that if monetary policy is made to respond correctly to short-term balances, these can play an important role in achieving payments equilibrium, especially when "the disequilibria are of the minor sort that arise under normal conditions" (Kindleberger 1937: 87–9).

As a general proposition, then, he treats gold movements, short-term capital movements, and exchange rate changes as substitutes in effecting a transfer of long-term capital. Both gold and short-term capital movements engender the monetary changes needed to effect the real transfer; and both can be expected to be reversed as the transfer is effected. This continues the Viner, White and Angell line of analysis. "The import surplus which the real transfer has evoked in the borrowing country must be paid for with gold or with short-term capital acquired from the lending country" (Kindleberger 1937: 97). In an extraordinarily thorough and comprehensive exploration of alternative causes of short-term capital movements and evaluation of their equilibrating (or disequilibrating) role, Kindleberger proceeds from the transfer problem to discuss the relationship of capital movements to what he called "foreign-exchange equilibrium," "undervaluation and overvaluation" (chronic tendencies toward disequilibrium) and "cyclical movement". "Abnormal movements" are treated separately.

In the discussion of abnormal capital movements, Kindleberger is in substantial agreement with Machlup (Kindleberger 1937: 155n) that abnormal movements are those taking place for "'uneconomic considerations'" but prefers the more precise rate-of-interest criterion: an abnormal capital movement is one in which capital moves from a higher to a lower interest market (see the discussion of Nurkse above). The reasons given for them, citing Marco Fanno's list (Kindleberger 1937: 155 ff) are: "(1) . . . reparations or war debts; (2) high taxes" or (3) fear thereof; "(4) . . . political or social motives; (5) distrust of the national banking system; and (6) fear of monetary devaluation." Kindleberger adds a reason of his own, which sounds as if it had been written this morning: A country which has borrowed so much that it can borrow no more and must service the debt will be in a position very similar to one involved in reparations payments. Such a country is likely at that time to be faced with very high interest rates, so that again capital will be moving upstream (Kindleberger 1937: 157–8).

Surveying the literature on the subject (particularly Machlup 1932 and Fanno 1935), Kindleberger notes that "abnormal" capital movements, because they are autonomous, will have to be transferred eventually, probably immediately through gold movement and eventually by commodity flows "in normal fashion" (Kindleberger 1937: 164). He takes issue with this and argues that abnormal capital movements are more likely not to be effected because of the probability that the inflow will be sterilized and hoarded in the receiving country. This was Keynes's complaint about the inflows into the United States (see Chapters 8 and 10); the United States explicitly made statements expressing fear that funds would have to be repatriated, with deflationary pressure, and therefore it was preferable not to let the inflow cause the "normal" inflation in the first place. (Note that the League of Nations 1932: 51, says something very similar when it argues that open market operations should be used to sterilize a temporary inflow, to prevent real effects from occurring which would later need to be reversed.) It is this which brings him closer to the crisis school, namely the argument that capital flows of this kind present a particular problem. Remember, however, that he includes reparations here as well as short-term hot money flights. The normal process of transfer, he says, involves

inflation of money incomes . . . in the receiving country. With normal capital movements, the major share of the adjustment falls on the borrowing country. With abnormal capital movements, the gold received merely increases excess reserves of the banking system in the country of refuge if the reduction in the country's foreign short-term assets does not lead to an increase in the national money income.

The engine of the transfer then is the "expropriation of basic banking reserves of the capital-losing country." This will stop only when the flight stops or the capital exporting country gives up and devalues, or introduces exchange control (Kindleberger 1937: 165–6).

Under freely floating rates (a paper standard with no intervention or control, in Kindleberger's terminology), speculative capital flows in the same direction as long-term capital, capital flight initiated by currency depreciation, and uncertainty about the future of the exchange rate, all are likely to be destabilizing, exacerbating any movement of the exchange rate away from equilibrium. Interest arbitrage will not occur without forward cover, and this is likely to be too expensive to make covered arbitrage profitable in a time of great uncertainty about exchange rates. Nevertheless, in spite of these and other reasons to worry about stability, Kindleberger is sanguine that in general short-term capital movements will flow in an equilibrating direction under a paper currency. The borrowers will convert the proceeds of their loans slowly in order to minimize their losses from sharp and rapid appreciation of their home currency (Kindleberger 1937: 93–5).

### Summation

It comes as no surprise that assessments of the international monetary scene written in the middle and late 1930s and the early 1940s should have been concerned with short-term financial capital flows and that writers would have centered their attention on such movements, their causes and effects.

With the turbulence of the 1920s and 1930s either fresh in their memories or still eddying around them, it would have been astonishing had they not responded.

As in the general economic literature, the pressing issues of the day were not thought to be optimum resource allocation and the study of long-run trade and payments patterns between economies individually operating at full employment equilibrium. The works discussed here, products of their age, deal with models in which rapid, real adjustment to real disturbances generally does not occur. They discuss either monetary shocks, or real shocks to which adjustment is not smooth. Short-term financial capital flows often, in this literature, tend either to exacerbate an already existing disequilibrium, or themselves constitute the disturbance, leading either to further monetary repercussions or to real adjustments, generally difficult, undesired and undesirable. They often occur in a situation of imbalance in the basic balance of payments, generally in a counter-financing direction; if they intrude themselves into a balanced payments pattern, they again constitute a disequilibrating force, requiring real adjustments away from equilibrium, away from optimum resource allocation, and away from what some, and perhaps all, of the participating economies would view as desirable levels of income and employment.

# 3

---

# Stream F

# The late classicals

We turn to an examination of the "Taussig school". Ohlin dubbed them the "Harvard school"; I prefer the label late classical. The books in question span (in terms of publication dates) the 1920s and most of the 1930s. I include here the following works by Taussig and his famous students: Williams (1920), Viner (1924) and (1937), Taussig (1927), and White (1933). Viner (1937) pursues a controversy with Angell, who had criticized the earlier book. I have also included Angell (1926), who would surely have objected strenuously. In terms of what he was aiming at, Bresciani-Turroni (1932) should perhaps have been included here, but I have concentrated on the people around Taussig. (Incidentally, a casual survey indicates that most of the important native-born American economists in the field of international economics until the post-World War II period were direct "descendants" of Taussig, since Kindleberger was Angell's student, and Bloomfield Viner's.)

All of these are basically classical in their approach, as distinct from neoclassical. I have labeled them "late classical", though perhaps "banking-system classical" would be appropriate. Unlike Hume, Mill, and Ricardo, they deal very explicitly with systems characterized by a modern banking system with the important characteristic of fractional-reserve banking. The relationship between reserve changes (specie flows) and changes in the quantity of money and credit was not only recognized by all of them; it plays a crucially important role in Viner's study and, as we shall see, is the subject of most of his debate and argument with Angell, *inter alia*. Nevertheless, I persist in using the classical label because (a) the role of endogenous short-term capital movements is generally played down and (b) the role of the central bank is ignored, as is, therefore, the policy-directed change in interest rates and its effects.

A second important aspect of the Taussig writers is that they held on to the assumption of constant costs. Viner (1937: 490–1) states that "Taussig, almost alone among modern writers, has adhered, with qualifications, to a labor-cost theory of value," with the justification that it is an adequate

223

approximation for practical purposes to a correct theory of real cost. Taussig himself (1927 [1928: 66]) dismisses land rent as an influence on comparative costs, but states explicitly that where capital endowments differ between countries *and* capital/labor ratios differ between industries, a capital-rich country will export capital-intensive goods. When pressed, that is, he enunciates something very like the Heckscher-Ohlin theorem, but considered relative labor costs a good empirical approximation to comparative advantage, as have many researchers since, including the present-day neo-Ricardians.

In both their real and monetary analysis the late classicals, like Ohlin, clearly operated in the framework of a three-commodity model, involving non-traded goods. This is noted, among others, by Iversen (1935: 306). (See, for example, Taussig's exchange with Wicksell 1918: 411–12, in which the distinction between "international" and "domestic" goods is heavily emphasized.) Third, some more than others, they formed the first arch of a bridge between the classical price theories and the keynesian income theories. They frequently revealed a less than complete belief in the smooth functioning of adjustments, the maintenance of full employment, and the rapid real-time adjustment to long-run equilibrium. This was particularly true of White and was hinted at strongly by Taussig himself, in his famous "misgivings", to be discussed below.

Viner, White, and Williams were, as noted, students of Frank Taussig's at Harvard, and the studies we are examining here were doctoral dissertations. Thus they were not tracts or pamphlets on contemporary issues, nor parts of Principles texts. They all purported to be simply "inductive" verification of the received classical doctrine, empirical tests of an established model; all pertained to major capital transfers during the pre-World War I period.

While at first it may be puzzling why they so consistently chose capital transfers as examples of exogenous shocks, on reflection it is not so surprising. Particularly in the absence of refined econometric techniques, the shock had to be large, temporally discrete, and clearly identifiable (as a change in tastes or technology might not be). They were constrained to relatively recent history, for which data were available: as it was, they performed Sisyphean labors compiling and processing their data. When they started their studies, during or just after World War I, there were probably not that many candidates for investigation. These were studies then of the restoration of long-run equilibrium and full adjustment to an exogenous shock, a capital transfer, and they showed only tangential interest in endogenous, financing capital movements during the process of adjustment. (This may have reflected, *inter alia*, the fact that adjustments in the pre-World War I gold standard were, as we have seen to be widely acknowledged, relatively smooth and rapid.)

## Williams

Williams's study (the first of the group, chronologically) deals with Argentina from 1880–1900, a period of rapid development, heavy foreign borrowing, a series of financial panics and crises, and, uniquely in this group, flexible exchange rates. The last point needs some clarification. Williams throughout the book took pains to emphasize that gold was not eliminated from the monetary scene, either domestically or internationally (see, for example, Williams 1920: 19–20). Gold convertibility of the peso was suspended, presumably temporarily, and so a premium on gold, in excess of the gold export point, was possible and did in fact obtain. But gold was used to buy foreign exchange, since Argentina was trading in a world of fixed, not fluctuating, exchange rates. The same was true in Britain during the nineteenth-century Suspension. He distinguishes emphatically between this situation and that in which the exchange is "dislocated," there are no gold shipments, and there is a truly fluctuating exchange rate and paper currency. He gives Chile as an example of this (Williams 1920: 258). He does not really clarify, however, what he thinks the difference between these two cases will be in terms of the adjustment mechanism.

He concentrates on the functioning of the adjustment mechanism under flexible exchange rates; the thesis was planned as an attempt to "verify" Taussig's (1917) statement of the theory. Williams states, almost in surprise, that gold movements under a paper currency cannot affect the domestic money supply, but that they yet affect the size of the premium on gold, that is, the exchange rate, and hence the balance of international payments. Since gold continued to be shipped, the considerations whether or not to ship it were the same as under a gold standard: the costs of shipping, which established the gold export point. The interesting theoretical question was, therefore, not the movement of gold, but the determination of the premium at which it traded in the home market and the feedback of this on the trade balance. The exchange rate, "the value of paper" was affected by international borrowing; this rate affected merchandise trade. But "on the other hand, the borrowings themselves emanated to a considerable extent from the paper money situation" (Williams 1920: 22).

Criticizing the writers who attributed the depreciation of the currency exclusively to the overissue of paper on the part of the government, Williams insists that although there indeed was overissue, "the *mere* increase of paper is not a sufficient explanation of the ups and downs of the gold premium, but . . . an important, and to my mind the controlling, element in the situation was the adverse balance of payments, in which the dominant factor was that of borrowings" (Williams 1920: 44). He expands on this to attribute a very sharp turnaround in the balance of payments, between 1883 and 1884, to large interest payments on the borrowed funds plus imported materials and inputs with which to effect the investment for which the borrowing was incurred, implying a very high marginal propensity to import (Williams 1920: 46 ff).

As for the borrowings, these were carried out by the government, both to pay its debts and to lower the price of gold (raise the price of its paper), though of course the accomplishment of one of these goals precluded the other; there was capital inflow into land speculation; and there was borrowing on the part of the railroads (Williams 1920: 71 ff). After studying all the numbers he was able to muster (a heroic task) he concluded that indeed "when borrowing exceeded interest charge, imports exceeded exports, and vice versa" (Williams 1920: 187). That is, the transfer was being effected, despite the flexible exchange rates.

In order to explain the mechanism he investigates (even more heroically) the movements of prices and quantities of exports and imports, and domestic costs, that is, wages. The theory suggests, he argues, that the premium on gold will raise export prices relatively to wages, raising the quantity of exports. The elasticity of exports was, however, not high, though it exceeded unity, and export earnings in terms of gold rose very little. His explanation of this is that European, that is world, prices were falling during the relevant period, 1890–5. In addition, there were natural disasters, such as locusts and excessive rain, in several years, which lowered the available quantities of agricultural exports. He concludes that on the export side "the Argentine case . . . is inconclusive." Convinced that, *ceteris paribus*, an increase would have occurred, he appeals to "the presence of other factors working at cross-purposes to the gold premium" which held them back (Williams 1920: 233–5). With respect to imports, the results are clearer cut. "As the price of gold rises, import prices rise more rapidly than wages, and power to purchase imports is thereby reduced. In other words, the Argentine import trade appears to offer complete verification of theory" (Williams 1920: 253).

One final problem in interpretation. Williams argues in his conclusion (1920: 254 ff) that the effect on exports and imports of the depreciated paper is an important but "further" aspect of the theory. More important, and critical, is "the interrelation between the balance of international payments and the value of inconvertible paper money" (Williams 1920: 255). For this to be anything other than the effect on the trade balance it must, perforce, be the effect on the capital account. Thus, as we shall see in the subsequent discussion, Williams gives a much more endogenous role to capital movements than the other writers in this group. What I take him to mean here is that there is a change in the overall structure of the balance of payments: the "excessive" issue of fiat money on the part of the government leads to an increase in the price of gold which draws gold to the home country, as arbitrage, the gold being exchanged for domestic assets. This is, therefore, a capital movement (not part of the "official settlements balance" as gold movements are regarded under fixed exchange rate regimes) and must be offset by a deterioration in the trade balance.

### Viner

Of the ex-Taussig trilogy, Viner's book on Canada (1924) is perhaps the most complex and has historically been the most controversial. This probably has to do, at least in part, with the specifics of the Canadian case. The period is 1900–13, so he is dealing with an economy which is a part of the British Empire and closely integrated with it and which imported large quantities of capital from the U.K. during that period. It had no central bank. And it dwelt in close physical and financial proximity to the United States. This seems to have much to do with the story, as Viner tells it.

In his enunciation of his view of the adjustment mechanism (1924: 147 ff) Viner gives short-term capital movements, stimulated by changes in exchange rates, an important role in the equilibrating process, stabilizing exchange rates within the gold points and thereby preventing, or minimizing the need for, specie movements. (Others in the late classical tradition and their "offspring", such as Kindleberger and Bloomfield, carried on with this view, as we saw in Chapter 11.) This is for him obviously the case when disturbances are "casual" and about to be "soon offset by disturbances in the opposite direction," so that specie movements, if they occurred, would shortly be reversed (Viner 1924: 148). But in the case of a more basic disturbance, such as long-term and protracted borrowing, the prolonged excess supply of foreign exchange will force the exchange rate to the gold import point and gold will flow. When it becomes evident that the exchange rate change will not be reversed soon, short-term capital flows will stop. He emphasizes that these financial capital movements are in fact the only forces keeping the exchange rates inside the gold shipping points; commodity trade will not respond sufficiently to such small movements of exchange rates. And he does not mention either interest rate changes or internal monetary adjustments in this context (Viner 1924: 149–50).

His main interest in this discussion, however, is not the importance of short-term capital movements but rather the argument over whether or not gold movements are *required* to restore balance of payments equilibrium in the face of a major disturbance. His argument is with those (like J. H. Hollander cited by Viner 1924: 150n and discussed 150 ff) who argued that current account balances are sufficiently elastic with respect to small changes in exchange rates so that movements in rates, inside the gold points, are enough to restore overall balance even without specie movements. It is this contention, together with Hollander's appeal to Ricardo for support, which

Viner, joining forces with Taussig, is challenging. Viner argues first, appealing to Taussig, that small changes in exchange rates cannot induce such large changes in commodity trade as would be required by this model; secondly, that exchange rates cannot change at all once they have reached the gold points, so that it is at best only at "the inception of borrowings" that their equilibrating influence might be felt (Viner 1924: 150).

However, the short-term capital movements which play a critically important role in Viner's account are of a very particular nature – Canadian banks' variations in their deposits with U.S. banks. In one version of the story Viner has the role of gold movements replaced by that of short-term deposits of Canadian banks abroad – typically in New York. He argues that this is unique to the Canadian situation, and that the adjustment process is as "automatic" as the classical explanation suggests, with the substitution of reserves for gold. An increase in Canadian borrowings in London, coupled with a desire on the part of the Canadian borrowers to spend the proceeds of the loan in Canada, results in an immediate increase in demand deposits in Canada (what Viner is later, in the *Studies* (1937), to refer to as a "secondary" expansion, omitting the primary expansion)[1] and a fractional increase in Canadian banks' assets consisting of increased deposits in New York banks. Thus, first the money supply in Canada, and then the price level, have increased prior to any major movements of gold. As the price level increases and the balance on current account deteriorates, there is an increased demand in Canada for foreign exchange. The banks meet this demand, reducing their deposit liabilities as they supply bills to their customers, draw down their deposits in New York and reexport the gold that has been imported. The stock of goods in Canada has increased, the transfer has been effected, and the initial flow equilibrium is restored. "Prices, deposits, cash reserves, outside reserves, will all be back to their levels prior to the flotation of the loan, and the borrowed capital will have moved into Canada in the form of commodities" (Viner 1924: 179).

If the transfer is under- or over-effected, on the other hand, there will be a rise or a fall, correspondingly, in the level of Canadian banks' reserves abroad. If gold and deposits abroad are viewed as perfect substitutes, Viner argues, the mechanism indeed is like "the generally accepted" theory. However, he ventures the guess that the specific and atypical Canadian pattern, "by preventing sudden inflows and withdrawals of gold, operated to bring about a steadier and smoother adjustment of price levels and trade balances in the face of huge and irregular borrowings abroad than would have been possible if gold movements into and out of Canada were as

---

[1]  There are many kinds of secondary expansion and contraction, depending on the type of institutional determinants of the reserve ratio, and on the extent of central bank intervention and sterilization, but there is only one kind of primary expansion: that related directly to a flow of specie, which we now refer to as the monetary base (Viner 1937: 394 ff).

automatic and free as they were elsewhere" (Viner 1924: 182). His metaphor for the role of the deposits in the United States is that of a shock absorber. The way he describes it, it sounds rather like an equalizer, smoothing out the monetary injections into the economy despite the lumpiness of the borrowings. If gold and correspondent deposits in New York were perfect substitutes from the point of view of the Canadian banks, this comment would not make sense. Viner clearly must be thinking of a model in which because of the ready availability of an intermediate liquid asset between non-income-earning gold reserves and interest-earning loans to Canadian businesses, Canadian banks had a lower elasticity of domestic lending with respect to their overall reserves than they would otherwise have had – or than banks in other countries had – so that domestic interest rate fluctuations were smaller. And it was presumably the time required to make trans-Atlantic transfers which made short-term deposits in the United States a more desirable reserve asset for the Canadian banks than deposits in London. Viner adds that these movements through the American banks apparently exacerbated "the financial difficulties" of New York at certain times. Except for this one comment, dropped as an aside, his is a small country model – as in fact all the late classical models are.

Finally, Viner disposes summarily of the possibility that trade in financial securities was an important part of the adjustment mechanism. The reasons are that "security transactions in Canada are predominantly of an investment character, and the market for 'floating securities' in Canada is too narrow to be much of a factor in settling trade balances." (This failure to distinguish between average and marginal changes seems un-Vinerian, to say the least.) A second reason is that it is temporary – put differently, that being a capital movement it cannot be part of the ultimate adjustment to capital movements. "[T]his would be equivalent to saying that a borrowing country facilitates the process of receiving its borrowings in a form other than gold, by lending to the lending country" (Viner 1924: 183). To which one is tempted to reply, with the hindsight derived from being familiar with the transfer problem literature, and the German reparations history – why not? In that last quotation, Viner seems to be taking a very narrow view of the adjustment problem. The distinction between goods and other kinds of assets is not a precise one, and a transfer which effects one kind of payment by increases in another is, of course, quite within the realm of plausibility. In fact, this is precisely what happened in the case of the spectacularly "successful" Franco-Prussian reparations (see the discussion of Taussig below).

## Late Viner

In the 1937 *Studies*, Viner returned to the Canada problem, defending himself against his critics, primarily Angell. White and others enter as minor participants in the debate. The discussion is centered around arguments about the behavior of Canadian banks, and empirical and statistical arguments about the timing of the increases in Canadian loans and deposits and only secondarily about the timing of the price increases and changes in the balance of trade. The main controversy seems to be about whether credit expansion preceded or followed the increases in bank reserves, not whether price movements, resulting from the credit expansion, were a necessary part of the mechanism. This last was taken to be axiomatic.

Viner repeats his argument that Canadian banks held the proceeds of the borrowings as short-term credits, partly in London, and partly in New York, and that these secondary reserves substituted for specie flows. As Arthur Bloomfield aptly expressed it (in private correspondence) "Canada was, in effect, on a U.S. dollar exchange standard managed by the Canadian commercial banks." These changes in secondary reserves could technically be labeled endogenous capital movements, but they stem, in Viner's analysis, from the institutional structure of Canadian banking rather than from responses to short-term interest rate differentials, induced either by the transfer itself or by central bank action. (Neither the U.S. nor Canada had a central bank at that time.) I do not deny, or assume that Viner would have denied, that some set of interest rate changes in Canada, Britain, and the United States would have resulted in a different set of events, but that is not the point. The point he is making is that the movements of the secondary reserves were an integral part of the borrowing process itself, rather than a step in the resultant adjustment.

An interesting amendment to the usual discussion of the transfer problem appears here when Viner concedes, fairly casually, that the long-term transfer (the loan) itself may have been endogenous, since "import surpluses may result from an internal . . . expansion of deposits made in anticipation of . . . borrowings abroad whose proceeds go to liquidate debit trade balances already incurred and to build up depleted reserves" (Viner 1937: 430–1). This point is not developed or elaborated, regrettably. It is essentially the model involved in many contemporary theories of foreign borrowing.

On the other hand, his criticism of the League of Nations Gold Delegation of 1932 indicates that he does not wish to carry the connection between foreign lending and domestic expenditure too far. In their report the Gold Delegation proposed a scheme for limiting short-term capital movements while preserving the gold exchange standard. Their recommendation would, Viner argues, essentially put an end to gold flows, and would imply that current account balances would never be liquidated, but would always be exactly matched by foreign lending. The report states: "While borrowing countries must thus watch and control the volume of their borrowings and assure that the funds obtained are devoted to productive purposes, it is necessary for lending countries to assure that foreign lending does not exceed or fall short of their net active balance on income account" (League of Nations 1932: 52). To contemporary ears this sounds as bizarre as Keynes's suggestion in 1943 (see Chapter 10) that capital transfers should be allowed only from countries with current account surpluses to those with deficits (Keynes 1940–4 [1980: 31]).

This notion of the endogeneity (and amenability to policy) of long-term capital movements is suggested casually and is developed in his discussion of the international transmission of business cycles. Viner's conclusion is that "anything can happen" when one considers both the effects of domestic expansion on interest rates, the effects of changes in interest rates on international capital movements, and the effects in other countries of changes in their trade balances on their domestic activity. If a capital-exporting country leads the rest of the world in its expansion, this may cause a reduction in capital exports as domestic investment is increased; it may even lead to capital imports. On the other hand, an increase in capital exports may lead and be the cause of an expansion (Viner 1937: 434).

Given this wide range of possibilities, I see no *a priori* grounds for expecting to find a significant correlation, whether positive or negative, between the fluctuations in the export of capital by particular countries and the fluctuations in their general level of business activity, unless there is ground for assuming that capital-exporting countries are typically countries whose business cycles always precede or always lag after world cycles, *or are countries in which fluctuations in the volume of foreign investment are major factors in initiating fluctuations in the internal level of business activity rather than by-products of the latter.* (Viner 1937: 435, italics mine)

On the role of capital flows in the propagation of business cycles we shall see more in Chapters 14 and 15 which deal with the contributions of Haberler (1937 [1941]) and of Neisser (1936), respectively.

Viner's view of the role (both actual and appropriate) of capital movements, especially of short-term capital movements, in the adjustment process, was that when they took place "in a reverse direction from the actual or incipient movement of specie" they were generally beneficial (Viner 1937: 403). This was most particularly true for countries with strong seasonal trade patterns, for smoothing out payments and avoiding reversible gold movements.[2] They were also important, and helpful, in cushioning the effect

[2] Viner here perceives a fallacy in the argument, which he attributes to both Goschen and Hawtrey, that the cost of shipping gold permits the exchange rate to deviate from par and hence discourages short-term capital movements in response to small interest rate differentials. Viner's point is that since short-term capital movements are here in the opposite direction to the incipient gold movements, as he calls them, they take place in the expectation of a reversal of exchange rate movements. If a currency is at the gold export point, presumably the expected exchange rate movement is in the direction of a return to parity, and this needs to be added to, not subtracted from, the interest rate differential. In fact, he

of a large and/or structural disturbance in the balance of payments – this is the familiar "buying time" argument. It is, he argues, particularly important for countries where long-term capital movements are large and lumpy.

These are very clear statements of the financing nature of short-term capital movements in the mechanism. The usefulness of the tool is limited, he argues, by the inelasticity of financial capital movements, resulting from the fact that "it is only a fraction of the short-term funds that is truly 'cosmopolitan'" (Viner 1937: 406n). He attributes this view, through Iversen (1935), to the Danish economist Axel Nielsen. But Viner's general stance in economic theory was sufficiently neoclassical to lead one to expect a sharper distinction between average and marginal shifts, and the importance of the latter, even when the averages are relatively small.

Viner rejects the argument, widely voiced, that short-term capital movements may abort the adjustment process by offsetting the credit reduction required for fundamental adjustment. This, he avers, ignores the point that short-term capital movements occur only if market interest rates rise, leading to reductions in both the demand for and supply of credit. The supply effect is attributed to unwillingness of banks to borrow additional reserves at the higher interest rates (Viner 1937: 406). But is not that the point? The tightness in the credit markets, part of the adjustment mechanism, is relieved, and interest rates lower than they would otherwise be, to the extent that a capital influx takes place. He agrees that short-term capital movements may reverse the stabilizing exchange rate movements, but since these are in any case small under fixed exchange rates, this is not an important consideration. More important is the disequilibrating role of short-term capital movements when they are speculative capital flights. This is the argument which I have attributed to the crisis group (see Chapter 11). He cites the experience both during the Napoleonic Wars and during the 1930s when such movements "influenced the international mechanism during a period of stress very much in the manner in which loose cargo operates on a ship during a storm" (Viner 1937: 407). Note the similarity to Keynes's language: "Loose funds may sweep round the world disorganising all steady business" (Keynes 1940–4 [1980: 31]; see Chapter 10, page 196).

Since the cause of such movements is non-economic, there is not much the authorities can do about it except recognize the problem and hold more reserves when their short-term indebtedness is large. Far from having done so, he says, central banks have "participated at least as actively as . . . other

says, with strong expectations as to future spot rates, the capital movements may be from higher to lower interest rate markets. This point about the stabilizing effect of speculation under fixed exchange rates, in contrast with the flexible rate case, is one which we shall encounter frequently.

banks and private individuals" in capital flights (Viner 1937: 10).
Particularly at fault, he argues, have been central banks operating their
reserves under the gold exchange standard. The defense of such a standard is
that it facilitates international payments and avoids the expense of physical
shipment of gold. He makes a strong argument against the gold exchange
standard, though it was supported by many people, including Keynes; his
opposition is based on the grounds that it either shifts the cost of carrying
non-interest-earning gold onto the center, reserve-holding countries, or else
it exposes those countries to excessive risks of drains on their reserves (Viner
1937: 411).

## Taussig

Taussig's own monograph on international trade is both real and monetary,
both analytical and empirical. His main interest is in the United States, but
he discusses events elsewhere. One in particular is closely related to Viner's
comment, cited above (page 229), in which he argued that a capital
movement cannot be part of the ultimate adjustment to capital movements
(Viner 1924: 183). I suppose, as always in economics, that the validity of this
depends on what we mean by ultimate. But to the extent that Germany paid
World War I reparations, she did it through borrowing, and an even clearer
case of paying reparations by borrowing was described by Taussig in the
story of the Franco-Prussian war and its aftermath in 1871. In describing
that incident Taussig notes that the tremendous speed and ease with which
the French paid their tribute to Germany was due at least in part to the fact
that they borrowed the means with which to do so. Actually, they dislent.
The French public had foreign securities; these they sold, and with the
proceeds they bought newly issued French government securities.[3] The funds
which the government acquired in this way it used to buy bills on other
currencies (foreign exchange) which it paid to the German government.
Government saving was matched by private saving; the counterpart of this
was that privately-held foreign assets were converted to government-owned
foreign assets which were then paid to Germany. Taussig suggests that many
of the foreign securities and bills which Germany thus acquired were
liquidated into specie and goods very gradually, over the next decade and
more (Taussig 1927: 266–79). The French presumably forfeited the import
surplus they could have enjoyed in later years through liquidation of those

[3] Iversen tells the same story, adding that the flotation of large issues by the French government
forced down the prices "not only of other French securities, but also of foreign bonds owned
by French capitalists. Consequently, it became a profitable business to buy such securities in
Paris and sell them abroad where their prices were higher. Thus the French capitalist by
converting his foreign holdings into French *rentes*, supplied the foreign exchange with which
the indemnity to Germany was paid" (Iversen 1935: 150).

assets, had they still owned them. Ultimately, therefore, Viner's criterion presumably holds and the capital was transmitted by the shipment of goods, but over a considerable period of time. On the Franco-Prussian reparations issue, Kindleberger has a nice note – Bismarck is cited to the effect that the next time they won a war the Germans would insist on paying reparations (Kindleberger 1984: 232).

A similar process was involved in the United States loans to the allies during the last years of World War I. The government borrowed from the public (the famous Liberty Loan) and lent to the allies. Since the transfer of goods occurred simultaneously with the granting of loans, there was no apparent transfer problem. But there was also, Taussig laments, serious misunderstanding and misplaced satisfaction with the results. It was argued that since the United States was not transferring "money" abroad, and was acquiring claims (they could not, perhaps, be blamed for not foreseeing that these claims would never be settled) she was getting the better side of the bargain. "[N]ever before was the nature of capital export more completely misunderstood. The country was supposed to receive much and to relinquish nothing; whereas in fact it parted with much and received nothing" (Taussig 1927: 316).

On the other hand, he expressed severe doubts in trying to explain the postwar pattern of payments. The inflow of specie which should have occurred shortly after the end of the war was delayed until 1920; then it came in "with a rush." But prices did not rise; we remember Keynes's inveighing against the Federal Reserve Board for sterilizing the flows. Eventually, Taussig insists, the gold inflow would have to affect the money supply, hence prices and thence trade. "But it was not eventually, it was promptly, that the equalization of the imports and exports took place." Exports to Europe fell off quite quickly; imports rose, but slightly; invisibles reacted in mixed ways. "But these ups and downs cannot be related to any general price movements of the kind contemplated in the theoretical analysis . . . To put it in the fewest words, things just *happened* so" (Taussig 1927: 332).

The mechanism he was interested in was, nevertheless, the classical one, or his interpretation of classical. According to Iversen he was one of the first to discuss the workings of a flexible exchange rate regime in response to real shocks (Iversen 1935: 302). Under fixed rates, he placed great importance, as I have indicated, on the role of the banking system. He agreed with Viner (or Viner with him) that the money supply can increase before the gold stock rises.

In all countries using deposits and checks freely, the looseness of the connection between bank reserves and bank deposits leads not infrequently to a chronological order different from that assumed in the Ricardian reasoning. An inflow of specie may follow, not precede, an enlargement of the circulating medium and a rise in prices. So it may be, at least, for a short time, even for a period of many months. Indeed, if there be further forces at work than those merely monetary, it may remain so for years. (Taussig 1927: 207–8)

In the longer run the money multiplier, a constant, determines the required specie inflow; not only the timing, therefore, but also the amount of the gold inflow, is an endogenous variable. Even if it is a deposit expansion which stimulates a price increase, neither can be sustained without the appropriate specie inflow, which depends on the size of the money multiplier (Taussig 1927: 208–9).

Like White, he argues that in continental countries such as France, the domestic money supply was not highly sensitive to gold drains abroad: the central bank kept high reserves on the one hand, and the circulating medium was primarily gold on the other, which implied that there was no pyramiding or multiple credit contraction. From this he concludes that in countries such as France, where most of the transactions currency consists of gold, "it is peculiarly difficult to trace the concrete working of the forces of international trade. There is nothing like the sensitiveness of the deposit-using countries, in which a great structure of credit money rests on a slender basis of reserves" (Taussig 1927: 211–12). This is an excellent example of the importance the late classicals put on the workings of a fractional-reserve monetary system in a classical model of adjustment.

I have referred throughout to Taussig's famous "doubts". Let me elaborate here somewhat on these. They are both germane to the subject and interesting for their unusual, probably unique aura of the confessional. On the one hand, reviewing Viner's Canada study, he concludes: "It is rare that the possibility of verifying the deductions of theory is found so successfully; and it is of no little significance that for this particular sort of situation the conclusions of theory prove to be so completely verified" (Taussig 1927: 235). And yet, he is troubled and remains agnostic. In a passage which all students of economics should be made to memorize when they begin to deal with methodology, he wonders at

the closeness and rapidity with which the varying balance of payments has found its expression in the varying balance of trade. The actual merchandise movements seem to have been adjusted to the shifting balance of payments with surprising exactness and speed. The process which our theory contemplates – the initial flow of specie when there is a burst of loans; the fall of prices in the lending country, rise in the borrowing country; the eventual increased movement of merchandise out of the one and into the other – all this can hardly be expected to take place smoothly and quickly. Yet no signs of disturbance are to be observed such as the theoretic analysis previses; and some recurring phenomena are of a kind not contemplated by theory at all. (Taussig 1927: 239)

He is particularly struck by the observation that equilibrating transfer-effecting movements of goods often seem to run upstream, as it were, with foreign lending and export surpluses often associated with rising, not with falling, prices. "It must be confessed that here we have phenomena not fully understood. In part our information is insufficient; in part our understanding of other connected topics is inadequate" (Taussig 1927: 239).

He goes further, confessing that what seems to be happening is that one "explain[ing] the facts in the light of a theory deemed sound, not . . . test[ing] the soundness of the theory by the facts." The specie movements are too small relative to the flow of merchandise, and they are often in the wrong direction. They show "oscillations that can be plausibly explained, but can hardly be said to be observably and specifically in accord with the formulations of theory" (Taussig 1927: 242–3).

There is much more in this vein. The trade flows respond with astonishing speed, "almost as if there were an automatic connection" between them and the financial flows which caused them. "Being roundabout, one would suppose that . . . [the process] would take time. And yet it appears to require practically none" (Taussig 1927: 261).

The French reparations, discussed above, puzzled him less than the British or German experiences, since there was a simple exchange of financial assets. He is, additionally, surprised by the smoothness and correctness of the adjustment in the United States from 1865 to 1879, although the country was not even on the gold standard during that period. This it was presumably which led him to explore, and to encourage Williams to study, the adjustment under a "paper currency".

## White

As a general statement, I would say that White's discussion of the adjustment mechanism is today fresher, less dated and, I would venture, more original, than that of any of the other late classicals.[4] Alone among the Taussig proteges, White was dealing with a case of capital exports rather than imports. He was studying the experiences of France as a capital exporter during the latter part of the nineteenth century. As Harrod was to argue that Britain had exported too much capital (see Chapter 9, note 5) he surmises that France was hurt by excessive lending abroad. The bias toward foreign investments he lays at the door of the "powerful French commercial banks" with the result that domestic investment and technological improvement lagged, particularly relative to Germany (White 1933: 300).

How was the adjustment to large-scale lending activities effected? White

[4] I do not know the details of White's biography, but the combination of government service and apparently related early death have deprived the profession of a major contributor.

seems unsure, unhappier with the received doctrine even than Taussig: he acknowledges the adjustment, but fails to observe evidence of any of the expected instruments. In reading his book, one is continually struck by the recurring tension between what he says he believes the adjustment mechanism to be, a product, apparently, of his training seasoned by his original thoughts on the subject, and what he feels he can document historically and factually.

He discusses several possibilities.

1   Unlike England in the nineteenth and the United States in the twentieth century, he says, the French did not experience much direct increase in demand for exports through the actual activity of investing abroad. Despite efforts on the part of the French government to link foreign lending to purchases of French goods, the effect was negligible (White 1933: 302).

2   He rejects the notion that exchange rate movements within the gold points could have had any significant effect.

3   He is left, therefore, only with price level changes (including intersectoral shifts in relative prices) to effect adjustment, that is, with the classical mechanism. He conjectures: "Shifts in demand schedules were doubtless a more effective medium" (White 1933: 303). But he could not find the evidence either way in the statistics. "The influence of sectional price changes as a force in the adjustment does not in the case of France appear to have played so prominent a role as is presupposed by the neo-classical doctrine. Nevertheless, the indications are that they were a factor" (White 1933: 303).

There does, indeed, appear to have been "some indication of a causal relationship between capital exports and movements of merchandise" but no evidence "that the price movements *were caused* by capital exports" (White 1933: 171, italics his). For causality he is impelled, therefore, to look at monetary and banking data. In this, he is a true late classical. But in the end he is stymied here, too. "Altogether analysis of French banking and monetary movements appears to show no definite relationships upon which can be based a satisfactory explanation of the connection between French capital exports and movements of sectional prices" (White 1933: 305).

He places great importance on the role of the Bank of France. I argued above that a characteristic of the late classical group (as distinct, for example, from the neoclassicals) is their disregard of the role of the central bank. It is just possible that had they been dealing, in their empirical work, with countries which did have central banks, they would have been candidates for the neoclassical category, though their emphasis on the domestic effects of interest rate changes was generally very light. Canada and the United States had no such institutions in the period discussed. Argentina likewise did not, but there was a good deal of banking legislation and supervision, emission of bank notes was limited to specific banks, and there were a number of semi-official provincial and national banks (see Williams 1920: 57–8). France had an old, long-established central bank, but half of White's book is devoted to a chronicling of its ineffectiveness in promoting and facilitating adjustment, in fact, its counter-productive sterilization (though he does not use the word) of money flows.

We conclude ... that in normal times the Bank of France exercised no influence on the contraction or expansion of credit. If any connection, then, is to be found between French net gold flows and changes in purchasing power, it must be sought elsewhere than in the activities of the Bank of France. (White 1933: 200)

The gold-flow-discount-credit-price sequence of the neo-classical theory appears to have been wholly absent. (White 1933: 223)

(This is, by the way, one of the examples I have noted of the use of the word "neoclassical" in the same sense I have used it.) However, the reason to which he attributes this is not that the "gold-flow-discount-credit-price" mechanism was inoperative but rather that it was jammed and adjustment impeded by the policies of the Bank of France. That institution first made every effort to prevent gold flows, and secondly, sterilized those that did occur. "The practice of the Bank of France of charging a premium on gold when a heavy outflow threatened thus constituted a formidable barrier (when the exchange rate was 'unfavourable') to the outward movement of short-term funds, and rendered the French gold holdings insensitive to movements of discount rates in foreign money markets" (White 1933: 185). He makes a big point of the active attempts on the part of the Bank of France to protect its gold reserves, even though these were large and generally in "excess" of needs, given the money supply and credit. When their gold stock was threatened, they raised their buying price. White notes that they employed this policy (known as the gold premium policy) much more frequently than they did discount rate policy (White 1933: 182). As we saw in Chapter 5, the Macmillan Committee and others in Britain frequently noted, slightly sourly, the greater freedom of the French to indulge in the use of various devices, such as the manipulation of gold prices, to protect their gold supply – devices which the British felt were not available to them, given their special role in world money and gold markets. He argues that according to the "neo-classical" theory an alternative to gold flows and their "automatic" effects should be variations in the discount rate, which would also affect domestic demand and hence prices (White 1933: 188). This policy also the Bank of France eschewed. The discount rate, he says, was raised rarely between 1880 and 1913, sometimes remaining unchanged for three, five, and even seven years (1900 to 1907). In the face of this "stability" one can hardly think of this as a major "link in the mechanism of adjustment for the international accounts" (White 1933: 198). When they did raise the rate it was by very little, seldom more than 1 percent in any given year; White doubts whether this could possibly have been instrumental in the adjustment process. He concludes that it was generally a defensive move, in response to higher rates abroad, and not intended to attract gold (White 1933: 188).

He alludes grudgingly to the possible use by the Bank of France of quantity restrictions on discounts; he does not think these important, however, because the market rate of interest remained below the penalty Bank of France discount rate during most of the period he studied (White 1933: 196–7). But just as central bank policy was not brought into play to aid in the adjustment, neither was it able to forestall it permanently. He emphasizes throughout the book the ill-developed state of deposit banking in France before the war (White 1933: 8) and the passive role of the Bank of France "which exercised no influence on the contraction or expansion of credit" (White 1933: 200). Nevertheless, he says:

Notwithstanding the varying degree of sensitivity of banking systems to bank reserves and the modifying effects of the cyclical movements of business activity, a sustained flow of gold out of the country eventually calls forth a rise in discount rates in the gold losing country, and a fall (relatively) in the gold receiving countries. (White 1933: 8)

As I have indicated, however, this somehow seems more a matter of faith with him than a conclusion arrived at from his study of events.

He similarly gives considerable pride of place, in his description of the "adjustment mechanism" in the abstract, to temporary short-term capital movements. And more than Williams, he endogenizes capital flows. Whether the difference is between White and Williams or between Argentina and France I am not quite certain, though I would guess the latter has something to do with it. Whereas Williams discussed the responses of government borrowing to exchange rate changes and the balance of payments, White built changes in "autonomous" capital flows into the adjustment mechanism. In fact, he explicitly treats them as alternative to gold flows as a means of effecting a transfer. "[T]ransfers are effected either thru gold flows or thru the movement of short-term loans." As a matter of fact, however, neither was very effective in the French case, according to White. Gold movements, on an annual basis, were small (intra-annual movements being reversed with great frequency), and short-term capital flows were discouraged by "[t]he absence of a free gold market, with the consequent increased risks of exchange" (White 1933: 147–9).

He ends his book with a recognition that "the neo-classical theory [as represented by Taussig] is not the complete explanation." I have argued, of course, that the Taussig tradition does not involve discount rate changes and internal interest rate effects as important parts of the process (see White 1933: 223). The problem, as noted above, is not that the mechanism would not work in an untroubled long run, but that it is hindered by "frictions and rapid changes characteristic of modern economic conditions" (White 1933: 306). In the course of outlining what a complete theory should include, he places heavy weight on endogenous long-term international investment (not short-term financial capital mobility), as developing countries may find themselves simultaneously borrowing abroad in order to grow while increasing imports "and thereby introducing disequilibrium."

Or a country having a large excess of exports brought about by capital exports may during a period of rapid business expansion consume more of its domestic commodities and thus cause exports to be curtailed (thru the medium of rapidly rising export prices). *The resulting disequilibrium* (the appearance or intensification of an unfavorable balance of payments caused by a decreased export surplus while the rate of foreign lending continues) *may in such a case be partially corrected by a decrease in the export of capital, the decrease in capital exports being caused by a greatly increased demand for capital at home.* (White 1933: 309–10, italics mine)

This is indeed endogenous capital mobility, but of a very different sort from the short-term financing that is usually implied by the term. (Both Taussig and Ohlin occasionally hint at something similar.) And here and elsewhere White comes closer to keynesian macro analysis than any of the others in the group. At the same time, he comes closer than any of the others to developing a truly full-fledged general equilibrium system. Here the comparison must be to Ohlin.

Another example of endogenous capital movements (indicating he considered this an important feature of the process) is the response to an exogenous shock such as a crop failure, which would consist of a reduction in savings and hence in foreign lending. This might, albeit accidentally, offset some or all of the decline in the trade surplus caused by the increased imports resulting from the same crop failure (White 1933: 309). This is indeed ingenious and startlingly original for its time. Having gone a long way (but not all the way) toward accepting the "income approach" rather than the price-specie flow approach to the adjustment mechanism, White judges the role of both gold flows and international capital mobility in terms of the effects of these on demand curves. He even has a term for income elasticity of demand, which he says "has been called," though he does not indicate by whom, "'flexibility' as distinct from elasticity" (White 1933: 18). In the closing sections of his book he has a very clear statement of the effects of flows of "gold or short-time balances" on trade "thru changes in demand schedules before prices have had time both to change and to modify merchandise movements," since prices change more slowly than demand schedules shift (White 1933: 308). Real changes can take place very quickly. Since demand shifts rapidly, one must examine the adjustment mechanism in terms of total, not net (annual), gold flows. Gold can flow out, *affect demand both at home and abroad,* and return to the lending country – all within the period of a year, and with no change in prices. There follows a beautiful discussion of the importance of *marginal* changes in demand, and other variables, for the adjustment process (White 1933: 31).

The discussion of the role of short-term capital movements, through changes in bank lending between countries, likewise is centered on the direct effects of such changes on merchandise trade. What is lacking is an examination of the mechanism which generates such international capital movements. What discussion there is of the effects of changes in interest rates on international lending (White 1933: 8–9 for example) appears in the context of the *result* of gold movements. That is, movements of gold must, sooner or later, as we noted above, affect central bank discount rates and lending rates in general and invite short-term capital movements. But why such capital movements might take place in the absence of gold flows is not discussed in much detail. That is, there is neither central bank "action" nor the "automatic" monetary effect of excess demand for foreign exchange, which, as we shall see, was the main focus of Angell's attack on the "Classical Theory". The one hint we have is in the introduction, where he sides with Viner against Angell on the question of substitution of short-term capital movements for gold flows as an institutional phenomenon (White 1933: 11–12).

White does, however, make some place for short-term capital movements of the neoclassical type, but specifically denies the internal effects of interest rate changes as part of the mechanism. Rises in the discount rate "[t]ogether with increases in the gold premium . . . served to check outward movements of gold when there was danger of any large efflux; they were intended not to curtail credit at home but to prevent short-time funds from being drawn to foreign markets when very high rates prevailed" (White 1933: 304). This is the same point he made specifically in describing the behavior of the Bank of France. It is not neoclassical but reminiscent of mid nineteenth-century views of the role of Bank rate in attracting short-term capital. But: "There was no trace of the gold-reserve-discount rate-volume-of-credit sequence held by the neo-classical theory to be the necessary chain connecting disequilibrium in the balance of payments with sectional price changes" (White 1933: 303).

### Angell

Angell was also a student of Taussig's, and he published his thesis in 1926. He argues throughout that he is rejecting the classical theory and is offering a counter-explanation of international adjustment. I suppose this is the reason he is not generally included in the Harvard School. However, I would classify him, in spite of himself, as a late classical. He is classical in three important respects.

1 His theory "rejoins the classical line of analysis only at the point where general price changes begin to appear" (Angell 1926: 414). I left the word "only" in the citation to avoid being accused of misquoting him; it is an important point at which to "rejoin the classical line of analysis" in my view. Disturbances lead to monetary adjustment which results in price level changes and hence in the restoration of equilibrium. To me that sounds "classical" enough.

2 There is virtually nothing in his model of the role of the central bank in setting monetary policy and aiding, or inhibiting, movement toward equilibrium. This certainly disqualifies him as a neoclassical.

3 Monetary responses to disturbances can lead to changes in discount rates and hence to short-term international capital movements, but these are relevant only for "temporary disturbances" (Angell 1926: 413) and he seems uninterested in this whole aspect of the problem. His main point seems to be that a shock to the balance of payments will directly and necessarily create monetary changes leading to price changes, in some cases before there are specie flows, and in some cases instead of specie flows.

An excess demand for foreign bills affects the exchange rate, in the first place. If that is not enough, he says, gold will flow, but this need not happen.

The volume of purchasing power in circulation in the creditor country will be built up, in consequence of the increase in the banks' holdings of bills . . . These changes, in turn, will operate upon the corresponding general price levels. The latter effect is often, though not always, strengthened by alterations in the discount rates. The movements in prices will then influence the commodity balance of trade, in ways long familiar, and will continue to do so until the change in the commodity trade has become great enough to offset and correct the original disturbance. (Angell 1926: 413)

We see here what Angell notes explicitly elsewhere, that his model, like the classical one, is stable – the mechanism is automatic and equilibrium always restored. To point out the monetary effects of an excess demand for foreign exchange was correct and useful, but it is excessively dramatic of him to argue, I think, that "[t]he critical factor in the maintenance of an international equilibrium . . . becomes the money market; that is, discount and exchange rates, not commodity markets and commodity prices" (Angell 1926: 140–1). Since the adjustment mechanism, as he sees it, necessarily involves price changes and adjustment in commodity trade to those price changes, it seems gratuitious to deny the importance of commodity markets and prices in the mechanism.

## Summation

Taussig and his famous students can quite legitimately be counted in the classical as distinct from the neoclassical camp. They are, as a group, characterized by concern for long-run adjustment, a conviction that stable equilibrium exists and is achieved through the workings of the price mechanism. Monetary factors are, of course, an integral part of the story, as they are in the classical mechanism, with the role of commercial banks being dominant. This is particularly true of Viner, though he argued that the importance of the banks and of their foreign-held deposits was unique to the Canadian experience. White, on the other hand, does devote considerable attention to the role, albeit an ineffective one, of the central bank in the mechanism. Though they did not succeed in incorporating income-expenditure effects into their models, most of them were, variously, aware of such interactions and in this sense they constitute the beginnings of the transition to the keynesian approach. Ohlin, as we shall see in Chapter 13, felt he had learned a lot from them about the connection between the structure of trade and changes in "purchasing power". A further link between them and Ohlin is their emphasis, greater than in the pure classical paradigm, on the importance of non-traded goods and of intersectoral structural shifts, both in demand and supply.

# Ohlin

### His place on the stage

Ohlin considered himself a late classical (he called the group the Harvard School), and I find this broadly acceptable, with many qualifications. One of his salient characteristics is, in fact, that he is difficult to classify. In a sense he has gotten a bad press, being widely regarded simply as a keynesian *manqué*, with a naive, pseudo-income approach to the balance of payments. I try to avoid psychological analyses, but I suggest that this characterization of Ohlin stems primarily from a tendency to read his controversy with Keynes over German reparations (Ohlin 1929), fit it into the matrix of pre-keynesian Stockholm economics, and let it go at that. The one-third of *Interregional and international trade* (Ohlin 1933a; less in the 1967 revision) devoted to the monetary as distinct from the real theory of international trade seems to be widely neglected. It is on this, primarily, that I base my discussion.

A word about dates, to put the work into its historical perspective. *Interregional and international trade* bears a 1933 copyright, but the preface is signed January 20, 1931. Ohlin's doctoral dissertation at Stockholm (entitled *Handelns Teori*) was presented and published in May 1924. Ohlin spent the year 1923 at Harvard and the preface acknowledges the comments and interest of Taussig, Williams, and Viner, and judging from an outline, contains the basic ideas embodied in the later English-language work.[1]

Economics is too young to indulge in scholarship for its own sake, but the dating of Ohlin's writing takes on added interest when we compare (Ohlin 1933a) with the 1933 paper "On the formulation of monetary theory" (Ohlin 1933b [1978]), translated only relatively recently from the Swedish

---

[1] Dr. Harry Flam was kind enough to provide me with a detailed summary of Chapters 9 through 13 of *Handelns Teori*. (He and I are currently collaborating on a complete translation.) It is certainly closely related to the treatment in *Interregional and international trade*. The detailed general-equilibrium analysis of the changes in commodity prices and factor prices, the effects of internal factor mobility and factor substitution – are not, apparently, spelled out. But the later work is rather an elaboration and extension of the earlier than an alteration.

and probably constituting his first major contribution to macroeconomic theory. The discussions of the flows of income and expenditure, saving and investment, are highly reminiscent of his treatment of the concept of "buying power" (Ohlin 1933a). It is indeed a macro article, as the second part of (1933a) is a macro treatment of international economics, but the emphasis is still on the causes of *price* changes, rather than on quantity adjustments. Shortly before he died, Ohlin compared himself and Keynes regarding their relative emphases on price and quantity changes, but mostly questioning whether Keynes was as exclusively quantity oriented, to the total exclusion of price changes, as Patinkin argued he was and as later keynesians indeed were according to Ohlin (Ohlin 1981: 206 ff). This is of course a major issue in the history of monetary theory (see the debates in *History of political economy*, Volumes 10 and 13, 1978 and 1981). In any case, when Ohlin prepared his thesis for 1933 publication he was not yet a full-fledged keynesian or, for that matter, a mature Swede, as far as international monetary theory was concerned. I must take the word of Swedish-reading experts that by 1934 his views were beginning to change; but I find support in the apt comment of Professor Hans Brems, in private correspondence: "A Keynesian Ohlin became in his macroeconomics in 1934, in his trade theory 1968." But the article of 1933 and the book, produced during the decade 1923–33, are of a piece.

Ohlin's treatment is neither formal nor mathematical, but it is the most complex general-equilibrium analysis of the subject of its day (with the possible exception of the ultra-formal treatments of Yntema (1932) and Mosak (1944)) – and thoroughly integrated as far as real and monetary analyses are concerned. The first part is in no way as "purely" real or as simple as students might think who have been brought up on the Heckscher-Ohlin-Samuelson theory of international trade; nor is the second part as exclusively monetary as may be believed by those familiar only with the 1929 *Economic journal* debate. This latter point is of crucial importance.

The monetary, balance-of-payments adjustment chapters of the book are entitled "The Mechanism of International Trade Variations and Capital Movements". This includes: various types of disturbance to equilibrium, some real and some monetary; aspects of adjustment, some monetary and some real, mostly private but some relating to the behavior of the monetary authorities; expenditure changes, involving changes in total demand and in the balance of trade directly, at constant prices; changes in demand and supply involving shifts between sectors (tradables and non-tradables) at constant prices; and the effect on and of prices on and of demand and supply shifts between sectors. It is general, detailed, with constant reference to historical and institutional "facts", both actual and stylized: a rich vein to be mined.

As we shall see in Chapter 15, Neisser and Modigliani (1953), in their brief survey of the literature, place Ohlin, along with Pareto and Polak, in the category of general equilibrium theorists of international macroeconomics. This is surely a defensible categorization of him. As indicated above, he is actively, constantly, and explicitly aware of the interactions between various markets for goods and services, at home and abroad. That "everything depends on everything else" is perfectly clear. What is less explicit is the existence of feedbacks, so that "everything also depends on itself". There are hints here and there which leave no doubt that Ohlin was aware of feedbacks (see for example the comment cited below about "secondary" changes in capital movements) but they tend to get left out of the discussion. Thus a change in demand for a country's export commodity will affect the prices of factors of production in a way that depends on myriads of elasticities and cross-elasticities of substitution in supply and demand; but the "final" effect on factor prices, at home and abroad, does not then feed back into the world demand for the commodity.[2] And it was only by dealing with feedbacks that Metzler (1942b [1973: Chapter 2]) was able to tidy up the Keynes-Ohlin debate on the transfer problem.

## Ohlin the late and neoclassical

Most of the disturbances Ohlin analyzes are real, the major exception being a brief discussion of "monetary variations" in which a credit expansion and price rise in one country is the proximate cause of imbalance. For the rest, he deals with the transfer problem (primarily long-term capital movements, in response to interest rate differentials, but also unilateral transfers such as reparations); changes in world demand for a country's export good; changes in technology, including changes in transport costs. Each is discussed in great detail, difficult to summarize; I shall try to convey the main thread and flavor of his argument.

Ohlin takes the counter position to Keynes, holding the view that in general commodity trade adjusts to long-term capital movements, rather than the converse.[3] In a general-equilibrium framework the question is meaningless, of course. It is, however, a sensible empirical question

[2] For a discussion of feedbacks (or lack thereof) in Stockholm School macroeconomics in general, see Hansen (1981 especially 267–8).
[3] There is a brief treatment of capital movements as endogenous, particularly when he is discussing very long-run trends. One example among many, which demonstrates the extent of what one may call Ohlin's general-equilibriumness, is the statement (Ohlin 1933a: 511) that an increase in the world demand for a country's exports may raise income and hence savings and, if labor from abroad is not available, lead to a fall in the rate of interest and a capital outflow. He suggests that this is the post-World War I story of Sweden, facing an increased world demand for its exports of both pulp and machinery.

specifically involving the size of the several parameters of the system. In Ohlin's words, long-term international capital movements "are due to differences in long-term interest rates and other comparatively permanent circumstances, and these circumstances are not *often* much affected by changes in the volume of imports and exports of goods and services" (Ohlin 1933a: 384, italics mine). Capital movements necessarily involve changes in the trade balance if capital is in fact to move. Changes in underlying conditions may lead to changes in both commodity trade and capital movements. However: "The point is that basic changes which primarily affect imports and exports seldom call forth *secondary* readjustments with regard to long-term lending, while the reverse *always* happens" (Ohlin 1933a: 384, italics mine). Keynes, on the other hand, argued that in general "the volume of foreign investment has tended . . . to adjust itself . . . to the balance of trade, rather than the other way round, the former being the sensitive and the latter the insensitive factor" (Keynes 1929a [1949: 167]).

Changes in trade or in long-term capital movements lead to expenditure (and hence commodity trade) changes directly and also indirectly through short-term capital movements and monetary effects. The latter are discussed in a manner which is close to the neoclassical. Ohlin's view has indeed much in common with many of the neoclassical theories. What is important here is that gold movements play only an occasional and minor role in this process.

A detailed discussion describes the foreign-exchange market and short-term capital movements, involving the relationship between interest rates, short-term financial indebtedness, and exchange rates. Short-term capital movements smooth out seasonal variations in payments and prevent exchange-rate movements. For other disturbances ("less regular") there is likely to be a change in interest rates and money-market tightness. Often this is integral to the cause of the disturbance itself: a crop failure, for example, leads to an increase in the trade deficit. But it also leads to a credit tightness since "farmers are unable to save as usual and instead have to ask for temporary loans to cover their expenses" (Ohlin 1933a: 388). The resulting rise in interest rates encourages short-term capital inflow and prevents exchange rate changes. Merchants, traders, exporters, respond to higher interest rates by seeking credit abroad, discounting their bills in the destination country. Higher interest rates lower the yield on securities and raise the cost of holding them, inducing international portfolio shifts.

If these market forces are insufficient, the authorities will raise the discount rate and/or sell securities in the open market. Foreign-exchange variations *within* the gold points call forth movements of short-term capital but not of gold. The resulting credit tightness will "reduce the volume of credit and buying power." Imports fall because traders buy less when credit is tight, and perhaps consumers buy less because their income is reduced. "Consumers use

their income, while traders use their capital or credit" (Ohlin 1933a: 392).
Exports may rise as domestic spending on exportables decreases.

Ohlin criticizes the "classical view of gold movements," aligning himself
with "Angell, Feis, Graham, Hawtrey, Keynes, Viner and others" (Ohlin
1933a: 396n). Gold movements are not essential to adjustment, if they occur
they may be sterilized (citing Federal Reserve policy), and finally when they
do occur it is not as a *cause* of central bank action but to restore the reserve
position of the central bank which has been affected by the adjustment.

A word about transport costs (which include tariffs and other impediments to trade). Ohlin argues that if there were *perfect* commodity arbitrage
there would be no transfer problem. A transfer of purchasing power would
shift the distribution of spending on the world's goods from the payer to the
receiver. This might or might not lead to a change in the relative prices of the
two countries' goods, depending on the taste pattern of the receivers as
compared with that of the payers (compare the Jones (1970)-Samuelson
(1971) debate on this issue), but there is no *a priori* presumption in either
direction. The contemporary reader is somewhat uncomfortable with a
theory based on the existence of impediments to trade, but the point is that it
is precisely these which create the distinction between traded and non-
traded goods, and it is the intersectoral shifts in demand and supply which
are crucially important in his view of the adjustment mechanism. He
classified goods as follows:

international goods, subject to international trade, competing home market goods, in
more or less close competition with international goods, and non-competing home
market goods, a large group with a less direct connection with other goods.
International goods may be either import or export goods, consequently competing
home market goods may compete with either the former or the latter. (Ohlin 1933a:
247)

### Ohlin as pre-keynesian: the concept of "buying power"

The prime mover in the adjustment process is a change in "purchasing
power" or "buying power." It is here that Ohlin can be classified as he ranks
himself, with some of the late classicals, the "Harvard School," particularly
Viner and Angell. He goes further than these writers, in that changes in
purchasing power need not lead to changes in prices, though they may do so.
But, as noted previously, not so far as Keynes, and for different reasons: when
prices remain unchanged, this is the result of substitutions in demand and
supply which render price changes unnecessary, not of keynesian-type
fixprice quantity adjustments. As an example of this distinction between
Ohlin and the late classicals, read in its entirety his citation of Angell, and his
own comments. He quotes Angell as saying that the "'key to the problem of

international equilibrium . . . lies in the effect . . . upon the volume of purchasing power in circulation, and through it upon the general level of prices.' I should like only to add: 'and upon imports and exports'" (Ohlin 1933a: 544n). I know of no other writer, except perhaps Iversen, whom I discuss below, who has used this concept. In fact, in the purely macro part of the analysis, I would view it as his most important single contribution to the theory. Ohlin refers back to Bastable (1889) and claims him as the originator of the notion (of buying power). But, he adds, "the concept 'aggregate of money incomes' is more useful than those *used in its place*: 'The height of money wages' (Taussig), 'The rate of efficiency earnings' (Keynes)" (Ohlin 1933a: 378n, italics mine).

It is puzzling to find Ohlin's "buying power" suggested as an alternative to "efficiency earnings" or "money wages," which emphasize the cost rather than the income aspect of the flows. In full-employment equilibrium the distinction between costs and income vanishes; but the emphasis on demand and expenditures, here and in the 1933 article, is what distinguishes Ohlin from the late classicals. And yet one foot at least was still firmly in the classical camp, as we see in the following citation from the 1933 paper. "Above all let us recall that in a study of prices what we are trying to explain by the generation of income among other things, are changes in the supply of and demand for various goods and services" (Ohlin 1933b [1978: 356]).

In the 1967 revision of *Interregional and international trade*, Ohlin was, not surprisingly, expressing more conventionally keynesian views: "The basic concepts and approach used here are well suited for a study of the influence of employment variations" (Ohlin 1967: 235n). Ohlin's definition of "buying power" follows:

the aggregate of money incomes and the flow of liquid capital during a certain period of time, increased by (1) the income drawn from the ownership in productive factors abroad, (2) new borrowings abroad, and (3) credit inflation; and reduced by (1) the incomes which people living abroad draw from productive factors in this country, (2) new lendings to other countries, and (3) credit deflation. (Ohlin 1933a: 378)

A footnote warns: "The part of the flow of income which is saved and thus becomes liquid capital must not, of course, be counted twice" (Ohlin 1933a: 378n). The "flow of liquid capital" has been earlier defined as follows:

Individuals may acquire buying power in terms of money in two other ways than by earning or borrowing it. In the course of the process of production a part of the capital, which has been invested, is made "free", i.e. liquid. This is a normal and important source of buying power. [The term "invested" is here used in a wide sense. Every sale of a commodity means that the monetary capital, invested in that commodity, is made liquid.] (Ohlin 1933a: 376, his brackets)

This is precisely the framework of the 1933 article, where we read: "Part of . . . [gross revenue] is spent on demand for consumers' goods, another part – freed capital plus new saving – goes into reinvestment and new investment, i.e., constitutes investment demand" (Ohlin 1933b [1978: 356]).

I have devoted a considerable amount of space to the definition and elaboration of "buying power" because it is both, to my knowledge, unique and an important step toward the development of the income approach. My interpretation of his definition of "buying power" is the flow of potential expenditure. The income he has defined, plus ownership of factors abroad, minus foreign ownership of factors at home, is net domestic product. The "flow of liquid capital" is clearly depreciation allowances (since new savings must not be included here, to avoid double counting). To the total, gross domestic product, he adds net foreign borrowing and the increase in the money supply. In the revised edition (Ohlin 1967) this interpretation is supported: "By 'buying power' I have meant not only variations in the national income of the different countries but also variations in the ability to make purchases that are directly associated with international capital transfers and with an inflationary or deflationary credit policy" (Ohlin 1967: 317).

I used the term "potential expenditure" to define buying power. It is not entirely clear whether Ohlin views expenditures as equal to buying power, which is most probable, or a function of it, with a coefficient less than or equal to unity. What is clear, however, is that total expenditure is not, in general, equal to total "demand for goods and services, produced in this country." An increase in buying power may be spent on foreign goods or home-produced exportables and affect, not the level of money income at home, but the balance of trade. At the same time, citing the debate with Keynes, Ohlin takes pains to note that an increase in purchases due to increased buying power may *cause* an increase in money income, in which case it would be misleading to attribute the increase in demand to the increase in income – the reverse, rather, is true (Ohlin 1933a: 407n).

Like Viner in his study of Canada (Viner 1924), Ohlin speaks of a "primary" and a "secondary" credit expansion pursuant to a transfer. When borrowers convert their foreign currency into domestic money and spend it, we have a primary expansion. The extension of bank credit based on the excess reserves thus created, and elicited by the demand for increased credit as home spending rises, constitutes the "secondary" expansion. Since the central bank acquires foreign-exchange reserves in this process it is likely to ease its credit policy, thus engendering a "tertiary" expansion. As a result of these increases in "buying power," there will be a rise in money incomes, the extent of which is unknown; there will necessarily be leakages into imports, but it is impossible to say in general how much. (Here is where the later, keynesian, contributions of Metzler and others become relevant.) Ohlin saw the problem of the relationship between expenditure and income: it is possible, he says, that most of the new spending takes place in securities and real estate markets, as occurred in the United States in 1928 and 1929. The "stage in the business cycle" determines both the direction and responsiveness of demand shifts and the mobility of factors of production between sectors (Ohlin 1933a: 407), since resource shifts are easier to effect during an expansion than a contraction. Furthermore, it makes a difference not only how much unemployment there is, but whether the unemployed resources are in the traded or non-traded goods sector (Ohlin 1933a: 424n).

### Ohlin unclassified: intersectoral price and quantity changes

Discussion of commodity markets starts with the simplifying assumption that, following a transfer from $B$ to $A$, world demand for each country's international goods is unchanged. The only change is that the demand for non-traded goods rises in $A$ and falls in $B$. This in turn influences the supply of exportables in each country and therefore their price, to an extent which depends on the demand elasticity in each country (since it is this that determines the rise in price of the non-traded goods). Demand elasticity depends on the "elasticity of wants" (which I understand to be the partial-equilibrium price elasticity of demand), on the elasticity of supply from other sources (from other countries, apparently), and on the "reaction of buying power" – the income effect of the changed factor prices resulting from the change in demand for non-traded goods.

Assuming, for the nonce, that all goods are produced with identical bundles of factors in fixed proportions, the rise in demand for and price of non-traded goods, demand for traded goods remaining fixed, will raise factor prices, hence costs of production of traded goods. This will shift some goods out of the exportable category, and conversely in the paying country, and will further limit the required movement in the relative prices of traded goods, that is, in the terms of trade (Ohlin 1933a: 419).

Dropping the assumption of fixed bundles of factors, Ohlin undertakes a detailed analysis of relative factor prices, involving such elements as heterogeneity of factors (assumed to be non-existent in the conventional, real, Heckscher-Ohlin trade model, by the way),[4] alternative uses of factors,

---

[4] Ohlin's view of the determinants of trade was a much broader one than that which has come down to trade theorists as the Heckscher-Ohlin-Samuelson model, or even than what de Marchi (1976) has labeled the Ohlin-Samuelson research program. In a brilliant survey of the post-Leontief pure trade theory literature, de Marchi shows that instead of naive falsification, the Leontief results led to a restructuring, by Samuelson and others, of the Heckscher-Ohlin factor proportions theory of trade. But I would argue that Ohlin had a sense of unity between real and monetary trade theory which has since become attenuated.

long- versus short-run elasticities of substitution, increasing returns, institutional frictions. It is all there, and again, not surprisingly, qualitative results are not derived.

In discussing the possible course of relative prices, Ohlin is similarly general-equilibrium, detailed, and "empirical". Adjustments vary with the extent of excess capacity in the several industries and the level of unemployed resources; frictions in the form of labor-union demands make their impact felt; the ratio of profits to factor costs varies between sectors; different stages in the adjustment process look different (Ohlin 1933a: 424–30).

We note recurrent emphasis on the difference between short- and long-run effects, on the time needed for various adjustments to work themselves out, on the different kinds of effects at different stages of the borrowing process. "A complete analysis of the effect of international capital movements upon the price system must be an account of a time-using process" (Ohlin 1933a: 426).

Both in my summary and in Ohlin's original, there is more emphasis placed on the adjustment in the receiving than in the paying country. He asserts that the effects are analytically symmetrical, but he argues that in fact the lending country will have a harder time of it, because contraction is always more painful than expansion. Continuing crisis in the paying country may, in fact, eventually force the country off the gold standard, or, perhaps, alternatively, cause a breakdown in union resistance to wage cuts. However it is done, "B may well lose much more from unemployment and other disturbances than from less favorable terms of exchange in international trade" (Ohlin 1933a: 428).

Finally,

the size of the capital movements in comparison with other aspects of economic life in the countries concerned has an important bearing on the dimensions of the changes in the price system . . . It is much easier to bring about a relative increase of imports and reduction of exports by 5 percent than by 50 percent. (Ohlin 1933a: 426–7)

Having listed all the possible results following a transfer, on the assumption that all the change in effective demand is concentrated on non-traded goods, Ohlin drops that admittedly "unrealistic" assumption and permits variations in the demand for each country's traded goods. He devotes little space to this case, however, since it is even more difficult than previously to get precise qualitative results.

Further "complications" which Ohlin examines in some detail include the

Samuelson (1982) in his obituary appreciation of Ohlin ignores the monetary section of Ohlin (1933a) and cites only the debate with Keynes as the locus of Ohlin's monetary views. The Ohlin-Samuelson program concerns itself with explanations and predictions of the direction of real trade flows. I am concerned here with Ohlin as contributor to the literature on the adjustment mechanism.

existence of third countries and the dependence of the precise nature of the transfer process on the trade and payments relations of the paying and receiving countries with the "third countries"; for example, when French and German capital exports to third countries slowed down, or stopped, after World War I, Britain's capital *goods* exports were adversely affected, and hence her income and her own capital exports declined (Ohlin 1933a: 456). Long-run growth is also dealt with, with emphasis on feedbacks from trade to terms of trade to income to savings to capital transfers, and back to trade again.

### Coda

Summarizing, Ohlin enumerates three mechanisms of adjustment, though we would be inclined to classify them slightly differently today. The first is changes in buying power, which shift the demand for traded goods. This has hints of keynesian income effects but also of the monetary approach to the balance of payments. His second and third are substitution effects between traded and non-traded goods in demand and in production. Additional help is to be expected from short-term capital movements, and from the fact that capital movements are often correlated directly with commodity movements, as when loans are extending to finance exports. (On this latter point, he comes very close to having a view of endogenous capital movements, at least for short-term capital.) Adjustment seems to work, and rather well – he cites Taussig and Viner and their empirical studies as support. A point he emphasized heavily and repeatedly in his debate with Keynes (Ohlin 1929a, 1929b) is that usually transfers are effected with no discussion and little fuss; the transfer "problem", it is suggested, is well-nigh unique to the German reparations controversy.

Many writers express the opinion that the readjustment has come about surprisingly quickly in some well-known cases of international capital movements. Such surprise is justified in the light of the classical description of the mechanism, where everything centres around the assertion that the lending country must offer its goods on cheaper terms of exchange in order to induce the borrowing country to buy a greater quantity of them and thus create an export surplus corresponding to the capital exports. The mechanism outlined above makes it much more understandable how the adjustment is brought about so smoothly. (Ohlin 1933a: 432)

One is reminded here of Taussig's soul searching and concern, dealt with in Chapter 12, over the excessive ease with which the major capital transfers of the nineteenth century apparently were effected (Taussig 1927: 260–2).

The important thing to Ohlin (again, citing Taussig for support and Keynes as the butt of his argument) is that in most cases the monetary transfer precedes both the real transfer and the price changes . . . changes in buying power are the ever-present *causa efficiens*, while the character of the price variations varies from case to case. Changes in buying power affect the balance of payments directly in several ways, even in the quite conceivable case where owing to great mobility and fluidity there are no relative price changes at all. It is true that in most cases price changes occur . . . but they hold a secondary position relative to the primary changes in buying power [which is indeed very like the monetary approach to the balance of payments]. (Ohlin 1933a: 432–3)

The discussion of capital transfers is followed by less complete, but equally general-equilibrium, analyses of the effects of other disturbances to international trade and payments: import duties – distinguishing between those levied primarily for revenue and those intended to be protective; there is also a second-best defense of their use to facilitate a transfer (Ohlin 1933: 487) – exogenous shifts in demand, changes in technology, and finally, monetary shocks. The story he tells is not, of course, the same in each case, but the analytical approach is. Thus, for example, credit expansion in one country will bring about price changes in the rest of the world, even without the "classical" influence of gold flows which affect the quantity of money abroad. Here the classical explanation "is to a certain extent correct, for if nothing else happened *before* all these reactions they would come into play. As a matter of fact, however, there are other reactions which is most cases bring about the price adjustment in a quicker and smoother way" (Ohlin 1933a: 541, italics his).

Finally, Ohlin ends with a discussion of flexible exchange rates and a critique of Cassel.

Changes in monetary policy, like the other variations, alter the supply and demand schedules in the foreign exchange market, and thereby, and only thereby, the exchange rates. Commodity prices are of course altered also; but it is uncertain whether the trade balance, the international movement of capital, or the price level is affected first. Changes in the volume of credit often affect the volume of imports or the size of capital transfers much more quickly than the height of home market prices. *Experience does not justify making changes in the price level the first step, and changes in the balance of payments the consequences of price variations.* (Ohlin 1933a: 550, italics mine)

To conclude, a few words on the earlier classification of Ohlin. Names are not important in themselves, but how we classify something says much about how we assess its significance. Ohlin's own characterization of himself as being in the late classical tradition is consistent with what I have noted earlier, and consistent with Metzler's view in which he traces a line from Ricardo through Wheatley, Longfield, Bastable, and to Ohlin, a line characterized by the notion that shifts in "purchasing power" and the direction of spending can effect a transfer and restore balance without any prior movements of gold. But, says Metzler, these writers all lacked a theory of employment or income, and were therefore unable to explain just how far the adjusting process could go. Some of the earlier explanations were vague and ambiguous as to the extent of income movements, while the later ones were frequently erroneous. There was a strong tendency . . . to cling to the *assumption that full employment prevails at all times*. (Metzler 1949 [1973: Chapter 1, 10], italics mine)

Metzler is correct in his comment, and none of the writers referred to, including Ohlin, spell out determinants of the mix of price and quantity changes. Ohlin was aware of this and by no means apologetic about it; Keynes's neglect of price changes he viewed as a fault (*Vide*, e.g., Ohlin 1981: 230).

If we must summarize, Ohlin parted company with the classicals in that he did not *assume* full employment; in this, and in his interest in the determinants of expenditure, he was keynesian. In his emphasis on the monetary mechanism he was classical. And (while the reader may on occasion wish he had a greater penchant for simplification and abstraction) in his awareness of the complexity of the general-equilibrium system and the importance of intersectoral adjustments he was unique.

### Addendum: Iversen

Finally, a brief appendix on the subject of Carl Iversen, if for no other reason than that his major work, *International capital movements* (1935), is so widely cited. It was his dissertation and it was written while he was in close contact with his friend, and colleague, Bertil Ohlin, whose influence is manifest. (This biographical detail I have from personal correspondence with Iversen's student, Professor Hans Brems.)

The book is of interest because it is a comprehensive critical survey of the literature, an extensive overview of history, and an enthusiastic promotion of what he calls the "modern approach", essentially Ohlin's position. I see him rather than Ohlin as forming a bridge between the classical and late classical on the one hand and the keynesian position on the other. Like the late classicals and Ohlin, he views the study of the transfer of capital as an essay in the theory of the balance of payments.

There is constant reference to "buying power", defined almost identically to Ohlin's definition, as real gross savings plus newly created credit (Iversen 1935: 30). At the same time, like Ohlin, he puts a good deal of weight on real intersectoral adjustments. Crediting Taussig with the awareness of the importance of non-traded goods, and Viner even more so for having developed and refined the analysis of relative, intersectoral prices (Iversen 1935: 233). Iversen perceives that the transfer problem (in the sense of effecting the transfer) can exist only because there are non-traded goods: if all goods were equally mobile internationally, the transfer would move purchasing power from one country to another, but that could not create difficulties. If some of the initial inflow is spent on non-traded goods, then "a roundabout process of readjustments is necessary in the productive systems [of both countries] . . . and perhaps even in that of outside countries as well" (Iversen 1935: 48). At the same time, on the Ohlinian path, he criticizes Taussig and all of the late classicals for having failed to note that the reason such a presumably difficult adjustment was in fact so apparently easy was the operation of that which they omitted to take into consideration: the transfer of buying power from one country to another. Making the point in terms of a critique of Marshall's trade theory, he notes the need to *shift* the offer curves of both countries (and probably to distort them as well) when exploring the effects of a transfer (Iversen 1935: 223).

Also reminiscent of Ohlin is his emphasis on the general-equilibrium interdependence between the capital and the current account and his complete awareness of the macroeconomic accounting identities of an open economy. Further, he agrees with Ohlin that in practice the capital account is the more likely to be autonomous. He alleges, almost in the same words as Ohlin, that in fact "basic changes which primarily affect the balance of current transactions *very seldom* call forth secondary readjustments with regard to long-term lending or borrowing, whereas basic changes which primarily affect the capital movements *practically always* lead to repercussions in the commodity and service transactions" (Iverson 1935: 66, italics his).

Like Ohlin he regards specie flows as important, not in their effect on the domestic money supply as such but because they are *"an actual means of transferring monetary buying power* from one country to another" (Iversen 1935: 515, italics his). Thus gold movements will reverse themselves during the course of effecting a transfer. At the same time, Iversen more than Ohlin deals with the relationships between specie flows, money supply, interest rates, and short-term capital movements. He is explicit about the distinction between what I have labeled the classical and neoclassical analyses. The emphasis on

changes in discount rates as the most powerful corrective of a drain of gold involves an *important modification of the classical doctrine*; it makes . . . equilibrium in the balance of payments dependent primarily on operations in the money market, so that an influencing of the commodity market becomes necessary only in extreme cases. (Iversen 1935: 221, italics mine)

But this is not the end of the story. For if and when short-term capital movements have direct effects on the supply of domestic credit, then in fact these substitute for gold and become part of the adjustment mechanism, so "ordinarily, the bulk of the monetary transfer takes place by means of short-term credits" (Iversen 1935: 516). This feeds into the domestic money supply and "the volume of purchasing power" directly. "This connection between the demand for and supply of foreign credits and the total volume of purchasing power in circulation is strongly emphasized by Angell" (Iversen 1935: 525). Foreign credits; not specie. He makes the same point here as Hayek does about the prewar gold standard: that the link between the changes in the volume of domestic credit and the gold holdings of a country was a variable and tenuous one (see Chapter 7). In view of this, however, it is not clear to me why he argues that "[a]n essential function of the short-term equalising capital movements is to postpone the real transfer and make it more gradual" (Iversen 1935: 522). To the extent that these capital flows replace specie flow *both* in balancing international accounts in the short run *and* in their effect on domestic credit, the transfer should be effected in the same way and in the same period of time as it would have been had there been gold flows under a pure specie standard.

This world-wide shift from specie to short-term credit "as the principal medium of international payment" he regarded as a major historical development. It was this which accounted, in Iversen's view, for the phenomenon which so troubled Viner in the Canada study (1924): the precedence of credit expansion over gold importation. Viner "and others have attempted to explain it merely as an adaptation of the classical mechanism to the conditions of modern deposit banking." Iversen viewed it as much more significant, as constituting "a dangerous menace to the maintenance of [the gold] standard" (Iversen 1935: 517–25). He was struck by the irony and "anomaly" of the fact that it was the solid foundation of the gold standard that was a "necessary prerequisite" to that large-scale mobility of short-term capital. Since the credit shifts are serving the same purpose as specie flows, and at least as effectively, one can only assume that he is using the word "dangerously" here ironically.

The most interesting aspect of his book, in my view, is that it is a survey of the literature, the only one of which I am aware, from the point of view of what he called the "new economics" of his day, which was essentially the Ohlin view, and closer to being a bridge to the keynesian approach than Ohlin himself. Given his interest in short-term capital movements, the precise determinants of changes in the domestic money supply, the importance of central bank policy, Iversen can in a sense be thought of as enunciating the P Stream version of Ohlin.

# The keynesians I

Keynes himself, as noted previously, nowhere presented a formal, precise statement of the application of the *General theory* model to an open economy.[1] The same point is made, *inter alia*, by Nurkse (1947a [1947: 264]). (And when Moggridge (1986: 57) defines the topics Keynes dealt with over time, he adopts a list drawn up by Williamson in the policy-oriented context of monetary reform.) When the applications did come, they came in a great rush. I shall not cover all of them, but have chosen from among them on the basis of seminal or path-breaking quality in the sense of stimulating other research and applications, frequent citations in the literature, or inherent interest.

We find the following types of works:

1   Surveys. These include those of Metzler, in his survey article (1948 [1973: Chapter 1]); Iversen (1935), assessing where the theory of international economics is, or should be, going after Keynes; and Haberler (1937 [1941]), in the international portions of *Prosperity and depression*. Nurkse (1944) includes a brief and cogent summary statement.
2   More narrow direct applications of the keynesian theory to the theory of international adjustment. The two striking examples here are Machlup (1943) and the two Metzler papers (1942a and 1942b [1973: Chapters 10 and 2]), which I have labeled "Early Metzler". Both are presented as explicitly analytical works, neither econometric nor prescriptive. Both deal with the dynamics of the adjustment; Metzler, in particular, places great emphasis on the discussion of stability conditions.

[1]   Bloomfield (1950: 257) says that Keynes applied the multiplier to international trade, citing Haberler (1941). But Haberler, presenting a lengthy and detailed discussion of the foreign trade multiplier (1941: 461–73) cites Machlup (1943), Robertson (1939), Clark and Crawford (1938), and Harrod (1939-Third Edition of Harrod 1933). His only citation of Keynes is from *The means to prosperity*, 1933, in which Keynes recognizes the relationship between government spending and the foreign balance. This is, of course, the period of the *Treatise*, and we have noted Keynes's continual awareness in the *Treatise* of the arithmetic of national income accounting in an open economy. This is however only a step in the direction of a full-fledged multiplier model of the balance of trade adjustment mechanism.

3   Direct application of keynesian concepts to empirical and econometric work in order to explain or predict trade patterns: Polak (1950) and (1954), and the enormous and ambitious undertaking of Neisser and Modigliani (1953).

4   Related to these are less quantitative, more informal attempts to use keynesian analysis as the foundation for discussions of policy. These particularly tended to appear during World War II, in reflections about the postwar period. Here William Salant and Kindleberger are cited as early *examples*. By the late 1940s there were many of these, so many that I make no attempt to cover them all.[2]

5   As I have hinted, the whole devaluation literature is in a real sense a keynesian (and not Keynesian) offshoot, but I make no attempt to survey it in any sense thoroughly; it has been ably analyzed in a number of more specialized surveys (see, for a first-rate example, Anne Krueger 1969, also Haberler 1955 [1961]). Yet I shall pay brief attention here to Joan Robinson's important and path-breaking work (1937) in that area and the closely related paper by Brown (1942).

6   The MMM literature is, of course, an outgrowth of the keynesian revolution, but I am treating it separately, in the closing chapter.

7   There are a few outliers who need to be included for historical reasons – people who were not developing full-fledged keynesian models, but who derived, early on, foreign trade multipliers and marginal propensities to import. Here I include Colin Clark (1938) and Frank S. Paish (1936).

8   Standing almost alone is the early Harrod statement (1933), which I find quite remarkable, primarily for its early dating, and secondarily for its early combining of keynesian (and pre-keynesian) ideas with the simple but important concept of endogenous money supply which was to reemerge thirty years later with the monetary theory of the balance of payments. Another lone figure, again astonishingly early, is Kalecki (1934 [1971]).

I shall discuss these groupings in roughly chronological order.

1   Pre-keynesian – Harrod (1933), and premature keynesian – Kalecki (1934 [1971]).

2   Early keynesian – the concept of the marginal propensity to import: Paish (1936), Clark (1938) and Robertson (1939).

3   Surveys – Nurkse (1944), Haberler (1937 [1941]).

4   Devaluation – the formal conditions and the beggar-my-neighbour concept: Robinson (1947 [1949]); more formal: Brown (1942).

---

[2]   See, for example, Part Five, "International economic relations," in Seymour E. Harris (1947), containing papers by Bloomfield, Harris, Nurkse, Robinson.

5   Analytical models, including the dynamics of adjustment and stability conditions – early Metzler (1942a, 1942b) and Machlup (1943).
6   Early wartime and postwar planning – Salant (1941), Kindleberger (1943).
7   Econometric applications – Polak (1950, 1954), Neisser and Modigliani (1953).

### Harrod: pre-keynesian

Harrod's work is particularly remarkable on account of its date. The first edition of his *International economics* appeared in 1933 and is startlingly prescient on some issues. It is a small book, half of which is devoted to real, and half to monetary issues of international economics. I have chosen to discuss it here for precisely the reason of its early date.[3]

In the fixed exchange rate case (which can be either a gold standard or otherwise pegged rates) there are two alternative mechanisms of adjustment, depending on whether one is in a fixprice or a flexprice world.

The flexprice adjustment has at first blush a classical aura. It is an equilibrium model, in the same sense that the postwar monetary approach to the balance of payments is, and the interwar keynesian approach, including the early Mundell models, is not. But the basic approach is that of an expenditure model. In a flexprice world, however, full employment prevails even when expenditure changes; in a fixprice world there can be permanent unemployment. Harrod states explicitly that if there is unemployment this is not "[f]ull equilibrium in one sense of the term . . . But there will be a new equilibrium in which receipts and expenditure, and exports and imports balance" (Harrod 1933: 109–10). In this, as in other respects, he is not here a full-fledged keynesian, since the straightforward keynesian model does not in general yield balance of payments equilibrium.

He begins with a simple model, in which there is neither investment nor saving (nor hoarding), expenditure being equal to income; this simplification, he says, does not affect the real analysis. There are three categories of goods, brought over from his real trade model: $A$: homogeneous traded goods, $B$: heterogeneous, differentiated, tradable goods and services, and $C$: non-traded goods. (Such distinctions, by the way, were not uncommon at

---

[3]  It purports to be a text, but is closer to being a monograph, despite his disclaimers, and those of Keynes in his Introduction to Cambridge Economic Handbooks, of which Harrod's work is Volume VIII. The second edition appeared in 1939, after the publication of the *General theory*, and is more conventionally keynesian. It has a longer and more detailed discussion of the multiplier mechanism, for instance. Almost all the references one sees in the literature are to this second edition. I emphasize the earlier one partly because of the piquant interest inherent in the early date, and partly because it is a fuller, more detailed, and more eclectic model than the later ones. The later work is more strictly speaking keynesian, and therefore, perhaps, less distinctive.

that time. We find them, as well, in Ohlin. The introduction of mathematics into economics has forced simplification which earlier writers found less compelling.)

Initially he considers the special case in which expenditure shares for each class of good are fixed. A real disturbance (a technological change abroad, reducing world demand for the home country's traded goods) requires a shift in the production and consumption of traded goods. If factor prices are flexible, full employment is maintained, all incomes are reduced, and trade is balanced. The deterioration in the terms of trade involves, obviously, a decline in real income.

If factor prices are not flexible downward, there will be unemployment until income has fallen by a multiple of the original shock. Here the analysis is very close to the later simple keynesian multiplier analysis. There is no leakage into hoarding, by assumption, but there is a "leakage" into consumption of the non-tradable goods. Total income must therefore fall, not by the amount of reduced demand for tradable goods output in the world, but by more than this, since expenditure shares are constant. The "result that, provided no one spends more than he receives in income, total income will be reduced sufficiently to curtail expenditure on imports by the amount that exports have declined has absolute generality" (Harrod 1933: 111).

The adjustment is symmetrical in the rest of the world; what is lacking, however, is any feedback impact on the home country of the foreign country's induced change in income. (See, for example, any edition of Kindleberger's *International economics*, spelling out the two-country foreign trade multiplier.)

If relative commodity prices change, the consequent shifts in expenditure shares will depend on price elasticities of demand; thus the change in income required to restore equilibrium will depend on the price elasticities of demand for the several types of goods. He applies this analysis specifically to a discussion of the effects of a transfer – an indemnity. This concern with elasticities presages the keynesian excursions into the devaluation issue and the importance of the excess demand elasticities in that literature (see the discussion of Joan Robinson below).

But the analysis of income and expenditure changes have to do solely with the description of the new equilibrium, that is, with the comparative statics. The dynamics are monetary. The new equilibrium implies a lower level of real income, through the decline in real factor rewards or by dint of unemployment, and hence a lower equilibrium level of money balances. This means that during the adjustment the country must be losing money through a deficit in the current account or having the domestic money supply reduced by the repayment of loans and the shrinking of domestic credit. Thus, the monetary contraction induced by a deficit becomes an integral part of the mechanism leading to contraction of income and attainment of the new static equilibrium. Here he is well "ahead" of the subsequent simple keynesian models; in income-absorption types of models, it was not until Tsiang (1961), to the best of my knowledge, that this mechanism was once more invoked.

Where it differs from both the classical and the later monetary approach (in the more general form which the latter adopts when it cuts its direct link with the quantity theory) is in the emphasis on causality and precedence in time. In the Harrod view equilibrium is not brought about by the monetary changes which lead to expenditure changes: rather, the expenditure changes imply a change in the quantity of money demanded. Nevertheless, where the similarity appears is in the assertion that equilibrium in real income with balanced trade, both at a new, lower level, implies a reduction in the money supply. Given a constant money multiplier, this means a deficit in the current account during the transition. The generalized version of the monetary approach turns the statement around and says that an economy is not in long- or even medium-run equilibrium so long as the international payments are not in balance because under these circumstances the domestic money supply is changing.

But whereas the equilibrium money supply depends on the demand for money, the way real balances will decrease depends on the central bank's reserves/liabilities ratio. The community's demand for high-powered money depends, of course, both on the demand for money functions of households and firms and on the institutional determinants of the "money multiplier".

If the central bank's proportion of reserve to liabilities is to be restored to its old level, there must be some internal deflation . . . [T]he proportion of the reduction in the total monetary holding of the community which is covered by a passive balance and by internal deflation respectively must be equal to the proportion of the central bank's reserves to the total monetary holdings of the community. (Harrod 1933: 131)

However, return to equilibrium is not guaranteed. During the transition, the deficit in trade may be larger than the total by which money balances need ultimately to be reduced. That is, the reduction in total spending may be insufficient, as people reduce their money holdings in order to maintain spending. The central bank may run out of reserves. It may therefore borrow abroad short-term or impose monetary restraint at home (Harrod 1933: 115 ff). That is, there is a possible role for "bank rate" and/or central bank policy to achieve domestic monetary tightening. The latter is likely to be necessary under these circumstances, since "the attraction of short loans from abroad . . . is only a suitable remedy for a passive [debit] balance if that is destined to be subsequently offset by an active [credit] balance." So there may have to be some internal deflation (Harrod 1933: 116–17).

Where the multiplier and the elasticities approach get intertwined explicitly is in the discussion of the transfer problem. Here again, Harrod was well ahead of his time, following hard on the clash between Ohlin and Keynes on the issue which can be said to be precisely about the elasticities as opposed to the multiplier, or rather the pre-multiplier, viewpoints. Whether a transfer will lead to unemployment, according to Harrod, depends on the extent to which factor incomes can decline. And the effect of the decline in factor incomes, of course, depends in turn on the elasticities.

Thus the burden of an indemnity is twofold. The paying country has to reduce its expenditure by an amount equal to the taxation required to cover the indemnity. In addition it must either allow an unemployment crisis to persist, with the resulting loss of output and income, or it must reduce the real reward to factors of production. (Harrod 1933: 121)

The most complete general-equilibrium statement of adjustment and, at least retrospectively, the most eclectic, appears in Harrod's discussion of the transfer problem where the transfer consists of net foreign lending. It is rich enough, I think, to merit some discussion. He seemed particularly interested in the problem, presumably because of his conviction that Britain had lent too much abroad, for too long (see Chapter 9, footnote 5).

If the lending country experiences a reduction in factor rewards, the story is the same as that of a gift or indemnity, with the elasticities playing a major role. If, however, it does not, there are again two possibilities: net domestic savings are increased by the amount of the lending, or not.

1   Where net savings are increased, the problem is the same as the multiplier analysis in the pure trade case, discussed above, since we have a reduction in domestic demand and a multiplier effect on income, the size of which depends on the marginal propensity to spend on traded goods.

2   If, however, there is not an increase in savings to match the capital export, the deficit will continue and there will be a loss of reserves. Once more there are two possibilities:

1   The central bank will offset the monetary effects of the reserve loss, maintaining the domestic money supply, in the hope that the reduction in reserves is temporary. "It can pursue such a waiting policy with greater equanimity if its reserves are very large" (Harrod 1933: 127).

2   The central bank does not sterilize the outflow. In this case

the banks will have to curtail their loans and interest rates will rise. This has the short period effect of inducing a reverse flow of short term loans to the country and the more far-reaching effect of checking the output of capital goods for the home market. This creates unemployment in the capital goods industries, which diffuses unemployment . . . until the purchase of . . . [tradable] goods is reduced by the amount of the net addition to foreign lending. At that point the contraction of loans will cease and with it the contraction of capital construction. Sufficient unemployment will have been created to generate an active trade balance, through the fall in income reducing the purchase of . . . [tradable] goods by an amount equal to the new foreign lending. (Harrod 1933: 127–8)

The longer-term adjustment thus includes neoclassical elements (the rise in the interest rate discouraging domestic investment) as well as keynesian (the reduction in domestic investment leading to unemployment and *hence* an improvement in the trade account). However, if this process is too slow, the central bank "may be impelled to accelerate the process of contraction by contracting its own credit" (Harrod 1933: 128).

But the specifics of the monetary theory are Keynesian, reminiscent of the *Treatise*. The chain of causality is from the quantity of money to the rate of interest to investment to prices. "Deflation operates through a rise of interest rates and a consequent fall in the output of capital goods." In equilibrium savings minus investment is equal to the current account surplus. "The equilibrium rate of interest . . . is that which limits the demand for new capital goods to this proportion" (Harrod 1933: 131–2).

Regarding the endogeneity of short-term capital movements Harrod stands between the neoclassical and some versions of the late classical positions. The central bank has only to be passive here, which is the same as if it did not exist; the neoclassical "bank rate policy" is not required. But the bank can activate such a policy and choose between drawing down its reserves or "operating on the market rate of discount to induce offsetting changes in the flow of short term loans" (Harrod 1933: 130).

This may at times be appropriate, in dealing with seasonal or transitory imbalances for instance, but in the long run it can be a mistake. After the return to gold in 1925 Britain increased her short-term borrowing and thus "the amount of internal deflation which the Bank had to apply was less than it otherwise would have been . . . [B]ut the gold standard was not re-established on a firm foundation." This was understandable, but its "natural consequence" was the Bank's inability to meet the demands placed upon its reserves in 1931. Like the Macmillan Committee before him and like Keynes preparing for Bretton Woods after him, he worried about the possibility of "abnormal capital movements" – capital flights. These might create problems that could be corrected only by exchange controls or abandonment of the gold standard (Harrod 1933: 118–30).

The interdependence of countries under fixed exchange rates was not lost on him; nor was the other side of the same coin, the dampening effect of openness when shocks originated internally. Thus, while a country with a closed economy could readily experience cumulative recession, in an open economy a balance of payments surplus would be "generated and recuperative forces would be set in motion tending to revive output". He recognized also that: "The world as a whole *is* a closed system" (Harrod 1933: 133). If central banks behaved asymmetrically (again we hear the theme that was so prominent in the Macmillan Report and which Keynes continued to elaborate on) with surplus countries not expanding as much as deficit countries contracted, large payments imbalances could in themselves be the cause of world deflation. This may, he thinks, be the (or a) cause of the depression (Harrod 1933: 134).

In such a situation, furthermore, real capital transfers are more helpful than uneffected financial flows. The surplus countries would do the world more good by expanding their own output (of capital goods) and hence increasing their imports than they would by extending foreign loans, since in that case the deficit countries have acquired debt and interest obligations. "Nothing can be more foolish than to make distress loans to an impoverished country while maintaining a tariff against her goods *or while reducing expenditure on development at home*" (Harrod 1933: 136, italics mine). The Macmillan Committee had made a similar point, arguing that the creditor countries would help the debtors by lending to anybody, not necessarily the most needy debtors; and in fact, they would benefit the common weal if they would merely expand their own domestic investment, provided it involved new capital formation (Macmillan 1931: 135–6).

Regarding the choice between floating and fixed exchange rates, Harrod was somewhat ambivalent. On the one hand, he noted that floating rates seem to give the authorities another tool: "Both unemployment and deflation can be avoided" (Harrod 1933: 138). For this reason he favored maintaining the more-or-less flexible rate regime, while continuing to strive for world cooperation which, like Keynes, he considered to be the only really viable solution. We saw above, in Chapter 7, how Hayek attacked him for this view.

And yet he recognized, what was generally forgotten for the next thirty years and more, that there is no clean float. His argument is different, however, from more recent ones (compare Flanders 1974) in that the problem for him arises not from the international mobility of financial capital but the multiplicity of "equilibrium" national outputs. This concept has fallen out of favor, both in the assignment literature, which assumed successful maintenance of full employment, and in the later new classicism which assumes that the equilibrium level of output is unique.

The government may wash its hands of the matter and declare that it will let the exchange find its natural level; but there is no natural level! There are an infinite number of possible levels. The level will be precisely determined by what the government and bank do. They may have no specific policy, but they cannot do nothing. Their behaviour may be actuated by irrelevant, subsidiary or even trifling motives; none the less it will decide that vitally important question, what the output and income of the community is to be. (Harrod 1933: 139)

Retreating to the gold standard is no solution, because then world gold prices depend on what all central banks do. He views the central bankers and governments of the world as ostriches, buried in the sand of *"laissez-faire"* which would one day again prove to be a viable and adequate policy. This hope, he averred, is "not likely to be realized". In that case: "It may well prove easier for one government to make an intelligent use of its own powers, than to persuade the whole collection to do so in concert" (Harrod 1933: 140).

## Kalecki: premature keynesian

Kalecki published a brief paper, "On foreign trade and 'domestic exports'" in Polish in 1934. It was not translated into English until 1967, and though subjectively original, it was unread, uncited, and hence cannot be said to have been influential or seminal. (In 1971 Kalecki noted, perhaps in sorrow but without comment, that three papers, of which this is one, contained "the essentials" of the *General theory*. (Kalecki [1971: vii]). Kalecki presents a precisely formulated foreign trade multiplier. The difference between it and the later, standard model is Kalecki's marxist assumption that capitalists save all their income and workers none (except for a parenthetical comment indicating that workers might also save), so that the marginal, equals average, propensity to save is represented in his formulation by the share of profits in output. The marginal, equals the average, propensity to import is the amount "indispensable for the expansion of production" (Kalecki 1934 [1971: 17]). He emphasizes that it is not exports but the export surplus that has the expansionary effect on income.

The "domestic exports" of the title is his term for deficit-financed government expenditures. He shows that the effect on aggregate output is the same for both "foreign" and "domestic" exports, since profits and imports constitute identical leakages in the two cases. He even draws analogies regarding methods of financing the expansion. A loan by capitalists to foreigners to finance an export surplus is the same as a loan by capitalists to the government to finance a deficit; inflow of gold or foreign exchange to finance the export surplus has the same effect as central bank financing of a government deficit.

The difference, however, is in the impact on the balance of trade of the two measures. He emphasizes in a slightly convoluted manner the fact that the secondary effects are the same in both cases, but, since the initial change is an increase in the export surplus in one case and zero change in the other, the total impact on the trade balance is favorable in the one case, unfavorable in the other; the ability to increase domestic output by government spending is therefore self-limiting. The same is true, he notes, of a "'natural' upswing based on the automatic increase in investment" in the course of the business cycle (Kalecki 1934 [1971: 25]).

In a few pages Kalecki touches on a number of major issues, such as: (a) the possibility of counteracting the trade deficit by devaluation, the effect of this on total earnings because foreign demand eventually becomes inelastic, the effect on domestic prices, and hence exports, and the impact on the terms of trade, diminishing the welfare gain of an expansion in output; (b) the possibility of capital flowing in to finance the deficit, encouraged by the higher rate of return in the expanding country, but deterred by expectation of devaluation or debt repudiation.

## Paish: early keynesian I

Paish (1936) is not generally classified as either a keynesian or a Keynesian. And the model here presented fits neither category. But it contains, explicitly, the concept of the marginal propensity to import, apparently for the first time (compare Haberler (1937 [1941: 472])). And for that reason I have included it here.

Paish starts from the position that, in the absence of central banking, any country with a deficit in its balance of payments requires an active response on the part of the banking system to the outflow of reserves caused by the deficit. As the banks call in loans and otherwise reduce their liabilities, they are likely to raise interest rates, at least to some borrowers; alternatively, borrowers whose loans have been called will go elsewhere for accommodation, at higher rates than they had been paying (Paish 1936: 408). The discussion is reminiscent of that of Angell (1926) in its emphasis on the immediate response of the banks, without the necessity of such intervening occurrences as specie flow. It is comparable to Whale (1937 [1953]) in its view of immediate and *endogenous* interest rate response as an integral part of the mechanism. The existence of a central bank makes no significant difference, unless it tries to offset the effects of the deficit and prevent the interest rate change; then the question becomes whether the central bank runs out of foreign exchange reserves.

How long the adjustment takes, and the extent to which banks have to call in advances and otherwise reduce their liabilities (and assets), depends on whether and in what manner individuals who initially are affected by the reduction in exports adjust their expenditures, which in turn rests in part on how temporary they think the reduction is. If all of the initial reduction in expenditure falls on imported goods, the effect is quick, since expenditure of foreign exchange is reduced quickly. This depends, "[t]o adopt a phrase of

Mr. Keynes . . . [on the] Marginal Propensity to Import . . . M.P.I. . . . In existing circumstances, it seems probable that advanced 'industrial' countries, such as Great Britain, would be found to have a relatively low M.P.I., and the 'raw material' countries, such as South Africa or New Zealand, a relatively high one" (Paish 1936: 414–15).

Short-term capital movements, which enable a country to delay or even to avoid the need to make domestic banking adjustments to balances of payments, are most characteristic of those countries which act as international banking centers. These are usually, he alleges, countries with a low marginal propensity to import, presumably for reasons having to do with the level of industrialization and the structure of their economy. Most of the masses of empirical work relating to both the average and marginal propensities to import of countries at different stages of development occurred after Paish's casual observations.

We get a gentle hint of the foreign trade multiplier: "[W]hile a favourable balance resulting from local developments may well be accompanied by a fall in local incomes, a favourable balance resulting from developments abroad will usually be accompanied by a rise." The higher the marginal propensity to import, the more rapid the adjustment and *the easier*, in the sense that there is less need (in the limit none) for a "fall in local prices or wages . . . expansion in exports . . . and increase in unemployment. The whole process of adjustment can be carried through rapidly, at the cost, indeed, of inconvenience to those who have to reduce their expenditures, but without any serious check to local business activity" (Paish 1936: 419–21). Once again, the proof of the partial nature of the keynesian adjustment was to come only later.

### Clark, Robertson – early keynesian II

Colin Clark and J. G. Crawford, in a pioneering attempt to measure national income magnitudes for Australia (and to explain, predict, and to recommend policy, as well as to make international comparisons) applied the multiplier to an open economy, in an exercise which was widely quoted and much debated for some time. They attribute the definition of the multiplier to "Mr. J. M. Keynes, Mr. Kahn or Mr. Harrod" (Clark and Crawford 1938: 90–103).[4]

In a critique of Keynes, and the "Keynes-Harrod" theory, Clark argued

---

[4] At the end of the discussion, however, they claim temporal precedence for several relatively obscure or anonymous writers: Professor Giblin in his inaugural lecture in Australia; in "unpublished memoranda submitted to the British government in 1930, and a quite independent and very thorough examination . . . in Germany (published in *Wirtschaft und Statistik*, Nov. 1933)" (Clark and Crawford 1938: 103).

that the multiplier should be related neither to real income nor employment but to money income (Clark 1938b: 437) since an exogenous increase could lead to higher prices, more output with a given level of employment, or a rise in employment. Clark and Crawford argue along different lines, holding that the received formula, which "works well under British and American conditions" is not appropriate for Australia. They preferred instead to "regard the 'multiplicand' as being made up of the four short period determinants." The argument, which, as we shall see, continued for several years and engaged a number of Greats, was essentially over whether one wanted a stable multiplier applied to frequently occurring and variable disturbances, or whether one was willing to accept a variable multiplier. The meaning of this will become clear when we describe the discussion, and computation, of the import function, below. They went on: "Of course Mr Keynes's theoretical analysis was concerned mainly with the conditions of a closed economy, and this alone would suggest that some modification might be required from the point of view of statistical technique" (Clark and Crawford 1938: 92).

D E T O U R: Here they quote extensively a letter from Keynes to Clark which I find it impossible to ignore. Keynes accuses Clark, first of all, of having confused "Kahn's employment multiplier and my investment multiplier . . . Your money income multiplier is substantially identical to my investment multiplier except that yours is in terms of money and mine of wage units . . . There is surely a greater presumption of stability of marginal propensity to consume or to import in terms of wage units or composite commodity units than in terms of money" (Clark and Crawford 1938: 92n). (So much for the accusation often levied against Keynes of having believed in the inexorability of price inflexibility, or in the widespread incidence of money illusion.) Turning to the open economy elements in Clark's definition, Keynes writes:

I like your analysis of the multiplier into several factors. Separating our foreign trade in the way that you do, I agree, has advantages – *I have not neglected it*. And if it is true, e.g. in Australia, that the marginal propensity to import is *often* stable your technique is instructive. (Clark and Crawford 1938 93n, italics mine)

Clark and Crawford disaggregate the shocks into changes in the following exogenous variables:

1   Investment.
2   The government deficit (which can be stretched to include situations in which individuals, as well as governments, decide to spend more than their income).

3   The value of exports, due to either volume or price changes.
4   Imports – here they specifically mean a shift in the import function as a result of tariff, exchange rate or other changes.

[This] . . . may be construed as implying that the national income can be increased almost indefinitely by the well-known economic process of discouraging imports. This is literally true. Be it noted, however, that we are here dealing with money national income . . . [not] real national income. The practitioner of import restriction and similar techniques sooner or later discovers the difference. (Clark and Crawford 1938: 95)

They are also aware of and alert to the concept of the marginal propensity, but consider the distinction between exogenous and endogenous import changes to be of great practical importance, at least for Australia. Computing the import function for the years 1922/3 to 1936/7, they derive two linear segments, one for 1922/3 to 1926/7, with a marginal propensity to import of 0.21, the second, for 1930/1 to the current date, 1937, much lower, with a slope of 0.25. The three years from 1927 to 1930 "were clearly a period of transition to a new state of equilibrium." They attribute the shift to the "industrialization of Australia, the cheapening of Australian manufactures in comparison with imports, and . . . higher tariffs" (Clark and Crawford 1938: 98–9).

In 1938, in a paper in the *Economic journal*, Clark made the same point. Arguing that both Kahn and Keynes had neglected *both* exports and imports he puts $(X - M)$ into the multiplicand (Clark 1938: 438). Furthermore, "it is necessary to divide changes in imports into *consequential* changes due to changes in national income, and non-consequential or autonomous movements in imports" (Clark 1938: 438, italics his ). The question then was, in essence, the problem of computation and of identification. One solution was to assume that the whole current account was exogenous, thus including, perforce, "consequential" imports. He computes the "'marginal propensity to import'" and the multiplier both ways, letting the reader decide on the method of choice. In one, he relates the "total balance of trade" to income; in the other he attempts to compute the incremental imports by aggregating from the input side: by estimating the average import content of output in various sectors and making heroic, but evidently well-informed, assumptions about the allocation of incremental income to consumption in the several sectors. It is an impressive performance.

He divided the period 1929–37 into two, 1929–33 and 1934–37, and derived the multiplier separately for each. It was quite a bit higher in the second period because of the reduction in profit shares and the higher savings rate of profit earners than of wage earners. Predicting backward, he was very pleased at the accuracy of his forecasts, though his predictions for the future were gloomy.[5] And yet when, in June of the following year, Robertson wrote a critique of Clark's paper in the *Economic journal* (Robertson 1939) Clark in his "Comment" claimed that he shared Robertson's scepticism and lack of sympathy with the whole approach of the multiplier.

Concentrating primarily on the issue of whether to put imports (or some imports) in the multiplicand or in the multiplier, Robertson argued that formally it was of no importance which procedure one followed, but he accused Clark of having tried to do both simultaneously.

> Moreover an "autonomous" change in imports, due *e.g.* to an alteration of tariff levels, is simply a manifestation of a change in the *q* factor [the average imported component of consumption]. Mr. Clark seems to want *both* to keep his *q* factor invariable *and* to take account of its propensity to change.

> I should perhaps add that this incursion by an agnostic into the realms of theology must not be taken to imply whole-hearted conversion to the doctrine of the multiplier as an instrument for the analysis of cyclical fluctuations. (Robertson 1939: 356, italics his)

Astonishingly, the same debate was revived, eight years later, between Haberler (1947b) and Polak (1947).

### Nurkse: survey I

A concise statement, frequently cited, of the transition from late classical to keynesian analysis is to be found in Nurkse (1944: 98 ff). While out of chronological order here, it really does belong, in my view, in the "survey" category.

He cites the doubts of Taussig and his students, elicited by the apparently excessive ease and smoothness of the adjustment, and presents "a more realistic and comprehensive explanation [which] has gradually emerged" (Nurkse 1944: 99). He emphasizes his view that this new explanation is complementary to the classical model, not a substitute for it. He makes the distinction, obvious but all too frequently neglected, especially theretofore, between financing and adjustment. Historically gold movements had seemed to be too small and too late to have constituted the main driving force to adjustment; this could be explained by the fact that short-term capital movements provided temporary financing. "Thus even under the gold standard . . . there were . . . other means of covering international discrepancies; these other means were quantitatively important; in a stable-exchange regime not based upon gold they would clearly be all-important" (Nurkse 1944: 100).

---

[5] In the book with Crawford he is, to me, surprisingly interventionist in terms of government fiscal and monetary policy alike, strongly advocating anti-cyclical measures (see particularly Clark and Crawford 1938: Chapter XII, "National income and future policy").

But this left unexplained the cause of the ultimate adjustment. The monetary effects of the classical mechanism may include endogenous long-term capital flows of an equilibrating nature, in addition to the widely recognized short-term flows, as a result of the interest rate changes attributable to specie flows. The effect on the current account, however, will be at best slow, since it must work through the effect of the interest rate changes on domestic investment. The gold standard mechanism probably functioned primarily by financing imbalances with short-term capital movements in response to interest rate changes, while "real adjustment" of the keynesian sort was taking place "through the direct effects of the balance of payments upon income and effective demand in the various countries" (Nurkse 1944: 104; see Chapter 11, page 211). Here is a statement of the now-standard keynesian view of the "gold standard" adjustment mechanism. Note that it is different from Keynes's view as described in Chapter 6, where the causality was reversed, a reduction in output and employment being necessary to bring about the indispensable change in prices.

It is only through this stimulus to domestic activity that . . . a higher level of costs and prices may come about by reason of a keener competition for the available means of production. The increased activity itself tends to close the gap by increasing imports and reducing exports. *The rise in prices is merely a by-product of the increase in activity . . . and is clearly not an indispensable prerequisite of the adjustment process.* (Nurkse 1944: 104, italics mine)

The monetary mechanism is retarded by the sluggishness with which long-term interest rates respond to changes in the money supply and the additional lethargy in the response of investment to interest rate changes (Nurkse 1944: 104). But it is not necessary to wait for that: the imbalance in payments involves not only changes in the stock of money but also in income and spending. These can take place through velocity changes even if the authorities pursue a policy of sterilization (Nurkse 1944: 100).

The foreign trade multiplier is enhanced with an accelerator, since "the rise in current domestic expenditure is likely to induce a higher rate of capital expenditure, which will tend to absorb the additional saving." He applies the multiplier to capital movements, as well as to current account shocks. Here he distinguishes between types of disturbance: autonomous, equilibrating, and disequilibrating. The first, he asserts, are readily transferred, since they result in direct expenditure increases, often immediately in increased imports. The second have no secondary adjustment effects, and serve only as "stop-gaps" until the demand adjustments result in "a change in imports sufficient to restore an even balance" (Nurkse 1944: 101–2). (This is, of course, mistaken, in that the foreign trade multiplier does not in general lead to complete adjustment. See the discussion of Metzler 1942a and 1942b, and Machlup 1943 in Chapter 15.) The third kind of disturbance tends to exacerbate existing imbalances or to create new ones (see the discussion in Chapter 11). He concludes his discussion by noting both that the keynesian mechanism explains the "synchronization of cyclical fluctuations in economic activity under gold standard conditions" and that the automatic mechanism is thwarted as countries attempt to insulate their domestic economies out of "growing concern for stability of income and employment" (Nurkse 1944: 104–5).

In an early, and very keynesian, version of the "dilemma literature" Nurkse emphasizes the direct income effects of current account imbalances. These obtain irrespective of attempts to sterilize the monetary impact of the imbalance. Later versions of the dilemma, on the other hand, assumed the effectiveness of expansionary domestic monetary policy in stimulating real activity. Nurkse argues, for example, that although the effect on other countries of capital inflows into France in the late 1920s, a monetary shock, could be offset by monetary intervention, the effect of the undervaluation of the franc and the resulting real impact, the French current account surplus, could not. "France's current surplus itself, as distinct from the accompanying shifts in currency reserves, affected income and employment adversely in other countries." Offsetting this would have required a "compensating stimulus," by which he obviously means an expansionary *fiscal* policy in France (Nurkse 1944: 106–7).

He describes, approvingly, early statements by the Federal Reserve Board and the Australian Monetary and Banking Commission, both declaring the goal of stabilizing domestic economic activity with all the means at their disposal, monetary, fiscal (the word was not used) and international. He takes it as self-evident, however, that domestic economic stability should not be sought at the expense of other countries, by tariffs, import restrictions, or "undue exchange depreciation." No beggar-my-neighbor policies here! But he worries about the ability to coordinate economic stabilization policies, even among the major industrial countries, and even granted the will and the willingness to attempt cooperation and coordination in the name of worldwide stability and "good employment." Differences in the structures of the several economies, the parameters of their macroeconomic functions, and their political and economic institutions, make synchronization difficult "even if the general objective of stable and adequate employment is accepted by all and even if some coordination of measures affecting national income and expenditure is recognized as desirable" (Nurkse 1944: 111). What is needed ultimately, therefore, is a mechanism for providing sufficient buffer stocks of the means of international payment so that countries could maintain their compensatory offsetting policies to protect themselves from imported depression.

If a particular country were subject to a recurrent tendency towards depression, an adequate volume of foreign lending would not merely stop the drain of currency reserves from the rest of the world but would also enable that country to maintain or increase its export surplus and thus to stimulate employment at home without prejudice to employment elsewhere. (Nurkse 1944: 112).

Writing a book to be published by the League of Nations, he was presumably too delicate to mention the United States by name in that context; he did not have to. Precisely when this was written, I do not know; it was published as the Bretton Woods Agreements were being drawn up.

In later writings, such as the contribution to *The new economics* (Nurkse 1947a), he worked out the algebra of the multiplier a little more fully and emphasized still more heavily the distinction between defensive and offensive exchange rate devaluation, but did not add in substance very much to the 1944 treatment.

## Haberler: survey II

In 1936 Haberler published a major survey of business cycle theory and history, *Prosperity and depression*, which had been commissioned by the League of Nations "with the object of analysing and sifting . . . the theories which already exist and subjecting those theories to the test of fact" and "an attempt to weave from those theories a general synthesis" (A. Loveday, "Preface," Haberler 1937 [1941: vi]). By 1939 an additional chapter, in the Second Edition, discussed some of the methodological issues involved in the Keynesian debates. And in 1941 the Third Edition added Part III, "Further Reflections on Recent Developments in Trade Cycle Theory," which contained extensive coverage of Keynesian literature including international repercussions and the foreign trade multiplier.

The earlier chapter (prepared for the 1939 edition), which we might call pre-keynesian, is perhaps the more interesting. It is highly reminiscent of Neisser's study (1936), which Haberler cites.[6] Starting with a single, undifferentiated, worldwide economy, he considers the effects of imperfect mobility of goods and factors, due to transport costs and tariffs (the latter being variable over the cycle). He then injects this additional constraint into the synthesis of theories of booms and depressions.

The concept of the marginal propensity to import is here attributed to Paish (1936). The foreign trade multiplier is not developed explicitly, though its germ is here. The size of the import propensity is specific to the individual country and its trade and consumption patterns. In addition it depends on

---

[6] The footnote in which he gives that citation is interesting. He refers to the increasing level of "cycle conscious[ness]" in recent international trade literature, citing Ohlin (1933), Nurkse (1935), Harrod (1933), Iversen (1935), and Viner (1937), as well as Oskar Morgenstern (1927) and A. v. Mühlenfels (1929).

the cause of the particular shock, whether it involves consumption or investment, and in what sector. The phase of the cycle is relevant as well – the only thing one can say with certainty is that "the further a local expansion goes the more it is likely to 'spill over' into other regions." This concern about the variability of the propensity to import, over time and between countries, is an important theme in his later discussion of the foreign trade multiplier (see below). Any expansion induces an accelerating increase in imports, due to the effect of bottlenecks in production and rising prices and costs as a boom continues (Haberler 1937 [1941: 411]). Transport costs (read any impediments to trade) retard the spread of prosperity and depression, so that under some circumstances the two may in fact coexist in different parts of the world.

In the context of analysis of the spread of business cycles, Haberler has the beginnings of the income-expenditure approach to the transfer problem. The greater the volume of trade between two countries (the higher the average propensity to import), the smaller the contraction in the paying country, and the smaller the expansion in the borrowing country, required to effect a transfer through a change in the trade balance.

The most interesting part of the chapter, in my view, is Haberler's treatment of the international propagation of business cycles in a general equilibrium context involving both current and capital accounts (Haberler 1937 [1941: 421 ff]). He asks: does capital mobility enhance or inhibit the spread of a boom initiated in country $A$? The answer, predictably, is that it depends. It is a brave attempt at general-equilibrium analysis of both the current and capital accounts, in the context of cyclical dynamic analysis. If capital has zero international mobility, a boom in one country is spread by the increase in its imports, implying a rise in exports for other countries and an increase in their income, stimulating the demand for investible funds. With capital immobile, $A$'s deficit implies an outflow of "money" from $A$, that is, credit ease and an increase in the supply of investible funds in the rest of the world. If capital is perfectly mobile, on the other hand, the upward pressure on interest rates in $A$ attracts capital; in the rest of the world, therefore, the supply of investible funds decreases, as capital is exported to $A$, while the demand for funds rises as a result of the increase in goods and services exports to $A$. Which effect is greater is, of course, in general unknown.

On the one hand, it might appear that capital mobility is bad for the rest of the world. This negative effect is mitigated if there is a liquidity trap during a recession, since in that case the shift in capital from the rest of the world to $A$ implies an increase in "active" balances worldwide. On the other hand, capital immobility limits and shortens the boom in the home country and hence offsets the stimulating effect this has on the rest of the world (a double feedback). "Thus, localisation of credit may easily have the effect of hindering the spread of a boom by hindering the boom itself"[7] (Haberler 1937 [1941: 421–2]).

Furthermore, imbalances in payments, and hence movements of money from one country to another, will have net effects which are either expansionary or contractionary depending on: the state of development of the several countries, the above-mentioned liquidity trap, the liquidity preference/money multiplier constellations and other institutional characteristics of the several countries, the industrial demand for credit. Many of these factors in turn depend, clearly, on the stage of the cycle in the respective countries. Where capital is imperfectly mobile internationally, additional complications arise, in that "we must abandon the simplifying assumption that the market for investible funds is completely homogeneous . . . [T]he markets for certain types of debts are much more international than the markets for others" (Haberler 1937 [1941: 423]).

The conclusion is that while hindrance to perfectly free and costless trade in commodities "tends definitely to disturb the uniformity of the cyclical movement in the world," the effect of increased capital mobility is ambiguous (Haberler 1937 [1941: 425]). The results here, uncertain as they are, are not particularly interesting. The complexity of the discussion and the awareness of the interactions, however, are. As is the preview of the Mundell-Fleming analysis (though without the policy variables).

Haberler carries out parallel analyses for alternative exchange rate systems – alternative, that is, to the initial assumption of a common currency which is equivalent to a full-bodied commodity standard. This includes drawing the distinctions (and showing the similarities) between the gold and other fixed rate standards, the primary difference being in the tendency to world inflation or deflation, which is different under the two regimes. He particularly emphasizes the symmetry of the gold standard as compared with the asymmetry (as between the reserve currency country and the satellites) of exchange reserve standards.

Next, flexible exchange rates (either administratively adjusted or freely floating). Like the crisis writers, he worries primarily about the destabilizing types of capital flows which are encouraged by flexible exchange rates (Haberler 1937 [1941: 436]). He distinguishes also between devaluation and free floating. Devaluation is discussed in connection both with trade balance improvements, which he expects will occur, and capital flights (speculatively destabilizing before the devaluation, stabilizing afterward). He worries about the stability of floating rates, not so much in terms of market elasticities of demand and supply of exports and imports but in terms of the currency in which claims are denominated – the now-familiar "J-curve" effect. He notes

---

[7] Interestingly enough, he here cites, in a footnote, the "Neo-Marxian Theory of Imperialism" developed by Rosa Luxembourg and others (Haberler 1937 [1941: 422n]).

that in the case of instability an exchange rate appreciation would improve the deficit country's balance but that a freely fluctuating market rate is unlikely to appreciate when faced with excess demand for foreign exchange. He assumes, by the way, what we might call a "super-Marshall-Lerner" condition – *each* country has elasticity of demand for imports greater than unity.

In the absence of capital mobility, there is no tendency for the business cycle to be propagated from one country to another under a floating rate regime. A rise in income normally leads to increased imports, exchange rate depreciation, and a rise in exports, thus strengthening the boom at home, compared with the fixed rate case, since there are no leakages, but by the same token eliminating the spread abroad. "The free-exchange system eliminates from the economic interchange of different countries the most important carrier of the boom and depression bacillus – namely, the flow of money across frontiers." Capital flows, however, are different. An exogenous shift in the demand for foreign securities immediately affects the exchange rate and hence the current account. The net effect is likely to be expansionary in the lending and contractionary in the borrowing country – the opposite of the gold standard case. The point is, he notes, that under fixed exchange rates, in contrast to flexible rates, the contraction in the lending country is what is required to generate the export surplus. The "intermediate phase is cut out under the operation of a system of free exchanges" (Haberler 1937 [1941: 446–7]).

Capital movements do make a difference under floating rates, but Haberler disagrees with Whale (1936) that they reproduce exactly the gold standard results. "On the contrary, they may produce exactly the opposite result from what we would expect under an international gold standard" (Haberler 1937 [1941: 449–50]). It is true that with capital mobile countries are not independent under a floating rate regime. But under the gold standard movements tend to be synchronized; under floating rates they are just as likely to be opposite. It can go either way, depending on the origins of the boom. Specifically it depends on what is happening to interest rates, which determine which way the capital will flow.

Characteristically for the period, there is again the distinction between different kinds of shock. The analysis could be extended, Haberler concludes, to other types of payment, including capital servicing and reparations, war debts, and so on. In that case, however, one must bear in mind that the "'propensity to consume' or the 'propensity to save' (to borrow these expressions from Mr. Keynes)" may respond differently than for private commercial capital movements (Haberler 1937 [1941: 451n]).

This variability of the propensities to consume – and to import – is the theme of his discussion of the multiplier in his Chapter 13, which was added in the Third Edition, completed in 1941. While essential in a survey, in my view it adds little of interest to what has gone before. The early post-*General theory* debates (particularly on issues such as the equality/identity between saving and investment and the multiplier) were replete with heated arguments which stemmed from uncertainty about whether one (or one's opponent) was doing comparative statics, period analysis, discussing functional relationships or identities, and, very importantly, just what was and what was not endogenous to the model at hand. One of the main issues in the early arguments about the multiplier was the distinction between comparative static and dynamic interpretations, and the related issue of the equality of the multipliers variously defined, and their stability over time (see, *inter alia*, Haberler 1947b, Polak 1947 for a spirited debate). This issue will excite, I think, few contemporary readers.

The second set of arguments had to do specifically with international applications of the multiplier. Just as some early applications to a closed economy took investment to be autonomous, while others viewed it as induced, and still others as both, so there were differences, in dealing with the foreign trade multiplier, as to (a) whether the trade balance was endogenous or not and (b) whether non-commodity items, such as capital services, should be included. There is a lengthy discussion, which a contemporary reader finds a bit discomfiting, on the issue of (a) above – essentially on whether or not to include imports in the multiplicand or in the multiplier, basically the question of the endogeneity of imports. There seem to be some misconceptions: Haberler argues strongly for or against any particular formulation on the grounds that a simpler formula is likely to be more stable and hence more useful – a comment which Polak drove to absurdum (which, frankly, it deserved) in their subsequent debate in the *American economic review*, 1947.

On the other hand, the question of the stability of the import function (over the cycle, for example, in the face of changes in domestic shortages and bottlenecks) is a real issue. A further question, hinted at but not discussed in detail, is that of feedbacks in a large country model (see the discussion of Metzler in Chapter 15) – imports cannot be regarded exclusively as leakages, he argues, citing Machlup (1939), if some of them "bounce back" because they "will affect favourably national income of the countries where they are exports. This will lead to increased exports – 'consequential exports' of the first country" (Haberler 1937 [1941: 470n]). This is essentially Polak's "reflection ratio". Meanwhile Haberler quotes Clark (1938) as arguing that autonomous increases in imports had the same effect on the multiplier as a reduction in exports, but that "consequential imports" were not a leakage, which seems remarkable (Haberler 1937 [1941: 469–70]).

He concludes with a wonderful brief foray into the history of thought.

Faced with a fairly large new apparatus and body of literature, he felt compelled to comment on the

relationship between the new type of analysis of the cyclical implication of foreign trade changes and the more traditional approaches on which Chapter 12 of the present study is based.[8] The concepts of the foreign-trade multiplier and the marginal propensity to import are new, but the underlying ideas can be traced back a long way in the history of economic thought, though sometimes only in a rudimentary form. (Haberler 1937 [1941: 471])

True, much of the traditional theory assumed full employment, but since a rise in prices implies a rise in money income, it follows that the theory did not really neglect income changes. Furthermore, it is easy to amend the traditional theory by allowing incomes to rise without price increases if there are unemployed resources. Again, the traditional theory emphasized gold flows, which are assumed to affect total spending, whereas capital flows are not. This, too, can be adjusted. If there is an infinitely elastic supply function for loanable funds, "an export surplus will bring about a rise in prices and/or income irrespective of whether it is financed by an import of gold or an export of capital" (Haberler 1937 [1941: 471]).

That two approaches with very different emphasis can often be made formally consistent within the framework of a more general model is, of course, commonplace. But the development of one of the approaches may nevertheless represent a significant departure from the path pointed to by the other. Having yielded much, perhaps too much, Haberler refers to real differences in approach. He notes that in the "traditional theory" capital movements tend to be treated as exogenous, whereas "[i]n the modern view this relationship is almost reversed." He notes however the conceptual difficulty of viewing any capital movement as purely financing or "induced" in the sense that somebody is holding foreign assets willingly.

As for the marginal propensity to import, Haberler insists that as an analytical concept it is a very old idea, and was an "integral part of the classical model of the international trade mechanism." The modern theory, starting with Paish, formalized it; what is new is the idea that the relation is a constant and stable one.

If we want to formulate the difference of the two approaches in one sentence we could say this: These new theories try to analyse sequences, transitions from one equilibrium to another in concrete terms, while the traditional theories were more interested in the description of equilibrium positions and have a tendency to minimise transitional processes. But it is a difference in degree rather than in kind. (Haberler 1937 [1941: 472–3])

---

[8] Chapter 12 was based on "traditional theories" but I think it yielded more to the "new approach" than the quotation suggests.

The distinction between comparative statics and dynamics as one which separates the classical from both the late classical and the keynesian points of view is valid, and one which I have emphasized from the beginning. But to assert that anything like a direct income effect on imports is "an integral part of the classical model of the international trade mechanism" seems to me to be stretching the usual meanings of the terms.

### Robinson: devaluation I

In his Survey (Metzler 1949 [1973: Chapter 1: 4]) Metzler cites Robinson (1947 [1949]) as part of the keynesian literature. The book it is taken from, *Essays in the theory of employment*, in itself is explicitly just that: "an attempt to apply the principles of Mr Keynes' *General theory of employment, interest and money* to a number of particular problems" (Robinson 1937, 1947 [1953: v]). But the chapter cited by Metzler is the famous "The Foreign Exchanges," and in a footnote at the beginning of that chapter (Robinson 1947 [1949: 83]) she refers, appropriately, to the *Treatise on money*, Chapter 21 as the source and motivation of the discussion.

The heart of the chapter is the development of the famous Bickerdike-Robinson-Metzler formula for devaluation,[9] which has led to unceasing controversy as to whether it is wrong or unestimatable: the latter is the case if in fact the model represents a complete general-equilibrium model. (For a thoroughgoing exploration of this question see Magee 1975, especially 222–32.) In any case in my view it is keynesian only in the general sense which I mentioned in Chapter 1: that the keynesian position precluded discussion of relative price or price level changes, leaving the exchange rate as the only movable price in the system; hence the interest in devaluation. Why Metzler cites it as keynesian is something of a puzzle to me.

Apart from the exchange rate formulation, the rest of the chapter is indeed akin to Keynes of the *Treatise*. Thus: short-term equilibrium at the given exchange rate involves equality of "recurrent lending" and the trade balance, with no short-term capital or gold movements. (Long-term equilibrium, she notes, is consistent only with zero lending, foreign or domestic.) But this can be attained only by the emergence of unemployment "and any reduction in the rate of interest, by stimulating activity, would set up a tendency for the exchange to fall. The third stage is not reached until *increased unemployment has brought about a fall in money wages in the home country*" (Robinson 1947 [1949: 101], italics mine).

She stresses the point that "[t]he notion of *the* equilibrium exchange rate is a chimera. The rate of exchange, the rate of interest, the level of effective

---

[9] To my knowledge she was the first to derive the formula. Alexander (1952 note 1) cites Brown (1942), Lerner (1944), Metzler (1949) and Robinson (1937).

demand and the level of money wages react upon each other like the balls in Marshall's bowl, and no one is determined unless all the rest are given" (Robinson 1947 [1949: 103]). All this is indeed very like Keynes of the *Treatise*.

The second chapter in that section of the book, "Beggar-my-neighbour remedies for unemployment," is in my view a better example of keynesian open economy economics, though it too is formally about devaluation (Robinson 1947 [1949: 393 ff]). We start with the proposition that a rise in the price of foreign exchange will improve the balance of trade and hence the level of employment. She refutes as irrelevant the argument that unrestricted free trade maximizes world output and efficiency since she is talking, she says, about the "division of a given total of employment between nations"[10] (Robinson 1947 [1949: 395]).

It will, however, improve the devaluing country's employment at the expense of that of other countries, and hence is an unneighborly act and likely to invite retaliation. However, any particular country will be forced eventually to enter into the game if it "has been played for one or two rounds" by others, since it will be faced with "intolerable" pressure of unemployment "and the demand for some form of retaliation [becomes] irresistible" (Robinson 1947 [1949: 396]).

The main part of the chapter is then a discussion of the considerations involved in choosing the weapon of retaliation: exchange rate depreciation, money wage reduction, tariffs, and quotas are all candidates, all intended to improve the balance of trade and hence the level of employment, but differing among one another in their impact on the level of employment, and in the income generated per unit of employment (which in turn depends on: (a) effects on productive efficiency and (b) the terms of trade. This in turn is a function of both the price and income elasticities of demand and supply for imports and exports. She is clearly more concerned here with relative price changes and their effects than were later keynesian expositors of international adjustment.

## Brown: devaluation II

A word or two here about Brown (1942), whose name is frequently mentioned in tandem with Robinson's in allusions to the devaluation literature. Mentioning the Robinson volume in his introductory note, he says he had not seen it when he wrote the article, "but her treatment is of a

---

[10] If that sounds somewhat specious, let us remind ourselves of the date; many people were expressing sentiments at that time which severely downplayed efficiency as compared with concern for the level of employment. In fact, Robinson was more concerned with efficiency and with income, as distinct from employment, than many writers of that period.

somewhat less general character than that attempted here" (Brown 1942: 57). His derivation of the elasticities conditions is more elegant than hers, and his attempt to sort out some of the necessary interrelationships between demand and supply elasticity conditions is more detailed, but the treatment on this score is essentially the same. He is as subject as she is to the accusation that it is uncertain how general-equilibrium the nature of the elasticities is intended to be. We find phrases such as: "The supply-function of British exports, ignoring for the moment the effect of prices of imports on their cost of production" (Brown 1942: 59), which indicate that he is not constructing a complete general-equilibrium model and is aware of that fact.

More interesting, however, is the second section of his paper, "The effect of the multiplier" (Brown 1942: 64 ff). Here he assumes less-than-full employment, variable employment/income ratios, and constant prices, which is to say, infinitely elastic supply functions. This last assumption he made, apparently reluctantly, to keep the model manageable. Injecting feedbacks through income and "income elasticity of demand for imports" he works out the general condition for stability and concludes that the "sensitivity of trade-balances to exchange rates is clearly diminished more the greater are the ratios . . . of reciprocal trade to national income in the two countries, and the greater are the multipliers . . . and the income-elasticities of demand for foreign goods." He applies his analysis to several types of disturbance, obviously the kinds of shocks which would have been on the mind of many an Englishman in 1942. The first is a permanent loss of British overseas shipping income, that is, a downward shift in the demand for exports. The income effects on the one hand work in an equilibrating direction, but on the other "increase . . . the depreciation which is necessary in order to achieve any given alteration in the trade-balance." In this case, if capital flows are unchanged, the restoration of equilibrium following a shock to the current account implies that at the new equilibrium income in both countries is the same as it was before the shock; here the elasticities condition remains the relevant one. He notes specifically that the elasticities have been defined to allow for the effect on import demands of the change in the terms of trade which the adjustment implies (Brown 1942: 66–7).

He does not undertake any formal monetary analysis, but he notes that in the case of a capital transfer, monetary repercussions may help the adjustment. Here he considers two kinds of capital movements. The first is a capital flight from Britain to America, as Americans withdraw their British holdings. If the money supply (credit position) is not dependent on the portfolio shift itself, then in the new equilibrium the capital flow will be matched by the current account change "and the credit positions in the two 'countries' will therefore presumably be restored to their previous conditions" (Brown 1942: 68). This is correct for his example of a "capital flight", a shift in asset preferences as between domestic and foreign assets on the part of American residents. It would not be valid for a gift or reparations transfer, in which real income has changed and hence, presumably, the equilibrium money supply.

The second alternative is a shift in real British investment from home to foreign locations, that is, increased foreign investment matched by a decrease in real domestic investment. If the transfer is completely effected, that is, there are no reserve changes, the new exchange equilibrium will take place with real output in both countries unchanged, since for Britain there is a substitution of the increased export surplus for domestic investment, and conversely in America.

Finally, he computes the effect of several shocks for British data. Using volume changes over pairs of periods, he estimates elasticities of British demand for imports. He assumes that the elasticity of demand for British exports is high, and assigns it the value of 1.5. Assuming that foreign supply of British imports is infinite, and that British supply of exports is that computed by Colin Clark, he proceeds to estimate the probable effects of devaluation. He then recomputes, taking into account the operation of a multiplier effect on income (assuming induced investment to be zero but the marginal propensity to import positive), thus making a move in the direction of applying general-equilibrium analysis to the problem of devaluation. The improvement is greater without the multiplier, but the difference is not large.

Here I must mention one final *curiosum*. Brown is explicitly aware that he is computing improvement in the export surplus pursuant to devaluation in terms of the currency of the devaluing country. Since his computations all show an elasticity of the surplus with respect to the exchange rate of considerably less than unity, the implication is that the earnings of foreign exchange will in every case *decrease*. That he can make this statement and not show greater concern over it can be interpreted only as a measure of the extent to which, at that late date, British economists were still completely sterling-oriented in their view of the world.

# CHAPTER 15

# The keynesians II

### Early Metzler: formal I

An early formal development of the keynesian model of an open economy was Lloyd Metzler's thesis (submitted at Harvard University in 1942), from which two chapters were published in the journals.[1] The two papers are clearly of a piece. They are different in style, as befit the respective journals (*Econometrica* and the *Journal of political economy*) at that time, but in content they are both studies in the application of keynesian analysis to the open economy problem. Distinguishing between various channels of adjustment, price (including price level, exchange rate, and interest rate changes), real income effects, and Ohlin-type expenditure and purchasing power changes, he concentrates his attention on the real income effects.[2] While not as rich as Machlup's study (see below) in the proliferation of disturbances and varying institutional environments, Metzler's two papers here are spare and elegant; they constitute a breakthrough in the formal application of the keynesian apparatus to the open economy.

The model is the same in both – a simple two-country keynesian model, in which consumption, imports, and investment are lagged functions of income. The first paper treats the issue of the dynamic stability of income in an open economy. If any parameter of the model changes, will income converge to a new equilibrium, given that the current account is

[1] The first was published in *Econometrica*, 10 (April 1942) 97–112, under the title "Underemployment Equilibrium in International Trade," and is reprinted as Chapter 10 in the *Collected papers*. The second appeared in the same year in the *Journal of political economy*, 50 (June 1942) 397–414, and appears as Chapter 2 in the *Collected papers*. See the editors' introduction to Metzler's *Collected papers*, 1973, signed by the editorial committee: Alice Bourneuf, Evsey Domar, Paul Samuelson, and Richard Caves. In the third chapter, unpublished, they find the seeds of the paper, "The Process of International Adjustment under Conditions of Full Employment: A Keynesian View," which I discuss in the next section, on the post-keynesian, MMM, literature.

[2] A number of early keynesian and peripherally keynesian writers, such as Iversen, did not distinguish clearly between the real income effects of the keynesian approach and the purchasing power emphasis of Ohlin, a distinction I have emphasized heavily in my discussion of Ohlin.

unconstrained? If stable, what will the new equilibrium for the two countries, and the world, look like? The second asks whether it is possible for income in the two countries to change in such a way that a transfer can be effected without the need for any prices (including exchange rates) to change. In this case, of course, the current account is not unconstrained. The question is rather whether there exist income changes which will generate, for the two countries, alterations in the current account equal to the exogenous shift in the capital account.

The first paper explores, as noted, the stability of a dynamic system in which savings and (induced) investment respond to changes in income, given exports and autonomous investment. He considers three cases, that of a single economy in isolation, that of a small open economy in which there is no feedback, so exports continue to be exogenous, and that of a two-country world. The results in the first and second cases are the now standard ones that stability requires a marginal propensity to spend on home goods for consumption plus induced investment less than unity, or a marginal propensity to hoard plus a marginal propensity to import greater than zero. In the third case, world income is stable even if one country is unstable in isolation if the other country has "sufficiently small" marginal propensities to save and invest, that is, the second country is, perhaps, "super-stable". This is analogous to the Marshall-Lerner conditions in which the inelasticity of one country's demand may be offset by the very high elasticity of the other (Metzler (1942a [1973: 264]).

From the stability results he works out the comparative statics of several parameter shifts: investment or government spending, the average propensity to consume, and the average propensity to import. The latter shift has two sub-cases, that in which the increase in the demand for imports is a movement away from home goods and that in which it constitutes a net increase in expenditure. The results are, of course, fairly complicated. They depend not only on whether the stability conditions hold, but on whether both countries are stable in isolation and, if only one is stable, on whether this is the country experiencing the parameter shift. However, almost all the results are determinate, if it be known which is the unstable country. Only the direction of change in investment is uncertain, because if domestic investment rises and the current account deteriorates, the change in total investment depends on the magnitudes of the two sub-changes. The movement of the current account depends on the configuration of stabilities between countries, but it is determinate (Metzler 1942a [1973: 265–74]). Remember that stability here does not mean the absence of unemployment, nor does it imply balance of payments equilibrium, since Metzler specifically assumes that each country has, or has access to, foreign exchange reserves, and can, and will, sterilize and offset the monetary effects of changes in those reserves. Stability simply means that income in both countries does not explode.

The second paper (1942b [1973: Chapter 2]), has to do with effecting a transfer, putting the cap on the Keynes-Ohlin debate of 1929. Again working out both the dynamics and the comparative statics, Metzler shows that whether the transfer is under-, over-, or precisely effected depends on:

1   The fiscal impact of the transfer, whether either the paying or the receiving country adjusts its government budget to allow the transfer to have an impact effect on expenditures. Thus, the transfer may or may not initially affect purchasing power and expenditures; the process may be aborted at the very beginning by governmental offsetting.
2   The expenditure effect, whether one or both countries is stable in isolation (the propensities to spend summing to less than one). The impact effect of (1) and (2) combined determines whether or not the transfer can be effected with no price changes; if not, then
3   the famous issue of the elasticities comes into play. Failure to make these distinctions clearly (though Ohlin was certainly struggling with them in his book) lay at the heart of the debates during the 1920s and early 1930s, especially the notorious Keynes-Ohlin exchange on the matter (Keynes 1929a, 1929b, 1929c, Ohlin 1929a, 1929b).

## Machlup: formal II

Machlup's book constitutes, I believe, the earliest attempt to present systematically a full treatment of the international adjustment mechanism based explicitly on keynesian foundations, specifically on the multiplier mechanism. His declared purpose was to "reconsider those parts of the theories of international trade and capital movements which can be profitably analyzed with the technique of the money-income multiplier" (Machlup 1943: v). A further innovation, he argued, was to develop it in terms of "really 'dynamic economics'" (Machlup 1943: vii) using, as did Metzler, period analysis. It is more detailed than Metzler's, both in terms of different kinds of disturbances and different institutional assumptions.

Taking great pains (necessary in 1943) to explain and define the concepts involved in national income measurement and accounting, and their extension to international economics, Machlup develops what are now the standard textbook expressions for the multiplier in an open economy. He rings the changes on the type of disturbance, the values of the several parameters (the marginal propensities to save and to import) and the inclusion of foreign feedback, even at one point extending the analysis to more than two countries. The most striking difference between his and more recent versions is the pains he takes to spell out the details of the adjustment through time.

### The multiplier working models

There is no need to present the multiplier formulas here. They are now, largely thanks to Machlup, the standard text-book formulations. They differ from the latter in having more different forms and variations, and in showing the period-to-period changes in the variables, which was generally fashionable in multiplier analysis in the 1940s. Showing the love of categorization and classification so characteristic of him, Machlup notes in a footnote that "[a]ll of the statistical 'determinations of the multiplier' in earlier [unnamed] writings were in fact *ex post* determinations of the multiplicand, because most of the repercussions which a certain amount of autonomous income-creating disbursement may have had were added to or deducted from that amount" (Machlup 1943: 10).

Not only are there various kinds of repercussions, but also there is importance attached to the nature of the multiplicand.

The "government-expenditures multiplier," the "private-investment multiplier" and the "foreign-trade multiplier" may be seen to have different values for one and the same economy at one and the same time, if dependent changes and repercussions are no longer assumed away or surreptitiously hidden away by *ex post* corrections of the multiplicand. (Machlup 1943: 9–10)

This kind of disaggregation did not reappear until the advanced stages of discussion of the assignment problem, when it was introduced by writers such as Jones (1968) and Niehans (1968), who broke down the instruments and the targets of stabilization policies into subsets. In Machlup's discussion of capital movements, as we shall see below, it is not disaggregation which distinguishes different kinds of disturbances, but rather the difference between real and monetary shocks. In this he follows closely in the Austrian tradition, along with Hayek, as we saw in Chapter 7.

Never a keynesian, he has a great deal of difficulty confining himself to the fixprice model, and the book is replete with apologia for his use of it. Indeed, the most interesting parts of the work are those in which he deviates from it, and injects discussions of price changes and interest rate changes. But in the formalization of the model, he manages to adhere to the assumption of constant prices, engaging in abstractions, presumably for pedagogical and expository purposes. (The book was intended to be, *inter alia*, a textbook.)

A complete analysis would not confine itself to income-induced changes but would also include price-induced changes in exports and imports if the price changes in question were in turn the result of "autonomous" changes in exports and imports. It has become fashionable to neglect these potentially resulting price changes and their consequences; the assumptions of unemployed resources, inflexible wage rates and perfectly elastic supply curves (and, it must be added, stable foreign exchange rates), are used as excuses for "assuming away" any repercussions via price. (Machlup 1943: 12–13)

### Domestic and foreign investment

Throughout, even as the models become more complicated, there is no induced investment (as distinct from Metzler, as he notes) no change in the interest rate, and no price changes. The model is keynesian; Machlup was not. "Commodity prices, foreign-exchange rates and interest rates are all likely to change to some extent in consequence of the change in the trade balance . . . Nevertheless, the separation of income effects from price effects . . . is methodologically sound" (Machlup 1943: 21).

He departs, however, from what has since become the standard treatment of foreign trade multipliers in introducing capital movements. Here the discussion is less formalistic and mechanical than elsewhere, though it is, like the rest of the work, highly taxonomic. Machlup cites the studies of Nurkse, Kindleberger, and Iversen on the distinction between accommodating the spontaneous capital movements, and the tendency for the latter to be met, at least on impact, by increases in the former in the opposite direction (Machlup 1943: 136–7).

However, this distinction is inadequate for him and he sub-classifies autonomous into "spontaneous" and "not spontaneous" autonomous capital movements (Machlup 1943: 135 ff). The issue here is the question of whether the buyer or the seller of securities, the lender or the borrower, takes the initiative. It may, of course, be both. This is important, he argues, because it implies something about the effects of the capital transfer upon domestic "disbursements", that is, expenditure.[3] Furthermore, foreign lending can take place at the expense of "(a) idle funds, (b) bank debts, (c) domestic investment or (d) consumption." He argues that in the first two "the spontaneous change in foreign lending may in fact not merely be balanced but also neutralized by the opposite accommodating change in foreign lending. In the last two cases, however, the balancing is not neutralizing" (Machlup 1943: 137).

This is the old and continuing debate of whether it is the capital or the

---

[3] Ohlin talks about differences in ease of adjustment between borrower and lender, but he does not relate this to the issue of whose initiative is responsible for the lending (see Chapter 13, page 253 and Ohlin 1933a: 427–9). Kindleberger and Bloomfield make some slightly analogous comments about the ownership of the assets which are traded in short-term capital movements, whether home country capital is being repatriated or foreign capital coming in (see Chapter 11).

current account which dominates. In the course of listing categories and possibilities he enunciates some significant asymmetries in the argument. A "spontaneous" capital flow may or may not result in a current account balance to effect it. (This is the whole issue in the transfer problem discussions and in the works of the Taussig school.) A "spontaneous" current account imbalance, under fixed exchange rates, on the other hand, *must* result in a capital movement in the opposite direction. The question becomes symmetrical "[o]nly if one were willing to . . . refer no longer to overall net capital flows but instead to certain types of capital flows, for instance long-term capital movements" in which case this movement (of capital in response to trade imbalance) would also become a question of "cause and effect" rather than a book-keeping identity. "[I]ts probability value, however, would be definitely inferior to that of the opposite proposition" (Machlup 1943: 141n). "This question cannot be decided merely by implicit theorizing; but the evidence presented by careful investigators points to the more frequent priority of capital movements" (Machlup 1943: 143). By this he means that the traditional transfer mechanism is much more likely to "work" than is the mechanism by which a current account surplus leads to long-term autonomous capital movements in the opposite direction. As noted above, Chapter 13 (pages 247–8), Ohlin makes some very similar remarks. Ohlin, however, depends less than Machlup does on accounting identities in making his argument.

In presenting the formal models of international adjustment to changes in investment, Machlup notes that

*trade* balances and incomes . . . will show exactly the same developments whether . . . the additional investment . . . is undertaken as part of an expansionary domestic policy or whether it is undertaken under the impact of an autonomous capital inflow. The *only* material differences between these cases will be in the international balance of payments and in the reserve positions of the banking systems. (Machlup 1943: 162, italics mine)

This is the complement of Harrod's comment that it is better for the world if the surplus countries engage in domestic expansion, thereby increasing their imports, rather than making "distress loans" (see Chapter 14, page 266).

The final topic Machlup deals with formally is essentially the issue of the propagation of business cycles. He asks whether several countries can expand in step with one another and maintain balance of payments equilibrium; the answer is that this depends on their respective marginal propensities to save (Machlup 1943: 187 ff).

### The transfer problem

There is a fairly extensive discussion of the transfer problem, both in terms of the general issue of the transfer of foreign lending and with specific reference to German reparations and the Keynes-Ohlin debate (Machlup 1943: 178 ff). Suppose the paying country has succeeded in solving the fiscal problem of raising the funds required by the transfer. The fact that this problem does not exist in the case of private lending is a major reason that transferring reparations is more difficult and more dubious than transferring private capital flows. Now there may be effects of the changes in disposable income on investment, effects of exchange rate change and price effects (both excluded by assumption), and income effects on the trade balance.

With the specific case of reparations under consideration he assumes a reduction in expenditure in the paying country, but no primary increase in expenditure in the receiving country. Citing the Metzler paper (1942b), he discusses some additional possibilities. If the paying country has a marginal propensity to save of zero, the transfer must eventually be effected through a decline in imports. This would be unrealistic, he argued, in that the reduction in income implied by this would be so great that the domestic fiscal problem of the transfer, collecting the taxes to pay it, would be insuperable. He notes, correctly (Machlup 1943: 184n) that Metzler gets the result of the transfer's being completely effected with no changes in price because he has induced investment offsetting the incremental saving. Machlup himself gets the transfer fully effected only when the marginal propensity to save is equal to zero.

But he escapes from the narrow confines of his model to argue that an increase in income in the receiving country, and the probable decline in prices in the paying country would together result in the transfer's being effected. He brings up the question of the several elasticities, extending the concept to include the case in which a decline in prices renders a new export profitable which was not previously so; this is tantamount to an infinite elasticity of foreign demand for that good. He therefore feels justified in rejecting the "pessimistic transfer theories of Lord Keynes and his followers." He concludes "that an expansion of primary disbursements in the receiving countries can do much to remove or ease all transfer difficulties; and that flexibility of prices, and particularly of costs, can greatly alleviate the squeeze in the paying country" (Machlup 1943: 185–7).

### Money

While not incorporating them formally into the analysis, Machlup is conscious of the monetary implications of a permanent imbalance in payments. The pressure on the banking system in the deficit country (and the excess reserves in the surplus country) are likely to lead to interest rate changes which result in changes in domestic investment, which in turn might (he says) influence trade flows in an equilibrating direction. This channel cannot be ignored. "The neglect of these matters goes back to the Keynesian idea of the perfectly . . . elastic lower end of the liquidity preference schedule and to the habit of regarding interest rates as independent variables." Nevertheless, for simplicity, he proceeds to ignore this effect as well, noting that it must "of course, be a factor not to be neglected when multiplier analysis is applied to a concrete situation" (Machlup 1943: 209–11). Though he does not pursue the point explicitly, he strongly implies that the addition of this monetary effect would be insufficient to assure balance-of-payments equilibrium (Machlup 1943: 171–4). In this he differs from the later (1960s) view of world monetarism, which took the position that as long as foreign exchange reserves, and hence high-powered money, were changing, one could not think in terms of internal equilibrium. Thus, in its weakest version, *any* positive relationship between the money supply and domestic expenditures (not necessarily the traditional quantity theory of money) assures that it is impossible under fixed exchange rates to think of equilibrium in the domestic economy as long as the balance of payments is imbalanced.

### *Wage-price flexibility*

Again, though not part of the formal structure, price and wage flexibility are too important to be ignored, in Machlup's view. He is prepared to accept the idea that wages are inflexible downward. What he argues against, citing Joan Robinson as an ally, is the assumption that in the face of unemployment wages will not be flexible upward. Unemployment will not deter labor unions from demanding wage increases. Thus the applicability of the multiplier model does not depend on whether there is unemployment. "The real issue is the upward flexibility of wage rates, which may come into operation long before anything approaching full employment is attained. An aggressive labor movement can always create conditions which would make the assumption of full-employment analysis applicable to an underemployment economy" (Machlup 1943: 208).

Finally, I note the following comment, supporting my own interpretation of the classical mechanism as necessarily involving price movements. Machlup finds in Longfield a statement, in 1840, of the importance of the marginal propensity to import. However, he adds: "The similarity between Longfield's exposition and more recent discussions, rather striking up to this point, ends here because Longfield proceeded to introduce price increases in the exporting country and price declines in the importing country" (Machlup 1943: 35).

### Salant: policy I

William Salant (1941 [1949]) presented a relatively early and clear statement of the keynesian model. He defines the foreign trade multiplier, attributed to Colin Clark, and applies it to the large country model, with feedbacks. In the face of a decline in exports, a country has a number of policy alternatives:

1   To do nothing.
2   To deflate. This is described as the "traditional gold standard behavior" (Salant 1941 [1949: 209]).
3   To offset the effect on income by domestic stimulation, at the cost of exacerbating the payments deficit.
4   To apply specific remedies such as devaluation, tariffs, or subsidies. As I noted in Chapter 1 it is precisely during that period, under the influence of the growing popularity of the keynesian view and the recent memory of the traumas of the 1920s and 1930s, that the discussion of devaluation became widespread.
5   To try to become less open, to trade less, and to divert trade more and more to bilateral channels, to barter, and to form blocs while effecting domestic expansion through internal measures. The idea of forming blocs and engaging in bilateral clearing is reminiscent of Keynes's suggestions along those lines in his proposals for the postwar era (see Chapter 10).

Though not using the term, he has a clear picture of the policy dilemma. Like Joan Robinson and, later, Nurkse, he puts the stamp of approval on domestic expansion coupled with (defensive) devaluation, to be distinguished from a "beggar-my-neighbor" policy of devaluation designed to stimulate the economy by creating an export surplus (Salant 1941 [1949: 209]). A country can have an independent monetary policy, he notes, if foreign trade accounts for a small share of its national income but it, in turn, is responsible for a sizable percentage of world trade. The exemplar of this, of course, is the United States. At the same time, the United States was in a sense too closed. Not only was it protected, by a small marginal propensity to import, from foreign disturbances; this same small propensity to import meant that it was unable to export much of its own domestically caused shock (the recession of 1937–8). A larger share in world trade would have lessened the impact of this shock on the U.S. economy (Salant 1941 [1949: 213–26]). He does not mention, however, that it would have caused even greater resentment than was already felt at the extent to which the United States was leading the world in, and into, depression.

## Kindleberger: policy II

Published in 1943, Kindleberger's paper deals with the issues expected to confront the world after the war. It is instructive, and perhaps not incidental, to note the complexity and interventionism in exchange rate management and schemes which were being planned for the postwar period. This is true of virtually all the discussions of a postwar monetary system. Faith in either a relatively unfettered fixed exchange rate regime or a floating exchange rate system was a rarity in that period.

Kindleberger's paper is not a deliberate exposition of the keynesian view. Rather it is a broad-ranging discussion of alternative plans for postwar international stabilization, as the title suggests, from a keynesian vantage point. What is keynesian is the basic tenet. Like many others, Kindleberger expected the major postwar problem to be a dollar shortage. (He was later (1950) to write a book by that name.) His major argument here is that this dollar shortage is unlikely to be eliminated by increased imports into the United States.

Like Salant, he assumes that the U.S. has a "low marginal propensity to import (low elasticity of demand for imports with respect to income)" and a small share of exports in income; its trading partners are characterized by the reverse: high propensities to import and heavy dependence on trade. Thus, at least as many dollars as the United States makes available to foreigners through imports will be spent; the dollar shortage will remain. This is a real problem, he says, and reducing tariffs is an inadequate solution. Thus "the earnest admonitions of the rest of the world to the United States that it 'live like a creditor nation' fail to come to grips with the fundamentals of the problem" (Kindleberger 1943: 380–1). In short, he is arguing that in terms of a real income model the world system, with feedbacks included, is unstable, or at best neutrally stable. There were people at that time who argued, more simply, that the world was so far removed from equilibrium (the excess demand for American goods and services so great) that any increase in the supply available would be taken up immediately. But this would explain only why an increase in U.S. imports would lead to an *equal* rise in U.S. exports; he seems to be arguing that a *greater* increase was equally likely.

The gold accumulated by the United States during the 20 years prior to the war has not succeeded in inducing an expansion of United States imports which was not followed by an equal or greater rise in exports. This gold represents an investment as cumulative and as barren as claims on foreign countries and is increasingly recognized as such by the man in the street and in vaudeville jokes. Perhaps claims on an international clearing office would provide a greater inducement than gold to stimulate imports. In any event, it may be doubted that increased imports would correct for long the world shortage of dollars. (Kindleberger 1943: 387)

At the same time, he recognizes and insists, albeit in a footnote, that a clearing or pooling arrangement involves adjustments which are essentially the same as those which prevail under the "gold standard", adjustments for which the gold standard has been "politically repudiated" but which would be just as necessary, and automatic, under a pooling arrangement: the surplus country is drawing from the [world] central bank "which directly enlarges national income and expands the credit base; the deficit country builds up idle balances at the central bank, which contracts money incomes directly and the credit base" (Kindleberger 1943: 386n). One of the plans which he discusses and rejects, and which he attributes to an anonymous writer, calls, as did Keynes at one point before Bretton Woods, for cancellation of credit balances which have not been spent by a certain time (in this case, seven years). Whether he was referring to Keynes's plan or not I do not know.

### Neisser and Modigliani: econometric I

I should, perhaps, explain why I am devoting considerable space to a work which is not generally regarded as a landmark in the literature under study. There are several reasons: First, partly because it has in fact been neglected and deserves attention. Second, because I find it interesting in and of itself. Third, because it constitutes an early struggle on two fronts: a new tool, econometrics, and a new model, the keynesian framework.

This is, to my knowledge, the first attempt ever to carry out an econometric model of world trade. They probed further and deeper than anybody before them, and for some time afterward, in attempting a multi-country, general-equilibrium econometric attempt to study trade flows. The model is estimated for the interwar period, with data gleaned primarily from the 1920s and 1930s. But they discuss extensions to the post-World War II period, and consider it applicable in principle to the pre-World War I period as well. It is an impressive work, the more so when one realizes the extent to which they were breaking new paths, analytically as well as econometrically. Both the scanty availability of data and the crudity of the computing hardware of the time (the late 1940s) make it a heroic effort technically.

It is an exercise in the study of the adjustment mechanism, not a description of the patterns of world trade nor a study in comparative advantage. It is deeply micro and general-equilibrium in its orientation. And yet it is explicitly, albeit perhaps reluctantly, keynesian. The book itself at times seems to be not entirely cohesive, analytically. This may be due to its having been written over a considerable period of time, or it may be that the authors were essentially carrying on a debate between themselves in its pages.

This apparent inner conflict of the book is partially explained by the history of its creation. The research was sponsored by the Institute of World Affairs of the New School for Social Research. In his preface to the book Adolph Lowe, Executive Director of the Institute, indicates that the work was formulated and started by Hans Neisser "as an extension of . . . his former work in international economics" (Neisser 1936). Since that earlier work was completed, however, "invaluable tools for this kind of analysis have been provided through the elaboration of the methods of econometrics, and through the theoretical contributions with which Keynesian thinking has enriched the theory of international trade" (Neisser and Modigliani 1953: v). He continues that Modigliani joined in the work a year later, and "made an important contribution in reformulating the underlying model of international trade" (Neisser and Modigliani 1953: vi). I mention these comments because on reading the book I was struck by the differences in emphasis (even the contradictions) between certain parts of it. At times it almost seems that the reader is privy to a dialogue between the authors. And it has to do with the micro as opposed to the macro nature of the work.

### Neisser's prelude

A reading of the earlier Neisser work (Neisser 1936) makes it much clearer (as Lowe suggests) what the analytical origin of the study was, so I shall devote a brief discussion to it before proceeding. It is a little like Haberler's *Prosperity and depression* in its eclecticism. He presents a fairly catholic view of the causes of cycles, discussing the under-saving, over-saving (and "Neo-Marxian") views, as well as "partial overproduction" and "structural unemployment". Keynes is little mentioned (once in reference to the *Tract*, once or twice referring to the *Treatise*), but there is some discussion of Kahn's formula for "secondary employment", that is, the multiplier (Neisser 1936: 47 ff).

Starting with a well-placed attack on the autarkical assumptions of most cycle theory (except for "the unsuccessful attempts of the Neo-Marxian theory of 'Imperialism'") (Neisser 1936: 1), he examines, both analytically and empirically, the issue of worldwide propagation of business cycles. He is particularly interested (for the period 1924 to 1932, the boom and the beginnings of the Great Depression) in the interrelations between the United States, Germany, Britain, and, to some extent, France, and the connection between all of these and the raw-material- and food-exporting areas of the world. These are precisely the geographical distinctions we find in Neisser and Modigliani (1953).

The United States, he argues, (and not Germany) was at the heart and cause of the general worldwide deflation (Neisser 1936: 105). How did it spread? The possible mechanisms are threefold: (1) the repatriation of capital, "withdrawing of loans", (2) a reduction in imports, of inputs, of consumer goods and of capital goods, (3) increasing competition for markets abroad as home demand shrank (Neisser 1936: 106). Thus, distracted by its tremendous domestic stock market boom, the United States stopped lending to Germany in 1929. The Germans had been heavy inporters of raw materials and foodstuffs. New investment which substituted for net lending to Germany was likely to involve the more finished capital equipment than the lending to Germany had done. If the substitutability in output between capital goods and commodities was not high in the short run, the result would be a bidding up of the price of the former and/or supply constraints in acquiring them. This shift in the composition of investment could lead to a decline in its total, that is, "oversaving" (Neisser 1936: 99–100).

Crucial to the propagation and to the links between economies are two concepts. First is that of *imposed* versus *autonomous* deflation. The issue is apparently whether the expenditure functions have shifted or not. As I understand it, imposed deflation is deflation forced by a reduction in the money supply, generally because of a gold outflow, and so related to a decline in exports, a reduction in new foreign lending, or a calling in of debts. Autonomous deflation, on the other hand, has to do with expectations and/ or discrepancies between planned savings and investment. Imposed deflation results from a reduction in the money supply. If there is autonomous deflation, "not all available money funds would be used for purchasing goods or hiring factors of production." Part of the money stock would be destroyed by domestic debt repayment, and part hoarded. However, the "dilemma" of the 1940s is lurking and any attempt at reflation might convert autonomous into imposed deflation "if the country lacked the means of paying for additional imports of producers' goods, and were not assisted by capital imports or by a simultaneous revival of the world's trade" (Neisser 1936: 111–12).

Secondly, he has the concept of the foreign trade multiplier. The idea of "a fixed ratio between the volume of exports (*and thus, other things being equal, of imports*) and the volume of national income" is attributed to Douglas Copland, in *The Australian Crisis*, 1934 (Neisser 1936: 48, italics mine).

The multiplier (secondary employment) has a supply component here: exports can lead to increases in "secondary employment" but only if imported raw materials are made available. So increased capital imports, permitting the increase in material (or capital equipment) imports, become the multiplicand. Then Copland's multiplier needs to be qualified, according to Neisser, as follows: some imported gold will be held as additional reserves; public spending is not automatically expanded when total expenditure increases; output (and labor) per employed person may increase rather than the number of employed; import versus domestic production at the margin may depend on the stage of the cycle; there are discontinuities due to the lumpiness in increasing capital equipment. Given these qualifications, it is not difficult to understand the later comments (see below) in Neisser and Modigliani (1953) regarding the microeconomic nature of the marginal propensity to import, or, stated alternatively, its instability as a macroeconomic parameter.

In quantifying the spread of the depression from the United States, Neisser attempts to estimate, for Germany and Britain, for 1930 and 1932, two kinds of induced increase in unemployment. They correspond, as suggested, to the simple multiplier effect of a reduction in exports on the one hand and, on the other, that caused by the supply constraint. The supply constraint in turn is due to both induced and autonomous deflation. The former (the multiplier effect) was never as large as the latter, he says (Neisser 1936: 128 ff). That is, the reductions in output and employment due to reduced imports of raw materials because of the balance of payments constraint and because of the expectational effect of the depression were greater than the reduction due to the export multiplier.

This does not fully describe the Neisser study, but I have attempted merely to show why, some eight years after its publication, Neisser was so happy to plunge in and exploit the "elaboration of the methods of econometrics." He was very clearly ready for a technique that would permit him to solve a set of equations for a number of individual countries, each with its own (preferably variable) parameters. What is less clear was whether he was equally comfortable with "the theoretical contributions with which Keynesian thinking has enriched the theory of international trade" (Neisser and Modigliani 1953: v).

### The Neisser-Modigliani model

In an early chapter on the theoretical aspects of an international trade model they explicitly discuss, and reject, the concept of the marginal propensity to import. Based on applications of the *General theory*, short-run theories of foreign trade have been formulated in which "the imports of industrial countries are usually regarded as a function of income alone. There are strong theoretical reasons, however, for believing that this is not adequate." The main reason is that the desire for imports is not (with the possible exception of goods such as French wine) a behavioral relationship stemming from consumer preferences. Since imports are the residual between consumption and production of any given commodity, they are a function not only of expenditure but also of domestic output. It follows from this, they argue, that in order that imports be a simple function of income, "not only domestic demand but also domestic production should be a simple function of income." In order to analyze demand and output, it is necessary to include prices as well as income as variables. To do this, one must turn to "the vast body of modern price theory as developed by the schools of Lausanne and Cambridge [Walras and Marshall]." But in fact, having decried the use of such a simple relationship, they discover an unexpectedly good fit (of imports on income), which they feel needs explaining. To their surprise, domestic production could be omitted, except in the case of food imports (Neisser and Modigliani 1953: 36–40).

Later in the book, however, they present their model as an explicitly keynesian, short-run, and disequilibrium one. Their exposition of this, in Chapter 18, "The Case for a Macro-Economic Model," is fascinating; it is the earliest attempt I know of to present an explicit justification for the building of a short-term, disequilibrium macroeconomic model with international interdependencies. Nevertheless they are always conscious of being in the shadow of the long-run, equilibrium, fully specified model which they know is there. This distinction is a very important one to them, and they take pains to emphasize it.

it should be stressed that variables which are exogenous in our model are not necessarily so in the wider framework of the total economic process, including its accompanying measures of economic policy. Similarly, our breakup of the time interval into subperiods, each with its own equation, is a statistical device imposed on the system, serving the purpose of an exogenous variable; but it cannot be concluded that the structural change described by this device is exogenous to the total economic process. (Neisser and Modigliani 1953: 335)

This last statement is interpreted to mean that if the model were enlarged to include financial variables and investment decisions, the "breaks" which appear in some of their functions over time, specifically the discontinuities which they observe during the great depression, would disappear: these changes would be endogenous to a more fully specified model. "Time lags in the process of investment determination, and in the formation of financial and other economic policy decisions, would contribute a dynamic element to such an expanded model" (Neisser and Modigliani 1953: 336). As we saw above, we find similar statements in Machlup recognizing the importance of financial, institutional, and other variables. The difference, of course, is that whereas Machlup was developing formal models, Neisser and Modigliani had to make empirical decisions for econometric estimation, regarding what was and what was not exogenous.

That which they label the neoclassical theory (the general-equilibrium modelling) of Pareto and, to a lesser extent, Yntema and Ohlin, has the analytical advantage of being more formal and "exhibiting clearly the mechanisms leading to a new long-run equilibrium" and making explicit what structural changes are required to achieve the new equilibrium (Neisser and Modigliani 1953: 330). If there has been a change in one of the fundamental parameters of trade (tastes, technology, even monetary conditions), price changes alone are not enough, they argue. Structural changes must occur, which require a decline in real wages, through a fall in money wages or by devaluation. This may take more time to effect than can be bought with the available foreign exchange reserves.[4] The reason the long run may be too long in real time, then, is that foreign exchange reserves may be inadequate to buy the necessary time. Much of the later discussion, in the 1960s, of the "adequacy of international reserves" was based on very similar analytical grounds: that there would be a long-run equilibrium achieved, that adjustment was possible, but that it might take a long time during which financing of imbalances would continue to be required. In this case other forms of adjustment are required during the short run, and they may result in underutilization of some plant and equipment and unemployment of labor. As a result there may be "a decline in real income beyond that caused by the change in the terms of trade. Since these short-run adjustment processes may be so severe, it is particularly necessary that we be able to learn something about their dimensions" (Neisser and Modigliani 1953: 332).

This can be done by extending to short-run problems the kind of general-equilibrium analysis which Pareto and others applied to long-run equilibrium. They cite Mosak's attempt, but note that he got "sufficiently concrete results" only for the specific case of the transfer problem and even that only in a two-by-two model. As a rule, these general-equilibrium analyses do not yield even qualitative results as to the direction of change. Still less do they provide solutions for the level of income, employment, and real wages consistent with short-run internal and external balance. "The micro-economic theory of short-run equilibrium, as it has been developed in analogy to the neoclassical theory of long-run equilibrium, does not give us a means of ascertaining even approximately either the nature or the size of these adjustments" (Neisser and Modigliani 1953: 332–3). They turn, therefore, to

the bold macro-economic system of the *General theory*, which, with a few equations, explains domestic short-run equilibrium by interrelating the basic aggregate quantities of income, consumption, investment, stock of money, and the interest rate. It is along these lines that our model has been developed, and within this context that its theoretical justification is to be sought. (Neisser and Modigliani 1953: 333)

In the long run, real income will vary only with the terms of trade, structural changes having to do with shifts in the environment, such as the world pattern of comparative advantage. These are not likely to be "related in a simple statistical fashion to the import aggregates". But in the short-run

---

[4] This is still an unsettled point in doctrinal debates today. The question is, what is the debate between the Keynesian and the new classical position about? Is it over the existence or not of an equilibrium solution (see Shackle 1967, Coddington 1976), the Keynesian position that we live in a disequilibrium world? The alternative view is that the real issue is the length of time needed to approach the long-run equilibrium, the Keynesian view presumably being that convergence is so slow that what happens on the road is important, the monetarist-new classicists arguing that the process is rapid in terms of real time so that what happens when the economy is out of equilibrium is not very important.

model they have developed, they derive the notion of the propensity to import "directly" from the keynesian approach, and complete it by assuming exports to be determined by the import propensities of the trading partners, assuming each country's share in the imports of its trading partners to be fixed. They thus argue that they have created a short-run macroeconomic model of the international economy, in which imports (and indirectly therefore exports) depend on income. Formally the model could also be inverted to derive equilibrium levels of income in the several countries as a function of the trade magnitudes, but this, they assert, is econometrically unfeasible in their framework (Neisser and Modigliani 1953: 333–4).

Treating prices and exchange rates as exogenous, as they do, may be considered inferior to endogenizing them, as in "the micro-economic system of neoclassical short-run equilibrium theory." This could be done, they argue, in their system as well. But whereas in a closed economy prices depend on money wages and the aggregate supply function, in the open economy model "international factors" impinge on aggregate income and output as well. To account for these income and output changes statistically, given their interrelationships and given the instability of the investment function, they found impossible. It is this complex of interrelationships and not the rigidity of prices that motivates their treating prices as exogenous (Neisser and Modigliani 1953: 334).

Thus, they are willing to assume that a country can vary its income, independently of what other countries do, by either of two methods, the "classical one of monetary policy, especially the discount policy of the central bank, or the Keynesian one of controlling the volume of domestic investment." But assumptions of independent price index movements must be made with great care: "a price change in one sector of the world economy may well be followed by price changes in other sectors" (Neisser and Modigliani 1953: 62).

With certain qualifications we obtained high correlations between imports and income, and also found a relative stability in the export participation coefficients. This would not be possible in a system that described long-run equilibrium . . . Such differences in real income as occur [in the long run] are not related in a simple statistical fashion to the import aggregates. The reason is that the very process of establishing an all-round equilibrium causes deep-reaching structural changes, and the effect of these on imports is not uniquely associated with their possible effect on real income. In the short run, however, the situation is different. When an existing equilibrium of the balance and of the domestic economy is disturbed by a change in the basic determinants, within the country and abroad, the economy will react by immediate changes in the degree of utilization and the level of income; and this income change will be associated with changes in the foreign-trade magnitudes. (Neisser and Modigliani 1953: 334–5)

The fact that they found, statistically, "such a close association between income and imports" leads them to the conclusion that price changes will not occur quickly enough" to prevent changes in foreign demand from affecting domestic income. *This conclusion challenges the optimistic tenet of classical theory that the balance of payments can be equilibrated without disrupting domestic equilibrium through a reduction of income and employment"* (Neisser and Modigliani 1953: 335, italics mine).

Their short-run model, then, is explicitly, I should say committedly, a *dis*-equilibrium one. While disclaiming originality in connecting equilibration of foreign payments with the worldwide transmission of income changes, they do assert that classical trade theory was prevented from dealing with these issues by its concern with long-run equilibrium. Here a footnote expresses astonishment that "[a]s recently as 1934 a theoretical treatise on international trade characteristically presented, as a mathematical model, a Lausanne equation system of general equilibrium, typified by a condition of 'equilibrium' in the balances of payments of the various countries included." The reference is to Ohlin (1933). As distinct from the classical theory, they state, the "popular contemporary approaches . . . deal rather vaguely with the struggle for export markets" and make no distinction between exports as a source of foreign exchange earnings on the one hand and exports as a stimulus to domestic production on the other. Furthermore these same popular writings typically ignore the impact of income changes on the terms of trade "which in the academic treatment has almost become a separate branch of international-trade theory" (Neisser and Modigliani 1953: 129). They repeatedly emphasize the fact that theirs is a short-run model which does not converge to equilibrium. They not only insist that full employment equilibrium for every country in the world does not imply balanced trade between them (a concept foreign to the classical paradigm), they even measure the disequilibrium in payments which would have resulted from the pursuit of full-employment policies in all the "leading industrial countries" (Neisser and Modigliani 1953: 335).

They play a number of very ingenious games with their model, of a type which was to become popular with economic historians, for example, ten to fifteen years later. One of these is to compute the international income multipliers (described briefly below), based explicitly on the "Keynesian foreign-trade multiplier" (Neisser and Modigliani 1953: 121). This exercise is of inherent interest, and it is an excellent demonstration of the nature of their model and the way in which they use it, so I shall discuss it briefly, as a sampler. The problem is to compute the likely effect, operating through the trade balance, of an exogenous change in country $i$'s income on the income of other countries.[5] "We refer to this as transmission via the volume of imports,

[5]  The countries in their model were as follows: Eleven industrial countries "whose exports of manufactured goods were . . . half or more of their total exports." 1. United Kingdom;

and it is the only transmission mechanism for which we can obtain quantitative indicators from our model." (Neisser and Modigliani 1953: 115).

The answer in general, is, as always: it depends. It depends, *inter alia*, on country *j*'s policy reaction, which is likely to be different in the case of an increase from its response to a contraction. Furthermore, it will depend on the availability (to a deficit country) of foreign exchange reserves (including gold) or financing possibilities. Secondly, it depends on price effects, which they discuss but do not attempt to incorporate into their estimates, for reasons made clear in the discussion above. Price effects are the effects of a change in prices in country *j*, in response to a change in income and prices in country *i*, and they involve, for *j*:

1  A change in domestic investment,
2  A change in the exports and imports resulting from its (*j*'s) own price change,
3  The direct effect of changes in terms of trade on income,
4  The direct effect of changes in the real value of nominally fixed international transfers on real income (Neisser and Modigliani 1953: 117–19).

Having thus duly noted the price changes, they assume them away and concentrate on the international transmission of income changes. These they compute under three alternative assumptions:

1  The first is the assumption that all countries except *i* remain "passive," there is no policy reaction, and deficits are financed through reserve changes, gold flows "or in invisible items that are not income-affecting." Here the relevant computation is that which they label the Clark multiplier (see Chapter 14, pages 269 ff above), in which "*j*'s balance change is directly reflected in its income" (Neisser and Modigliani 1953: 119–121).
2  The second assumption is that country *j* takes policy steps to correct its trade balance by altering its income level; the question then is how much it has to change its income in order to do this. This would depend on what price effects had taken place, though these would show up in the computations as exogenous.
3  As in the second case, *j* adjusts its income in order to maintain its trade balance, but third countries are experiencing effects on their income

2. United States; 3. Germany; 4. France; 5. The remaining seven (Italy, Japan, Sweden, Belgium, Switzerland, Czechoslovakia, Austria); 6. The rest of the world (except for the Soviet Union), the "Non-industrial" or "primaries" countries (Neisser and Modigliani 1953: 9). For France they were unable to compute "reliable" import functions (Neisser and Modigliani 1953: 87), so France was omitted from the multiplier computations.

through changes in their trade balances. These third countries, however, are not reacting in terms of policy.

They compute the coefficients of $j$'s income change in response to $i$'s income change for their sample countries, for the years 1928, 1932, and 1935. Despite these multilateral effects (which are basically what the IMF study described by Polak and discussed below was trying to achieve) they felt that their model had done inadequate justice to inter-country dependence in fluctuations because it lacked a monetary mechanism, which meant that they could not treat "the process of international credit inflation or contraction that may be set in motion by a large country – and during the great depression this process was probably of *greater significance* for the level of a country's income *than was the transmission of income changes through import demand*" (Neisser and Modigliani 1953: 336, italics mine). A closely related application is the computation of the effects of full employment policies on the trade balances of the industrial countries (Neisser and Modigliani 1953: 135 ff).

The values of the model are projected forward to estimate the postwar situation, and in particular to estimate ". . . the level at which the United States trade balance would be in equilibrium" (Neisser and Modigliani 1953: 148–9). In this connection it should be noted that they specifically consider "adjustment" to involve changes in the trade balance to eliminate imbalances caused by shocks. They recognize the possibility of short-term financing through movements of capital and of gold. "Consideration of the second mechanism of equilibration, which affects the non-speculative capital flow via the interest rate, would complicate the discussion without affecting the results" (Neisser and Modigliani 1953: 329–30). That is, they are not interested in short-term capital movements, exploring the effects of shocks only on the trade balance. The distinction between induced private financing of trade deficits on the one hand and government financing, by drawing down foreign exchange reserves, is not considered germane to the questions which interest them. This may be part of the general syndrome of the early postwar decades of considering private capital movements in general to be a thing of the past.

Another exercise is to examine the prewar depression (the late 1920s and the 1930s) and to pose the question: could the major industrial countries, Germany, Britain and the United States have adopted, in 1918 and in 1937, expansionary domestic policies to achieve full employment and have financed the ensuing trade deficits by reducing their capital exports and/or gold imports? (This harks back to Neisser's attempts to analyze this period in Neisser 1936.) (Neisser and Modigliani 1953: 135 ff). They conclude that the United States could have done so. Britain could not (even if all three countries had adopted expansionary policies in concert) because her commodity exports were to a large extent a function of her capital exports, both being directed heavily to the primary producing countries; the feedback of a reduction in British capital flows to these countries on British exports through the declining income of the primary producing countries would prevent Britain from expanding to full employment without loss of foreign exchange reserves. Germany could have managed it in 1928 if Britain and the United States followed suit, and if she could have dispensed with gold imports, which were an essential part of the post-inflation recovery process and were in fact capital imports (Neisser and Modigliani 1953: 139).

In the interwar period, the financial position of the major European lenders was weakened. The United States took over the British role as lender of surpluses, but did it much less effectively and smoothly than Britain had done. In the 1920s Britain and the U.S. were operating in tandem, but when the United States' capital markets "collapsed" in 1929, there was no other center available. Britain was not in a position to take over; France had never played such a role and was not likely to start at that point. This is highly reminiscent of the Macmillan Committee's discussion, treated in Chapter 5, page 91 and footnote 2, about the failure in the late 1920s of the United States and France "to employ the receipts in the way in which Great Britain had always employed hers, namely, either in the purchase of additional imports or in making additional foreign loans on long-term" (Macmillan 1931: 107). As I noted in that discussion, Keynes emphasized that point frequently, both in his testimony to the Macmillan Committee and in his pre-Bretton Woods writings, for example, where he argued that there must be a mechanism encouraging, or forcing, countries to lend their surpluses (see especially Keynes 1940–4 [1980: 21 ff]).

This passage is highly revealing of their view of the historical workings of the mechanism. It rejects the idea that either specie flow or short-term capital movements are part of the "normal working" of the gold standard. No other country had the necessary "resources" (presumably surpluses) so there was nothing to prevent "the spreading of the American depression over the world, both via prices and via the volume of United States imports . . ." (Neisser and Modigliani 1953: 133–4). Thus, without assuming policy reactions, they have developed a very general-equilibrium analysis.

They then perform an additional exercise, and conclude that if either the U.S. or the U.K. had tried to expand employment in 1928 or in 1937 and lowered export prices to offset the deleterious effect on the trade balance, they would have had to lower the export price index by 2,144 and 473 points respectively. Since 1928 was their base year for price indices, the index for that year was 100. For the United States the comparable figures were declines of 160 and 229. And if the two countries had orchestrated a simultaneous expansion in 1928 the United Kingdom would have had to lower its price index by 1,796, the United States by 2 (Neisser and Modigliani 1953: 143). They allow these numbers to speak for themselves.

Finally, recomputing tentatively for the few postwar years, they conclude that U.S. civilian trade would be balanced "at an income level only about 20 percent higher than that of 1951 . . . [This] suffices to justify a greater optimism concerning the problem of the dollar scarcity than is frequently voiced" (Neisser and Modigliani 1953: 149). On this optimism they were correct, though not for the right reason.

## Polak: econometric II

Similar in goal to Neisser and Modigliani, but much simpler, is an early attempt by Polak at the International Monetary Fund "to construct a multicountry model which would give a satisfactory explanation of the international transmission of fluctuations in economic activity." It is reported on briefly (telegraphically) in Polak (1950), and extensively in Polak (1954).

It is a very rudimentary keynesian model. It is multicountry, but not multilateral, in the sense that the Neisser and Modigliani model is. For $n$ countries there are $3n$ equations in real income, consumption, and imports. Exports are a given share (specific to the country) in world trade, exogenously determined. It is this assumption, that world trade is exogenous, and not the sum of the imports of every country from every other, which makes his model simpler and less multilateral than theirs (see Polak 1954: 17n). Exports plus autonomous investment times the multiplier equal income; imports are equal to the marginal propensity to import times consumption and induced investment (the marginal propensities being in general different for the investment and consumption sectors). Exogenous shocks to income come from changes in "autonomous investment" or government spending; fluctuations in agricultural output or in commercial policy constitute shocks to the import equations. Relative prices and government restrictions on trade, including changes in commercial policy, are treated as shift parameters. Prices are never treated endogenously (Polak 1954: 13–46).

In the aggregative world model, the feedback comes from the additional imports resulting from an expansion in income due to increased exports. The ratio of the incremental imports to the exogenous increase in exports which caused them is labeled the "international reflection ratio", and is measured by $\mu(\delta+\mu)$, where $\mu$ is the marginal propensity to import and $\delta$ is the marginal propensity to hoard ("not to spend" in Polak's words). This ratio, the product of a country's marginal propensity to import and its foreign trade multiplier, represents the "intensity with which the country under consideration reflects back into the world impulses it receives from the rest of the world" (Polak 1954: 42).

Polak implies and assumes, but does not emphasize, that if the reflection ratio is unity the adjustment mechanism is fully stabilizing, since the balance of payments will return to equilibrium after a shock. Note that this can happen only if δ is zero, that is, the country would be unstable in isolation, or if the indirect reflection ratio is made to include a government response of tightening or loosening restrictions (such was the standard view of the world as late as the early 1950s). He notes further that government adjustment, the loosening or tightening of restrictions can, if there are lags in adjustment, lead to overshooting (Polak 1954: 42–4).

Although for a single country a reflection ratio of unity would assure that the balance of trade would be in equilibrium, world stability requires that the weighted average of the reflection ratios be less than one. Otherwise, with one increase in exports, world income would take off to infinity. This is yet another way of demonstrating that the payments adjustment in a purely keynesian income model is incomplete in a stable world (see the discussion of Metzler above). Here again, remember that stability refers to income, not to the balance of payments.[6]

The data are for twenty-five countries for the interwar period. For each country a parameter is estimated indicating the response of its exports to a change in the exogenously determined total of world trade. From this the multiplier computes the effect on the income of each country, and hence its imports, which are endogenous. "Of all the relationships used in this study, that between national income and imports is the most widely known and accepted." The fit, he concluded, was surprisingly poor. Part of the reason seems to have been a downward shift in the function in the 1930s as

---

[6] He had earlier studied the payments stability problem from the point of view of an individual country. In an (unfortunately) relatively neglected paper (1943 [1949]) he applied the foreign trade multiplier to the problem of the ability of countries to repay loans taken to finance development, taking into consideration the effects of borrowing and investment on output, consumption, and the trade balance and building in the impact of debt service payments on the current account required for equilibrium. Since the borrowing was assumed to be directed at financing investment (for postwar reconstruction) an important question was what the investment was used for, since this would affect the final balance of trade. Where the new investment finances an increase in the output of traded goods in excess of their increased consumption, the effect on the balance of trade is positive. Where it leads to an even greater increase in the output of non-traded goods (such as publicly provided goods and services, or consumers' durables), it leads to a worsening in the balance of the trade, since imported inputs are required and no exports emerge from the "operation". Where "goods sold on the home market replac[e] similar goods previously sold on the home market, and goods sold abroad replac[e] similar goods previously sold abroad" the effect is neutral. The respective weights of these three types of investment spending determine the total impact on the trade balance and hence the viability of the borrowing progam (Polak 1943 [1949: 468–70]).

compared with the 1920s (Polak 1954: 161–2). When he broke the period into two sub-periods the results improved. The reflection ratios were typically significantly less than unity, indicating stability of the model. His results are the opposite of those of Neisser and Modigliani, who, as we noted above, were skeptical of the marginal propensity to import as a theoretical artifact and astonished by the goodness of the fit.

For the aggregative world model there are two types of exogenous (autonomous) shocks: those which change the volume of world trade and those which merely redistribute it. The former are disturbances such as changes in autonomous investment in any country. Also in this category are changes in the level of import restrictions. Changes in relative prices, on the other hand, have a less certain effect on the volume of world trade, according to Polak, who assumes the impact to be of second order of magnitude, in contradistinction to Frisch (Polak 1954: 58–9).

Like Neisser and Modigliani, Polak, in the country studies, pays attention to the different commodity structure of the various countries' trade patterns, but he does this on the export side, dividing world trade into two categories, one for primary products and the other for manufactures (Polak 1954: 68). Changes in the level of domestic expenditure obviously have a greater international impact the bigger the country and its role in world trade; here the United States is singled out as particularly significant. Polak estimated the effect on world trade of the United States' depression. Imports fell by 39 percent between 1929 and 1932. Since the United States accounted for 15 percent of world trade, this decline constituted a decline of 6 percent of total trade. From the average of the "reflection ratios" Polak estimates the world trade multiplier to be about 2, meaning that an autonomous rise in imports would be expected to result in a total increase in world trade of double the original amount. So the decline in United States imports, initially 6 percent of world trade, should result finally in a decline of 12 percent in world trade. Since the volume of trade declined by 25 percent, Polak concludes that roughly half the reduction in world trade could be attributed to the exogenous shock of the United States' depression (Polak 1954: 164–9). This is consistent with the result stated by Neisser and Modigliani, though they emphasized the other side of the statement: that not all of the reduction in other countries' trade was due to the reduction in United States imports.

## Summary

The keynesian writings took various forms: formal, quasi-normative policy-oriented writings, and econometric studies. We have examined samples of all of these, though I have not tried to cover them encyclopedically. The models of adjustment which I have described in these two chapters constitute the essence of what was, from the late 1930s into the late 1950s, the "received doctrine" of balance of payments theory. It is, as I have emphasized frequently, primarily a model of disequilibrium in payments. Prices are rigid, resources are not fully employed, monetary effects of imbalances are stifled, and changes in real output and employment constitute the link between nations.

In such a world the size of reserves and the ability to finance disequilibria for substantial periods of time became a major issue. The aggregated version of that problem, the optimal size of world "international liquidity" and the appropriate method for controlling, adjusting, and increasing it, was the subject of lively debate into the 1960s and even beyond. Closely related was the question of the optimum policy mix and level of control and intervention in order to live with the famous "dilemma" of policy. I said "live with" and not "solve" or "eliminate" the problem, which was generally viewed as unsolvable. The one possible solution was exchange rate change, typically devaluation, which explains the emergence of the devaluation theories during that time span. After the publication of Alexander's paper in 1952, however, the general-equilibrium complexities involved in a devaluation became increasingly evident.

A natural outcome of such a view is the concept of the policy dilemma. Particularly in the light of the optimism of early keynesian thinking about the efficacy of macroeconomic policy in achieving full employment (inflation at less than near-full employment not being conceived as a problem), it was clear that a major – if not the major – constraint on the pursuit of such policy was the availability of foreign exchange reserves. The need to conserve one's limited resources of international means of payment, or to refill an emptied treasury, was seen as a serious potential brake to the achievement of an otherwise attainable desideratum. The policy discussions of the war years and early postwar era are full of attempts to deal with this problem, primarily in terms of various kinds of international cooperation, lending, clearing, and recycling. This was premised, generally, on the assumption, often implicit, that in the long-run equilibrium in international payments was readily attainable, that if necessary a change in exchange rates would achieve it, and that the problem of financing disequilibria, though a serious one, was also a temporary one. Thus when what we currently call the Mundell-Fleming models pointed the way for the authorities of an individual country to break this constraint and achieve the twin goals of "internal and external balance" simultaneously, without official intergovernmental borrowing arrangements, they were briefly hailed as panaceas. We turn to the development of these ideas in the next chapter.

Finally, a postscript about the technicalities of the foreign trade multiplier. There were a number of heated arguments which, when reread today, make us aware that there has indeed been some progress in economics: some things we no longer argue about. There were debates as to the relative merits of the "Clark" and "Keynes" multipliers on the grounds of the inclusion in the former, but not in the latter, of autonomous imports. For the rest the debate seems to have involved, as Polak (1947) and Haberler (1947b) recognize in their joint statement in the *American economic review*, the distinction between dynamic analysis (with either discrete or continuous time) on the one hand, and comparative statics on the other; and to have demonstrated that it is necessary to be specific about what variables are endogenous and which exogenous, since a given accounting magnitude or statistical datum such as imports, or consumption, can have components of endogenous and exogenous change. Furthermore, at one point, Polak's objections to Haberler seem to stem from his, Polak's, assumption that the marginal propensities to consume and to import always necessarily sum to unity. In addition, the balanced budget theorem not yet having been proven, the analogous expansionary effect of a balanced increase in trade was a subject for debate. The names in this all-star act include, of course, Clark (1938), Haberler (1947b), Harrod (1939), Kahn, Keynes (1936), Machlup (1943), Metzler, Neisser, Polak (1947), Robertson (1939), Stolper (1947). The impatient contemporary reader should bear in mind the intensity and furor of the debates only a few years earlier about the equality of savings and investment. What every freshman knows today he or she learned by studying the cave drawings which these artists have left behind.

# 4

## The confluence

# CHAPTER 16

# Post-Keynes: MMM

The group of writers labelled MMM consists of Metzler (1960 [1973: Chapter 8]), Meade (1951a and 1951b), and Mundell (1968). The first two wrote about 1950.[1] Mundell was later but he winds up this era with the beginnings of what is known as the Mundell-Fleming model. Mundell was concerned primarily with policy recommendations, and the Mundell-Fleming literature, which I do not propose to survey extensively, is generally interpreted as being based on a text-book type of IS-LM analysis. Meade's important work has for some reason dropped out of the limelight; it is, like most of his work, too detailed and "complete" to serve as a useful hand-book. Presumably, also, the fact that it puts "wages and incomes" policy on the same footing as "financial" (fiscal plus monetary) policy made it somewhat alien to the spirit of western, particularly anglophone, economics in the post-World War II period.

Metzler's work is on an entirely different analytical footing from the others. It is called "Keynesian" but is much more Wicksellian. Unlike the others, it is not at all policy-oriented. The role of the central bank is simply to buy and sell foreign exchange in order to peg the exchange rate; it is therefore applicable to any regime where exchange rates are fixed and the money supply varies with the balance of payments. I shall deal with it first.

### Metzler[2]

Metzler's contribution in this area is the paper, "The Process of International Adjustment under Conditions of Full Employment: A Keynesian

---

[1] The dating of Metzler's paper is, unfortunately, problematic. It was presented at an Econometrics Meeting in 1960 and was probably written considerably earlier than that – quite possibly as early as 1950, which is about the time he became ill. There is fairly clear evidence that the paper is incomplete; it is certainly edited much less carefully and elegantly than his published papers. The Editors of Metzler's *Collected papers*, in their introduction, hint that, like the two papers discussed in Chapter 15, it had its origins in Metzler's dissertation.

[2] The redrafting of this section has been very heavily influenced by the discussions I had with Jonathan Eaton in the course of our work on a joint paper (1987) of exposition and elaboration of the Metzler article.

View." As published, it presents problems to the analyst, because it is a draft rather than a finished product. Several aspects of the model are as yet imperfectly worked out. Nevertheless, I believe it to be a seminal work, of major importance, and worthy of some effort at exegesis.

One of its several innovations is that it presents, to my knowledge, the first formal integration of capital movements into the adjustment mechanism, as opposed to treating them as part of the financing, accommodating process. In the classical paradigm it is absent; in the neoclassical tale it appears as a result of central bank action. Here,

a country which has a deficit in its balance of payments will eliminate this deficit partly by a rise of interest rates, relative to interest rates in the rest of the world, which will lead to a capital backflow, and partly by an outflow of money which will lead to deflation at home, inflation abroad, and an improvement in the country's balance of trade. (Metzler 1960 [1973: 232])

The very title appears paradoxical at first blush: "The Process of International Adjustment under Conditions of Full Employment: A Keynesian View."[3] What is Keynesian in this model is, explicitly, "the Keynesian monetary rate of interest" (Metzler 1960 [1973: 209]). The model is one of full employment: prices move in response to excess demand. There are two countries, with different real rates of return on capital.[4] Saving and investment at full employment are functions of the rate of interest, and these by assumption intersect at a positive rate of interest; this is the Wicksellian natural rate, $r_n$.

The saving and investment schedules represent the (flow) demand and supply functions for new securities and determine, as noted, the natural rate of interest, $r_n$. The market for the stock of existing securities is cleared by the monetary rate of interest, $r_m$. This last sentence is, in fact, the liquidity preference theory which makes the model Keynesian, in Metzler's interpretation. Since the stock of securities is very large relative to current increments, any short-run divergence between $r_n$ and $r_m$ will be settled by the dominance of the market rate (see Shackle 1967, Chapter 15 for a detailed discussion of the development of this issue in the *General theory*). However, in the long run the natural rate dominates, "through changes in the price level which alter the real value of cash balances" (Metzler 1960 [1973: 213]). That is, if the market rate of interest is too high, there is a deflationary gap,

---

[3]  It is, however, wholly consistent with that interpretation of Keynesian economics which developed during the 1960s and views the contribution of Keynes's writings in general, including the *General theory*, to be something other than the assumption of rigid prices and wages (see Coddington 1976).

[4]  Metzler labels the countries "advanced" and "underdeveloped" ($A$ and $U$), but this classification has no purpose other than to allow for differences in the natural rate of interest. The countries are treated symmetrically in every other respect.

prices fall, real balances increase, and the monetary rate of interest (hence the market rate) falls. This continues until the market (monetary) rate of interest equals the natural rate.

Metzler devotes a fair amount of space to developing the macroeconomic definitions for an open economy which have become standard (and which Keynes approaches in the *Treatise*), but I believe his is the first explicit statement of the connection between these and Walras's Law: considering the market for foreign exchange (the overall balance of payments), the market for securities, and the market for goods and services, he notes that if two of these markets are balanced, the third is, perforce, also in balance.[5] Now he connects the two countries. The link is the interest rate differential between them, which induces capital flows, that is, trade in securities. For every rate of interest each country has an equilibrium excess of savings over investment, or balance of trade surplus. Collect all the pairs of interest rates for which one country's surplus is equal to the other country's deficit and you have a function, *BB*, which is the "natural balance of trade". Where *BB* intersects *CC*, the market clearing equation for securities trade, the capital and current accounts are equal and the overall balance of payments is in equilibrium.[6] A balance of payments deficit leads to a reduction in the money supply and hence to a rise in the monetary interest rate. This discourages both capital outflow and domestic expenditure (investment). The latter effect causes a decline in prices and an improvement in the current account.

Here Metzler has revived a notion which had been dormant for some years; except for Harrod, it had been virtually moribund since Keynes's *Treatise*: that the money supply is endogenous under a regime of fixed exchange rates. It is different from the classical endogeneity of the money supply, since there the rate of interest was not part of the mechanism. In the neoclassical version it was. But here, in Metzler, there is none of the

---

[5] His frame of reference, general-equilibrium analysis both formal and less formal, is indicated by his comments here that this is "a special application of Walras's well-known proposition" but also that "it is a slightly generalized treatment of Professor Alexander's conception of 'income absorption,' which states that currency devaluation will not be effective in improving a country's balance of payments unless it is accompanied by measures to reduce the demand for goods and services" (Metzler 1960 [1973: 219]).

[6] He never worked out satisfactorily (nor to his own satisfaction) the relationship between capital movements and interest rates, in the sense that he took capital mobility to be a function in interest rate *differentials*, but he drew the diagrams with absolute levels of interest rates on the axes. This bothered him, but he did not work out a solution to the problem. He insisted, correctly, that in fact the system was not overdetermined, and that in equilibrium there was one pair of interest rate which satisfied both the interest-rate differential required to clear the market for foreign securities and the interest rates required to equate domestic saving and investment in both countries. See Eaton and Flanders (1987) for a formal demonstration of this point. Holmes (1973) criticized him for permitting flows to stop before interest rates are equalized, but I would argue that the choice between the assumption of perfect and imperfect capital mobility is one of taste rather than of correctness.

neoclassical policy element. There is no discussion here of central banks, monetary authorities, or any kind of policy tools. The full employment assumption vitiates the need for them.

Metzler addresses himself to the question "whether most of the adjustment will take the form of interest-rate changes and a backflow of capital or whether changes in prices and an improvement in the deficit country's balance of trade will be the dominant factor in creating an even balance of payments." (Metzler 1960 [1973: 223]). This depends, he argues, on the type of disturbance and on the several parameters of the model. Regarding disturbances, he distinguishes between parameter shifts involving changes in preferences with respect to commodities on the one hand and those involving financial capital flows on the other. It turns out that the former have no permanent effects, whereas the latter do.

A word here about this question of the type of disturbance, since there is more discussion of the importance of different types of shock than is typical in the literature. The results are perhaps on the face of it counter-intuitive in that, in Metzler's example, it is the real shock which has no permanent effects and the monetary shock which has; but the distinction that carries through the analysis is not really that of real as opposed to monetary disturbances; it is rather that between shocks which directly involve securities markets and those which do not. Eaton and Flanders (1987) extend the analysis to other disturbances, and the pattern persists. Anything that shifts either of Metzler's market clearing functions $BB$, involving savings and investment, or $CC$, the desire to hold foreign as distinct from domestic securities, leads to a new equilibrium. Shifts in preference for domestic relative to foreign products, or shifts in the demand for cash balances, prices being flexible, have no permanent effect on any of the variables. The first leaves all the variables unaltered; the second changes the distribution of the world's money supply. This is not only interesting *per se*; it further justifies treating models which involve interest rate effects separately from those which do not.

As noted above, savings and investment are functions of the rate of interest, and the difference between them, in an open economy, is the "natural balance of trade". For some pair of interest rates this will be of equal magnitude and opposite sign in the two countries. The interest rate differential also determines the desired financial capital flow between the two countries. When this is equal to the balance of trade, the world is in equilibrium. Considering first the change in tastes, Metzler argues that a switching from home to foreign goods, given the saving and investment schedules, leaves the equilibrium capital account and the natural balance of trade unaltered, so the adjustment must ultimately take place entirely through price changes "and an adaptation of $A$'s balance of trade to a fixed capital movement" (Metzler 1960 [1973: 224]). The impact effect will be a deficit in the overall balance of payments, implying a money flow from the deficit to the surplus country. This causes the market rates of interest (in both countries) to change and capital flows to respond accordingly (in his example, the capital outflow is reduced). The rise in the interest rate also creates, temporarily, a deflationary gap, which leads to a fall in prices, restoring the balance of trade.[7] In short, since nothing has happened to affect autonomous capital movements, and prices are flexible, a change in tastes affects only the merchandise account of the balance of payments. The conditions of demand (the elasticities of demand for imports) affect, not the incidence of change between the trade and capital accounts but rather the terms of trade deterioration required to restore the trade account to its original value (Metzler 1960 [1973: 233]).

Metzler notes here that "the system seems to behave rather like the traditional theory in which the balance of trade adjusted itself to fluctuations in capital movements through movements in the quantity of money and corresponding changes in prices." Thus, the classical model with its quantity theoretic foundation becomes a special case of Metzler's model. When tastes for goods change we get the Hume mechanism: the money supply is endogenous and the Marshall-Lerner elasticities conditions determine the change in the terms of trade. Since neither the "natural balance of trade", determined by the savings and investment functions, nor the preference function for foreign securities, has changed, both the market and the natural rates of interest (which must be equal to each other in equilibrium) must return to their pre-disturbance values. This means that real balances must be the same as they were initially. This in turn implies that the change in prices must "be proportionate to the loss of nominal balances attributable to the deficit". In this instance "a reasonably good case could . . . be made for the classical, quantity theory of money" (Metzler 1960 [1973: 225]).

An issue Metzler does not deal with here is the size of the specie flow (the duration of the imbalance) as a function of the relative size of the two countries and of their money multipliers. The Marshall-Lerner conditions dictate the change in the terms of trade required to restore equilibrium. The price changes will be proportionate to the changes in the money supply. But though the real money supply must be unchanged in both countries, the nominal money supply will change, in general, in different proportions in the two countries, since the absolute change in nominal balances is the same.

Therefore the amount of specie flow which is needed and, as a result, the

---

[7] The model is also Keynesian-Wicksellian in that the money supply, the stock of real cash balances, affects spending through the rate of interest and the savings and investment functions, rather than directly as in the more straightforward quantity equations. In equilibrium, there is, of course, a unique relationship between the size of cash balances and the level of spending in any case.

length of time required, depend on the relative sizes of the money stocks before the disturbance and the size of the money multiplier in each country (if this is not equal to unity). Metzler assumes that the money multiplier is unity (as if there were a specie standard) and he seems implicitly to assume that the two economies are of the same order of magnitude. It is formally easy to define liquidity preference as the demand for specie holdings, combining the institutionally determined money multiplier with the preference function of agents for money over other financial assets.

Where the disturbance is a change in the autonomous capital flow, on the other hand, the long-run equilibrium position is not unaffected. Consider country $A$ (advanced) with a relatively low rate of the interest and a capital outflow equal to its export surplus; now suppose the capital outflow is increased, leading to a balance of payments deficit and, again, a reduction in the money supply. Part of the adjustment is a rise in interest rates and a backflow of capital, and part takes place through a decline in prices and an increase in the commodity export surplus. While Metzler does not state explicitly what the shift toward foreign securities is *away from*, it is evidently a shift from domestic securities, since he assumes that the parameters of the commodity market functions are unchanged. This will eventually influence domestic investment, but indirectly, through the change in the interest rate, which will in turn influence the equilibrium level of savings and investment.

In this case, however, the interest rate change "rather than being a temporary force to get the required changes in prices . . . is a permanent part of the new adaptation" (Metzler 1960 [1973: 226]). Since the parameter shift involved autonomous capital movements, the export surplus is permanently greater than it was previously, so there must be a permanent increase in the excess of savings over investment, which means a higher interest rate in equilibrium.[8]

It is here that the model becomes "keynesian" in the sense that the role of liquidity preference becomes crucial: the interest rate enters as an argument in the demand function for money. Since the interest rate in both countries is permanently changed, equilibrium real balances will have changed. Nominal balances must then change by a percentage different from the change in prices required to restore balance-of-payments equilibrium. "Thus the introduction of liquidity preference creates a certain inertia in the system. Prices do not react as readily to movements in the nominal quantity of money as they would in the classical system" (Metzler 1960 [1973: 228]).

This effect is, of course, greater, the more elastic the demand for real cash

---

[8] Once again, we note the use of the word "permanent" as being somehow different from the contemporary one. A permanent capital flow may be inconsistent with the notion of long-run equilibrium. The distinction which Metzler is making, between autonomous and accommodating capital flows is nevertheless, in my view, a relevant one.

balances. The more elastic the demand for real balances, the longer the adjustment will take, and the greater the change in the nominal money stock. Since real balances must fall, the nominal money stock must fall by more than prices (the effect of the deficit in reducing the money supply must outweigh the effect of the falling prices, which is to raise real balances). In the limit, we have the "keynesian liquidity trap" with infinitely elastic demand for money, and money flows never lead to equilibrium.

Since prices are rising in one country and falling in the other, the question arises as to which country experiences the greater price change. The answer is, the one with the lower elasticity of demand for money. In the country with a highly elastic liquidity preference schedule, a given interest rate change is associated with a large change in real balances. Similarly, in the country with a relatively inelastic liquidity preference schedule a small change in real balances is called for. But the change in nominal balances is the same in both countries (except for sign); so the difference must lie in the change in price levels. The country with the relative large change in real balances must experience a relatively small change in prices. Here again, however, Metzler ignores the fact that the same absolute change in the money supply in the two countries in general represents different proportional changes. Metzler emphasizes the difference in the extent of price change in the two countries, and its dependence on the relative elasticities of liquidity preference. This is the contribution which the theory of liquidity preference has made to the analysis, he argues. The rest of the analysis, that imbalance is eliminated partly by "a rise of interest rates ... which will lead to a capital backflow, and partly by an outflow of money, which will lead to a deflation at home, inflation abroad, and an improvement in the country's balance of trade" has been known, he says, since the *Treatise* (Metzler 1960 [1973: 233]). This is true, but it seemed to have been forgotten during the intervening twenty or thirty years; hence the concern for so long about the dilemma and the breakthrough which the assignment solution provided. More important, even in the *Treatise* the interest rate changes are not endogenous – it takes liquidity preference added to the demand function for money to achieve that, a step Keynes did not take formally until the *General theory* (see Shackle 1967). When Metzler says he is exploring the contribution of Keynes to the theory of adjustment, he clearly is referring to the contribution of the *General theory*. The role of liquidity preference, then, is the injection of "a degree of inertia" into the system. "The way in which relative [between countries] prices are transformed into absolute prices thus depends in an important way upon the nature of the demand for money" (Metzler 1960 [1973: 232]).

Stated another way, Ricardo's concept of the "natural distribution of money" (1811 [1951: 53–54], 1821 [1951: 137]) which is the theoretical counterpart of the Hume price-specie flow mechanism, and of the latter-day monetary theory of the balance of payments, is modified by the addition of Keynesian liquidity preference, so that the equilibrium distribution of money depends not only on the size and respective levels of economic activity of the several countries, but also on their respective elasticities of liquidity preference. On the other hand, "whether most of a deficit is eliminated through prices and the balance of trade or whether it is eliminated through interest rates and the balance of capital movements does not depend upon the external conditions of the demand for imports but upon the internal conditions of saving and investment" (Metzler 1960 [1973: 232]).

Metzler viewed this paper as an exercise in "deciding whether Keynes's ideas have made a substantial contribution to the concept of monetary adjustment" (Metzler 1960 [1973: 233]). I see it in somewhat broader terms as: (a) a Wicksellian analysis of the role of natural and market interest rates in the international adjustment mechanism, and (b) a revival of the Keynesian (and Ohlinian) views of the *Treatise* and of *Interregional and international trade*, of the interrelationships between capital and current accounts, which had fallen by the wayside during the crisis mentality and pseudo-*General theory* keynesianism of the 1930s and 1940s. It led the way to the postwar rediscovery of the role of capital movements as an integral part of the balance of payments adjustment mechanism, not confined to being either purely exogenous (as in the transfer literature) or purely financing and accommodating, with no feedback into the basic balance. It is perhaps not too extreme a statement to say that he brought the subject back into a general-equilibrium framework from the brink of partial analysis on which it had hovered in the keynesian and early devaluation literature.

## Meade

In 1951 James Meade published the first of two volumes (the seeds of which can be found in two earlier papers in the *Economic journal* (1948), (1949)) aptly subtitled *The theory of international economic policy*. And this is exactly what they were. The first, *The balance of payments*, is the one of interest here; the second deals with trade and commercial policy. His acknowledgments in the "Preface" support my placing him here, close upon the writers treated in Chapters 14 and 15, since most of them are cited here. And indeed, the work is a direct outgrowth and combination of the keynesian income analysis and the elasticities approach that came out of the devaluation literature. Like many, if not most, economists in the immediate post-World War II era, Meade was not thinking of a self-adjusting system, and in this sense as well the work qualifies as keynesian. He has refined the multiplier, contrasting it in (1949) with Machlup's (1943) formulation; Meade defines the marginal propensity to import as a function of expenditure rather than of income. This implies a two-stage decision, first between spending and saving, and then, given the level of spending, establishing its composition.

Additionally, he has the concept of induced foreign investment, arguing that while this appears to be the same at first as induced imports, the effect on the foreign country's income, and hence the feedback on the home country, will be different in the two cases (Meade 1949: 37–9). But the keynesian income effects, with all the foreign-trade multipliers worked out, are combined with price effects and Marshall-Lerner stability conditions (Meade 1951a: 125–48; Chapter XI).

He notes somewhat apologetically that his model is exclusively one of comparative statics, quoting Hawtrey as having "emphasized strongly the inadequacy of dealing with these problems by the method of comparative statics rather than dynamically" (Meade 1951a: x). Formally it is a general-equilibrium model, but both in the mathematical supplement and the verbal discussion so many parameters are assumed to be either zero or infinity that the analysis becomes, in fact, more partial than at first appears. The reason is the usual one of manageability; this is particularly important here since he deliberately and persistently draws policy conclusions from the analysis. Throughout, in the verbal treatment and the more formal *Mathematical supplement* (1951b), his is a two-country model, so repercussions and feedbacks abound.[9]

Meade's formal statement of the gold standard adjustment mechanism is classical rather than neoclassical, in the sense that it is an equilibrium system with an endogenous money supply. It is generally applicable to any fixed exchange rate system in which the money supply in each country responds "in a more or less automatic manner when there is a persistent inflow" or outflow of gold (Meade 1951a: 178). There is a detailed account of the different systems under which this may be achieved: 100 percent reserve banking at one extreme, fractional-reserve banking at the other (the "normal" system, he says), and between them, the fiduciary-issue system, reminiscent of the Bank Act of 1844, in which there are fractional reserves, but a ratio of unity at the margin between changes in gold and induced changes in the domestic money supply (Meade 1951a: 181–4). Note that if the central bank has a fiduciary-issue system and the commercial banks engage in fractional-reserve banking, the system as a whole operates on the fractional-reserve system. This, as we saw in Chapter 7, was a matter of great concern to Hayek. If both countries have a fractional-reserve system, the burden of adjustment will be greater for the country with the larger money

[9] An even more heroic attempt, in my opinion, to include formally many of the general-equilibrium details in a model with changing exchange rates (an analysis of devaluation) and the impossibility of making any sort of qualitative generalization in such a case can be found in Stuvel (1950). See also the review article by Harberger (1952).

multiplier, since its monetary system will respond more to any flow of gold between the two countries. For analogous reasons, adjustment will be more gradual and hence, presumably, easier, under 100 percent reserve banking than under fractional-reserve banking. There is a detailed discussion of the implications of the gold-exchange standard, and Meade concludes that either (a) it does not really economize on gold for the world as a whole, or (b) it places a very great strain on the reserve currency country. (At the time the book was written, the sterling balances which the overseas Sterling Area countries had accumulated during World War II were a cause of much concern in Britain.)

His view of the mechanism under fixed exchange rates, when money wages are flexible, is a highly eclectic one. The endogenous changes in the money supply pursuant to a shock to the balance of payments, assumed to be a shift in foreign lending, affects first of all the rate of interest and the short-term capital flows. The change in the rate of interest, however, also affects domestic expenditure and, directly, the trade balance, depending on the sum of the marginal propensities to consume and to import in the two countries (the condition for a transfer to be effected). If this is not enough to restore balance of payments equilibrium, there will be excesses of supply (demand) in the commodity and labor markets, causing prices and wages to fall (rise). If the Marshall-Lerner conditions hold, there will be a further movement toward equilibrium in the balance of payments (Meade 1951a: 191–3). The system is stable, because the movement of gold will continue as long as imbalance in international payments prevails. Under a managed fixed exchange rate standard, any rule that requires the money supply to vary *pari passu* with reserve changes means that "there will be a deflation of the money demand for goods and services so long as the deficit on the balance of payments continues" (Meade 1951a: 189). The argument is, of course, symmetrical with respect to the surplus country. But remember that the assumption here was flexible money wages, an assumption essential to the simultaneous achievement of internal and external balance, defined as full employment with balance of payments equilibrium.

Flexible exchange rates will give the same real result, "though in a different order and by rather different means" (Meade 1951a: 194). He assumes here that the flexible rates are combined with a "financial policy" to achieve "internal balance". A balance of payments shock will affect, first of all, exchange rates, and therefore commodity trade, again assuming that the Marshall-Lerner conditions hold. This changes total effective demand in each country, forcing the authorities to undertake expansionary (or contractionary) financial policies to stabilize expenditure. The result is that interest rates in the two countries change, and foreign lending is altered accordingly, again in an equilibrating direction. The lending country was the one which experienced a depreciation of the currency, an increase in net exports, an expansion in demand, a contractionary monetary policy, and hence rising interest rates, causing some backflow of capital. Simultaneously the movement in interest rates affects total expenditure and hence imports in the two countries, once more in an equilibrating direction.

While the fixed rate system requires flexible money wages, he notes that flexible (variable) exchange rates implies that *real* wages must be flexible, since any adjustment through exchange rates would affect the terms of trade. This implies, *inter alia*, wages could not be tied to the cost of living under a flexible rate regime (Meade 1951a: 201–3). In general, flexible money wages are not taken for granted here: this is essentially the whole point of the exercise. Price adjustments as a policy measure are defined as "alterations in the general level of prices which are brought about as an act of policy by the authorities . . . expressly in order to exert an influence over the internal or external balance of the country concerned." At the same time, relative prices, in Meade's view, are flexible, and change readily in response to "spontaneous change[s] in productivity or as the result of a change in employment and output leading to an alteration in real labour costs and so, at constant money wage rates, to an alteration in money costs and prices" (Meade 1951a: 151). I interpret this to mean that commodity markets function quite efficiently and competitively; the problem lies in the labor market.

Meade rings the changes on a number of different disturbances, with varying assumptions as to the sums of the marginal propensities to import, which determines whether the transfer can be effected without price changes. The Marshall-Lerner conditions he assumes always to hold. He notes that the adjustment mechanism is somewhat different when the shock is a transfer than when it is a change in tastes for the several commodities. If there is a change in tastes, there must be a change in the terms of trade. If there is a transfer, and the sum of the marginal propensities to import is equal to unity, the transfer is effected with no change in price (as Metzler demonstrated in 1942b). Meade puts it very succinctly: "This may help to explain why in some cases it has been found that equilibrium has been restored without unemployment but with surprisingly little of the 'classical' mechanism of price adjustment" (Meade 1951a: 200n).

The model, as noted, is heavily oriented toward policy discussion, and he is very explicit about delineating alternative policies. A "neutral" economy, in which the authorities do not engage in policy responses, involves fixing the following: the level of public demand for goods and services, the rate of taxation, monetary policy,[10] the exchange rate, the money wage rate and

---

[10] This meant stabilizing the rate of interest. The early years of the debate involving Mundell, Fleming, *et al.* were plagued by misunderstandings and apparently conflicting results, until it

commercial policy (fixed import taxes and export subsidies and no exchange and import controls) (Meade 1951a: 47–9). The question then is, what effect do "spontaneous", that is, exogenous, changes have on the general level of employment, on the balance of trade, and on the capital account?[11]

I shall not attempt to summarize. Meade's full model, as noted above, is a general-equilibrium one, with many variables. It is a two-country model, so that we have feedbacks; there are non-traded goods (like Ohlin, Meade has two traded goods produced at home: exportables and import-substitutes), and elasticities of substitution between factors in production of the two goods, in demand between both home-produced and the import good, in factor supplies to the two home industries. There is a monetary sector, liquidity preference, and demand for foreign securities. The full model is presented in a separate volume, the *Mathematical supplement* (1951b), and there is no attempt at a general solution. The main text consists of a verbal discussion of its several components.

Meade argued that there was a distinction between the effects of fiscal and monetary policy, and even between different kinds of fiscal policy, such as tax changes and expenditure changes, and their differential impact on the balance of payments. He anticipated the assignment problem, for example:

[T]his difference between fiscal and monetary policy is likely to be particularly marked if domestic expenditure is not in fact very sensitive to changes in the rate of interest, i.e. if it needs a very large fall in the rate of interest to induce any required increase in domestic expenditure; for in that case the very large change in interest rates is likely to have a relatively large effect upon foreign lending. (Meade 1951a: 104)

Having said this, however, he proceeded to ignore it and lump fiscal and monetary instruments together into "financial policy for internal balance" which was defined as "the control of total domestic expenditure by fiscal or monetary measures for the purpose of achieving whatever is considered *on domestic grounds* to be the best form of stability of demand for home production and for home employment." Financial policy (fiscal *cum* monetary) when used for external balance involves "the control of total domestic expenditure for the purpose of preventing a deficit or surplus in the balance of payments" (Meade 1951a: 106–7, italics his). He takes great pains to spell out the

was noticed that some writers were referring to a constant interest rate while others had in mind a constant domestic money supply (see Krueger 1965). "[F]ollowing the tradition of British central banking and monetary theory, Meade identified monetary policy with the fixing of the level of interest rates, a procedure that automatically excludes consideration of the monetary consequence of devaluation by assuming them to be absorbed by the monetary authorities" (Johnson 1976: 151).

[11] I believe he was the first to ask the question about the capital account that way, although a number of writers (among them Goschen) had included endogenous changes in the capital account through interest rate variations (without central bank action required to effect this).

differences in the results, depending on whether the financial policy applied is fiscal or monetary, but he stops short of recommending (as Mundell and others did) using them differentially. Thus if internal balance requires expansion and external balance requires contraction there may be a problem, particularly since this is, as noted, a two-country model with foreign repercussions. In this connection, there is some discussion of the problem of coordination or cooperation between countries in their policy. However, in some situations the problem may be intractable regardless of the extent of coordination of policy tools. Thus, for example, if the deficit country is depressed and the surplus country inflated no financial policy combination can bring internal and external balance to both. This is the traditional dilemma case (Meade 1951a: Chapter X, Table X, 117). In such a case, an additional policy tool is required (that is, to repeat, financial policy is a single tool), such as money wage rate changes, exchange rate changes or direct controls.[12]

### The effect of capital mobility

In the first case in which he discusses capital mobility, Meade starts with what resembles the Mundell-Fleming argument. In a flexible rate regime, monetary policy is effective if capital is immobile. With some capital mobility an expansionary monetary policy lowers the interest rate, inducing a capital outflow, which in turn leads to an exchange rate depreciation. The resulting current account surplus (matching the capital outflow) is that which, in the Mundell models, actually stimulates output and employment. Meade does not spell this out, though it is consistent with his analysis. He does worry, however, about the feedbacks, his being a two-country model, and concludes that in the end the marginal propensities to import in the two countries may be inadequate to effect the capital transfer. In this case, country $A$'s terms of trade must deteriorate, "whereas if capital had been completely immobile there would have been no balance-of-payments adjustment necessary at all" (Meade 1951a: 257). Thus, whereas, as we shall see below, capital mobility is a boon in the Mundell-Fleming world, it is a hindrance in Meade's, in this instance at any rate. Note, however, that Meade simply assumed flexible real wages when he described the working of a flexible rate economy. If this assumption does not hold, then the "dilemma" of policy translates, for the flexible exchange rate case, into the possibility that full employment may be incompatible with price stability: if the existing exchange rate is not the

[12] This last comment is of a piece with Meade's famous argument in favor of flexible exchange rates, which was based on the welfare loss resulting from the shrinking trade which would result from direct controls on trade, these probably being often the only feasible alternative, according to Meade, to exchange rate changes (Meade 1955). In the work under consideration here, the argument in favor of flexible exchange rates is more guarded and more conditional.

equilibrium rate at full employment, expansionary financial policy may, in the absence of capital movements, lead to a depreciation of the exchange rate which will threaten domestic price stability. I am not familiar with any discussions of this form of the dilemma during that period, other than Meade's own remark, noted above, that the untrammeled working of a floating rate system implied real wage flexibility. In fact, any sort of stickiness in the ratio of traded to non-traded goods prices would jeopardize price stability in such a model.

If the initial shock is a shift in demand for traded goods (away from country $A$'s exports), the exchange rate will change to clear the commodities market – that is, to shift demand back to $A$'s goods. $A$'s terms of trade will deteriorate, but the whole adjustment will presumably take place in the commodities markets, the exchange rate being the only price to move. Whether capital mobility exists or not makes no difference in this case, according to Meade: in any event capital will not move and interest rates and money supplies in the two countries will not change. Note that this implies that the government accommodates any change in the demand for money occasioned by the shifts involved, including the change in real income implied by the movement of the terms of trade.

Capital mobility aids adjustment where the disturbance is an unrequited transfer (referring, presumably, to the reparations debate). Both countries maintain internal-balance-preserving policies, so the real effects of the transfer are not allowed to take place. "There will be a deficit in $A$'s balance of payments equal to the unrequited transfer, but otherwise everything will be unchanged" (Meade 1951a: 257–8). The payments imbalance will lead to exchange rate and terms of trade changes, which in turn will affect expenditures in the two countries. That is, the currency of $A$, the paying country, will depreciate, its current account will be in surplus, and inflationary pressure will be generated internally. To preserve internal balance the authorities will raise the interest rate (the reverse is happening in $B$, of course), and if capital is mobile it will flow from $B$ to $A$, financing the transfer. (This is what Ohlin was arguing, in 1929a, 1929b, had happened with respect to German reparations.) This is an interesting argument in the light of current concern with intertemporal optimization: the argument would be currently phrased in terms of a country which, faced with an unanticipated one-time payment (such as reparations), decides to borrow currently in order to effect the payment, essentially spreading the payment and consequent reduction in absorption out over a number of years (see the forthcoming work of Adam Klug).

In discussing capital movements (and the desirability of controlling them) Meade distinguishes between different types of capital movements, ranging from direct investment abroad (matched by a reduction in investment at home) through various combinations, to short-term financial movements involving holdings of "idle money" in one or another currency.

A capital transfer from B to A may therefore be directly associated with a fall in domestic expenditure in B ranging from 0 to 100 per cent of the total transfer and it may be directly associated with a rise in domestic expenditure in A ranging again from 0 to 100 per cent of the total transfer, these two percentages being quite independently determined. (Meade 1951a: 292–3)

In the ensuing analysis he assumes that either the capital transfer comes about because of, or concomitant with, a rise in expenditure in the receiving country and a fall in the paying country, or that both countries pursue policy measures which involve such increases and decreases in domestic expenditure as necessary to maintain balanced trade with no exchange rate change. The two assumptions, he argues, are interchangeable, since they yield the same results. The question then is, is there any reason to interfere with such capital movements? He considers several cases: If there is a sudden large movement from B to A, the authorities in the two countries can allow the gold standard "to work itself out with a deflation of demand and so of money wage rates, costs, and incomes in B" and the reverse in A (Meade 1951a: 295); or B can impose exchange controls and restrictions; or one or both countries can sterilize the capital movements. Since the first may require very large and sudden, albeit temporary, real adjustments, and the second a mass of bureaucratic interference, the third, in this situation, is preferable. This may require A's cooperation, since B might run out of A's currency to supply to the speculators (Meade 1951a: 294–6).

The same three alternatives face the respective countries in the case of variable exchange rates, but the analysis differs as between freely floating rates on the one hand and an adjustable peg on the other. If there is an adjustable peg and the speculative capital flight is caused by a correct expectation of devaluation of B's currency, then only strict exchange controls could contain it. Freely fluctuating exchange rates, on the other hand, would not require exchange controls, because the capital flight would cause an immediate depreciation of B's currency. However, since the price effects would be expected to affect the balance of trade slowly, there might be overshooting. (Compare Dornbusch 1980, where the different speeds of adjustment in commodity and capital markets lead to overshooting of exchange rates.) Exchange controls, however, as before, are considered inefficient and bureaucratic; Meade suggests that again the optimum policy might be "official 'counter-speculation'" (Meade 1951a: 296–8).

Regarding non-speculative capital movements, that is to say, long-term transfers, Meade notes that one argument in favor of control drops out: the expectation of imminent reversal of the capital flow is not present, as it is in the case of speculative flows. In considering whether to limit long-term capital exports, thus preventing the deterioration in the terms of trade which, Meade argues, will accompany them, a country needs to consider: (a) the possibility of retaliation (thus, the net, not the gross flows, are what is relevant), (b) the improvement in the terms of trade that will accompany the repayment of the loan, and (c) the higher income which is presumably being earned on the foreign investment and which should be offset against the terms of trade deterioration. In addition to these considerations, an argument in favor of controls obtains if the social return on capital is higher in the capital-exporting country, but the private return is lower because of different "fiscal arrangements" (Meade 1951a: 298–303).

Meade presents an analysis, still timely today, of the difficulty, nay, impossibility, of effecting strict capital controls while leaving current transactions free of all supervision. However, it is technically possible to avoid restricting current transactions, provided that "the exchange control authority is prepared to lay down some arbitrary rules as to what constitutes a current payment and if it is given the power to supervise all foreign payments." It is even possible to have floating exchange rates while controlling capital movements, he argues. This would require complete non-resident convertibility plus the existence of limited funds available to residents for use in forward market speculation (Meade 1951a: 302–3). In practice, sometimes this has taken the form of a pool of funds available for foreign investment, which is one form in which one can engage in exchange rate speculation.

Meade concludes the volume with a discussion of the relative advantages of discrimination and non-discrimination, arguing that there are arguments in both directions, but that a more important issue is whether to use direct controls at all (either discriminatorily or not) to attain external balance, "or whether reliance should not rather be placed upon price adjustment in one form or another. . . The author of this work makes no attempt to conceal his own view that, if possible, reliance should be placed upon measures other than direct controls" (Meade 1951a: 423).

This requires, as conditions, "reasonably successful" internal balance policies in at least the major countries, price rather than quantity adjustments if a country wishes to protect a particular sector, and internationally agreed-upon methods for changing exchange rates, whether free floating or an adjustable peg (Meade 1951a: 424). This last requires that money wage rates "must not be so tied to the cost of living that domestic costs and prices automatically follow the price of imports." And this in turn requires that social justice and equality be achieved through internal policy measures other than wage policies.

The conditions for the successful use of the mechanism of money and prices for the achievement of external balance are . . . not at all easy of achievement. But their attainment is worth the effort. Their absence would make inevitable a perpetual structure of direct trade controls whose only justification was the regulation of international payments; and it will be a chief purpose of Volume II to show *how great can be the wastes of unnecessary obstacles to trade*. (Meade 1951a: 425, italics mine)

By 1955 he was recommending flexible exchange rates, for this very reason (Meade 1955).

## Mundell

Between 1960 and 1963 Robert Mundell and Marcus Fleming (1960) wrote a number of papers which became known as the Mundell-Fleming model. Mundell's work has been reproduced, with at most minor changes, in his book (1968). In my view, Chapter 15, first published in *Kyklos* in 1961, titled "The International Disequilibrium System" best captures the spirit of what the model is about, and places it most aptly in its proper perspective in the development of ideas. It flows most naturally, I think, out of the Metzler headwaters, and it is an elegant statement of what the other models are about. That chapter (as well as the "Preface" to the book) open with a very revealing statement, which I cite:

The fundamental proposition of classical international trade theory, that there is an automatic mechanism ensuring balance-of-payments equilibrium, enabled the classical economists to isolate the short-run, dynamic process of international adjustment from the long-run, static theory of international barter. (Mundell 1968: 217)

We know today that this separation of statical, barter theory from dynamical, monetary theory was carried too far, in the sense that it cannot be maintained, as the classical school seemed to hold it could, that the trade equilibrium established under conditions in which money is used and trade equilibrium reached under conditions of barter are identical. (Mundell 1968: 4)

In my view, he here exaggerates the short-run quality of the classical balance-of-payments theory. Nevertheless, he himself, in the models treated here, does take a very short-run view of adjustment. This is, by the way, a frequent criticism levied at the Mundell-Fleming model. Mundell was himself explicitly aware of this when he wrote the papers (Mundell 1968: 232) but it tended to get lost frequently in subsequent descriptions and applications.

The "Disequilibrium System" is essentially a generalization of the protomodel (see Chapter 1) to include the rate of interest as an endogenous variable (in this sense it approaches, for example, Whale 1937 [1953]). The money supply is changing as long as the balance of payments is not equal to zero, "and to show that the results are not dependent on the quantity theory of money, we assume that a change in the money supply affects the level of effective demand and the balance of payments only insofar as it first affects the rate of interest" (Mundell 1968: 219). This is very close to the path of adjustment we found above in Meade. Positing a simple model of three markets, we have equilibrium in the markets for goods, for foreign exchange, and for money depending on real income and the rate of interest. The dynamic adjustment process may be unstable; even if "all signs are 'normal', stability depends . . . on the relative speeds of response in the three markets and on the banking reserve ratio" (Mundell 1968: 221). The important point, however, is that the equilibrium exists, and it exists independently of the assumption of price flexibility. So long as, for one reason or another, the balance of payments depends on the level of expenditures, expenditures depend on the quantity of money, and the money supply on the balance of payments, there will be an equilibrium combination of payments balance, money supply, and rate of interest. This is as true in what he calls the "*income-specie-flow* mechanism of Keynes" as it is in the Hume price-specie flow.

The question manifestly is at what level of income the goods market is equilibrated at this balance-of-payments equilibrium. Which is again another way of stating the famous dilemma. Mundell turns the story around a little in the telling, but this does not change it. The equilibrium will be blocked if, either "automatically" or by discretion, the impact of the gold or foreign exchange flow on the domestic money supply is thwarted or sterilized, in brief if the money supply is not really endogenous, or in Mundell's words, if "the monetary authorities . . . divorce the money supply from the balance of payments" (Mundell 1968: 225). Mundell spells out the dilemma: depression and a payments deficit, or inflation with a surplus. In these cases the policy designed to achieve internal equilibrium will only exacerbate the foreign payments imbalance.

What saves the day here is the mobility of capital, international trade in financial assets. It is for this reason that I have drawn the line from Metzler to Mundell, although Metzler did not deal with policy questions, having assumed full employment with flexible prices. Assume that international capital flows are also a function of the rate of interest. This means that while total expenditures affect demand for goods, both domestic and foreign, in the same keynesian way, the interest rate has a differential effect. It influences the balance of trade both indirectly through expenditures and *hence* the marginal propensity to import (the simple keynesian approach) and additionally directly through the capital account. It is precisely this which is to give fiscal and monetary policy tools differential effects on the trade balance. We shall have statements analogous to the statement of comparative advantage in real trade theory: the ratio between the effectiveness of fiscal policy (expenditures) and monetary policy (the rate of interest) is different for home expenditures than the ratio of their relative effectiveness in maintaining foreign balance equilibrium. Mundell calls this "assignment" of policy tools according to their comparative advantage the "principle of effective market classification". It is, as he notes, an extension and addendum to Tinbergen's well-publicized dictum (itself a special case of a basic theorem in linear algebra) "that to attain a given number of independent targets there must be at least an equal number of instruments." The extension is necessary because Tinbergen's rule, he says, is about the existence of equilibrium, not its dynamic stability (Mundell 1968: 169–70; 239).

Thus, in the case of Britain in 1957, a contractionary monetary policy could have restrained a capital outflow and improved the balance of payments; it would also depress domestic expenditures. But if combined with an expansionary fiscal policy, the monetary contraction, the higher interest rate, would attract foreign capital to finance the trade imbalance caused by the higher expenditure. Result: overall payments equilibrium, at least in the short run.

The other papers are similar in tone and in spirit. They spell out the dynamics of the adjustment and the appropriate policy mixes under both fixed and flexible exchange rate regimes, both for small countries and for two-country models. Not surprisingly, but very agreeably, the fixed and flexible rate cases turn out to be perfect duals of one another. Thus, if capital is less than perfectly mobile, with fixed exchange rates, as we have seen, full employment can be achieved by an expansionary fiscal policy; the resulting trade deficit is then financed by a capital inflow induced by a tight monetary policy. If capital mobility is perfect, the tight money policy is unnecessary: the pressure on interest rates imposed by the expansionary fiscal policy will induce the capital inflow required to finance the deficit and satisfy the higher demand for cash balances on the part of the public.

Under flexible rates, on the other hand, an expansionary monetary policy increases income while a contractionary fiscal policy offsets the downward pressure on interest rates, inducing the inflow necessary to finance the current account deficit resulting from the income increase. When capital mobility is perfect, the second policy tool again becomes redundant; expansionary monetary policy itself will improve income by inducing a capital outflow and exchange depreciation, with the ensuing improvement in the balance of trade stimulating domestic income. (See Flanders 1974 for an elaboration of some of the implications of this process.)

The model has had a wide popularity and long ascendancy despite the fact that many users of the approach often forgot Mundell's own admonitions:

In the first place the deficit has been cured by borrowing, usually a temporary solution. And second, the domestic rate of investment is lower (because the rate of interest is higher) . . . a factor that may conflict with the policy aim of maximizing the rate of growth of the private sector of the economy. (Mundell 1968: 232)

## Comments and summary

Meade did not go as far as Mundell, Fleming and others, in that he did not separate fiscal and monetary policy into two distinct tools, so any additional tools had to consist of various unsavory wage and price controls, changes in commercial policy, or exchange controls. There are those today who feel that he was right, in the sense that there may not really be two independent tools, or, more generally, that there is a shortage of tools when matched up against goals. Nor was he as sanguine about the ease and smoothness of capital movements as the Mundell-Fleming tradition (if not their authors) implied. Further, he was taking, I think, a longer-run view than the Mundell-Fleming models did, Mundell's caveat to the contrary notwithstanding. His model is fuller and richer, in that the Mundell-Fleming story is one of a strictly fixprice world, whereas Meade builds flexible relative prices and changeable (through policy) price and wage levels. Mundell takes the degree of capital mobility as a given; Meade considers the desirability of either capital controls or various forms of counter-speculation, as did Keynes, to change it, generally to decrease it.

Metzler, as I have argued, is quite different in that his is not at all a policy model. His place in this group comes from the fact that he opened the way to handle endogenous capital flows and to reinstate monetary considerations in the balance-of-payments literature.

The Mundell-Fleming model (or models) has proved to be a little like the famous *IS-LM* diagram from which, in a sense, it sprang; everybody criticizes it but everybody uses, and, especially, teaches it. It has proved a hardy work-horse. Criticisms began to be raised soon after it appeared, regarding its short-term nature, which Mundell himself recognized; the problem of its sustainability in terms of the balance-of-payments effects of repayments and of debt servicing; the questions of the true independence of tools; the appearance of new, quasi-institutional constraints, such as the apparent robustness of inflation even at less than satisfactorily high levels of employment; the proliferation of goals, such as growth rates (again recognized by Mundell).

Today it is being attacked on three fronts: first, its short-term nature and lack of micro-foundations in terms of intertemporal optimization (see Frenkel and Razin 1987); second in terms of its neglect of expectational factors, particularly in the present era of floating exchange rates; and third on the question of the consistency of the goals and plans of the several countries, a subject that is gaining increasing, and increasingly sophisticated, attention. Nevertheless, it is still found by many people to be a useful starting point. I classify it as a confluence because it merges the F and P streams, the policy orientation with the positive, equilibrium, analysis.

In a sense, the recent interest in intertemporal optimization has given the Mundell-Fleming model and its derivatives a new lease. A few years ago we were prone to dismiss as hopelessly short term any model which implied perpetual borrowing; today, though for different reasons than those set forth in the Mundell-Fleming models, this is no longer true.

I end with the MMM stream because it did constitute a takeoff point, both in time and in analytical style, into the present. It brought money back into the story, after its relative neglect during the keynesian preoccupation with multipliers. It also brought back capital mobility, as wholly endogenous or at least amenable to government policy measures. This in turn prepared the ground for the movement toward portfolio analysis, asset choices, and stock adjustments. From this it was a short step to the monetary approach to the balance of payments and from there into the 1970s and 1980s.

# Ex post

I have done. A summing up is considered in order. A waggish colleague on reading my Introduction proposed that it should come at the end. A flippant solution therefore would be to suggest to the reader to return now to Chapter 1, in the hope that my intentions will be clearer. I can draw no conclusions as such, nor can I summarize what I have written.

A brief afterword must therefore serve, in part, as a confessional. First, a guilty mention of those whom I have not (for various reasons) included, except perhaps in briefest passing. The list includes the following: Bastable; Beach; Bresciani-Turroni; Cassel; Cairnes; Fisher; Goschen; Gregory; Johnson; Mosak; Pigou; Wicksell; Yntema. The German and French economists have probably not received their due.

Topics I have not dealt with extensively include devaluation, and hence the work of Alexander, Harberger, Stuvel, Tsiang. The development and controversy over the purchasing power parity doctrine is not here; nor is the Keynes-Ohlin controversy on the transfer problem. Nor the discussions of the 1950s as to the permanence of the dollar shortage, nor those of the 1960s about the "adequacy of international liquidity". Nor the debates involving the optimum exchange rate regime, including the still timely issue of the optimum currency area, the optimum fixed exchange rate constellation.

The choice of which writers to include was difficult. I made it on the basis of my own interest and, I dare to hope, the reader's, the originality of the work, its importance or seminal nature, or, in some cases precisely its failure to have achieved the widespread recognition which I felt was deserved. I lay claim to no revisionist revelations. More modestly, I have tried to write a simple history of the development of ideas during a period not so very long ago, but far enough into the past that young professionals and their graduate students no longer read them. I think it rather wasteful that as a profession we feel the need to rediscover the wheel every generation; we might perhaps progress faster if we were more prone to build on what went before and "stand on the shoulders" of the giants who came before us. (The likely retort to this is that various ideas have died precisely because they came before their time, either historically or scientifically. There is a literature on the cyclical nature of scientific discovery, summarized by Adam Klug in his forthcoming dissertation.)

In the telling of the tale I have grouped, combined, separated, and distinguished various people and ideas in the way that seemed most sensible and appealing to me. Not everyone would do it that way, or agree with my classifications. As I indicated in Chapter 1, some sort of classification was essential. Though I found the one I adopted very easy and natural, I cannot claim that it is unique. Furthermore, though I have quoted liberally, to let people be heard in their own voices, I have, by editing and selecting, imposed my own evaluations of what was important. I do not apologize for this.

Finally, a few Treppwörter – the words spoken as one goes down the stairs and thinks of what one neglected to say before. They consist of some musings on an appropriate projected research program:

I have placed heavy emphasis throughout on the way various writers, or groups of writers, treated capital movements, trade in assets. In particular, I have paid attention to how they treated short-term capital movements, and why. The reason for this is that my subjects demand it, in my view. The issue of whether there are short-term capital movements, whether they are important, and whether they are endogenous and accommodating or exogenous and often destabilizing – this issue pervades the literature. I have argued that the differences in treatment of this item in the balance of payments are systematic, symptomatic of alternative points of view. To the researcher of formal bent and perhaps a new classical outlook who retorts that none of these things matters, that agents are optimizing and making decisions about alternative allocations of their endowments over time and over space, generally under conditions of certainty or with known expected values of alternative events, I answer: precisely. This is one point of view. Different people at various times and places have had others, and it is these differences which I am describing. It is this, for example, which distinguishes the classical-late classical position from the neoclassical, a distinction between an equilibrium and a disequilibrium view of the mechanism; and, somewhat modified, the distinction between the crisis writers and mainstream keynesian analysis.

However, regarding the highlighting of capital movements, a number of questions yet remain unanswered.

1  Why has it always seemed natural, both within the profession and without, to treat the current and the capital account as the basic modular units of the balance of payments? The question arises naturally, as indicated above, from the distinctions I have made in the book; it came even closer to the forefront of my mind as a result of correspondence I have had with Ronald Jones, which stimulated further thoughts about it. In what sense can the purchase of foreign firms, or the building of foreign subsidiaries, be said to finance a current surplus of exports of manufactured goods over imports of raw materials? More puzzling, what do we say about a situation such as that which characterized the United States' balance of payments during the 1950s and early 1960s, for example, when the current account surplus was

smaller than long-term capital exports, and the resulting overall deficit was financed by short-term capital inflows? Surely here the simple notion of movement of goods and services above the line and movement of a particular factor of production below the line is muddied. And even when there is a simple equality between long-term capital movements and current account imbalances the causality is often reversed, as in the contemplation of the transfer problem, where the capital flow constitutes the exogenous, autonomous shock.

2 Why do we readily simplify the theory of international macroeconomics, at least for pedagogic purposes, by discussing the demand and supply for foreign exchange on the assumption that there is no trade in financial assets? We seldom make the reverse assumption, even for "simplification". Some of the newer literature on intertemporal optimization does something very close to that, by assuming for "simplicity" that there is only one good being traded and the direction of the net flow of goods is the same as that of the net lending; the concept of comparative advantage in production is dispensed with here. But this is considered to be slightly bizarre, in some quarters, and it has certainly not worked its way into the textbooks.

We can carry that one step further. It is common to find models of the balance of payments which seek simplification in the assumption that there simply are no capital flows. I have never seen the reverse. The study of balanced trade in goods is in fact the matter on which "pure" trade theory is based and has been so for 150 years. The analogy, balanced trade in different types of assets, is virtually never treated.

3 Why do we find it so easy and natural to combine short- and long-term capital movements into a "capital" account? Since the balance of payments is drawn up for a specific period, generally a year, a fortuitous imbalance in the current account as of the last day of the period is recorded as a short-term capital movement, considered to be a "financing" or "adjusting" variable, though often no particular specific decision has been taken regarding "capital flows." (This is not wholly fair, since obviously such flows would not occur if we lived in a cash-in-advance world; the point is that the normal granting of short-term trade credit on open account, coupled with the accidents of the calendar, is enough to give rise to "capital flows.") This is quite different in its motivation and decision-making background from either the purchase of foreign short-term financial assets or the acquisition of a portfolio of long-term assets or yet again the purchase or founding of a company abroad.

One of the implications of the above is that the "basic balance of payments," defined as the current account plus long-term capital flows, both direct and portfolio, is in a sense a more meaningful way of looking at the balance of payments than others. But what of short-term financial assets? Much trade in them is certainly "autonomous" and indistinguishable in motive from either commodity trade or long-term capital flows. No economist can be happy with a classification that depends on whether the due date on a financial asset is more or less than one calendar year into the future. Somehow we have two phenomena occurring simultaneously: one is the act of providing financing services and the other is the international movement of a factor of production. Only at a high level of abstraction, in a world of putty-putty capital and long-run equilibrium, are these formally identical.

Real trade theory is based on the assumption that all goods are perfectly mobile and all factors immobile. This implies the definition of equilibrium as a zero balance in the current account, with no capital movements. This was indeed the assumption of trade theory through most of the history of the subject. The assumption has, of course, been challenged from time to time. Ohlin wrote both of international mobility of factors and domestic immobility. In 1929 Williams made this point the core of a trenchant criticism of the pure theory of international trade. Arguing simultaneously for a study of international trade as part of a dynamic theory of growth involving trade between countries at different stages of development and for a recognition that factors of production were often both immobile domestically and mobile internationally, he stated that "the international movement of productive factors has significance relative to comparative prices, incomes, positions of nations, at least equal to that of the trade in goods . . . even today . . . capital movements are discussed mainly in connection with the balancing of payments . . . and . . . not . . . as transfers of productive power" (Williams 1929 [1949: 255]). One of the features of this neglected paper was that it predicted much of the "trade and growth" literature which blossomed in the 1960s, in which the existence and structure of trade was itself a cause of increase in a country's capital stock and a change in the rate of growth.

There have been arguments, as I noted in the text (for example the diametrically opposed casual empiricism of Keynes and Ohlin), over whether changes in the capital account tend to dominate or whether it is changes in the current account which lead to capital account changes. Which, in a general-equilibrium model and a general-equilibrium world, is more likely to be the disturbance and which part of the adjustment? In recent years we heard similar arguments about whether the exchange rate drove the current account or "depended on" it.

4  Why have economists been so nearly unanimous for two hundred years about the desirability of relatively free trade in goods and services and so much less united in their objections to capital controls? Turn the question

around: What can we obviously say about the advantages of international trade in goods that we cannot say equally obviously about international trade in capital, in terms of world optimum allocation of resources both over space and over time? The answer must clearly be: nothing. And yet, why was Keynes, *inter alia*, much more willing to condone, or advocate, controls on capital movements than on commodity trade? Few economists or public figures will argue that a particular country has opened itself to trade too much. But we often hear that a country has imported too much capital. Or exported too much capital. And can both exports AND imports of capital be BAD?

There are two fundamentally separate types of argument in favor of controlling or limiting international capital flows. The first type is that discussed above, involving either the correction of distortions of one kind or another, or an argument analogous to the optimum tariff position. In terms of long-term portfolio or direct investment, arguments about importing too much capital extend all the way from the contemporary discussion about the optimal level of foreign debt to the semi-political issue of "foreign control" when there is direct investment. We have examples aplenty in recent years of governments telling home offices that their subsidiaries abroad may or may not sell certain goods to particular buyers, or even pay taxes in the host country. If we add to this the distinction between national product and domestic product, and remember that profits tend to be repatriated, and that profits may be a high percentage of value added in many cases of direct foreign investment, even if transfer pricing is done totally "fairly", then it may be easier to understand why some countries wish to limit foreign incursions. Add further the idea that foreigners will invest to maximize relatively short-term profits whereas home investment could be directed to maximizing the rate of growth, for example. These arguments frequently combine with marxist notions of control in society being associated with control of the means of production (or communication, for example) resulting in often strident objections to almost all foreign investment.

If it is undesirable to import capital under certain circumstances, what is the argument for limiting capital exports? Here we must be on different ground. If Harrod and White argued that Britain and France respectively exported too much capital in the nineteenth century, and if it is argued that the United States did the same in the 1950s and 1960s, this must rest on something else. If British capital could earn more abroad than at home, why not? The only plausible reasons involve some sort of market failure, such as: a bias in institutions or taxation that drives capital overseas even at lower rates of return; unemployment at home, so the real cost of the labor employed by the extra capital is zero; externalities such that the social return on investment at home is higher than the private return.

Externalities, distortions, and market failure play a major role in a spate of recent writing on the subject, triggered by Tobin (1978), in favor of limiting (primarily short-term) financial capital flows; Tobin's suggestion involved a uniform (across country) tax on all foreign currency conversions, thus particularly penalizing short-term capital flows. These arguments, focusing as they do on distortions, are analogous to the distortions arguments (proposed by Haberler and developed further by Bhagwati) for trade restriction. For a brief but excellent comment on and bibliography of the recent literature in this area (as well as in interesting contribution to it) refer to Tornell (1988). As Tornell puts it, what is common to all of these arguments is the presumption that "factors other than fundamentals are the driving force in financial markets." Rumors and "news", expectation of increased taxes on earnings on assets (including expropriation), fear of capital controls in the future, may lead to short-term capital flight (very much like that discussed by the crisis writers). An alternative story (Tornell's) is that the relative irreversibility of investment in physical capital, compared with that in financial assets, imposes an additional bias against real investment. In the face of expectation of tax increases, the bias in favor of investment in foreign (untaxed and reversible) financial assets is strengthened. Taxation or other limitations on the acquisition of such assets is a second-best corrective to this distortion.

5 In a wholly different vein, why is it argued that a high degree of capital mobility makes it difficult for a country to engage in an independent monetary policy? What would a country want that it needs to get by an independent monetary policy? With perfect markets, zero inflation, and no unemployment anywhere, any "policy" is presumably unnecessary, so independence in policy is vacuous. There must, therefore, be something else involved, some sort of disequilibrium.

Here is a hypothesis to try on. Most policy-makers and economists feel sufficiently confident that transport costs, market imperfections, product differentiation, differences in business organization, all constitute barriers between countries so that even "free trade" will not equalize the returns to factors of production. (There are a few exceptions: economists who favor tariffs and protectionism precisely because they take factor-price equalization seriously and fear that the North will be impoverished by free trade with the South.) Financial assets, on the other hand, are becoming increasingly homogeneous; transport and transactions costs in them are rapidly shrinking. It follows that, under any kind of exchange rate regime, maintaining an "independent" monetary policy is becoming increasingly difficult, virtually impossible, if capital flows are uncontrolled. Economists and policy-makers who still believe that some sort of macroeconomic policy is "necessary" or desirable will, if forced, opt for some sort of limitation on capital flows which enable a country to pursue such a policy. The totally committed non-interventionist will have no problem.

I argue, therefore, that there are two issues involved in attitudes toward capital mobility. One is the position taken on genuine foreign investment. The optimal solution for the world is that interest rates be equal everywhere. But, analogous to the optimal tariff argument, there may be a gain to maintaining a difference (this was the Jones and Kemp argument). There may be external effects of domestic investment that argue for exporting less capital than this would imply (Harrod, White). There may be political reasons for importing less capital (also involved with the dynamics of optimum growth policy) than the "optimal".

But these arguments for limiting the movement of capital as a factor of production are historically and conceptually different from the attitude toward capital flows that involves monetary policy and its independence. Here are quotations from two famous antagonists, Keynes and Hayek, both supporting my point.

First, Hayek, discussing

the differentiation between moneys of different degress of acceptability or liquidity, the existence of a structure consisting of superimposed layers of reserves of different degrees of liquidity, which makes the movement of short term money rates, and in consequence the movement of short term funds, much more dependent on the liquidity position of the different financial institutions than on changes in the demand for capital for real investment. It is because with "mixed" national monetary systems the movements of short term funds are frequently due, not to changes in the demand for capital for investment, but to changes in the demand for cash as liquidity reserves, that short term international capital movements have their bad reputation as causes of monetary disturbances. And this reputation is not altogether undeserved. (Hayek 1937: 62)

And Keynes noted that because the current account (foreign investment) must equal the capital account (which he called foreign lending):

it has been assumed that no serious problem presents itself . . . All this, however, neglects the painful, and perhaps violent, reactions of the mechanism which has to be brought into play in order to force *net* foreign lending and *net* foreign investment into equality . . . If, therefore, a country adopts an international standard, it is a question just how international it wishes to be. (Keynes 1930 II: 319)

And in the pre-Bretton Woods writing, when he was most vociferously plumping for controls on capital movements, he was also supporting "genuine new investment." But "[f]loating and liquid funds" other than trade acceptances and other funds involved in current banking business "shall only be lent and borrowed between central banks" (Keynes 1940–4 [1980: 54]).

For a while, as we know, the idea was current that floating exchange rates extricated one from this "trap" and that a country could have its own monetary policy if it would only let the exchange rate go. Milton Friedman championed flexible exchange rates on this ground, very persuasively, in a model in which there were no capital flows (Friedman 1953). And I submit that much of the disappointment which developed over the years with a flexible rate regime stemmed from unrealistic expectations because not much thought had been given, seriously, to the implications of very mobile capital in a flexible rate world, particularly one in which full employment and price stability were two goals rather than one (see Flanders 1974). Both the United States in the early 1980s and Britain in the late 1980s are examples of the problems involved in trying to pursue an "independent monetary policy" in the face of flexible rates and mobile capital.

To sum up briefly I am suggesting, as a research program, exploration of the idea that there are various reasons for the historical distinction between capital flows and current account flows in balance-of-payments modelling and policy alike. Part of it has to do with the idea that some capital flows originate in the need to provide temporary financing of imbalances. Part of it has to do with the economic-political aspects of "foreign ownership", part with the idea of keeping one's resources "at home" to stimulate growth. And part, in a narrow macro policy sense, stems from unwillingness to accept a common world interest rate because this limits the governments' ability to exercise an independent monetary policy; still operative today is Keynes's old idea that the interest rate (and money supply) compatible with full employment is different in different economies.

Note that if all interference with capital flows is excluded except that which emanates from the second-best arguments, we are still left holding the bag of the inability of a country to carry out independent monetary policy in a world with perfectly integrated capital markets. This is by no means necessarily a "bad thing" but the consequences should be spelled out and faced up to.

We know that for the world as a whole, the optimum economy is the world, with all trades permitted over time and space. Without factor immobility of some sort there would be no theory of international trade. Given this constraint, free trade in goods is best for the world as a whole. In the Heckscher-Ohlin world free trade in goods is as good as mobility of factors: the final result is the same. In a Ricardian world it is a second best – perfect factor mobility would yield a higher world income than free trade. Given the constraint, free trade is the best that can be accomplished. Why is trade in capital, the perfect mobility of one factor, not optimal for the world? The answer must be that it is optimal. This conclusion is independent, I would argue, of the definition of capital. If it is one of two factors of production, free trade in capital restores the capital/labor ratio to what it would be if both factors were mobile. If we think of the trade in capital as equalizing the rate of time preference worldwide and the rate of return to new investment, it again is optimal. Does this mean that any remaining argument in favor of interference is (a) irrational, (b) purely political, (c) an optimal tariff argument, (d) a consequence of a struggle to redistribute income within a country, (e) justified only by market imperfection? The answer is, I think, yes: most, if not all of the above.

# Bibliography

Alesina, Alberto and Guido Tabellini (1988), "Credibility and politics," *European economic review*, Volume 32, March, Number 2/3, 542–50.

Alexander, Sidney S. (1952), "Effects of a devaluation on a trade balance," International Monetary Fund *Staff papers*, Volume II, April, 263–78.

Angell, James W. (1922), "International trade under inconvertible paper," *Quarterly journal of economics*, Volume XXXVI, May, 359–412.

Angell, James W. (1926), *The theory of international prices; history, criticism and restatement*, Cambridge, Mass: Harvard University Press.

Angell, James W. (1928), "Equilibrium in international trade: the United States 1919–26," *Quarterly journal of economics*, Volume XLII, May, 388–433.

Ashton, T. S. and R. S. Sayers, Eds. (1953), *Papers in English monetary history*, Oxford: Clarendon Press.

Backus, David K. and Patrick J. Kehoe (1987), "Trade and exchange rate dynamics in a dynamic competitive economy," Queen's University Discussion Paper Number 684, April.

Bagehot, Walter (1873), *Lombard Street: A description of the money market*, London: Henry S. King and Company.

Barro, Robert J. (1986), "Recent developments in the theory of rules versus discretion," *The economic journal*, Volume 96, Supplement, "Conference papers," 23–37.

Barsky, Robert B. and Lawrence H. Summers (1985), "Gibson's Paradox and the gold standard," Harvard Institute of Economic Research, Discussion Paper Number 1175, July.

Bastable, C. F. (1889), "On some applications of the theory of international trade," *Quarterly journal of economics*, Volume IV, October, 1–17.

Bernholz, Peter (1982), "Flexible exchange rates in historical perspective," Princeton: *Princeton studies in international finance*, Number 49, International Finance Section, Princeton University.

Bickerdike, C. F. (1920), "The instability of foreign exchange," *Economic journal*, Volume XXX, March, 118–22.

Black, Fischer (1970), "Banking and interest rates in a world without money: The effects of uncontrolled banking," *Journal of bank research*, Volume 1, Number 3, Autumn, 9–20.

Blaug, Mark (1985), *Economic theory in retrospect*, 4th Edition, Cambridge University Press.

Bloomfield, Arthur I. (1950), *Capital imports and the American balance of payments, 1934–1939: a study in abnormal international capital transfers*, Chicago: University of Chicago Press.

Bloomfield, Arthur I. (1959), *Monetary policy under the international gold standard, 1880–1914*, New York: Federal Reserve Bank of New York.

Bloomfield, Arthur I. (1963), "Short-term capital movements under the pre-1914 gold standard," Princeton: *Princeton studies in international finance*, Number 11, International Finance Section, Princeton University.

Bloomfield, Arthur I. (1968a), "Patterns of fluctuation in international investment before 1914," Princeton: *Princeton studies in international finance*, Number 21, International Finance Section, Princeton University.

Bloomfield, Arthur I. (1968b), "Rules of the game of international adjustment," in C. R. Whittlesey and J. S. G. Wilson, Eds., *Essays in money and banking in honour of R. S. Sayers*, Oxford: Clarendon Press, 26–46.

Board of Governors, Federal Reserve System (1947), *International monetary policies*, Postwar Economic Studies, Number 7, September, Washington.

Bordo, Michael David (1983), "Some aspects of the monetary economics of Richard Cantillon," *Journal of monetary economics*, Volume 12, Number 2, August, 235–58.

Bordo, Michael David (1984), "The gold standard: the traditional approach," in Bordo and Schwartz, Eds., 23–120.

Bordo, Michael D. and Anna J. Schwartz, Eds. (1984), *A retrospective on the classical gold standard, 1821–1931*, Chicago and London: The University of Chicago Press.

Bowley, Marian (1973), *Studies in the history of economic theory before 1870*, London: Macmillan.

Bresciani-Turroni, Costantino (1932), *Inductive verification of the theory of international payments*, Cairo.

Bresciani-Turroni, Costantino (1937), *The economics of inflation: a study of currency depreciation in post-war Germany 1914–1923*, London: George Allen & Unwin.

Brown, A. J. (1942), "Trade balances and exchange stability," *Oxford economic papers*, Number 6, April, 57–75.

Brown, William Adams Jr. (1940), "The international gold standard reinterpreted 1914–1934" (2 volumes), New York: National Bureau of Economic Research.

Buiter, Willem H. and Richard C. Marston, Eds. (1985), *International economic policy coordination*, Cambridge University Press.

Butlin, N. G., A. Barnard and J. J. Pincus (1982), *Government and capitalism: public and private choice in twentieth century Australia*, Sydney: George Allen & Unwin.

Cairnes, J. E. (1874), *Some leading principles of political economy newly expounded*, London: Macmillan.

Cameron, Rondo (1961), *France and the economic development of Europe, 1899–1914*, Princeton: Princeton University Press.

Canada, Dominion of (1923), Joint report of the Canadian Delegates to the Genoa Conference for the Economic and Financial Reconstruction of Europe, presented in Ottawa, 1922. Sessional Paper Number 35, Sessional Papers volume 6, second session of the Fourteenth Parliament.

Cannan, Edwin (1925), *The paper pound of 1797–1821: A reprint of the Bullion Report, Report from the select committee on the high price of gold bullion, 1810,* reprinted with an introduction by Edwin Cannan, Second edition, London: P. S. King and Son, Ltd.

Capie, Forrest and Alan Webber (1985), *A monetary history of the United Kingdom, 1870–1951, Volume I – Data, Sources, Methods*, London: George Allen & Unwin.

Cassel, Gustav (1916a), *Germany's power of resistance*, New York: Jackson Press.

Cassel, Gustav (1916b), "The present situation of the foreign exchanges," *Economic journal*, Volume XXVI, Number 101, 62–5.

Cassel, Gustav (1916c), "The present situation of the foreign exchanges," *Economic journal*, Volume XXVI, Number 103, 319–23.

Cassel, Gustav (1917), "The depreciation of gold," *Economic journal*, Volume XXVII, Number 107, 346–54.

Cassel, Gustav (1918), "Abnormal deviations in international exchanges," *Economic journal*, Volume XXVIII, Number 112, 413–15.

Cassel, Gustav (1920), "Memorandum on the world's monetary problems," International Financial Conference, Brussels, *Documents of the conference*, V. Reprinted in Cassel (1921).

Cassel, Gustav (1921), *The world's monetary problems; two memoranda*, London: Constable.

Cassel, Gustav (1922), *Money and foreign exchange after 1914*, London: Constable.

Cassel, Gustav (1936 [1966]), *The downfall of the gold standard*, Oxford: The Clarendon Press, 1936; New York: A. M. Kelley; London: Frank Cass, 1966.

Caves, Richard E. (1978), "Bertil Ohlin's contribution to economics," *Scandinavian journal of economics*, Volume 80, Number 1, 86–99.

Caves, Richard E. and Harry G. Johnson, Eds. (1968), *Readings in international economics*, Homewood, Illinois: Richard D. Irwin, for The American Economic Association.

de Cecco, Marcello (1984), *The international gold standard: money and empire*, New York: St Martin's Press, first edition, 1974. Italian, 1971.

de Cecco, Marcello (1987), "Gold standard," entry in *The new Palgrave: a dictionary of economics*, John Eatwell, Murray Milgate, Peter Newman, Eds., London: Macmillan.

Clark, Colin (1937 [1965]), *National income and outlay*, London: Macmillan; New York: Augustus M. Kelley, Reprint.

Clark, Colin and J. G. Crawford (1938), *The national income of Australia*, Sydney and London: Angus and Robertson.

Clark, Colin (1938), "Determination of the multiplier from national income statistics," *Economic journal*, Volume XLVIII, Number 191, September, 435–48.

Coddington, Alan (1976), "Keynesian economics: the search for first principles," *Journal of economic literature*, Volume XIV, Number 4, December, 1258–73.

Cohen, Daniel (1988), "The management of the developing countries' debt: guidelines and applications to Brazil," *The World Bank economic review*, Volume 2, Number 1, January, 77–103.

Cohen, Daniel and Jeffrey Sachs (1986), "Growth and external debt under risk of debt repudiation," *European economic review*, Volume 30, Number 3, 529–60, and "Comment" by William D. Nordhaus, 561–4.

Copland, Douglas (1934), *Australia in the world crisis. 1929–1933*, New York: Macmillan; Cambridge University Press.

Cowen, Tyler and Randall Kroszner (1987), "The development of the new monetary economics," *Journal of political economy*, Volume 95, Number 3, 567–90.

Cukierman, Alex (1986), "Central bank behavior and credibility: some recent theoretical developments," *Review* of the Federal Reserve Bank of St. Louis, Volume 68, Number 5, May.

Cunliffe Committee (1918), "The interim report of the committee on currency and the foreign exchanges," Command 9182 vii, August, London: HMSO.

Cunliffe Committee (1919), "Final report of the committee on currency and foreign exchanges after the war," Command 464 xiii, December 3, London: HMSO.

Davis, E. G. (1981), "R. G. Hawtrey, 1879–1975," Chapter 7 in D. P. O'Brien and John R. Presley, Eds., *Pioneers of modern economics in Britain*, London: Macmillan, 203–33.

Domar, Evsey (1950), "The effect of foreign investment on the balance of payments," *American economic review*, Volume XL, Number 5, December, 805–26.

Dornbusch, Rudiger (1974), "Real and monetary aspects of the effects of exchange rate changes," in Robert Z. Aliber, Ed., *National monetary policies and the international financial system*, Chicago: University of Chicago Press, 64–81.

Dornbusch, Rudiger (1980), *Open economy macroeconomics*, New York: Basic Books.

Dornbusch, Rudiger and Jacob A. Frenkel (1984), "The gold standard and the Bank of England in the crisis of 1847," in Bordo and Schwartz, Eds., 233–64.

Dow, Sheila C. and P. E. Earl (1981), "Methodology and orthodox monetary policy," Paper presented at the Cambridge Journal of Economics conference on the New Orthodoxy in Economics, Cambridge, June, 1981.

Driffill, John (1988), "Macroeconomic policy games with incomplete information: A survey," *European economic review*, Volume 32, Number 2/3, March, 533–41.

Dutton, John (1984), "The Bank of England and the rules of the game under the international gold standard: new evidence," in Bordo and Schwartz, Eds., 173–95.

Eaton, Jonathan and M. June Flanders (1987), "Metzler on the process of international adjustment: an unfinished classic in international monetary theory," Unpublished: University of Virginia.

Eaton, Jonathan, Mark Gersovitz and Joseph E. Stiglitz (1986), "The pure theory of country risk," *European economic review*, Volume 30, Number 3, 481–513.

Eaton, Jonathan and Lance Taylor (1986), "Developing country finance and debt," *Journal of development economics*, Volume 22, Number 1, 209–65.

*Economic essays in honour of Gustav Cassel, October 20th, 1933*, London: Frank Cass and Co.

Eichengreen, Barry (1985), "International policy coordination in historical perspective: a view from the interwar years," in Buiter and Marston, Eds., 139–78.

Eichengreen, Barry and Richard Portes (1986), "Debt and default in the 1930s: causes and consequences," *European economic review*, Volume 30, Number 3, 599–640.

Ellis, Howard S. (1934), *German monetary theory, 1905–1933*, Cambridge, Mass: Harvard University Press.

Ellis, Howard S. (1941), *Exchange control in central Europe*, Cambridge, Mass: Harvard University Press, Reprinted 1971, Greenwood Press.

Ellis, Howard S. (1943), "Removal of restrictions on trade and capital," in Harris, Ed., 345–59.

Ellis, Howard S. and Lloyd A. Metzler, Eds. (1949), *Readings in the theory of international trade*, Philadelphia: Blakiston for the American Economic Association.

Fama, Eugene F. (1980), "Banking in the theory of finance," *Journal of monetary economics*, Volume 6, Number 1, January, 39–57.

Fama, Eugene F. (1983), "Financial intermediation and price level control," *Journal of monetary economics*, Volume 12, Number 1, July, 7–28, "Comments" by Elhanan Helpman, 29–32 (Conference on Alternative Monetary Standards).

Fanno, Marco (1935), *I transfermineti anormali dei capitali e le crisi*, Torino, Giulio Einaudi, Editore.

Fanno, Marco (1939), *Normal and abnormal international capital transfers*, Studies in Economic Dynamics, Number One, November, Minneapolis: University of Minnesota Press.

Feis, Herbert (1926), "The mechanism of adjustment of international trade balances," *American economic review*, Volume XVI, Number 4, December, 593–609.

Fetter, Frank W. (1965), *Development of British monetary orthodoxy 1797–1875*, Cambridge, Mass: Harvard University Press.

Flanders, M. June (1969), "International liquidity is always inadequate," *KYKLOS*, Volume XXII, Fasc. 3, 519–29.

Flanders, M. June (1974), "Some problems of stabilization policy under floating exchange rates," in George Horwich and Paul Samuelson, Eds., *Trade, stability and macroeconomics; essays in honor of Lloyd Metzler*, New York: Academic Press, 111–27.

Flanders, M. June (1986), "The balance-of-payments adjustment mechanism: the doctrine according to Ohlin," *History of political economy*, Volume 18, Number 2, 237–57.

Fleming, J. Marcus (1962), "Domestic financial policies under fixed and under floating exchange rates," International Monetary Fund *Staff papers*, Volume IX, November, 369–79.

Ford, A. G. (1962), *The gold standard 1880–1914; Britain and Argentina*, Oxford: Clarendon Press.

Fratianni, Michele and Franco Spinelli (1984), "Italy in the gold standard period, 1861–1914," in Bordo and Schwartz, Eds., 405–41.

Frenkel, Jacob A. and Harry G. Johnson, Eds. (1976), "Introductory essay: the monetary approach to the balance of payments, essential concepts and historical origins," *The monetary approach to the balance of payments*, Toronto: University of Toronto Press.

Frenkel, Jacob A. and Assaf Razin (1987), "The Mundell-Fleming model a quarter century later: a unified exposition," International Monetary Fund *Staff papers*, Volume 34, Number 4, December, 567–620.

Friedman, Milton (1953), "A case for flexible exchange rates," in *Essays in positive economics*, Chicago: University of Chicago Press, 157–203.

Gervaise, Isaac (1720 [1954]), *The system or theory of the trade of the world*, London: A. Woodfall, 1720; Baltimore: Johns Hopkins University Press.

Goodhart, Charles A. E. (1984a), *Monetary theory and practice, the U.K. experience*, London: Macmillan.

Goodhart, Charles A. E. (1984b), "Comment" on John Pippenger in Bordo and Schwartz, Eds., 222–6.

Goschen, G. J., Viscount (1861 [1920]), *The theory of the foreign exchanges*, London: Effingham Wilson.

Graham, Frank D. (1921–2), "International trade under depreciated paper. The United States, 1862–79," *Quarterly journal of economics*, Volume 26, February, 220–73.

Graham, Frank D. (1930), *Exchange, prices and production in hyper-inflation: Germany 1920–3*, Volume 1, Princeton: International Finance Section Publications.

Gregory, T. E. (1964), *Selected statutes, documents and reports relating to British banking, 1832–1928*. Selected and with an introduction by T. E. Gregory, New York: Augustus M. Kelley.

Haberler, Gottfried (1937 [1941]), *Prosperity and depression*, first edition 1937, second edition 1939, third edition "enlarged by Part III," 1941, League of Nations. Reprinted in 1946 and 1952 by the United Nations, New York.

Haberler, Gottfried (1947a), "Comments on 'National central banking and the international economy'" by Triffin, in Board of Governors, Federal Reserve System (1947).

Haberler, Gottfried (1947b), "Comment" on Jacques J. Polak, "The foreign trade multiplier," *American economic review*, Volume XXXVII, Number 5, December, 898–906, and joint with Polak, "A restatement," 906–7.

Haberler, Gottfried (1955 [1961]), *A survey of international trade theory*, Special Papers in International Economics, Number 1, 1955, Revised and Enlarged Edition, 1961, Princeton: International Finance Section, Princeton University.

Hansen, Bent (1981), "Unemployment, Keynes, and the Stockholm School," *History of political economy*, Volume 13, Number 2, Summer, 256–77.

Harberger, Arnold C. (1952), "Pitfalls in mathematical model-building," *American economic review*, Volume XLII, Number 5, December, 855–65.

Harris, Seymour E., Ed. (1943), *Postwar economic problems*, New York: McGraw-Hill.

Harris, Seymour E., Ed. (1947), *The new economics: Keynes' influence on theory and public policy*, New York: Alfred A. Knopf.

Harrod, Roy F. (1933), *International economics* (Cambridge Economic Handbooks, Number 8), London: Nisbet; New York: Harcourt Brace and Co.

Harrod, Roy F. (1939), *International economics*, substantially Revised Edition of Harrod (1933), London: Nisbet; Chicago: University of Chicago Press.

Hawtrey, Ralph G. (1919, 1923, 1927, 1950), *Currency and credit*, London: Longmans, Green.

Hawtrey, Ralph G. (1932), *The art of central banking*, London: Longmans, Green, Second Edition, London: Frank Cass, 1962.

Hawtrey, Ralph G. (1933), *The gold standard in theory and practice*, London: Longmans, Green.

Hayek, Friedrich A. (1932 [1984]), "The fate of the gold standard," First published as "Das Shicksal der Goldwährung," in *Deutsche Volkswirt*, February 1932, pages 642–65 and 677–81. Reprinted as Chapter 5, in Hayek, *Money, capital and fluctuations: early essays*, Edited by Roy McCloughry, London: Routledge and Kegan Paul, 118–35.

Hayek, Friedrich A. (1931 [1935]), *Prices and production*, Second Edition, London: George Routledge and Sons.

Hayek, Friedrich A. (1937), *Monetary nationalism and international stability*, London: Longmans, Green.

Hayek, Friedrich A. (1976), *The denationalisation of money*, Hobart Special Paper, London: The Institute of Economic Affairs.

Helpman, Elhanan (1981), "An exploration in the theory of exchange rate regimes," *Journal of political economy*, Volume 89, Number 5, October, 865–90.

Helpman, Elhanan and Assaf Razin (1979), "Towards a consistent comparison of alternative exchange rate systems," *Canadian journal of economics*, Volume XII, Number 3, 394–409.

Henderson, Hubert D. (1943 [1955]), "International economic history of the inter-war period," December 3, 1943, in *The inter-war years and other papers*, Henry Clay, Ed., Oxford University Press.

Hicks, John R. (1953), "An inaugural lecture," *Oxford economic papers*, Volume V, N.S. Number 2, June, 117–35.

Hicks, Sir John (1967), "Thornton's *Paper credit*," Chapter 10 in *Critical essays in monetary theory*, Oxford: Clarendon Press.

Holmes, James M. (1973), "The process of international adjustment under conditions of full employment: A Keynesian view revised," *Journal of political economy*, Volume 81, Number 6, 1407–29.

House of Commons (1922), Accounts and Papers, Comnd. 1667, Great Britain.

Hume, David (1752), "Of the balance of trade," from *Political discourses*, in *David Hume: writings on economics*, Eugene Rotwein, Ed., Madison: University of Wisconsin Press.

International Bank for Reconstruction and Development (1985), *World Development Report*, New York: Oxford University Press.

International Monetary Fund (1977), *The monetary approach to the balance of payments*, Washington, D.C.

Iversen, Carl (1935), *Aspects of the theory of international capital movements*, Copenhagen: Levin and Munksgaard; London: Humphrey Milford, Oxford University Press.

Jastram, Roy W. and E. S. Shaw (1939), "Mr. Clark's statistical determination of the multiplier," *Economic journal*, Volume XLIX, Number 194, June, 358–65.

Johnson, Harry G. (1976), "The monetary approach to balance-of-payments theory," in Frenkel and Johnson, Eds., 146–67. Reprinted from H. G. Johnson, *Further essays in monetary theory*, London: George Allen & Unwin, 1972.

Jones, Ronald W. (1967), "International capital movements and the theory of tariffs and trade," *Quarterly journal of economics*, Volume LXXXI, Number 1, February, 1–38.

Jones, Ronald W. (1968), "Monetary and fiscal policy for an economy with fixed exchange rates," *Journal of political economy*, Volume 76, Number 4, Part II, July/August, 921–43.

Jones, Ronald W. (1970), "The Transfer Problem Revisited," *Economica*, Volume 37, Number 146, May, 178–84.

Jones, Ronald W. (1975), "Presumption and the transfer problem," *Journal of international economics*, Volume 5, Number 3, August, 263–74.

Jones, Ronald W. (1976), "Terms of trade and transfers: the relevance of the literature," in D. Leipziger, Ed., *The international monetary system and the developing nations*, Washington, 99–114.

Kalecki, Michal (1934 [1971]), "On foreign trade and 'domestic exports'," in Polish, source unknown, translated and published in *Studies in the theory of business cycles, 1933–1939*, Oxford: Basil Blackwell (1967), and in *Selected essays on the dynamics of the capitalist economy, 1933–1970*, Cambridge University Press, 15–25.

Kemp, Murray (1966), "The gain from international trade and investment: a neo-Heckscher-Ohlin approach," *American economic review*, Volume LVI, Number 4, Part I, September, 788–809.

Kenen, Peter B. (1960), *British monetary policy and the balance of payments, 1951–1957*, Cambridge, Mass: Harvard University Press.

Kenen, Peter B. (1986), *Financing, adjustment, and the International Monetary Fund*, Washington: Brookings Institution.

Keynes, John Maynard (1913 [1971]), *Indian currency and finance, Collected writings*, Volume I, Elizabeth Johnson, Ed., London: Macmillan.

Keynes, John Maynard (1920–2 [1977]), *Treaty revision and reconstruction, Collected writings*, Volume XVII, Elizabeth Johnson, Ed., London: Macmillan.

Keynes, John Maynard (1922–9 [1981]), Testimony before the Committee on the Currency and Bank of England Note Issues, *Collected writings*, Volume XIX, Chapter 4, "The return to gold and foreign lending," 238–356. Chapter 5, "The economic consequences of Mr Churchill," Donald Moggridge, Ed., London: Macmillan.

Keynes, John Maynard (1923), *A tract on monetary reform*, London: Macmillan.

Keynes, John Maynard (1929–31 [1981]), *Activities 1929–1931; rethinking employment and unemployment policies, Collected writings*, Volume XX, Donald Moggridge, Ed., London: Macmillan, Cambridge University Press.

Keynes, John Maynard (1929a [1949]), "The German transfer problem," *Economic journal*, Volume XXXIX, Number 153, March, 1–7, reprinted in Ellis and Metzler, Eds., 161–9.

Keynes, John Maynard (1929b), "A rejoinder to 'The reparation problem: a discussion,' by Professor B. Ohlin," *Economic journal*, Volume XXXIX, Number 154, June, 179–82.

Keynes, John Maynard (1929c), "A reply to a criticism on 'Mr. Keynes' views on the transfer problem,' by J. Rueff," *Economic journal*, Volume XXXIX, Number 155, September, 404–8.

Keynes, John Maynard (1930), *A treatise on money*, Two volumes, London: Macmillan.

Keynes, John Maynard (1931), *The international gold problem*, London.

Keynes, John Maynard (1931 [1972]), *Essays in persuasion, Collected writings*, Volume IX, Elizabeth Johnson *et al.*, Eds., Chapter III, 5, "The Economic Consequences of Mr Churchill" (1925), London: Macmillan.

Keynes, John Maynard (1936), *The general theory of employment, interest and money*, London: Macmillan.

Keynes, John Maynard (1940–4 [1980]), *Activities 1940–1944; shaping the post-war world: the Clearing Union, Collected writings*, Volume XXV, Donald Moggridge, Ed., London: Macmillan, Cambridge University Press.

Keynes, John Maynard (1941–6 [1980]), *Activities 1941–1946, shaping the post-war world, Bretton Woods and reparations, Collected writings*, Volume XXVI, Donald Moggridge, Ed., London: Macmillan, Cambridge University Press.

Kindleberger, Charles P. (1937), *International short-term capital movements*, New York: Columbia University Press. Reprinted by Augustus M. Kelley, New York, 1965.

Kindleberger, Charles P. (1943), "International monetary stabilization," in Harris, Ed., 375–95.

Kindleberger, Charles P. (1950), *The dollar shortage*, New York: Technology Press of Massachusetts Institute of Technology.

Kindleberger, Charles P. (1968), *International economics*, 4th Edition, Homewood: Richard D. Irwin.

Kindleberger, Charles P. (1978), *Manias, panics, and crashes: a history of financial crises*, New York: Basic Books.

Kindleberger, Charles P. (1984), *A financial history of Western Europe*, London: George Allen & Unwin.

Kindleberger, Charles P. and Jean-Pierre Laffargue, Eds. (1982), *Financial crises: theory, history, and policy*, Cambridge University Press.

Krueger, Anne O. (1965), "The impact of alternative government policies under varying exchange systems," *Quarterly journal of economics*, Volume LXXIX, Number 2, May, 195–208.

Krueger, Anne O. (1969), "Balance-of-payments theory," *Journal of economic literature*, Volume VII, Number 1, March, 1–26.

Laidler, David (1987), "English classical monetary economics in the 1870's," Undated ms. University of Western Ontario.

Latsis, Spiro J., Ed. (1976), *Method and appraisal in economics*, Cambridge University Press.

League of Nations (1930a), *Selected documents*, Gold delegation.

League of Nations (1930b), *Interim report of the gold delegation of the financial committee*, Geneva, September 8, League of Nations Publications, II, Economic and Financial, 1930.II.26.

League of Nations (1932), *Report of the gold delegation of the financial committee*, Geneva. (C.502.M.243.1932II.A.12).

League of Nations (1944), *International currency experience, lessons of the inter-war period*, Princeton: Princeton University Press. See Nurkse (1944).

Lerner, Abba P. (1944), *The economics of control*, New York: Macmillan.

Lutz, Friedrich (1936), *Das Grundproblem der Geldverfassung*, Stuttgart and Berlin: Kohlhammer.

Machlup, Fritz (1928), "Währung und Auslandsverschuldung", *Miteilungen des Verbandes österreichischer Banken und Bankiers*, Volume 10, 194 ff.

Machlup, Fritz (1932), "Die Theorie der Kapitalflucht," *Weltwirtschaftliches Archiv*, Volume 36, 512–29.

Machlup, Fritz (1939), "Period analysis and multiplier theory," *Quarterly journal of economics*, Volume LIV, November, 1–27.

Machlup, Fritz (1943), *International trade and the national income multiplier*, Philadelphia: the Blakiston Company.

McCloskey, Donald and J. Richard Zecher (1976), "How the gold standard worked, 1880–1913" in Frenkel and Johnson, Eds., 357–85.

Macmillan Committee (1930–1), *Report of the Committee on Finance and Industry*, June 23, Command 3897, London: HMSO.

Macmillan Committee (1931), *Minutes of evidence*, Two volumes, London: HMSO.

Magee, Stephen P. (1975), "Price, incomes, and foreign trade," in Peter B. Kenen, Ed., *International trade and finance: frontiers for research*, Cambridge University Press, 175–252.

Maloney, John (1985), *Marshall, orthodoxy and the professionalisation of economics*, Cambridge University Press.

de Marchi, Neil (1976), "Anomaly and the development of economics: the case of the Leontief Paradox," in Latsis, Ed., 109–27.

Marshall, Alfred (1887 [1926]), "Memoranda and evidence before the Gold and Silver Commission," reprinted in *Official papers*, London: Macmillan for the Royal Economic Society, 17–196.

Marshall, Alfred (1888 [1926]), "Evidence before the Indian Currency Committee," reprinted in *Official papers*, London: Macmillan for the Royal Economic Society, 263–326.

Meade, James E. (1948), "National income, national expenditure and the balance of payments, part I," *Economic journal*, Volume LVIII, Number 232, December, 483–505.

Meade, James E. (1949), "National income, national expenditure and the balance of payments, (continued)," *Economic journal*, Volume LIX, Number 233, March, 17–39.

Meade, James E. (1951a), *The theory of international economic policy, Volume I, The balance of payments*, London: Oxford University Press.

Meade, James E. (1951b), *The theory of international economic policy, Volume I, The balance of payments, mathematical supplement*, London: Oxford University Press.

Meade, James E. (1955), "The case for variable exchange rates," *Three banks review*, Volume 27, September, 3–27.

Metzler, Lloyd Appleton (1942), "Interregional income generation," Ph.D. dissertation, Harvard University.

Metzler, Lloyd A. (1942a [1973]), "Underemployment equilibrium in international trade," *Econometrica*, Volume 10, April, 97–112. Reprinted as Chapter 10 in *Collected papers*, Cambridge, Mass: Harvard University Press.

Metzler, Lloyd A. (1942b [1973]), "The transfer problem reconsidered," *Journal of Political Economy*, Volume L, Number 3, June, 397–414. Reprinted as Chapter 2 in *Collected papers*, Cambridge, Mass: Harvard University Press.

Metzler, Lloyd A. (1947 [1973]), "Exchange rates and the International Monetary Fund," in Board of Governors, Federal Reserve System (1947). Reprinted as Chapter 5 in *Collected papers*, Cambridge, Mass: Harvard University Press.

Metzler, Lloyd A. (1948 [1973]), "The theory of international trade," in Howard S. Ellis, Ed., *A survey of contemporary economics*, Homewood, Illinois: Richard D. Irwin, 210–54. Reprinted as Chapter 1 in *Collected papers*, Cambridge, Mass: Harvard University Press.

Metzler, Lloyd A. (1960 [1973]), "The process of international adjustment under conditions of full employment: a Keynesian view" (Delivered before the Econometric Society, December 1960; reprinted in Caves and Johnson (1968), Chapter 28.) In *Collected papers*, Cambridge, Mass: Harvard University Press.

Mill, John Stuart (1849, 1871, 1909), *Principles of political economy*, 1909 edition by Sir W. J. Ashley, London: Longmans, Green; Reprinted New York: Augustus M. Kelley, 1961.

Mlynarski, Feliks (1931), "The functioning of the gold standard" (Memorandum submitted to the gold delegation of the Financial Committee of the League of Nations), Geneva.

Moggridge, Donald E. (1972), *British monetary policy, 1924–1931: the Norman conquest of $4.86*, Cambridge University Press.

Moggridge, Donald E. (1982), "Policy in the crises of 1920 and 1929," in Kindleberger and Laffargue, Eds., 171–87.

Moggridge, Donald E. (1984), "Comment" on John Pippenger and on John Dutton in Bordo and Schwartz, Eds., 195–8.

Moggridge, Donald E. (1986), "Keynes and the international monetary system, 1909–46," in Jon Cohen and G. C. Harcourt, Eds., *International monetary problems and supply-side economics, essays in honour of Lorie Tarshis*, Basingstoke and London: Macmillan.

Morgenstern, Oskar (1927), "International vergleichended Konjunkturforschung," in *Zeitschrift für die gesamte Staatswissenschaft*, Heft 2.

Morgenstern, Oskar (1959), *International financial transactions and business cycles*, Princeton: Princeton University Press.

Mosak, Jacob L. (1944), *General equilibrium theory in international trade*, Bloomington: Indiana University Press.

Mühlenfels, A. v. (1929), "Internationale Konjunkturzusammenhänge," in *Jahrbücher Nationalökonomie und Statistik*, 130, Band III, Folge 75, I.

Mun, Thomas (1621), *England's treasure by forraign trade*, reprinted in J. R. McCulloch, Ed. (1856), *Early tracts on commerce*, 1952 reprint. Reference in Bowley (1973).

Mundell, Robert A. (1968), *International economics*, New York: Macmillan.

National Monetary Commission, 61st Congress, Second Session, 1910, Senate document number 405, Interviews on the banking and currency systems of England, Scotland, France, Germany, Switzerland, and Italy. Document number 492, The English Banking System by Hartley Withers, Sir R. H. Inglis Palgrave and other writers, Volume 18. Washington: GPO.

Neisser, Hans (1936), *Some international aspects of the business cycle*, Philadelphia: University of Pennsylvania Press.

Neisser, Hans (1946), "The significance of foreign trade for domestic employment," *Social research*, Volume 13, Number 3, September, 307–25.

Neisser, Hans and Franco Modigliani (1953), *National incomes and international trade: a quantitative analysis*, Urbana: University of Illinois Press.

Niehans, Jürg (1968), "Monetary and fiscal policies in open economies under fixed exchange rates: an optimizing approach," *Journal of political economy*, Volume 76, Number 4, Part II, July/August, 893–920.

Nurkse, Ragnar (1933 [1961]), "Causes and effects of capital movements" in Nurkse (1961), 1–21. Originally "Ursachen und Wirkungen der Kapitalbewegungen," *Zeitschrift für Nationalökonomie*, V (1933), 78–96.

Nurkse, Ragnar (1935), *Internationale Kapitalbewegungen*, Vienna: Julius Springer.

Nurkse, Ragnar (1944), *International currency experience, lessons of the inter-war period*, League of Nations, Princeton: Princeton University Press. See League of Nations.

Nurkse, Ragnar (1945 [1949]), "Conditions of international monetary equilibrium," Princeton: *Princeton essays in international finance*, Number 4, Spring, International Finance Section, Princeton University. Reprinted in Ellis and Metzler, Eds., 3–34.

Nurkse, Ragnar (1947a [1947, 1961]), "Domestic and international equilibrium," in Nurkse (1961), 41–71, and in Harris, Ed., 264–92.

Nurkse, Ragnar (1947b [1961]), "International policy and the search for economic stability," *American economic review*, Volume XXXVII, Number 2, May, 569–80. In Nurkse (1961), 72–86.

Nurkse, Ragnar (1952 [1961]), "Review" of Meade's *Balance of payments*, *Political science quarterly*, Volume LXVII, Number 4, December, 604–8. In Nurkse (1961), 352–6.

Nurkse, Ragnar (1954 [1961]), "International investment to-day in the light of nineteenth century experience," *Economic journal*, Volume LXIV, Number 256, December, 744–58. In Nurkse (1961), 134–50.

Nurkse, Ragnar (1956 [1961]), "The relation between home investment and external balance in the light of British experience, 1945–1955," *Review of economics and statistics*, Volume XXXVIII, Number 2, May, 121–54. In Nurkse (1961), 151–220.

Nurkse, Ragnar (1961), *Equilibrium and growth in the world economy: economic essays by Ragnar Nurkse*, in Gottfried Haberler and Robert M. Stern, Eds., Cambridge, Mass: Harvard University Press.

O'Brien, D. P., Ed. (1971), "Introduction," *The correspondence of Lord Overstone*, Three Volumes, Cambridge University Press.

Obstfeld, Maurice and Alan C. Stockman (1985), "Exchange-rate dynamics," in Ronald W. Jones and Peter B. Kenen, Eds., *Handbook of international economics*, Volume II, Amsterdam: North-Holland Press, 917–77.

Ohlin, Bertil (1924), *Handelns teori*, Stockholm: Akademisk Avhandling.

Ohlin, Bertil (1929a [1949]), "The reparation problem: a discussion," *Economic journal*, Volume XXXIX, Number 154, June, 172–8, reprinted in Ellis and Metzler, Eds., 170–8.

Ohlin, Bertil (1929b), "A reply to a criticism on 'Mr. Keynes' views on the transfer problem', by J. Rueff; a rejoinder from Professor Ohlin," *Economic journal*, Volume XXXIX, Number 155, September, 400–4.

Ohlin, Bertil (1933a), *Interregional and international trade*, Cambridge, Mass: Harvard University Press.

Ohlin, Bertil (1933b [1978]), "On the formulation of monetary theory," translated from the Swedish by Hans J. Brems and William P. Yohe. From *Ekonomisk Tidskrift*, Volume 35, Number 2, 1933, 45–81. *History of political economy*, Fall, A Bertil Ohlin Symposium, Volume 10, Number 3, Fall, 353–88.

Ohlin, Bertil (1967), *Interregional and international trade*, Cambridge, Mass: Harvard University Press, Revised Edition.

Ohlin, Bertil (1974), "On the slow development of the 'Total Demand' idea in economic theory: reflections in connection with Dr. Oppenheimer's note," *Journal of economic literature*, Volume XII, Number 3, September, 888–96.

Ohlin, Bertil (1981), "Stockholm and Cambridge: four papers on the monetary and employment theory of the 1930s," Otto Steiger, Ed., *History of political economy*, Volume 13, Number 2, Summer, 189–255.

Oppenheimer, Peter (1974), "Non-traded goods and the balance of payments: a historical note," *Journal of economic literature*, Volume 12, Number 3, September, 882–8.

Paish, Frank S. (1936), "Banking policy and the balance of international payments," *Economica*, Volume III, N. S., Number 12, November, 404–22.

Patinkin, Don (1978), "Some observations on Ohlin's 1933 article" (Ohlin 1933b), *History of political economy*, Volume 10, Number 3, Fall, 413–18.

Perlman, Morris (1986), "The bullionist controversy revisited," *Journal of political economy*, Volume 94, 745–62.

Persson, Torsten and Lars E. O. Svensson (1985), "Current account dynamics and the terms of trade: Harberger-Laursen-Metzler two generations later," *Journal of political economy*, Volume 93, Number 1, February, 43–65.

Persson, Torsten (1988), "Credibility of macroeonomic policy: an introduction and a broad survey," *European economic review*, Volume 32, Number 2/3, March, 519–32.

Pippenger, John (1984), "Bank of England operations, 1893–1913," in Bordo and Schwartz, Eds., 203–22.

Polak, Jacques J. (1943 [1949]), "Balance of payments problems of countries reconstructing with the help of foreign loans," *Quarterly journal of economics*, Volume LVII, February, 208–40. Reprinted in Ellis and Metzler, Eds., 459–93.

Polak, Jacques J. (1947), "The foreign trade multiplier," *American economic review*, Volume XXXVII, Number 5, December, 889–97, and "Comment" by Haberler, 898–906. Jointly, "A restatement," 906–7.

Polak, Jacques J. (1950), "An international economic system," *Econometrica*, Volume 18, January, 70–2. See brief comment by H. Neisser, Volume 18, 286.

Polak, J. J. (1954), *An international economic system*, London: George Allen & Unwin.

Pressnell, L.S. (1982), "The sterling system and financial crises before 1914," in Kindleberger and Laffargue, Eds., 148–63.

Reddaway, W. B. (1970), "Was $4.86 inevitable in 1925?" *Lloyd's Bank review*, Number 96, April, 15–28.

Review Committee (1965), "The balance of payments statistics of the United States: a review and appraisal," Report of the review committee for balance of payments statistics to the Bureau of the Budget, Edward M. Bernstein, Chairman, April, Washington: U.S. Government Printing Office.

Ricardo, David (1811 [1951]), "The high price of bullion, a proof of the depreciation of bank notes," in Piero Sraffa, Ed., *The works and correspondence of David Ricardo*, Volume III, *Pamphlets and papers, 1809–1811*, Cambridge University Press, 47–127.

Ricardo, David (1821 [1951]), *Principles of political economy and taxation*, Piero Sraffa, Ed., *The works and correspondence of David Ricardo*, Volume I, Cambridge University Press.

Ricardo, David (1821–3 [1952]), Piero Sraffa, Ed., *The works and correspondence of David Ricardo*, Volume IX, *Letters, July 1821–1823*, Cambridge University Press.

Robertson, Dennis H. (1939), "Mr. Clark and the foreign trade multiplier," *Economic journal*, Volume XLIX, Number 194, June, 354–6. "Comment" by Colin Clark, 356–8.

Robinson, Joan (1937, 1947 [1953]), *Essays in the theory of employment*, New York: Macmillan; reprinted Oxford: Basil Blackwell.

Robinson, Joan (1947 [1949]), "The foreign exchanges," Chapter 1 and "Beggar-my-neighbour remedies for unemployment," Chapter 2, Robinson (1937, 1947

[1953]), reprinted from the 1947 edition, in Ellis and Metzler (1949) 83–158, 393–407.

Rogoff, Kenneth (1987), "Reputational constraints on monetary policy," in *Carnegie-Rochester conference series on public policy*, Volume 26, Spring, Amsterdam: North-Holland, 141–82.

Sachs, Jeffrey D. (1981), "The current account and macroeconomic adjustment in the 1970s," *Brookings papers on economic activity*, Number 1, 201–68; discussion, 269–82.

Sachs, Jeffrey (1982), "The current account in the macroeconomic adjustment process," *Scandinavian journal of economics*, Volume 84, Number 2, 147–59.

Sachs, Jeffrey (1984), "Theoretical issues in international borrowing," Princeton: *Princeton studies in international finance*, Number 54, July, International Finance Section, Princeton University.

Salant, William A. (1941 [1949]), "Foreign trade policy in the business cycle," in C. J. Friedrich and Edward S. Mason, Eds., *Public policy, a yearbook of the Graduate School of Public Administration*, Cambridge, Mass: Harvard University, Graduate School of Public Administration, 208–31. Reprinted in Ellis and Metzler, Eds., 201–28.

Salter, W. E. G. (1959), "Internal and external balance: the role of price and expenditure effects," *Economic record*, Volume XXXV, Number 71, August, 226–38.

Samuelson, Paul A. (1971), "On the trail of conventional beliefs about the transfer problem," in Bhagwati *et al.*, *Trade, balance of payments and growth*, Amsterdam: North-Holland, 327–51. Reprinted in *Collected scientific papers*, Volume 3, Cambridge, Mass: MIT Press, 1972, 374–98.

Samuelson, Paul A. (1982), "Bertil Ohlin: 1889–1979," *Journal of international economics*, Volume 12, January, Supplement, 33–49.

Sargent, Thomas J. and Neil Wallace (1982), "The real-bills doctrine versus the quantity theory: a reconsideration," *Journal of political economy*, Volume 90, Number 6, 1212–36.

Sayers, R. S. (1936 [1970]), *Bank of England operations 1890–1914*, Westport, Connecticut: Greenwood Press.

Sayers, R. S. (1953), "Ricardo's views on monetary questions," in Ashton and Sayers, Eds., 76–95.

Sayers, R. S. (1960), "The return to gold 1925," in L. S. Pressnell, Ed., *Studies in the industrial revolution; presented to T. S. Ashton*, London, University of London: the Athlone Press, 212–327.

Sayers, R. S. (1976), *The Bank of England, 1891–1944*, Three Volumes, Cambridge University Press.

Schacht, Hjalmar (1927), *The stabilization of the Mark*, London: George Allen & Unwin.

Schumpeter, Joseph A. (1959), *History of economic analysis*, New York: Oxford University Press.

Shackle, G. L. S. (1939), "The multiplier in closed and open systems," *Oxford economic papers*, Number 2, May 1929, 135–44.

358     Bibliography

Shackle, G. L. S. (1967), *The years of high theory: invention and tradition in economic thought 1926–1939*, Cambridge University Press (Paperback, 1983).

Simons, Henry C. (1936), "Rule versus authority in monetary policy," *Journal of political economy*, Volume XLIV, Number 1, February, 1–30.

Siven, Claes-Henric (1985), "The end of the Stockholm School," *Scandinavian journal of economics*, Volume 87, Number 4, 577–93.

Skidelsky, Robert (1983), *John Maynard Keynes, volume one, hopes betrayed, 1883–1920*, London: Macmillan.

Smith, Bruce D. (1988), "Legal restrictions, 'sunspots,' and Peel's Bank Act: the real bills doctrine versus the quantity theory reconsidered," *Journal of political economy*, Volume 96, Number 1, February, 3–19.

Stolper, W. F. (1947), "The volume of foreign trade and the level of income," *Quarterly journal of economics*, Volume LXI, February 285–310.

Stuvel, G. (1950), *The exchange stability problem*, Leyden: H. E. Stenfert Kroese N. V. Uitgeversk-Maatschappij, Reprinted 1951, New York: Augustus M. Kelley.

Svensson, Lars E. O. and Assaf Razin (1983), "The terms of trade and the current account: the Harberger-Laursen-Metzler effect," *Journal of political economy*, Volume 91, Number 1, February, 97–125.

Swan, Trevor (1960), "Economic control in a dependent economy," *Economic record*, Volume XXXVI, Number 73, March, 51–66.

Swan, Trevor (1963), "Longer-run problems of the balance of payments," in H. W. Arndt and M. W. Corden, Eds., *The Australian economy: a volume of readings*, Melbourne: Cheshire Press, 384–95.

Taussig, Frank W. (1915, 1919), *Principles of economics Volume I*, New York: Macmillan.

Taussig, Frank W. (1917), "International trade under depreciated paper: a contribution to theory," *Quarterly journal of economics*, Volume XXXI, May, 380–403.

Taussig, Frank W. (1918), "International freights and prices," Reply to Wicksell (1918), *Quarterly journal of economics*, Volume XXXII, February, 410–14.

Taussig, Frank W. (1927), *International trade*, New York: Macmillan.

Thirlwall, A. P., Ed. (1976), *Keynes and international monetary relations: the second Keynes Seminar held at the University of Kent at Canterbuy 1974*, London and Basingstoke: Macmillan.

Thornton, Henry (1802 [1965]), *An enquiry into the nature and effects of the paper credit of Great Britain*, Edited with an Introduction by F. A. v. Hayek, New York: Augustus M. Kelley.

Tobin, James (1978 [1982]), "A proposal for international monetary reform," *The eastern economic journal*, Volume 4, Numbers 3–4, July/October, 153–9. (A presidential address at the Washington meeting, April 1978.) Reprinted in *Essays in economics, theory and policy*, Cambridge, Mass: MIT Press, 488–94.

Tornell, Aaron (1988), "Real vs financial investment: can Tobin taxes eliminate the irreversibility distortion?" Unpublished ms. Columbia University.

Triffin, Robert (1947), "National central banking and the international economy," Washington: Board of Governors, Federal Reserve System.

Triffin, Robert (1964), *The evolution of the international monetary system: historical reappraisal and future perspectives*, Princeton: *Princeton studies in international finance*, Number 12, International Finance Section, Princeton University.

Tsiang, S. C. (1961 [1968]), "The role of money in trade-balance stability: synthesis of the elasticity and absorption approaches," *American economic review*, Volume LI, Number 5, December, 912–36. Reprinted in Caves and Johnson, Eds., Chapter 24.

United States Senate, Commission of Gold and Silver Inquiry (1925), Foreign currency and exchange investigation, Serial 9, Volume I, *European currency and finance*, Washington.

Viner, Jacob (1924), *Canada's balance of international indebtedness, 1900–1913*, Cambridge, Mass: Harvard University Press.

Viner, Jacob (1937), *Studies in the theory of international trade*, New York: Harper and Brothers.

Viner, Jacob (1951), *International economics*, Glencoe, Illinois: the Free Press.

Whale, Barrett (1932), *International trade*, New York: Henry Holt and Company; London: Thornton Butterworth.

Whale, P. Barrett (1936), "International trade in the absence of an international standard," *Economica*, Volume III, N.S., Number 9, February, 24–38.

Whale, P. Barrett (1937 [1953]), "The working of the pre-war gold standard," *Economica*, Volume IV, N.S., Number 13, February, 18–32. Reprinted in Ashton and Sayers, Eds., 151–64.

White, Harry Dexter (1933), *The French international accounts 1880–1913*, Cambridge, Mass: Harvard University Press.

White, Lawrence H. (1984), *Free banking in Britain: theory, experience, and debate, 1800–1845*, Cambridge University Press.

White, Lawrence H. (1987), "Accounting for non-interest-bearing currency: a critique of the legal restrictions theory of money," *Journal of money, credit, and banking*, Volume 19, Number 4, 448–56.

Wicksell, Knut (1918), "International freights and prices," *Quarterly journal of economics*, Volume XXXII, February, 404–10.

Wicksell, Knut (1936), *Interest and prices (Geldzins und Güterpreise): a study of the causes regulating the value of money*, London: Macmillan.

Willett, Thomas D. and Francesco Forte (1969), "Interest rate policy and external balance," *Quarterly journal of economics*, Volume 83, Number 2, 242–62.

Williams, John H. (1920), *Argentine international trade under inconvertible paper money 1880–1900*, Cambridge, Mass: Harvard University Press.

Williams, John H. (1922), "Foreign exchange under depreciated paper," *Journal of the American Bankers Association*, January, 492–4.

Williams, John H. (1922a), "German foreign trade and the reparation payments," *Quarterly journal of economics*, Volume XXXVI, May, 482–503.

Williams, John H. (1929 [1949]), "The theory of international trade reconsidered," *Economic journal*, XXXIX, Number 154, June, 195–209. Reprinted in Ellis and Metzler, Eds., 253–71.

Williams, John H. (1934), "The world's monetary dilemma – internal stability versus external monetary stability," *Proceedings of the academy of political science*, Volume XVI, Number 1, April, 62–8.

Withers, Hartley (1909), *The meaning of money*, London: Smith, Elder and Co.

Withers, Hartley (1910), *The English banking system* (prepared for the U.S.A. National Monetary Commission in 1910).

Wright, Quincy, Ed. (1932), *Gold and monetary stabilization*, Chicago: University of Chicago Press.

Yntema, Theodore O. (1932), *A mathematical reformulation of the general theory of international trade*, Chicago: University of Chicago Press.

Young, Allyn A. (1928), *An analysis of bank statistics for the United States*, Cambridge, Mass: Harvard University Press.

# Index